Aladdin ELECTRIC LAMPS

By J. W. Courter

Printed by
Plain Talk Publishing
Des Moines, Iowa 50309

Other books by J. W. Courter
Aladdin—The Magic Name In Lamps
Aladdin Collectors Manual & Price Guide
A-ladd-in Service Newsletters (reprint)
Mystic Light of the Aladdin Knights (newsletter)

Aladdin Electric Lamps

Library of Congress Catalogue Number 87-071101

ISBN 0-9618879-0-7

Printed and bound in the United States of America

Copies of this book may be obtained from the author and publisher:
J. W. Courter
Route 1
Simpson, Illinois 62985

To Treva

Contents

Foreword

Bill Courter is truly Aladdin's Boswell. How fortunate for all of us!

I am proud that Bill asked me to write the foreword to *Aladdin Electric Lamps*; however, he knows far more about Aladdin lamps than I. That reminds me of an old cartoon showing a distinguished Shakespearean scholar lecturing on the life of the Great Bard. Every student was depicted in varing degrees of indifference: no one was taking notes except one who was writing at a furious pace in the rear of the room. It was William Shakespeare in his Elizabethan dress!

Because his first book, *Aladdin—The Magic Name in Lamps*, was an invaluable source of information for confirmed Aladdin collectors, they will certainly be eager to read his new book. *Aladdin Electric Lamps* will be even more rewarding for new collectors if it stimulates their interest in the pleasure of that hobby and if it opens up new friendships with Aladdin Knights in all walks of life and from all sections of our country.

For those of us who have made Aladdin part of our business life, this book is like picking up a long-forgotten diary: it brings back a flood of memories about many persons and events.

Bill's own professional career as a horticulturist has developed his keen appreciation of nature's cycle of growth, renewal, and change. I suspect that helps to explain his emphasis on growth, renewal, and change at Aladdin. As Aladdin diaries, the Courter books help us appreciate how fortunate we were to inherit the priceless legacy left by those who preceded us. The books also make us even more mindful of our obligation to those who follow.

To those Aladdin Knights I've met in the past and to all in the future—I hope to see you at a Gathering someday.

V. S. JOHNSON, JR.

Chairman of the Board, Emeritus
Aladdin Industries, Inc.

Preface

This book tells the story of Aladdin electric lamps made by The Mantle Lamp Company of America. Included are reprints from original catalogues, and many photographs, drawings, and lists to aid collectors in studying and identifying the lamps. In the companion piece *Aladdin—The Magic Name in Lamps*, published in 1971, early company history and production of kerosene lamps were emphasized. Some electric lamps were included, but only through 1942. Collectors frequently write to me about lamps they have found that are not in my first book. They should be pleased with this new book, which identifies nearly all of the Aladdin electric lamps sold from 1930 to 1956.

I began my research on Aladdin lamps in 1966 with an intense interest in the kerosene mantle lamps. At that time I knew nothing about glass, glassmaking, or even that Aladdin also made electric lamps. Many Aladdin employees, past and present, have contributed to my knowledge over the score of years since my earlier research. They have encouraged and educated me in so many areas, especially where I lacked enough background to even ask intelligent questions.

Collecting information for this book as been akin to putting together a giant jigsaw puzzle over the past twenty years. Pieces of the puzzle have been found in catalogues, price lists, engineering drawings, advertising, and through personal interviews. Aladdin electric lamps and shades are illustrated on more than 450 pages of catalogues and brochures. I have selected catalogue pages for the Appendix that show the greatest numbers of lamps. No catalogues are reproduced in their entirety. I have omitted pages that are repeated in different years and pages that illustrate only shades. Some catalogues are yet to be found, and collectors will undoubtedly be eager to search for them.

Henry Hellmers, Aladdin glass-house superintendent from 1935 to 1942, and I first met through the letter he sent to me on September 26, 1970. We corresponded and visited many times during the next eight years. Even today, I still learn new information as I study his letters and records. I have tried to acknowledge his role in making glass for Aladdin lamps, as well as his contributions to the glassmaking industry.

Other retired Aladdin glassworkers taught me many things also. With the help of Ken and Aggie Thatcher, we invited Henry Hellmers to Alexandria, Indiana, in 1973 for a reunion of glassworkers and other retired employees. This gathering of old friends opened the way for a lively exchange of greetings and past memories that none of us will soon forget. All of these friends have helped me in some way to prepare this book.

As collecting Aladdin lamps became increasingly popular, collectors wanted more information to improve their knowledge. This demand resulted in a newsletter, *The Mystic Light of the Aladdin Knights*, which I started in May 1973. That same year, Aladdin collectors gathered in Nashville, Tennessee, to trade lamps and stories, and to make new friends. Our annual meetings, known as Gatherings, are attended by hundreds hailing from forty-nine states, Canada, England, and Australia.

I first wrote about Aladdin electric lamps in a 1975 issue of *The Mystic Light*. However, the seeds for this book were planted in 1981 at the Gathering of Aladdin Knights in Amana, Iowa, where the

Aladdin glassworkers' reunion, Alexandria, Indiana, 1973. *Front row (left to right):* Bud Trout, Fred Peterson, Fred Kean, Bill McElfresh, Agnes McElfresh, Carolyn Phillips, George Dauenhauer, Lavere Kean, Glen Kean, Henry Hellmers. *Back row (left to right):* Izzie Ryan, Carl Antrim, George Jones, Bill Durr, Ralph High, Ken Thatcher, Ernest Phillips, S. B. Huse, Earl Durr, Jack Collins, John Green.

Knights presented me with signed petitions to write a book on Aladdin electric lamps. I started the research and presented an illustrated talk at the following year's Gathering in Hopkins, Minnesota, to give Knights a glimpse of the book's content. Writing and further research were well under way in 1982.

My well-intended plans, however, were delayed when my wife, Mary, was struck down by cancer. She died in 1985. I deeply appreciate my family and friends, who gave me support, understanding, and encouragement while showing great patience during this time. Now back on track, this book finally documents why Aladdin became one of the leading manufacturers of electric lighting beginning in the Depression years of the 1930s.

Most of this book was written and revised by the light of an ivory and gold Aladdin 3962 floor lamp. It is just as beautiful and useful as when it was made thirty-nine years ago.

This text was also enlightened by many Knights who have enthusiastically shared their information, knowledge, and collections. Several of the catalogues reprinted here were loaned to me. I could not have completed *Aladdin Electric Lamps* without these generous contributions.

Acknowledgments

I wish to thank the following people for their contributions and help in making this book a reality:

V. S. Johnson, Jr., and Aladdin Industries, Inc., for their cooperation and for permission to reprint advertising, catalogues, and photographs.

Past and present Aladdin employees and their families: Herman Durr for his enthusiasm and tireless search of company files and records; S. B. Huse, Ralph High, and Ernest and Caroline Phillips, who provided much information about the history of Alexandria and Aladdin's early years; William McElfresh, George Dauenhauer, John Green, Fred Peterson, and J. Glen Kean, glassworkers who taught me about their craft; Henry Hellmers, who enjoyed his retirement privacy and garden in Port Allegany; Mary and Ann Hellmers, who gave me Henry's books, notebooks, and papers; Helen Hellmers Adams, who helped with family history; and several others who provided information about the company—Ruth Young, Roy Hall, Carl Bramming, Byron Morgan, Herman Mack, Mary Williams, J. D. Pruden, George E. Miller, Ethel Wimmer, Rosemary Freeman, William Hollis, Scott Waymire, and K. E. Cox.

Aladdin Knights and collectors: Tom Teeter and Ken and Aggie Thatcher, who encouraged me to write this book before I knew I would; Robert Calvin for library research; Bruce Wood for research in early company history; Jim Bell for information on the Portland branch office; Donald and Diane Carey, who furnished lamps and their home for color photographs; Aggie Thatcher for research on the Town of Aladdin; and many others—Dave Corbissero, Steve Lolley, Joe DeMatteo, Dr. Moody Jacobs, Grace Farr, Robert Wachtel, Gary Smith, Jack Burns, Irvin Pogue, Robert Evans, Tom Lees, Robert Wind, Forrest Perkins, Gladys Wilke, Mary Engler, Eva Kelley, and all collectors of electric lamps who created the need for this book.

A. von Plachecki, Koopman-Neumer, Inc., who saved original advertising, photographs, and catalogues of electric lamps; Robert E. Johnson for information about his father; Anne Serio and Lorene Mayo of the Smithsonian National Museum of American History.

Sheila Ryan and Margery Suhre for their valuable editorial suggestions; Donald Carey for his technical review; and Bruce Shulman and Gary Shaw for typesetting and printing.

One person deserves enormous credit for her support and help in completing this book. She is my wife, Treva, who gave me encouragement and shared the commitment to meet the pressures of publication deadlines. During our first year together, she took on the job of typing, revising and formating the entire text while learning to operate our new computer. She also drew all the finials and line illustrations. Her support and love made this project a joy that we accomplished together.

I appreciate, too, the understanding of our children when we were busy. Thank you, Kathryn, David, Kym, and Karla.

The sources of photographs and illustrative literature that appear in this book follow.

Illustrations: Averil Mathis, logo; Roy Hall, Figure 3; Herman Durr, Figures 10, 11, 71; S. B. Huse, Figure 12, 95; Donald Carey, Figure 15; Aladdin Industries, Inc., Figures 34, 35, 36; Helen Hellmers Adams, Figure 37; Jack Roads, Figure 45; Jim Bell, Figures 51, 69; William Hollis, Figures 56, 70; Gary Moor, Figure 63; V. S. Johnson, Jr., Figure 66; J. D. Pruden, Figure 73; Larry Sundberg, Figure 81; Gary Smith, Figure 82.

Lamps photographed from personal collections: Donald and Diane Carey (including the cover photograph), Ken and Aggie Thatcher, Steve Lolley, Robert Wachtel, Jim Bell, Dave Corbissero, Kent Stratton, Gary Smith, and J. W. Courter.

Advertising: Scott Lombard, Figure 6.

Catalogues: George Foree, 1935 (pages 75 to 77); Smithsonian Institution Collection of Advertising History, 1939 and 1940 (pages 86 to 109); Steve Lolley, 1940 (pages 110 to 122); Dennis Black, 1947 (pages 143 to 151), 1948, 1949, 1950, and 1951 (pages 156 to 193); Ken and Aggie Thatcher, 1955 (pages 217 to 223).

Introduction

By the time The Mantle Lamp Company of America began marketing Aladdin electric lamps in the early 1930s, the name Aladdin had long been associated with excellence in home lighting.

In 1908 the company had introduced a new kerosene mantle lamp with the Aladdin trademark. "The best rural home lamp in the world," the advertising read. "Make your home bright and cheerful. There is an Aladdin for every room in your home. . . Be wise, Aladdinize and save your eyes."

These advertising claims were justified by the bright, white, steady light, equivalent to that of a 75-watt bulb, emanating from the lamp's mantle. Through the years, the company kept improving its models and thus the quality of light available to rural America.

By 1945 rural electrification had reached most areas of the country, and kerosene lamps were shelved for use during infrequent power outages. But Aladdin kerosene lamps continued to provide light in remote areas of this country, as well as in many other parts of the world.

The company's decision to manufacture electric lamps came at a time when the country was in a severe depression. Business was slow and competition was strong not only from domestic manufacturers, but also from importers of foreign-made lamps. However, rural electrification and the sales potential in America's cities made the decision inevitable for a company that had established its reputation in home lighting.

1. The Mantle Lamp Company of America

For nearly eight decades, the name Aladdin and home lighting were linked with two men: Victor Samuel Johnson, Sr., and, in later years, Victor Samuel Johnson, Jr. Together they saw an industry flourish and produce lamps that, today, are widely sought by collectors.

The Johnsons: Father and Son

The elder Johnson, an energetic and determined young man from Nebraska, first made his mark as an outstanding salesman for the Iowa Soap Company in Burlington, Iowa. His interest in lamps dated back to those early years. While traveling for the soap company, he came across a little-known German kerosene lamp, the Practicus. Compared with domestic lamps, the mantle burner gave off a superior white light. In 1907 Johnson decided to form

Fig. 1. V. S. Johnson as shown in the company's 1925 program of *Aladdin Knights of Mystic Lights.*

the Western Lighting Company to sell the improved burner. He was only twenty-five years old at the time.

Johnson then went on to find a manufacturer in this country who could make a complete lamp, along with an improved version of the kerosene mantle lamp burner. He sold this new lamp under the Aladdin trademark. In 1908 Johnson formed The Mantle Lamp

Company of America in Chicago, Illinois. During the company's first year, he marketed both Practicus and Aladdin lamps.

Cortland W. Davis joined the company in 1909 to establish a research department. The purpose of the department was to improve the lamp and the design of its important components: the mantle, wick, and burner. As Johnson hired competent people in management, research, and sales, The Mantle Lamp Company of America grew and prospered. As a result, many models of Aladdin kerosene mantle lamps were developed over the years.

On August 29, 1943, Johnson died suddenly at the Willard Hotel while on a business trip in Washington, D.C. The following morning, vice-president Cortland Davis discussed the situation with managers in Alexandria, Indiana. He assured them that Aladdin Industries would continue to operate under the local leadership of himself and plant manager Tom Blain. Vice-president J. O. White took over management of the home offices in Chicago. Although Johnson's death came as a shock, company management continued with little noticeable impact on the business.

On September 3, Victor S. Johnson, Jr., at age twenty-seven, was voted to succeed his father as president of the company. A second lieutenant in the army at the time, the younger Johnson was a graduate of the Yale Law School and had passed the Illinois bar exam before entering the service. After his discharge in 1945, he made a smooth transition to the role of president, as several retired Aladdin employees recalled.

Johnson, Jr., guided the company through many significant changes, much as his father had done before him. For forty years, until his retirement in 1985, the company continued to prosper from his innovative marketing and manufacturing of new product lines. (Additional information about the Johnsons can be found in *Aladdin—The Magic Name in Lamps* by J. W. Courter, 1971.)

Kerosene Lamps

When V. S. Johnson formed The Mantle Lamp Company of America in 1908, he chose the Aladdin trademark for his new kerosene mantle lamp. At the time, excitement over the

Fig. 2. Aladdin Alacite kerosene mantle lamp, B-75, 1940.

horseless carriage was running high, and the magic of electricity held wonderful promise for the future. Both the automobile and electricity were to have a profound effect on the quality of life in America.

During an era when the prairies and plains were being developed for agricultural production, Aladdin lamps brought a much needed white light to farm homes beyond the electrical high lines. The kerosene lamps were also used in train cabooses, lighthouses, and wilderness cabins. As late as 1939, the lens in the Turkey Point Lighthouse in Maryland was illuminated by an Aladdin lamp.

During World War II, the Aladdin kerosene burner made it possible for the famous Servel and Electrolux refrigeration units to preserve serum and plasma on the battlefield. Also during the war, Aladdin was granted special permission by the War Production Board to use copper. The reason behind the decision was that Aladdin kerosene mantle lamps would save much wiring that would otherwise have been required for electric high lines and to electrify rural homes.

As the kerosene lamps were sold in countries around the world, international affiliates were established. The first was in Toronto, Canada, in 1910, followed by Greenford, England, in 1919, Sydney, Australia, in 1921, and Buenos Aires, Argentina, in 1925.

The Mantle Lamp Company was a pioneer in radio advertising. One of the first paid commercial radio messages in the Midwest broadcast the story of Aladdin lamps. It aired in 1927 on Station KFNF in Shenandoah, Iowa, for $500 and prompted 2,200 letters asking for more information. The Mantle Lamp Company sponsored live broadcasts of the Barn Dance Frolic on WLS in Chicago and on WHO in Des Moines, Iowa. In the early 1930s Smilin' Ed McConnell promoted Aladdin kerosene lamps with remarkable success over WLW in Cincinnati, Ohio. He became a well known radio personality as "The Aladdin Lamp Man" who sang, told stories, and sold Aladdin lamps over the radio waves. By 1948, 145 ABC stations were subscribing to his fifteen-minute programs. Smilin' Ed's humor, songs, and music were condensed into a five-minute program especially for electric lamp dealers. Through his personable style, Smilin' Ed touched the lives of millions of housewives. He said in one program, "Honey, a house without an Aladdin kerosene or electric lamp is like a house without a door. Incomplete!" Then he described the current lamps available from Aladdin and closed the program by singing a hymn. In 1933, 153 of these hymns were collected into a hardbound book called

Fig. 3. Smilin' Ed McConnell.

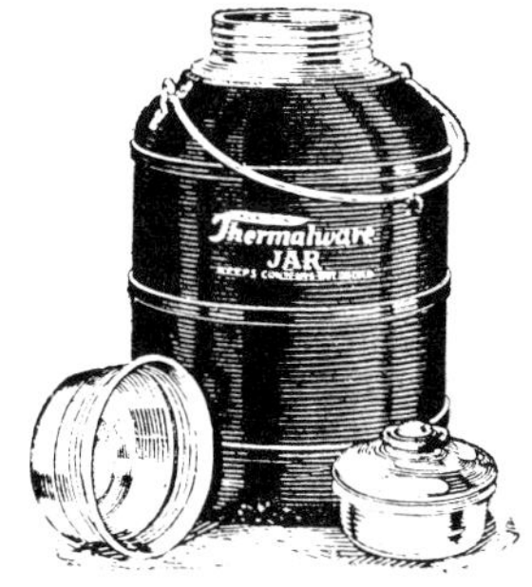

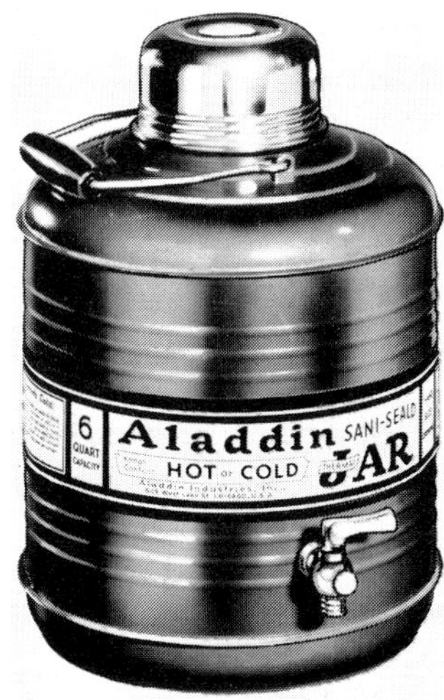

Fig. 4.
New products developed in the 1920s and 1930s: Thermalware jar (1922), Sani-Seald jar (1930s), Sani-Seald vacuum bottle and lunch box (1930s), Model 75 Blue Flame Heater (1939).

Smilin' Ed McConnell's Favorite Radio Hymns, published by the Rodeheaver Company, Chicago and Philadelphia.

Ironically, The Mantle Lamp Company enjoyed its best sales of kerosene lamps during the same years that it began to manufacture and sell electric lamps. Adept in advertising to rural and farm people, the company touted the quality light and proclaimed that the kerosene lamp could be converted instantly into a modern electric lamp with an Aladdin converter. The sales tactic hit the mark: it helped convince prospective customers who were hesitant because electrification was "just around the corner." Consequently, the sale of kerosene lamps continued even while rural electrification was spreading throughout the Midwest. In *Nickel's Worth of Skim Milk*, Robert Hastings described this era: "When Smilin' Ed McConnell sang and described the Aladdin 'magic' lamp, he made everyone with electric lights wish he were living in the country so he could buy one of those kerosene lights that were so easy on the kids' eyes and so hard on rural darkness."

Early in the company's history, Johnson had established a research and development department. Because of his foresight, seventeen models were developed in the United States as the company steadily improved its lamps. Model 12 Instant Light (1928) and Model B (1933) Aladdin mantle lamps were significant improvements in dependable kerosene light. Although the lamps were relatively expensive, Aladdin's claims were not overstated. The lamps were high quality, dependable, economical to operate, and decorative. Thus the Aladdin name and trademark became widely known for excellence and quality in home lighting.

In 1908 ten manufacturers and sixty-five companies distributed kerosene mantle lamps. Today only one remains, still making Aladdin kerosene mantle lamps and replacement parts.

New Products

As early as 1915, Johnson thought it wise to diversify. First he tried to sell Sambo Starters, a mechanical starting device for the crank-start Ford and similar to those now used on outboard motors. This effort failed.

Aladdin next made insulated cooking dishes for the U.S. armed services during World War I. Encouraged by this experience, the company began manufacturing Aladdin Thermalware jars, which had an aluminum or steel jacket enclosing a one-gallon heavy glass receptacle. The space between the jacket and receptacle was filled with ground cork. With this product, the company ventured into heat- and cold-retaining receptacles. Aladdin Industries, Inc., was founded in 1919 as a subsidiary of The Mantle Lamp Company of America to sell the Aladdin Thermalware jars and dishes. The first Aladdin vacuum bottles were later introduced in the early 1930s.

During the 1920s, efforts to diversify continued with the founding of the Pathfinder Radio Corp., the Cadillac Phonograph Corp., the Aladdin Chemical Corp., and the Aladdin

Phonograph Corp. Although these companies failed, another one, Johnson Laboratories, Inc., was successful. It developed a radio-tuning principle, which was the forerunner of the push-button automobile radio. In 1925 the Aladdin Radio Manufacturing Company was formed to make transformers and other related components for the new radio industry. The name was changed to Aladdin Radio Industries, Inc., in 1934, and then to Aladdin Electronics in 1951, when it became a division of Aladdin Industries in Nashville, Tennessee.

The purchase of the Lippincott glass factory in Alexandria, Indiana, in 1926 permitted Aladdin to manufacture its own lamp chimneys, lampshades, and kerosene fonts. Before this time, Aladdin contracted for the manufacture of most of its lamp components, with the exception of mantles and wicks. The cost to modernize the old factory gave management the opportunity to consider the manufacturing of new products.

Fig. 5. V. S. Johnson depicted as "Master Builder" in a cartoon drawing in the company's 1926 annual program.

Extensive research was undertaken at the refurbished Alexandria plant. New products that were developed in the early 1930s included the Sani-Seald vacuum bottles, Whip-o-lite and Parvelour parchment shades, kerosene heaters, and a new electric line with its multitude of molds. This expansion strained company finances at a time when labor problems were occurring and plant workers were unionizing. Mr. Johnson stated that Aladdin's patented mantles and wicks were the only profitable lines made at Alexandria in 1936. In addition to these concerns, a court battle was in progress with a rival firm in Muncie, Indiana, over the right to use the Aladdin trade name. Mr. Johnson met the challenges head-on, and Aladdin's new electric lamps found a strong market as the company developed unique glass (Opalique and Alacite), one-piece floor lamps, and new designs of the electric table lamps.

Aladdin introduced kerosene heating stoves in 1937-38. Aladdin Blue Flame Heaters, greenhouse heaters, and oil radiators became known worldwide for their efficiency and quality. The company developed pressure lanterns and during World War II developed conversion units to permit army lanterns to burn regular leaded gasoline. Also, during the war Aladdin won an army contract for a 20-ounce midget ski-stove that burned either leaded or white gasoline.

In 1950 Aladdin introduced its "character" school lunch kits. Until then, children's lunch boxes had been drab and unexciting. Decorated with action scenes of America's favorite cowboy, Hopalong Cassidy, Aladdin's creation set a new trend in colorful lunch boxes.

On May 24, 1965, Aladdin announced the

Fig. 6 Hopalong Cassidy ranch house lamps and lunch kits, about 1950. This ad appeared in a comic book.

acquisition of the Stanley Division of Landers, Frary and Clark. The world-famous Stanley stainless steel vacuumware has since been manufactured in Nashville by Aladdin.

Aladdin Electronics expanded into many fields of electronics. Known throughout the industry as one of the leaders in the micro-miniaturization of transformers, Aladdin supplied components used in several of our country's missile and space projects. Aladdin has been issued more than 200 patents, ranging from components of space-age transformers to radio-telephone filters.

Today, Aladdin Industries is a worldwide company headquartered in Nashville, Tennessee. It is a major manufacturer of thermosware products, the world leader in institutional distribution systems, and a major manufacturer of electronic components and heating and lighting products.

Aladdin Industries, Inc.

Aladdin Industries was incorporated on October 24, 1919; it was located at 348 North Ashland Avenue, Chicago, Illinois. The principal stockholder was V. S. Johnson. The company's stated purpose was "to manufacture and deal in (wholesale and retail) bottles, vacuum containers, thermos bottles, thermalware, kitchen utensils, fixtures for restaurants and kitchens, and all kinds of merchandise and equipment used in connection therewith, lamps and lighting devices, and phonographs, to own and control patents; to operate under royalty agreements, and to grant licenses on royalty basis."

In 1921 the principal place of business was moved to 609 West Lake Street, which also was the address of The Mantle Lamp Company of

America. In September 1936, the company moved to 223 West Jackson Boulevard, where it occupied the entire seventh floor of the Brooks Building.

When Aladdin Industries, Inc., merged into The Mantle Lamp Company of America on May 1, 1949, the name of Aladdin Industries, Inc., was retained. The principal place of business was moved to 1106 Merchandise Mart, but later the same year the permanent offices were moved to Murfreesboro Road, Nashville, Tennessee. The company became a Delaware corporation in 1969.

The Alexandria Works

Although only touched upon in a previous section, the company's move to Alexandria, Indiana, was a momentous event in the Aladdin story. For it was here that the colorful glass kerosene and electric lamps were manufactured over a twenty-year period.

Located about forty miles to the northeast of Indianapolis, Alexandria was little more than a rural village of 700 people in the 1880s. But the discovery of natural gas in 1887 stimulated a boom, and the town grew almost tenfold during the next decade.

Many factories were built in Alexandria, among them the Harper and Cruzan Glass Company, the DePauw Plate Glass Company, the Lippincott Glass Company, the Union Steel Company, the Kelly Axe Company, Banner Rock Products, as well as two brick plants, four small glassworks, and a paper mill. The town became known as "the largest window glass manufacturing center in the world" and "the home of rock wool." Banner Rock Products, which created the process to make rock wool

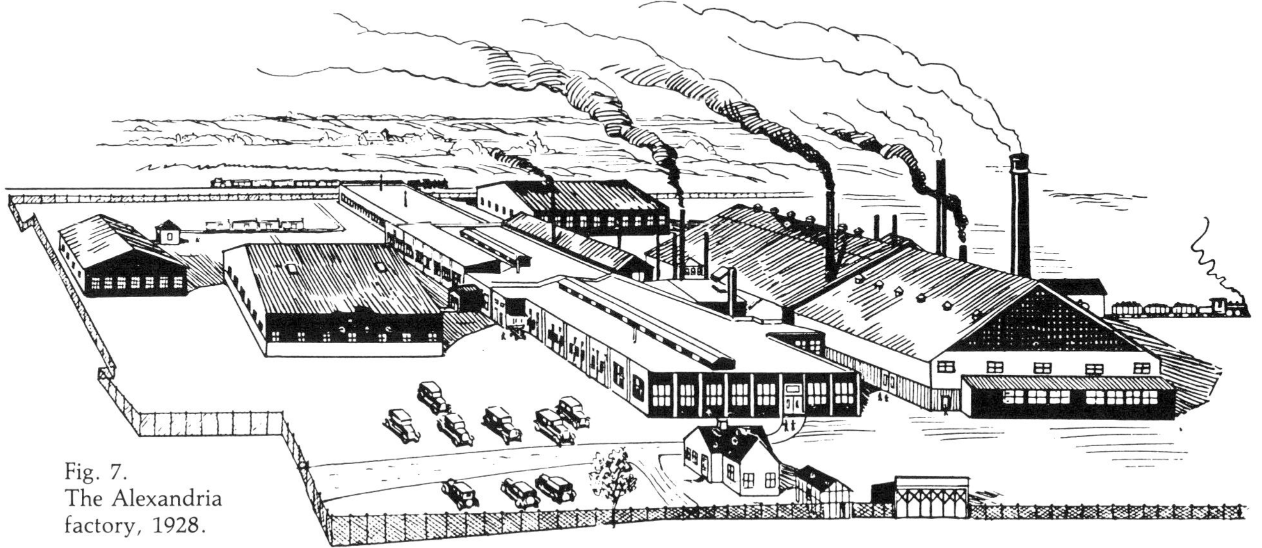

Fig. 7.
The Alexandria
factory, 1928.

Fig. 8. The general office and mantle building on Washington Street in the Town of Aladdin.

insulation, was eventually sold to the Johns-Manville Corporation.

In 1892 the Lippincott Glass Company moved to Alexandria from Findlay, Ohio, after the gas failure there. People thought that an "unexhaustible supply" was to be found at the Indiana location. The Lippincott factory became one of the largest makers of lamp chimneys and vacuum bottles in the world. They also made other products, including electric bulbs, lantern globes, and glass tubing. Lippincott was known for fine crystal stemware during the 1920s. Some of Aladdin's glass chimneys were made by Lippincott, but we do not know in which years or in what quantities.

After Lippincott went into receivership and was finally closed, Aladdin Industries purchased the old plant in September 1926. Aladdin started glass operations there in 1927 after extensive renovation. Although the management did not intend to manufacture anything except lamp chimneys, the plant soon began making many other products. In 1928 the Aladdin mantle factory moved to Alexandria from Chicago. Later, all lamp parts were made in the renovated plant. These parts included wicks, glass and paper shades, kerosene lamp fonts, metal casting for electric lamp stands and bases—not to mention new product development, testing, and quality control. The glass items made at Alexandria included chimneys, glass shades, kerosene lamps, vacuum bottle blanks, vacuum bottle tubing, glass stoppers and liners for jugs, and electric lamps. Diversification was necessary to maintain sufficient volume to keep the glass plant efficient.

S. D. Goodwin was the first factory superintendent at Alexandria. Others who moved with him from Chicago included Fred Reiss, chemist; F. W. Spangler, chief inspector; W. T. Rahe, foreman, vacuum bottles; and C. T.

Wright, supervisor, mantle department. Eugene Schwarz, designer, and W. B. Engh, kerosene lamp research, moved to Alexandria probably in late 1930 when the new Mantle Building and Machine Shop Building were completed. Others who followed from the Chicago office were C. W. Davis, vice-president, research; and T. A. Blain, traffic manager.

The officers of The Mantle Lamp Company in 1928 were: V. S. Johnson, president; B. S. Presba, vice-president; C. W. Davis, vice-president; A. H. Glantz, treasurer; and W. H. F. Millar, secretary (and attorney). All were headquartered in Chicago at that time.

Alexandria was designated "Small Town U.S.A." in a booklet published by the Office of War Information. "To know Alexandria is to know the American small town." The city was portrayed as a typical midwestern community, where most of the residents supported the war either on active duty or through war-related manufacturing. The booklet was translated into several languages and distributed worldwide.

Alexandria was called "Alex" by those who lived and worked there, although the nickname is seldom seen in print. In 1949 the *Alexandria Times-Tribune* headlined the town as the "Home of Rock Wool and Aladdin Mantle Lamps."

Town of Aladdin

The town of Aladdin was incorporated in 1928 to save money on taxes. It was comprised of 15.9 acres with twenty-two residents, seventeen of them voters, living within its boundaries. Containing the manufacturing plant of Aladdin Industries, Inc., Aladdin was almost completely surrounded by Alexandria and was the smallest town in Indiana. Except for taxation and voting, the town was in reality a part of the larger city. Aladdin obtained its water, fire, and police protection from Alexandria and paid a negotiated amount for those services.

Residents of Aladdin in 1928 were:

Lena and Edna Schaefer
Willard, Augusta, and Howard Disbennett
Hugh and Mae McElfresh
John and Galena Diehl
H. W. and Mary Bireley
Joe, Mona, and Virgil K. Eader
Earl, Etta, Clarence, and James Lynch
William, Bertie, William L., and Bertha Thais

According to the 1940 census, Aladdin had a population of seventeen persons living in five houses. Only five babies were reported to have been born to residents of the town.

Associated Companies

During the time that Aladdin Industries was beginning to flourish, company literature listed the following "Associated Companies and Branches":

- The Mantle Lamp Company of America
  223 W. Jackson Blvd., Chicago 6, Illinois
- Aladdin Industries, Inc.
  223 W. Jackson Blvd., Chicago 6, Illinois
- Aladdin Radio Industries, Inc.
  501 W. 35th St., Chicago 16, Illinois
- The Mantle Lamp Company of America
  1726 N. Flint St., Portland 12, Oregon
- The Mantle Lamp Company of America
  1244 Dufferin St., Toronto 4, Ont., Canada
- Aladdin Industries, Inc.
  1244 Dufferin St., Toronto 4, Ont., Canada
- Aladdin Industries, Ltd. (London Office)
  Greenford, Middlesex, England
- Aladdin Industries Pty., Ltd.
  61-71 Bourke St., Waterloo, Sydney, Australia
- Aladdin Industries, Inc.
  Washington St., Alexandria, Indiana

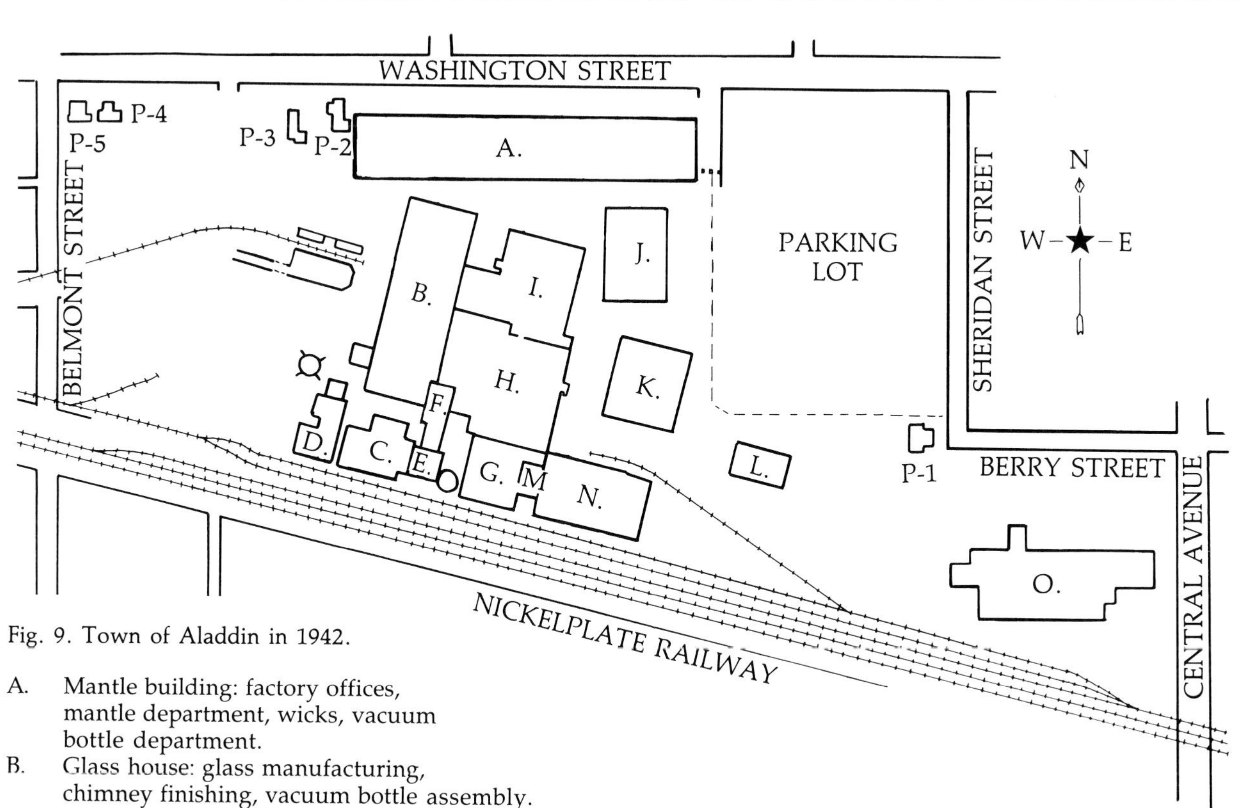

Fig. 9. Town of Aladdin in 1942.

A. Mantle building: factory offices, mantle department, wicks, vacuum bottle department.
B. Glass house: glass manufacturing, chimney finishing, vacuum bottle assembly.
C. Batch house and storage for glass raw materials.
D. Fine-iron for radio manufacturing.
E. Boiler.
F. Factory maintenance.
G. White-metal casting and buffing.
H. Metal plating, punch press, and lacquering.
I. Electric lamps assembly: Eugene Schwarz's office, white-metal and glass-mold shops.
J. Machine shop and engineering.
K. Sheet metal warehouse.
L. Small sheet metal warehouse.
M. Gum (resin) manufacturing.
N. Warehouse and shipping (two floors and basement).
O. Metal products building and material storage.
P. Residences: P-1, P-2, P-3, P-4, P-5. P-1, originally the office when Aladdin purchased the plant from Lippincott, was moved from the site where the machine shop was built.

Fig. 10. Office supervisors and office workers, July 22, 1929. *Front row (left to right):* Alden Higgins, draftsman, tool design; Thelma Baker, office manager; Ruby Antrim, clerk, payroll and distribution; Genevive Blake, clerk, payroll and distribution; Helen Huse, clerk, payroll and distribution; Zura Zink, group leader, mantles and wicks; Helen Reeves, group leader, mantles and wicks; Sarah Culbertson, floor lady, mantles and wicks; Pauline Bowman, group leader, mantles and wicks; Wallace Rahe, foreman, vacuum bottle department. *Back row (left to right):* Joe Sohm, foreman, glass grinding and decorating; Lester Horner, foreman, warehouse and shipping; Byron Morgan, foreman, warehouse and shipping; Robert Sloan, laboratory technician; Jesse Said, foreman, glass manufacturing; Eddie Weiss, foreman, chimney finishing; Harry McCune, foreman, maintenance; Herman Durr, inventory control; S. D. Goodwin, factory superintendent; George Goss, supervisor, machine and tool design; Earl Durr, laboratory technician; Albert Ingram, laboratory technician; Art Stafford, foreman, punch press department; Fred Reiss, chemist, laboratory supervisor; Clarence Cox, foreman, tool and die shop; Merle Zedeker, laboratory technician.

Fig. 11. Office supervisors, office workers, and factory workers in the machine shop, glass finishing, plating, maintenance, laboratory, and warehouse, July 22, 1929.

Fig. 12. Factory workers who made mantles, wicks, and flame spreaders, July 19, 1929.

2. Electric Lamps

Throughout the 1930s, electric lamps became increasingly more practical and fashionable. Many companies competed on the market to give consumers electric lighting of a scientifically determined quality. They also competed for consumers who wanted either reasonably priced or high priced lamps. The Mantle Lamp Company of America joined the competition in 1930.

A New Era in Home Lighting

In 1930, the first lamps designed specifically for electricity were the 781A pedestal lamps (later the E-200 series) and the 786 vase lamps (later the E-300 series). Examples of these lamps were most likely sold during the fall and winter of 1930-31. Sales must have been encouraging, because 783, 784, and 789A vases soon came off

---

Aladdin sold its first electric lamps in 1915 as conversions of Style 150 kerosene floor lamp. This Model 6 lamp was furnished with an elegant silk shade and priced at $60, but it was too expensive for Aladdin's customers. The company electrified the kerosene lamps and sold them in the higher priced city market where electricity was available. We do not know the selling price or if literature was printed for the electric version.

---

the drawing boards. *E* numbers were assigned to distinguish them from the kerosene lamps. The first *G* numbers, which began a twenty-year-long series of Aladdin electric table lamps, were sold in 1933 (Table 1). The chronology of Aladdin electric lamp production is in Appendix A. Letter designations and their meanings are in Appendix B.

The large Model 12 kerosene vase lamp (785) was introduced in May of 1930, and it is possible that this vase, modified for electricity, was the first one sold to test the market. In any event, the 785 electric vase lamp was sold in 1931 and stimulated creation of the new designs mentioned above.

When The Mantle Lamp Company began selling electric lamps, the company was

uncertain how to market them. The question arose because of franchise agreements with dealers who were already selling Aladdin kerosene lamps. Some dealers were in a favorable position to carry the electric lamps, but others were not.

The first lamps appeared on the market without benefit of the Aladdin name or trademark. They were sold without a trademark until the name Vogue was used in 1932. Beginning in 1933, the company sold its complete line of electric lamps and Whip-o-lite shades under the name Aladdin.

Along with kerosene lamp promotion, the electric line was illustrated in sales brochures sent to dealers. The company emphasized that

Everything that goes into the manufacture of Aladdin Electric Lamps and Aladdin Whip-o-lite shades is made right here in the good old U. S. A. We use no imports of any kind. And with the exception of such items as sockets, electric cords, etc., these lamps are produced right in our own factory at

Table 1. Aladdin Electric Table Lamps, 1930 to 1933

Sales no.[a] (vase no.)	First year	Description
E-200 (781A pedestal)	1930	Vogue pedestal
E-300 (786 vase)	1930	Vogue vase
Unknown (783 vase)	1931	Table lamp
Unknown (785 vase)	1931	Modified kero. vase
Unknown (789A vase)	....	Vase neck lamp
E-310 (784 vase)	1932	Table lamp
E-340	1932	Table lamp
E-360	1932	Table lamp
E-380	1932	Table lamp
E-390	1932	Table lamp
E-410	1932	Boudoir lamp
G-1	1933	Boudoir lamp
G-2	1933	Table lamp
G-3	1933	Table lamp
G-4	1933	Table lamp
G-6	1933	Table lamp
G-7	1933	Table lamp
G-10	1933	Modified G-1
G-12	1933	Modified G-4
G-15	1933	Modified G-6
G-16	1933	Table lamp
G-17	1933	Modified G-7
G-18	1933	Table lamp
G-19	1933	Table lamp

[a]We do not know the identity of the missing sales numbers or if they were produced.

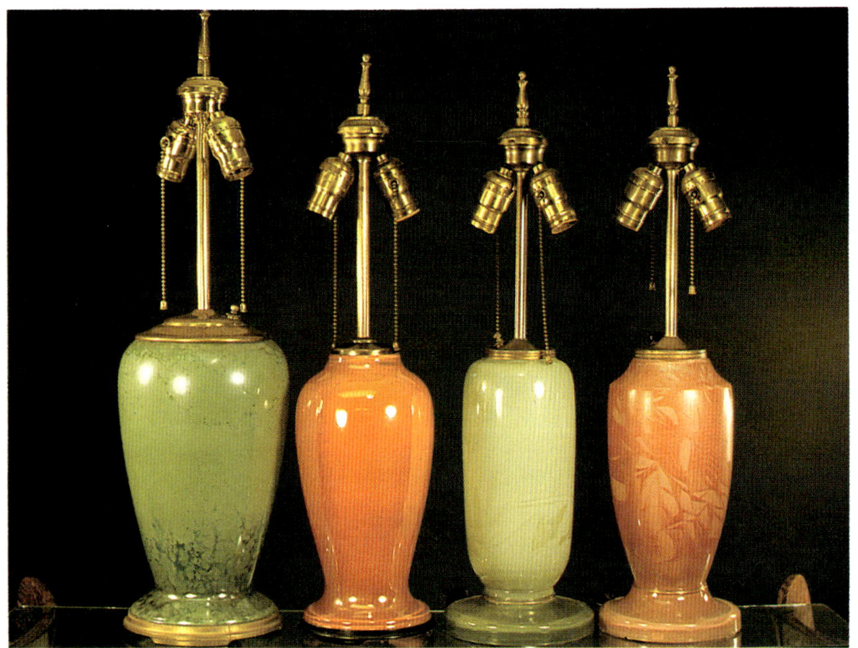

Fig. 13. Early vase lamps *(left to right):* 785 vase, E-300 series (786 vase), 783 vase, E-310 (784 vase)

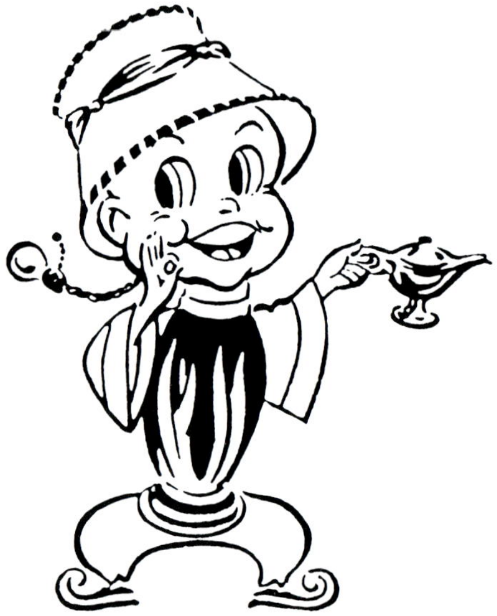

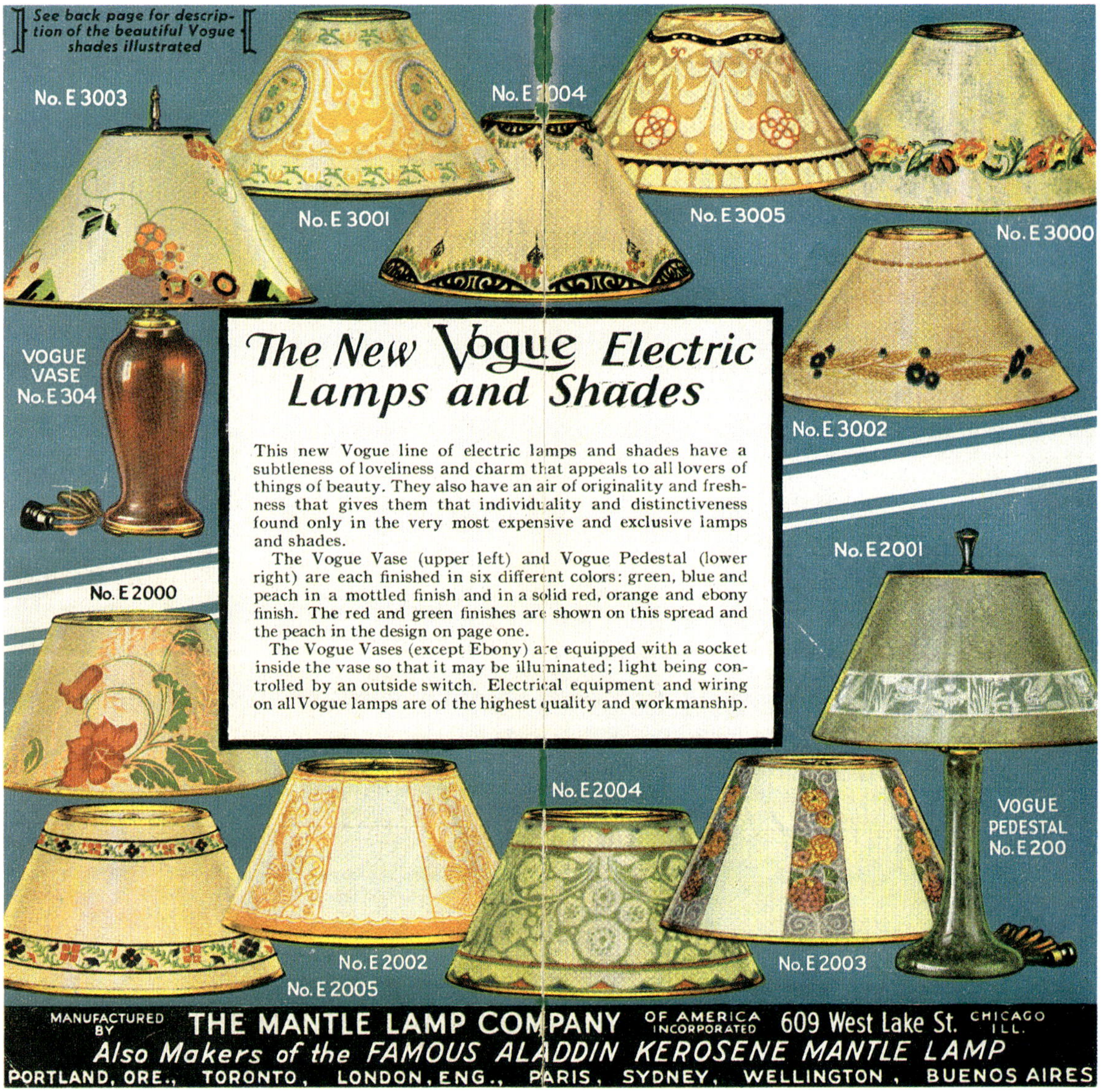

See back page for description of the beautiful Vogue shades illustrated
No. E 3003
No. E 3004
No. E 3001
No. E 3005
No. E 3000
VOGUE VASE No. E 304
The New Vogue Electric Lamps and Shades
This new Vogue line of electric lamps and shades have a subtleness of loveliness and charm that appeals to all lovers of things of beauty. They also have an air of originality and freshness that gives them that individuality and distinctiveness found only in the very most expensive and exclusive lamps and shades.
The Vogue Vase (upper left) and Vogue Pedestal (lower right) are each finished in six different colors: green, blue and peach in a mottled finish and in a solid red, orange and ebony finish. The red and green finishes are shown on this spread and the peach in the design on page one.
The Vogue Vases (except Ebony) are equipped with a socket inside the vase so that it may be illuminated; light being controlled by an outside switch. Electrical equipment and wiring on all Vogue lamps are of the highest quality and workmanship.
No. E 3002
No. E 2001
No. E 2000
No. E 2004
VOGUE PEDESTAL No. E 200
No. E 2002
No. E 2005
No. E 2003
MANUFACTURED BY THE MANTLE LAMP COMPANY OF AMERICA INCORPORATED 609 West Lake St. CHICAGO ILL.
Also Makers of the FAMOUS ALADDIN KEROSENE MANTLE LAMP
PORTLAND, ORE., TORONTO, LONDON, ENG., PARIS, SYDNEY, WELLINGTON, BUENOS AIRES

Fig. 14. Vogue vase and pedestal lamps and shades, 1932.

Fig. 15. Vogue vase lamp (E-304 Bengal Red), 1932.

Fig. 16. G-18 table lamp, 1933.

Fig. 17. G-28 table lamp, 1934.

Fig. 18. G-31 table lamp, 1935.

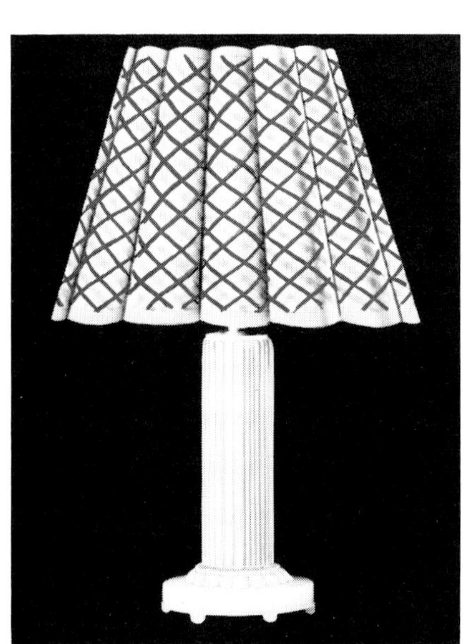

Fig. 19. G-32 boudoir lamp, 1935.

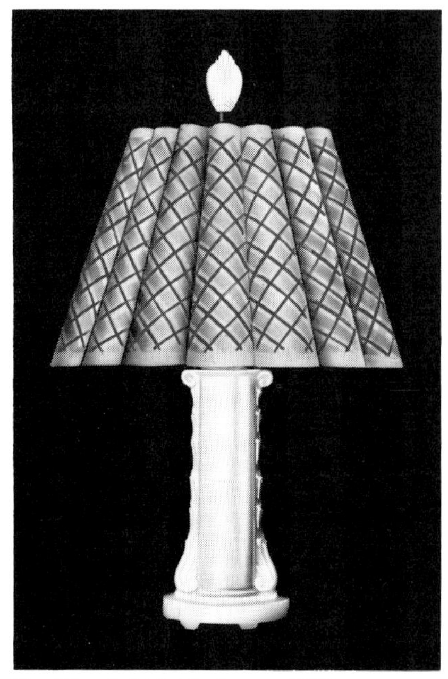

Fig. 20. G-34 table lamp, 1935.

Fig. 21. G-36 table lamp, 1935.

Fig. 22. G-82 table lamp, 1936.

Fig. 23. G-90 boudoir lamp, 1936.

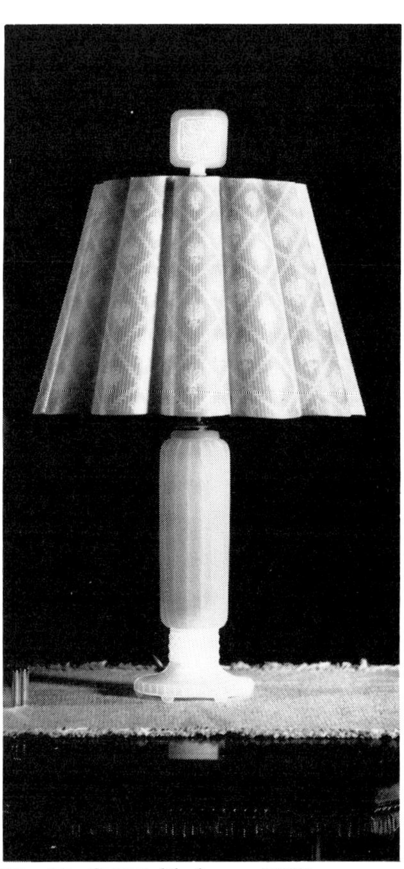

Fig. 24. G-98 table lamp, 1937.

Fig. 25. W-148 boudoir lamp, 1937.

Fig. 26. G-170 table lamp, 1938.

Fig. 27. Sales number unknown, 1940.

Fig. 28. Early electric lamps *(left to right):* G-16 (1933), G-17 (1933), G-12 (1933), sales number unknown (about 1935).

Fig. 29. G-6 in white semi-opal and marblelike glass colors, about 1933.

Fig. 30. Early table lamp, sales number unknown, about 1933.

Fig. 31. Early boudoir lamps *(left to right):* G-23 (1934), G-153 (1937), G-92 (1937), G-32 (1935).

Alexandria, Indiana. We even make our own glass and our own metal castings, develop in our own Art Department our exclusive designs. So Aladdins are quality products in every sense of the word.

The Alexandria facilities were claimed to be "America's largest and most complete lamp manufacturing plant" in 1937, with almost a quarter of a million square feet of floor space.

The Mantle Lamp Company quickly developed a variety of lamp styles. They were exhibited in the National Chicago Lamp Show from January 4 to 16, 1932, in competition with 155 lamp manufacturers, and again in the first New York Lamp Show from August 15 to 19, 1932, with 161 manufacturers. At that time, Chicago was considered the furniture capital of the United States. Furniture buyers purchased lamps when visiting the salesrooms at the Merchandise Mart and the American Furniture Mart. These showrooms, plus the seasonal lamp shows in New York, Chicago, High Point (North Carolina), and San Francisco, were the primary sales outlets for electric lamps throughout the 1930s and 1940s.

Catalogues and brochures for Aladdin lamps were printed through 1955. The line was changed every six months to coincide with the major shows, and the January and July catalogues featured the new lamps. A catalogue supplement was sometimes published. The price lists were printed separately.

V. S. Johnson, Sr., took a great interest in the new electric lamps. Meetings were held in Alexandria so that he could review each new style. Eugene Schwarz designed and assembled potential models complete with shades. Ralph High and Herman Durr then calculated the costs, which they discussed with Johnson, Schwarz, Jim White (sales manager), Paul Einwalter (assistant sales manager), and Auggie Etchison (salesman). Together, this group determined the new spring-summer and fall-winter lines. The procedure was followed from the early 1930s until 1943.

In 1928 The Mantle Lamp Company decided to sell only through franchise dealers. This was a significant change in their marketing strategy as mail orders and traveling sales agents were discontinued. Aladdin's franchised kerosene system of more than 10,000 dealers blanketed the United States.   Aladdin electric lamps were not only known as quality products on their own merit, but benefited greatly by the loyalty of hundreds of thousands of families who had been reared by the white light of the magic Aladdin kerosene lamp. Obviously, in the thirties and early forties, this gave Aladdin a great advantage in reaching a significant market that was not as readily available to competition;

Fig. 32. Neck table lamp (789A vase), 1931. We do not know if this lamp was produced.

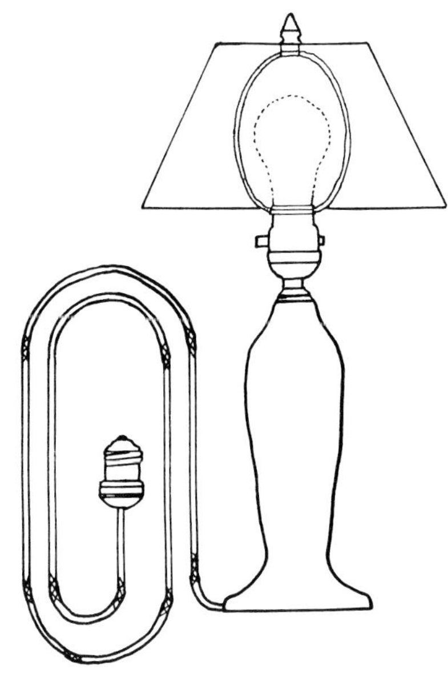

Fig. 33. Boudoir lamp, 1930. We do not know if this lamp was produced.

no competitor could possibly support such a sales force. Even in the urban centers, Aladdin electric lamps enjoyed a very fine reception.

The Crest Line

The Mantle Lamp Company was noted for reasonably priced electric lamps, but had requests for higher quality lamps from its dealers. To supply this market, the company purchased the Crest Company in October 1934. A Chicago firm since 1915, Crest was known for manufacturing the highest quality electric lamps. A Crest "Hallmark of Quality" advertisement in 1938 stated: "There is hardly anything in the world that some men cannot make a little worse and sell a little cheaper, and the people who consider price only are this man's lawful prey."

The two companies maintained separate display rooms at the Merchandise Mart, and their lines were targeted for sales to distinctly different clientele. No apparent relationship was discernible in their ads. The Mantle Lamp Company did, however, sell some lamp parts to Crest, along with at least one silver-plated table lamp similar or identical to M-175.

The Crest line featured eighteenth century period designs, as well as Kenton Hills and Saxony porcelains, Rookwood Ceramics, Old English Silver, Lenox, Spode, English Moorcraft, Chinese Cloisonnes, and other fine imported wares. Some were limited editions of twelve lamps, and others were signed by known artists.

The Mantle Lamp Company sold Crest Company to Fred A. Savage in 1939. Crest continued to prosper, and in 1941 the company moved to larger facilities at 1020 West Adams Street in Chicago, where they manufactured complete lamp units in one plant. John Wanamaker of Philadelphia featured expensive Crest lamps in 1947 advertisements showing a French Lalique lamp at $550 and a Sevres silver urn lamp at $595.

The Science of Seeing

A turning point in the philosophy of home lighting occurred in 1933. Said to be "going off the gold standard," lamps were henceforth to be considered for their lighting efficiency as well as for their decorative features. Using the concept of better lighting as the best way to sell lamps was spearheaded by the General Electric

Home Electric Lighting in 1934

The lighting conditions in a rural home about thirty miles from New Orleans were described by the Louisiana Power and Light Company:

The house, a four room bungalow style, looked typical of the majority of homes in the village. The total connected load in this house was 200 watts. An old fashioned bridge lamp was connected to a drop cord in the living room. The combination kitchen-dining room was lighted by a drop cord holding a two-way socket with 2-25 watt lamps. Both bedrooms had similar drop cords. An extension cord was fastened to one so that a light might be carried into the bathroom when necessary. The fifty watt lamp found in one bedroom, used at night as a sewing room, was so antiquated that when tested in the home lighting kit, it only gave 1/6 the light of the one in use in the living room bridge lamp. This represented the entire lighting facilities of a home inhabited by a man and his wife who spent most of their evenings at home reading and sewing. (*Lighting & Lamps*, May 1934)

Company. In 1934 *Lighting* magazine reported that "the lamp business is virtually in the process of a revolution." General Electric brought "Science of Seeing" facts to the public through its advertising. The information was based on research that the G. E. Lighting Research Laboratory conducted at Nela Park near Cleveland, Ohio. Their foot-candle standards for illumination created promotion opportunities for lighting engineers and salesmen alike. As *Lighting* magazine reported in 1934:

The new tables, which propose a reduction in the toll of crippled eyesight and a conservation of human energy, logically divide themselves into several distinct classifications depending upon the various visual tasks to be considered and offer recommended values for each and every task common to stores, offices, factories, schools and outdoor areas.

The new tables are extremely conservative when compared with intensities that are to be found outdoors. They are based, however, on practical considerations and economic justification.

The Illuminating Engineering Society (I.E.S.) set design specifications for portable floor and table lamps to provide superior lighting. Lamps that conformed to these requirements were known as I.E.S. lamps. Manufacturers designated them by an I.E.S. tag, which guided consumers in purchasing better lighting for their homes. Lamps certified by I.E.S. were advertised widely, and Aladdin began to participate in the program in 1934.

I.E.S.-approved table and floor lamps were fitted with white glass reflectors. Aladdin's 1935 literature shows 18-and 19-inch I.E.S. paper shades; lamps without glass reflectors and with Whip-o-lite shades were not I.E.S. approved. To meet I.E.S. specifications, The Mantle Lamp Company made special parchment shades for the approved lamps. Later, the company dropped out of the I.E.S. program. The following form sales letter stated the reason why:

Immediate shipment is being made of your order dated (date) and we hope it reaches you promptly. Thank you very much for this additional business.

However, these lamps will not carry the I.E.S. tags. We do not use them on Aladdin Electric Lamps or Aladdin "Whip-o-lite" shades.

When the I.E.S. movement was first started by the Illuminating Engineering Society we entered into it enthusiastically. Raising lamp manufacturing standards was "right up our alley." There was so much shoddy merchandise being put on the market—both lamps and shades that were built down to a price rather than up to a standard—that we felt that anything that would force lamp manufacturers, as a whole, to use approved cords, approved plugs, approved sockets and other parts that would insure trouble free service was something that was badly needed in the lamp industry.

Later they began setting standards for shades. They refused to approve Aladdin Whip-o-lite because it permitted too much light to pass thru. It was then that we made our decision to withdraw. Aladdin Whip-o-lite softens and diffuses light. Compared with the old style oil parchment shades which were so popular for so many years, you can use a 25 watt lamp under an Aladdin Whip-o-lite shade and get as much light from it as you would get from an ordinary oil parchment with a 50 watt bulb. So use of Aladdin Whip-o-lite shades actually effected a saving in current. That was contrary to the desires of the utilities. They were interested in developing lamps that would use more current because that's what they were selling.

You will find Aladdin Electric lamps and Aladdin Whip-o-lite shades made in accordance with the highest standards. You will find them equipped with approved cords, approved plugs, approved sockets, approved reflectors—the very best obtainable —because Aladdins are built up to a standard and not down to a price.

The Better Light Better Sight Bureau was a nonprofit organization formed in New York City in 1934 to promote improved home lighting. Financed by General Electric, Westinghouse, Sylvania, and the Edison Electric Institute, the bureau was established to "foster a better understanding of the relationship of light and sight." It sponsored educational programs and published the *Better Light Better Sight News* magazine.

About one hundred lamp manufacturers, including The Mantle Lamp Company, were members of an organization called the Certified Lamp Makers (C.L.M.), which developed new specifications for improved lighting in 1947. This program came after the I.E.S. and Better Light programs. The principal differences between C.L.M. lamps and I.E.S. lamps were the reflector shapes, reflector brightness, and the distribution of light to provide higher foot-candle values. I.E.S. lamps distributed 60 percent of their light upward and 40 percent downward. Light distribution in C.L.M. lamps was just the opposite—40 percent upward and 60 percent downward. I.E.S. reflector bowls had a maximum brightness of 3 foot-candles per square inch, while the C.L.M. glassware had an average bowl brightness of 5 foot-candles per square inch. A lamp that met C.L.M. specifications was permitted to carry a tag stating "This is a Certified Lamp."

The Mantle Lamp Company was quick to take advantage of the Better Light Better Sight Bureau's information and the C.L.M. program in advertising and promotion of their home light products.

The War Years and After

In 1940 the war in Europe curtailed foreign imports. As a consequence, American crystal, glass, and china lamps gained in popularity. Following Pearl Harbor in 1941, the War Production Board (WPB) cut the manufacture of domestic incandescent lamps by 20 percent and again later that year by 60 percent. The July New York Lamp Show was cancelled, and in December 1942 the WPB forbade the manufacture of all portable electric lamps and shades. Many lamp manufacturers started making giftwares and decorative accessories instead. Exhibitors at the Merchandise Mart were said to be "more than ankle deep in the gift field."

The Mantle Lamp Company was granted

Fig. 34. Store merchant's display of Aladdin electric lamps, Pine Bluff, Arkansas, 1936.

Fig. 35. Store merchant's display of Aladdin electric lamps, Hannibal, Missouri, 1949.

permission to continue manufacturing glass kerosene mantle lamps, and some burner parts were made of steel rather than brass. The company made Alacite glassware and smoking items for a short period. Most of these giftware items were soon discontinued, however, when the company developed ski-stoves and lanterns for the armed services.

Following World War II, a huge Victory Lamp Show was held in November 1945 in New York City. The Mantle Lamp Company exhibited its 1946 lines. Several of these lamps, mostly Alacite, were the same styles that were sold before the war. Collectors can easily distinguish prewar lamps made of old formula Alacite from the postwar lamps made without uranium oxide in the glass. The ones containing uranium glow under ultraviolet light.

During 1947 and 1948, Aladdin faced severe competition in the electric line. More than 2,000 electric lamp manufacturers were competing for the estimated $200 million market. Meanwhile, rural electrification was taking its toll on the Aladdin kerosene market. With the significant reduction in the number of farms after World War II, the U.S. kerosene lamp sales dramatically declined. No longer could Aladdin's kerosene lamp business support the old sales efforts. Electric lamps would have to pay their own way. Aladdin therefore no longer enjoyed its unique, integrated production and distribution of kerosene and electric lamps which previously had been a decided advantage. Both the kerosene and the electric product lines were to diminish in only a few years.

V. S. Johnson, Jr., made decisions that would affect the future of the Chicago and Alexandria operations. In 1948 he began construction of new offices and manufacturing facilities to produce vacuum bottles in Nashville, Tennessee. The new plant opened in 1949, and the general offices were moved from Chicago to Nashville.

One interesting post-war change in distribution was the party plan initiated by Stanley Home Products in Massachusetts. In one year in the late 1940s, Stanley used more than 300,000 Aladdin electric lamps, principally as a gift for the party givers. These lamps were a Chartreuse (lime-green) G-322 and a DuBonnet (maroon) G-311.

Fig. 36. This Magic Touch lamp turned lamps on and off in Aladdin's display room, 1950.

End of an Era

In 1950 a touch device was built into an Arabian Nights style lamp. With dramatic flare, the device was used to turn on and off an entire display of lamps in wholesale showrooms. Visitors to Aladdin's Nashville showroom could walk up to the lamp, rub it, and lo and behold! brilliant light from every table and floor

Aladdin Booklet for Homemakers

A new booklet giving advice to homemakers on the selection and arrangement of portable lamps for the home is issued by Aladdin Industries, Inc., 705 Murfreesboro Road, Nashville, Tenn., under the title "Decorator Guide."

This book was written by Robert Burton, Chicago designer who has recently designed many of the lamps in the new Aladdin Lamps line. It is stated that it embodies the results of research of point-of-purchase and on-the-spot interviews with both store personnel and women puchasers. It is available, without charge from Aladdin Industries. (*Lighting & Lamps*, December 1951)

lamp instantly filled the room. Another touch, and all the lights went out.

The touch device built into Magic Touch table lamps in 1954 and 1955 was patented by Fred Schumann and assigned to Aladdin Industries of Nashville. At least four design models were sold. Priced from $19.95 to $24.95, they were expensive at a time when most of Aladdin's table lamps carried wholesale price tags from $3.95 to $7.95.

The Magic Touch lamps were the grand finale. Not only were they expensive, but they turned on and off by themselves with any surge in electrical power during storms or when appliances were used in the home.

Aladdin ceased operations at Alexandria, Indiana, in June 1952 after twenty-five years. At the time, there were 431 workers with a weekly payroll of approximately $25,000. Aladdin continued the electric line in Nashville, but nearly all the lamp components were purchased and assembled. They were made of pottery, wood, metal, and plastic. Most were of a "modern" design but none was unique: other companies had similar products. The last sales catalogue of electric lamps was printed for the 1955 line. Aladdin electric lamps were discontinued in 1956 because they were unprofitable.

Aladdin Glass

Glass, which was first made in ancient times, is a hard, amorphous product of fusion, varying widely in its composition. Most commonly, however, glass is a mixture of sand, soda ash, and limestone that does not form crystals when cooled. Various chemicals may be added to color it and impart desired physical properties.

In 1920 James Gillinder, a renowned glassmaker, said that it was practically impossible to define glass. Until Gillinder's time, the chemical basis of glassmaking was an emerging science. Proven formulas were simply passed from generation to generation with little knowledge of the chemical changes involved. Today we know that even a small change in the proportion of substances in the batch, the furnace temperature, the rate at which glass cools, and the amount of impurities can make a great difference in the appearance and properties of glass.

Specialty Glass

Glassmaking is an ever-changing technology improved by scientific research. When Henry Hellmers, Aladdin's glass superintendent from 1935 to 1942, graduated from the University of Michigan in 1921, only about eighty elements were known; about half of them were useful in

Fig. 37. Henry Hellmers, 1921 graduate, University of Michigan.

glassmaking. Yet despite these early limitations, the industry was beginning to develop glass for special uses, for machine manufacture, and improved colors with new ingredients.

Aladdin made many types of glass in either day tanks or continuous tanks:

Chimney glass (boro-silicate): generally a transparent, semi-heat-resistant glass for chimneys, vacuum bottle blanks, and gallon jug liners.

Ordinary lime glass: a transparent or colored crystal that melts at a lower temperature and is easier to work than boro-silicate glass. Soda-lime glass was used for vases, shades, and lamp fonts. Made into chimneys, it produces a whitish, effervescent bloom on the surface when heated.

Marblelike glass: made of colors blended in marblelike tones of green and amber. The inside of the lamp base was usually painted to match these colors. The glass was described by the predominant color. As far as we know, this glass was not named for the retail trade. Lamps made of marblelike glass can be found in several designs, but they are scarce.

Moonstone: an alabaster glass that is semitransparent. Hellmers described moonstone as "a misty translucent glass similar to true moonstone." Aladdin made its moonstone glass mostly in white, pink, green, and yellow. It was commonly known among workers in the glass industry during the 1930s and 1940s.

Reflector glass: a white opal glass made for reflectors and shades. I.E.S. glass had to meet the light transmission standards of the Illuminating Engineering Society.

Opal glass: named Alacite for marketing purposes and extensively used for Aladdin electric lamps. Alacite is an opaque ivory glass. Being a true opal glass, it emits fiery opal colors under strong light or through the thinner parts of the glass. Opal glass can range widely from opaque to nearly transparent in the density of whiteness. Hellmers, classifying it as a type of glass rather than a specific color, recorded formulas for seventeen major colors of opal glass in his batch book.

In their textbook on glass, Hodkin and Cousen (1925) have this to say about opal glass: "Whilst being semi-opaque, [it] gives transmitted light an opal or fiery colour, whilst 'alabaster' glass diffuses the light without materially altering its colour." They go on to say that opal glass can result from different batch formulations. These include emulsions, solid suspensions, and devitrification, as well as the use of unique opalescing agents that create cloudy or milky glass. The procedure used can also affect the properties of the glass.

Alabaster and opalescent glass: formulas for both types grouped under this single heading in Hellmers's batch book. This group was separate from his formulas for moonstone. We therefore surmise that they were special for making glass with cloudy opalescence. Whether opalescence is produced depends on the temperature or rate of change in the temperature while making the glass, according to Hodkin and Cousen (1925). Alabaster glass can also be made in this way, depending on the skill and intention of the glassmaker. This glass was later named Opalique for marketing purposes.

In 1935 the cost of raw materials for making Aladdin glass ranged from $12 to $48 a ton. The purity of the ingredients is the main reason for the difference in cost. The following are in approximate decending order of the volume of glass made at that time:

Purpose	Cost per ton	Purpose	Cost per ton
Chimney glass	$19.33	White moonstone	$27.12
Green crystal	12.16	Rose moonstone	43.19
Amber crystal	12.96	Green moonstone	35.20
Reflector white	48.10	Black Glass	18.53

Mantle Lamp Features Etched Moonstone

The Mantle Lamp Company, with showrooms in the Merchandise Mart, Chicago, reports marked activity in several of its lamp lines. Etched moonstone is something new and popular in bases. The moonstone when acid etched closely resembles alabaster.

Another unusual type of lamp displayed by this firm boasts a supplementary light in the base. This not only adds to the general attractiveness of the lamp, but when only the base light is used the lamp serves as an excellent night lamp. A soft glow is shed through the rough glass base. (*Lighting & Lamps*, April 1935)

Fig. 38. G-84 Velvex lamp with floral finial.

Fig. 39. Velvex vases in 10-inch size with G-84 in a mottled peach color.

Trade Names

To boost sales, salespeople named some Aladdin glass to give it an identity of its own for advertising. The workers who made the various glasses usually did not know them by the names advertised in the retail trade.

Velvex: coined by Aladdin Industries for vases developed for the giftware trade in 1935. The glass was mottled, with one or more colors incorporated during manufacture. The vases were made in various sizes and colors. Some were etched, many were not. The etched ones were made of mottled colors on a clear glass background. Those that were not etched were mottled on a moonstone background.

Velvex vases were made in April 1935, according to George Dauenhauer, who received one as a wedding gift. S. D. Goodwin is generally given credit for the idea of making Velvex vases from old molds left over from the Lippincott plant. These vases were made for less than six months. Although the small bud vase was said to be popular, most of the line did not sell and Velvex vases were quickly discontinued.

In a letter to the author, Henry Hellmers described how Velvex was made:

In Figure #38 of your book (*Aladdin—The Magic Name in Lamps*), you show a glass mentioned as Velvex. This was one glass that I experimented with that I thought would be quite readily acceptable. However, it did not take too well. You might be interested in how it was produced. The glass was gathered on a pipe as a ball and while still hot, the ball was rolled on a plate that was covered with powdered glass of a different color. Then the ball of glass was blown into a shaped mold. After the top was cut off and the rough edges ground and finished, the piece of ware was dipped into a frosting solution to be acid etched. Personally I thought it to be a very pretty piece of ware.

Electric lamps were made of a moonstone glass mottled with color similar to the Velvex vases, although at the time the lamp bases were not called Velvex in the literature. Even so, a collector might find one of the lamps with a Velvex sticker similar to those occasionally found on the vases.

Because of the glass, lamps G-67, G-68, G-81, G-84, and G-124 are classified as Velvex lamps

Fig. 40. Assorted colors of Velvex vases in 12-,14-, and 16-inch sizes. Each vase is a different shape.

Fig. 41. Assorted colors of Velvex vases in 10- and 14-inch sizes. The 10-inch vases often vary in height. Each vase is a different shape.

Fig. 42. Velvex table lamp G-81, 1936-37.

Fig. 43. Velvex table lamp G-124, 1937-38.

Fig. 44. Velvex table lamps G-67 and G-68, 1935.

(see Table 2). The first ones (G-67 and G-68) were offered in an August 15, 1935, sales brochure and possibly were sold in 1936. As far as we know, no Velvex lamps were etched in the same way that many of the vases were treated.

Opalique: the name coined for special glass made by Aladdin. The name first appeared in sales literature dated July 1, 1938, but I suspect that Opalique was the "special glass" that Hellmers originally developed for Susie and Lulu figurines in 1936. In 1938, G-17 was offered in Crystal Glass or Opalique Glass, but the color was not specified. From 1938 to 1940, Opalique lamps were offered in several decorated colors (Table 3).

The glass is opalescent and is usually decorated with paint on the inside and sometimes on the outside of the glass base to provide color. The opalescent quality suggests that the original prefix of the name Opalique was derived from the word opalescent. In his batch book, Hellmers recorded Aladdin formulas for opalescent glass between 1938 and 1941. Company sales literature proclaimed:

Lamps in Opalique are another Aladdin

Table 2. Velvex Aladdin Electric Lamps, 1935 to 1938

Stock no.	Years sold	Height, inches Base	Height, inches Harp[a]	Diameter of shade, in.	Decorated color[b]
G-67	1935	$12\,^3/_4$	$20\,^7/_8$	13, 14	Amber, green, white
G-68[c]	1935	$12\,^3/_4$	22	16	Amber, green, white
G-84	1936	11	$20\,^1/_2$	14	Amber, green, rose
G-81	1936-37	$13\,^7/_8$	$21\,^7/_8$	13, 14	Amber, green, white
G-124	1937-38	$12\,^1/_8$	$19\,^7/_8$	13, 14	Amber, white

[a] Height measured to the washer at the top of the harp.
[b] These colors, applied to the inside of the base, are visible through the glass. The moonstone glass is pale white mottled with black. G124 has also been found made of white moonstone mottled with green.
[c] Two-light cluster

Table 3. Opalique Aladdin Electric Lamps, 1938 to 1940

Stock no.	Years sold	Decoration colors[a]	Other glass used
Boudoir Lamps			
G-16	1939	Not specified	Etched crystal, Alacite
G-17	1938-39	Not specified	Crystal
G-18	1939-40	Green, rose, blue	Crystal, Alacite
G-19	1939	White, blue	Alacite
Table Lamps			
G-165	1939-40	White, tan	Moonstone
G-166	1939-40	White, green, blue, peach, yellow	Moonstone
G-171	1939-40	Green, peach, white, yellow	Moonstone
G-173	1938-40	Ivory, green, clear, blue	None
G-178	1938-39	Ivory, green, tan, blue	None
G-179	1938-40	White, tan (etched)	None
G-181	1938-39	Ivory, amber (etched)	None
G-183	1939	Blue, yellow	Alacite
G-184	1939-40	Clear, white, amber	None
G-185	1939	Amber, white, blue	Alacite
G-186	1939-40	White, amber, blue	Alacite
G-187	1939-40	White, amber, blue	Alacite
G-189	1939	Green, amber, clear	None
G-190	1939-40	White, peach, blue	None
G-191	1939-40	Amber, blue	Alacite

[a] G-16, G-17, G-178, and G-184 were not listed as color-decorated in the price literature, implying that the glass color is ivory, green, blue, amber, and so forth.

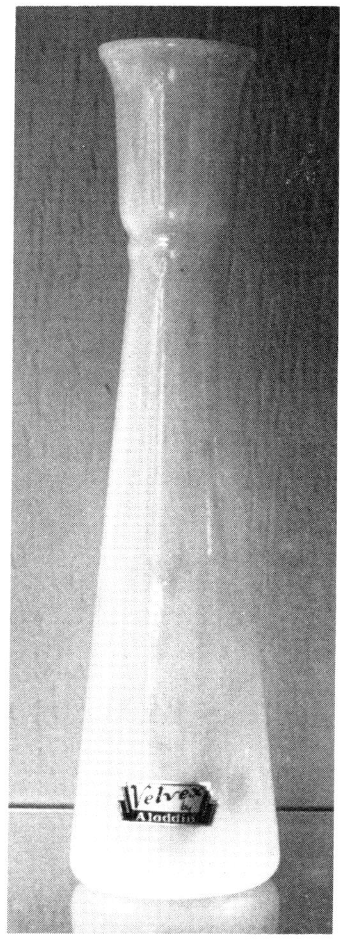

Fig. 45. Label found on some Velvex vases.

Fig. 46. G-184 in Opalique colors show the opalescence in the thicker parts of the glass, 1939-40.

Fig. 48. G-130 in light green Opalique.

Fig. 47. G-16 figurines showing opalescence in the thicker part of the glass.

Fig. 49. G-16 figurines in various kinds of glass: Alacite, clear crystal, etched clear crystal, Opalique colors, and experimental colors. These figurines are also found in other colors.

creation which appeals very strongly to lovers of the artistic and beautiful. In character, it is comparable only to genuine Lalique--a product of a famous French maker of the most expensive and exclusive glassware. Opalique is available in Aladdin Table and Boudoir Lamps in its natural color (clear), etched or in tantalizing tones of Amber or Green. Opalique in any color has sparkle, life and vitality, and molded in Aladdin's original designs becomes a thing of beauty and a joy forever. Ask your dealer to show them to you.

Note that lamps G-130 (1936 to 1938) and G-163 (1937 to 1939) were not called Opalique in the sales literature. They were described as "Clear Etched Crystal" or "Clear Crystal," although we now know that the G-130 was made in several Opalique colors. The G-163 has not been found in any Opalique colors. The G-16 was offered in 1939 in "Etched Crystal" or "All Opalique Glass" with no color specified. The G-16 figures are found in several Opalique colors.

Today, the similarity of Aladdin's etched glass figurine lamps to Lalique seems obvious to collectors, who sometimes call them Opalique even though the lamps are made entirely of clear crystal. Current research suggests that Opalique correctly refers only to clear or transparent colored glass of a milky opalescence.

The opalescence is intensified in the thicker parts of the glass. The thin parts are almost clear of any opalescence. The characteristics of Opalique are therefore best appreciated in figurines and lamps artistically designed to allow the opalescence to develop in the thicker parts, as in G-184. Lamps made without variations in glass thickness do not show the strong opalescence. They were painted on the inside to provide color and to hide the electrical cord. Some lamps were also etched to achieve opacity. Unfortunately they conceal the real beauty of the Opalique glass.

Aladex: coined for Aladdin's moonstone glass in the late 1930s. Many of the Aladex glass lamps were white moonstone and were color sprayed on the inside of the glass base. The color was visible through the glass. In the July 1938 illustrated catalogue of 1939 designs, the following lamps were advertised as Aladex glass: G-26, G-33, G-63, G-69, G-95, and G-153. However, in the corresponding "Dealers Wholesale Price List," the name Aladex was not mentioned. Short-lived, the name Aladex is

Fig. 50. Aladex table lamp G-95, 1939.

not found in company literature printed after 1938. All moonstone lamps, decorated or etched, were simply called moonstone after that date.

Alacite: first appeared in the sales literature on January 1, 1939. Alacite lamps were either decorated or undecorated. The decorated lamps were often painted on the inside as well as painted or stained on the outside of the glass base.

Alacite was the first truly opaque glass that Aladdin made for lamps, with the exception of a very few made of black glass in earlier years. A registered trademark, Alacite was described as follows:

Alacite is the trade-mark applied to a startlingly beautiful lamp base and pedestal material discovered by Aladdin after many months of research. It is quite impossible to adequately describe it in words. It resembles many of the semi-precious mineralites in texture. It has much of the softness, and tone of tusk (genuine ivory)—the only color in which it is yet available. You're sure to like Alacite. It has character, class and plenty of personality. Ask to see the charming boudoir and table lamps in which ALACITE is now available.

Some twenty-seven Alacite designs were offered in 1939. It was the predominant glass for nine production years (excluding the war years), from 1940 through 1951. The popular Alacite lamps were offered in several applied colors to accent the glass design. They often had lighted bases, which appealed to the housewives of that time.

Henry Hellmers stated that Alacite was one of three similar opal glasses that he developed. The others were an ivory for Arko Agate in 1928 and the glass named Cambridge Crown Tuscan in 1930. He said that all were a very similar type of glass.

The original Alacite formula contained uranium oxide, which, along with red lead, imparted its characteristic ivory tint. Alacite was not intended to be white, pink, or brown. The original Alacite produces a characteristic

Aladdin Introduces ALACITE
(Trade-Mark)

After many moons of intensive research and experiment in quest of a new and distinctive material of character and individuality for use in connection with the manufacture of lamp bases and pedestals, Aladdin now introduces Alacite to the public for the first time.

Alacite, at present produced in one color only - Old Ivory- has infinitely more charm and lure than is found in most semi-precious mineralites, and possesses all the seductiveness and mystery of the Orient. Alacite can not be compared with any other present day material, but rather to some of those rare and unusual materials produced in the "lost art" ages, centuries ago.

Alacite is instantly captivating in appearance. When skillfully molded as it now is into these artistically designed Aladdin boudoir and table lamps, shown herein, it gives them an irresistible and everlasting eye-appeal. Its attractiveness and fascination sets these lamps apart and above all others in customer preference. You are certain to find it so. (*Electric Lamp and Shade Catalog Supplement*, Jan. 3, 1939)

yellow glow under ultraviolet light. The Atomic Energy Commission did not permit the use of uranium during or after the war; therefore, Floyd Pruden's revised formula after World War II did not contain uranium. This change in composition, along with construction of a continuous Alacite tank, made it difficult to match the original color closely. Lamps made after the war varied in color, and the Alacite will not glow under ultraviolet light.

Before the Alexandria plant was closed, two continuous glass tanks were in operation: one large 45-ton clear tank and one 20-ton Alacite tank. No other colored glass lamps were made after Hellmers left Aladdin in 1942. Some colored glass finials were made in 1949. All ivory or cream-colored glass is not Alacite made by Aladdin. Collectors will find lampshades, torchieres, dishes, inkwells, and glassware made of a similar colored glass. Other companies made this glass, and although similar, it is not Alacite.

Aladdin Deco

In the eyes of many Aladdin collectors, the figurines produced in the 1930s and 1940s were among the finest electric lamps made from Aladdin molds. Their design and making was no accident—the necessary ingredients were all in Alexandria, Indiana. The time, the place, and the people were right for The Mantle Lamp Company to create unique lamps.

Influence of Art Deco

According to Katharine Morrison McClinton (1972), the art form that became known as Art Deco was most popular between 1925 and 1935. The new style was made prominent by the Exposition Internationale des Arts Decoratifs et Industriels Modernes, which was held in Paris in 1925. A symmetrical style often using modern materials and bold colors, Art Deco touched all phases of architecture, as well as furnishings, clothing, jewelry, art objects, transportation, lighting, and advertising.

Lamps popular during the Art Deco period often featured nudes, some with illuminated backgrounds and others supporting lighted globes or lighted columns. While studying McClinton's text, one cannot help but be impressed by the striking similarity of some Aladdin lamps (G-77, G-130, G-163, G-375, for example) to the artistic designs found in glass lamps, vases, and other objects made during the Art Deco period.

It was fortunate that Eugene Schwarz was Aladdin's chief designer. Trained in Europe, he was familiar with the art movements there. As the Art Deco style became popular in the United States, Schwarz blended the concepts of Rene Lalique with those of Art Deco to create some of the finest lamps Aladdin ever made.

Lalique--Opalique

Aladdin obviously tried to equate the artistic design of its lamps with the concepts of Lalique, who made art glass in France from the 1890s to the 1930s. Lalique glass is often a combination of pressed and blown ware and may include human figures, birds, or other pressed designs. The use of nudes and etching was typical of much Lalique glass, which was popular for its unique quality.

Aladdin Deco Lamps

Alacite became popular for many of Aladdin's electric lamps. Several Aladdin Deco styles are shown to advantage because the glass exhibits an opalescent or fiery quality through the thinner parts or through the edge of the glass. Cupids, figurines that were risque in their time, flower and leaf designs, and other decorations all show the fire of Alacite or the opalescence of Opalique in their relief. Aladdin Deco lamps were also made of moonstone, as well as clear and etched crystal glass.

The Alacite G-16 figurines, which do not have a hole in the glass for an electric cord, have five decorative rings in their base instead of four. We do not know whether these items were made for use as figurines by themselves or for some special lamp.

Aladdin pressed G-16 figurines in many colors of glass made in the Alexandria plant. New colors were tested by pressing the figurines, and the colorful samples lined the walls of T. A. Blain's office so that he could refer to them when choosing colors for new lamp designs. The figures remained there until the plant closed in 1952. At that time, one of the employees was instructed to throw them away. The employee took two bushelbaskets of the colorful figures home for sentimental reasons, and it was ten years later before the order was finally carried out. One day a hired boy cleaning

Fig. 51. G-70 frosted crystal figurine, 1935.

out the garage was told to take the baskets to the dump with other old things of no value. Thus countless G-16 figurines now rest somewhere amid the rubble and garbage of the Elwood city dump.

The double-nude lamp base (G-163) was sold as a glass vase (GV-162) in 1937. But all other Aladdin's glass figure designs were sold for use as lamps. We have no record that the company ever sold the figurines without lamp fixtures for their decorative value alone.

The G-77 Susie figurine lamp was designed with a lighted base. Most, however, are found today without this feature.

The term Aladdin Deco was coined by this author and first published in *The Mystic Light* newsletter in 1976 and then in *Hobbies* magazine in 1978.

Fig. 52. Alacite G-309 with leaf motif, about 1950.

Fig. 53. G-70 decorated figurine. We do not know if this irridescent finish was put into production.

Fig. 54. G-50 powder-dish lamp in white moonstone, 1935.

Fig. 55. M-143 with original shade, 1937.

Fig. 56. Aladdin Service awards 1949. *Front row (left to right):* Byron Morgan, S. D. Goodwin, Pearl Smith, Ethyl Dyer, Elsie McKowen, Sarah Culbertson, Mrs. V. S. Johnson, Sr., Helen Huse, Nettie Wheeler, Lillie Gaither, Herman Mack. *Back row (left to right):* T. A. Blain, Bud Hall, Frank "Shock" Hughes, F. W. Spangler, V. S. Johnson, Jr., Herman Durr, Earl Durr, B. Engh, Clarence Cox, Harry Delong, Eugene Schwarz, Albert Ingram, W. H. F. Millar.

Fig. 57. G-163 double nudes, 1938.

Fig. 58. G-130 frosted crystal figurine, 1937.

Fig. 59. G-375 Alacite dancing ladies urn, 1942.

Fig. 60. G-77 decorated moonstone, 1936.

Fig. 61. Moonstone figurine lamp, sales number unknown, about 1936.

Fig. 62. G-79 crystal rooster table lamp, 1936.

Fig. 63. G-77 in etched crystal glass, ribbed base, 1936.
The shade is not original.

Aladdin Floor Lamps

The first floor lamps, designed in June 1932, were assembled from parts purchased from other manufacturers. Only the paper shades were made by Aladdin. Bases, ornamental spindle parts, and finials were made after the company set up its white-metal department in 1933. Some finials were designed specifically for floor lamps.

Eventually, Eugene Schwarz perfected the one-piece cast floor lamp spindle, which gave Aladdin a competitive edge in manufacturing cost. The company was unique in the industry at that time, because all one-piece floor lamps were made by Aladdin. The white-metal formulation from which the lamps were cast was also claimed to be exclusive. Given the trade name Calzite, the metal was said to be strong, durable, and sharp in ornamental detail. As a result of research, improvements, and new designs each year, floor lamps became a significant part of Aladdin's electric lamp business.

Aladdin made standard (full size) and Junior floor lamps, which were shorter and had smaller dimensions. Aladdin modified the standard floor lamps to build Bridge lamps (arm or swing arms), Reflector lamps (addition of glass or metal reflectors), and Torchere lamps (large glass bowl for indirect lighting). The same base and spindle may be found on all of these styles.

The last floor lamps sold featured natural wood or steel designs. As in 1932, these lamps were purchased as components and assembled by Aladdin.

We have no records that Aladdin attempted to become dominant in the design and manufacture of electric hanging and wall-mounted lamps. One hanging lamp with parchment shades was designed in 1933, but it was probably never produced.

Fig. 64.
Eugene Schwarz improved the methods to cast the white-metal floor lamp spindles; compared in this display with the previous "antique" method.

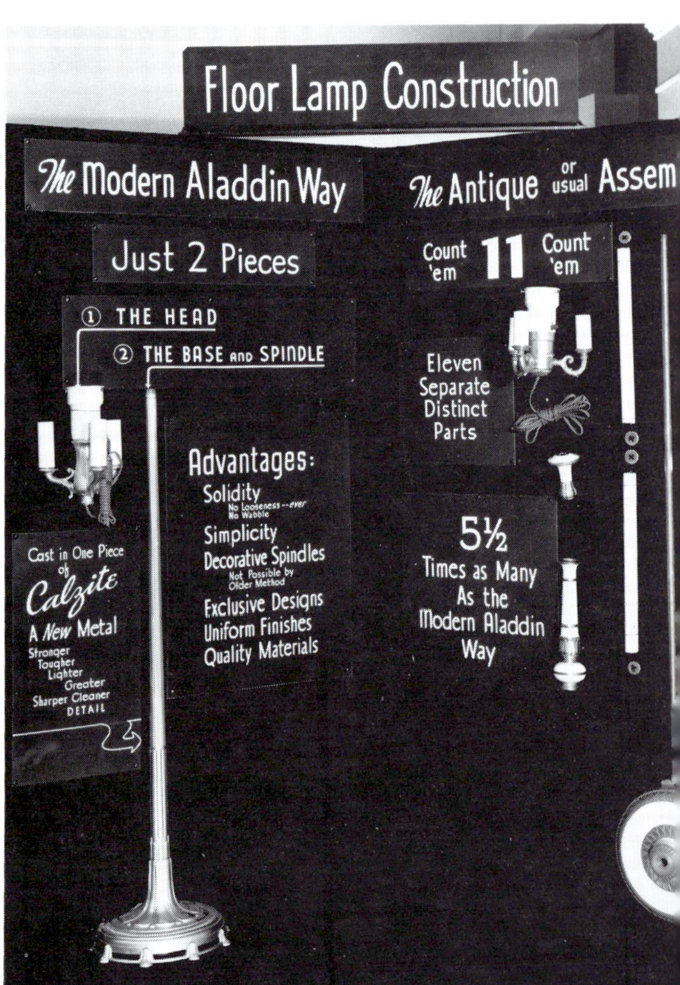

Fig. 65. Aladdin electric Whip-o-lite shades.

Parchment Shades

The Mantle Lamp Company began selling parchment shades in Chicago in 1929. Called Aladdinite in the advertising literature, the early shades were oily and turned dark with the heat of the kerosene lamp. No parchment available in the industry could stand up to the heat of the Aladdin. According to S. B. Huse, castor oil and chemical dryers were used to impregnate the paper for the early shades. He remembered this fact vividly because he loaded a truck with four barrels of castor oil when he moved the shade department to Alexandria about 1930.

The Aladdin parchment shades were colorful and popular, so much so that customers asked dealers for Aladdin's shades fitted for their electric lamps. Because of these requests, The Mantle Lamp Company began selling their shades for electric lamps as well as for kerosene mantle lamps. Some dealers wanted to buy electric lamps complete (shade and base), and this demand prompted the company to design electric lamps in 1930.

Whip-o-lite shades were introduced in June 1933 at the National Lamp Show at the Merchandise Mart in Chicago and a month later at the New York Lamp Show at Hotel New Yorker. The new parchment shades did not contain the traditional vegetable or mineral oils. Instead, highly transparent, synthetic resin developed by The Mantle Lamp Company provided transparency and light diffusion to impregnated paper. Whip-o-lite shades were claimed to be equal to those made of fine white opal glass.

The name Whip-o-lite was selected in honor of Allen D. Whipple, who developed the synthetic, organic resin and the paper-impregnating process. Applying for patents in 1931, he was granted patents #2,137,993, #2,137,994, and #2,137,995 on November 22, 1938. Others involved in this development were Cortland W. Davis, who helped make the machinery to impregnate paper (patent #2,065,636), and Fred O. Reiss, who patented the

A CENTURY of PROGRESS

In just 4 short years

That's the story of "Whip-o-lite" an amazing new shade material.

For over a hundred years parchment shade makers have sought a shade material that would overcome all of the many undesirable features in a parchment shade made of paper impregnated with oil. Just four short years ago our corps of lighting engineers and chemists set about solving this problem. Today after ceaseless, tireless effort and the expenditures of much money for special designed machinery for its manufacture, we present that perfect shade material "Whip-o-lite" as a complete answer. But "Whip-o-lite" not only far outstrips parchment but it also supplies a material of even greater illuminating qualities than the finest opal glass which heretofore has been regarded as the standard of comparison.

Thus in a single stride "Whip-o-lite" now takes its place far in the front of all known shade materials.

There is no oil, either vegetable or mineral, in "Whip-o-lite"; its transparency and diffusion of light is astounding, and for permanency and lasting qualities it is unapproachable.

The development of "Whip-o-lite" is undoubtedly the principal reason why Aladdin "Whip-o-lite" shades dominate the "quality" shade field. Other reasons, however, such as expert designing fascinating combinations in fadeless colors, patented designs for dealer's protection, and painstaking and careful workmanship have set Aladdin shades apart and above all others. And while Aladdin "Whip-o-lite" shades are "quality" products, they are modestly priced, and present an opportunity for quick profit taking by dealers everywhere. (*Lamps*, June 1933)

Fig. 66. Allen Whipple, who developed the process to make Whip-o-lite paper.

special parchment paper (patent #2,041,485) used in the process.

The cost of research to develop Whip-o-lite, not including the tools and machinery, was reported to be more than $49,000. In 1930 this was a substantial investment in research and development and reveals Johnson's concern to improve Aladdin's products in the marketplace.

The first Whip-o-lite shades were made in the conventional style, with sized top and bottom rings to give the shades a slope. Later, fluted, pleated, and cylindrical shades were made for specific lamps.

Designs were printed on the paper by the silk screen process. Eugene Schwarz prepared the new shade designs. For each color of the finished shade, he made a separate drawing of the design in India ink. The process could require six or seven drawings, each painstakingly accurate to prevent any overlapping of colors. Each ink drawing was then photographed onto a sensitized silk screen. When fixed and developed, minute openings were left in the screen where the design transferred through to the shade. The remainder of the screen was coated to prevent color from passing through. This long and expensive silk-screening procedure was later improved by using a photographic process.

Many shades were sent through a "flocking machine" after the final color was applied. In the machine, tiny particles of rayon fiber were blown onto wet lacquer to create a raised plush texture on the finished design. These shades were named Parvelour when introduced in 1937. Eugene Schwarz was granted patent #1,992,676 on February 26, 1935, for this process. Schwarz also laminated fancy cloth to Whip-o-lite paper to create new decorative shapes and designs.

The paper used to make the shades was supplied by Millers Falls Paper Company, Millers Falls, Massachusetts. Whip-o-lite parchment for shades was sold to the Crest Company and to Buckley Studios in Chicago, manufacturers of very high grade lamps and shades. True Whip-o-lite shades have not been made since the Alexandria plant was closed.

Handmade silk shades purchased from other companies were also sold on Aladdin electric lamps for a premium price. Later, Schwarz developed techniques to sew silk shades on machines, and Aladdin made them in the less intricate designs.

Lamp Finials

Aladdin electric lamps were sold complete with a shade and a finial if required. Shades and finials were also sold separately and in assortments to dealers so that housewives could improve any of their lamps at home. The

Fig. 67. Lamp finial assortment, 1938.

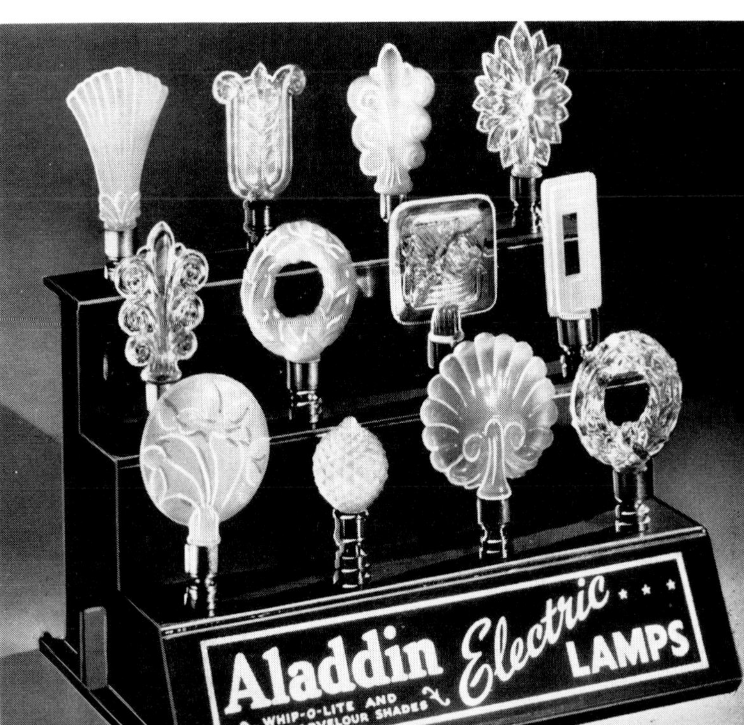

Boudoir, Bridge, and Torchere floor lamps did not use finials.

Lamp finials were made of wood, metal, glass, and glazed porcelain. They were often decorated or made in colors to complement and enhance the lamps being sold. A specific glass finial may therefore be found in different kinds of glass, different colors, etched, and sometimes even painted.

Aladdin designed and made most of its glass finials and many white-metal finials after setting up a white-metal-casting department. Before that time, they purchased all of the metal finials, as well as metal lamp parts. Aladdin continued to purchase some metal finials throughout its electric lamp production. All of the wood and plastic finials were also purchased. Because the purchased finials were not made exclusively for Aladdin, they can be found on other brands of lamps as well.

Smoking Stands and Related Items

Aladdin made several smoking stands, ashtrays, and cigarette containers as accessories to their electric lamps. The first ones were a four-rest ashtray and a pressed glass cigarette container in April 1934. Neither of these items has appeared in catalogue literature found to date.

Smoking stands fitted with Alacite ashtrays were made in 1939 for the 1940 season. Several other pieces of Alacite glassware were also made (see *Aladdin—The Magic Name in Lamps*), including cigarette containers probably intended to be Bridge lamp accessories. Smoking stands were offered throughout the years and were included in the last catalogue printed in 1955.

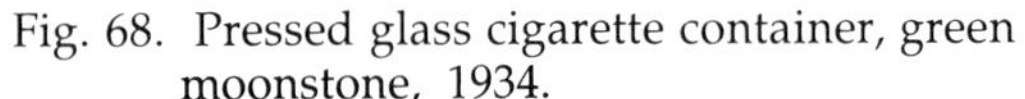

Fig. 68. Pressed glass cigarette container, green moonstone, 1934.

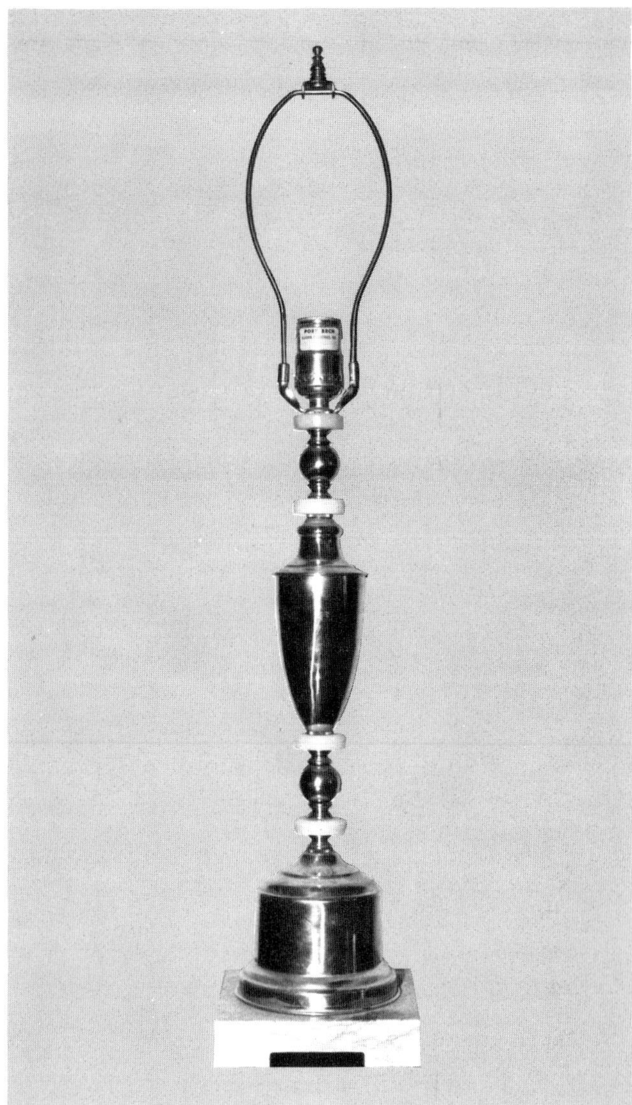

Fig. 69. Brass and marble "Aladdin" electric lamp designed and assembled by Sid Wellman in Portland, Oregon, about 1950.

Other Aladdin Electric Lamps

The Portland, Oregon, branch office was opened by H. O. Johnson, V. S. Johnson's brother, in 1909. It was closed by S. F. Wellman in 1958. In the later years, Wellman assembled four or five somewhat similar brass and marble electric lamps in the basement of his home. These "Aladdin electrics" were sold at the Portland office. When one of the Chicago executives saw Wellman's operation, he said, "If electric lamps can be designed and manufactured in basements, we might as well get out of the business."

Aladdin also manufactured electric lamps in England, Australia, and briefly in France. Lamp parts made in the United States were shipped to Canada and assembled there in the late 1940s.

3. Two Men Who Left Their Mark

Nearly all of the collectible Aladdin lamps eagerly sought today owe their creation to two men: Henry Hellmers, who formulated the glass, and Eugene Schwarz, who designed the shapes into which the glass was molded. Between them, these men served Aladdin for more than two decades.

Eugene Schwarz

Schwarz immigrated to the United States from Germany sometime after World War I. Before moving to Alexandria about 1930, he was employed by The Mantle Lamp Company in Chicago. We do not know when he became involved with the emerging electric lamp. One person suggested that Schwarz designed the Model 12 kerosene vase lamp and then modified it to create the first Aladdin electric lamp. In any event, the manufacture of electric lamps was started on an experimental basis in 1930, simultaneously with Model 12 vase lamps.

Ambidextrous, Schwarz could draw circles of identical size and write his name forwards and backwards with both hands at the same time. He liked horses and often would draw them. The influence of his European training is reflected in his design of many Aladdin lamps, especially Aladdin Deco.

As The Mantle Lamp Company's lamp and shade designer at Alexandria, Schwarz was knowledgeable in all phases of design and production. His unique mechanical ingenuity and artistic talent enabled him to make many improvements in the mold-making process and lamp manufacture. Seldom did he let a technical problem influence or limit what he felt should be done aesthetically. Instead, he found a new way to accomplish his idea. His name appears on many patents assigned to the company, the first of which were granted on August 16, 1932. Among them were patents for numerous ornamental lampshade designs.

Schwarz's patent for the Fluted Shade (application filed August 28, 1933) was granted on March 5, 1940. He designed the shade to use scrap paper left over after cutting round shade blanks from large rolls of Whip-o-lite paper. These shades were such a success that the scrap could not supply the demand. His first designs for fluted shades appeared in the *Official Gazette* on June 5, 1934.

Schwarz improved the process to slush-cast white metal for table and floor lamps in a fine-grain castiron mold similar to those he used for glass lamps. Previously, expensive bronze molds had been advocated and improved by Allan H. Bell of Alexandria. Both men were awarded patents for their work on November 17, 1936. These castiron molds reduced cost significantly and allowed more new designs to be created each year. Schwarz also developed a pressure pot for melting the white metal and filling the molds by air pressure. This process made it possible to cast hollow floor lamp spindles in one piece and thus to reduce the cost of manufacturing to the point where the selling price was very attractive.

Schwarz also improved the glass-molding process. On March 5, 1940, he was granted a

Fig. 70. Aladdin BE-10 horse bookends were finished in antique silver (shown) or oxidized bronze, 1937. This horse was also made into M-150 table lamp in 1937.

Fig. 71. Ethyl Wimmer, draftswoman, and Eugene Schwarz, chief designer, about 1950.

patent for a "one-piece mold-finished pressed boudoir and table lamp." The application had been filed in October 1938. The new lamp, similar or identical to G-17, had a straight solid stem with an open groove to contain the electrical wire. This innovation was quickly followed by a "pressed tubular glass structure" (application filed in February 1939), which meant that Aladdin could now blow an opening through slender glass lamps for the electrical wire. This patent, awarded on February 24, 1942, gave Aladdin the edge in the manufacture of a variety of decorative boudoir and table lamps. Schwarz was called a genius in making press-blow glassware. Some of his design patents were granted after he died in 1952.

Whether Schwarz refused to move from Alexandria to Nashville in 1948 is a matter of speculation. His rare combination of skills were still needed in the lamp manufacturing operation at Alexandria. However, his possible refusal may explain why final plans to move all electric lamp manufacturing to Nashville were not made until after his death. It was said that "the [Aladdin] electric lamp business, for all practical purposes, died with Gene Schwarz."

Henry Hellmers

Henry Theodore Hellmers was born in New York City in 1897. He attended Styvesant High School and later Rensselaer Polytechnic Institute to study civil engineering. After serving during World War I, he was graduated from the University of Michigan as a chemical engineer in 1921. The following year, he married Mary Sherman in Clarksburg, West Virginia, where he began his career in glassmaking with the Akro Agate Company.

From a collector's point of view, Hellmers had an interesting career in glassmaking, and his ability and achievements were recognized within the industry at the time. The 42-year record of his employment that follows was compiled from personal interviews. This record, illustrated with some of his recollections, speaks for itself.

1921—Akro Agate, Clarksburg, West Virginia. Fresh out of college, Hellmers moved to Clarksburg to begin the first of two terms with Akro Agate. He said that it was "an exciting challenge unlike many companies with limited lines. We made hundreds of colors for marbles." He recalled that the marbles were handmade primarily of crystal green, amber, and blue striped with white. "Machine-made marbles came about 1926 and we developed new colors for them."

Akro Agate also made marbles for roadside sign reflectors and graining balls used to remove the grain from lithograph plates for the Ault and Wilborg Company. Some 200,000 of these green glass balls, which were about one inch in diameter, were dumped in a nearby gully when the lithograph process became antiquated.

In 1973 Hellmers wrote to me that "the Akro book [*Akro Agate* by Dr. Budd Appleton, 1972] was quite a surprise to me. Had no idea anyone was collecting it. Around 1930 three of the Akro employees plus the sales manager quit and formed Master Marble Company. They were Messrs. Early, Grimmett, Moulton and Israel. They took a lot of my knowledge with them."

1930—Westite, Weston, West Virginia. Hellmers always referred to Westite as "Balmer-Westite." The J. H. Balmer Company, Newark, New Jersey, was an important wholesaler of Westite wares. He consulted with Westite on weekends and was employed by them full time briefly in 1930. Hellmers made opal as well as green and pink crystal glass for bathroom fixtures and nested ashtrays. The ashtrays I saw were etched to give a satin finish.

1930—Cambridge Glass Company, Cambridge, Ohio. Hellmers often acknowledged the excellent quality of glass made at Cambridge. He referred to Cambridge glass as "pot glass" made in smaller batches under more closely controlled conditions than for "tank glass," which was the procedure used at Aladdin.

Hellmers stated that "at the time I was employed there [at Cambridge], the emphasis was mostly on tableware, such as dishes, plates, cups and saucers, and the like. . . . Many colors were altered by me. . . to make glasses heat resistant in order that hot foods or drinks could be served on them. The idea that Cambridge made some lamps for Aladdin in various times is not true. Alacite was the last in a series of opal glasses that I developed [at Aladdin]."

He listed several improvements and developments in Cambridge glass during his tenure: he revised amethyst; made black (ebony) heat resistant for tableware; revised Willow Blue; revised Peach Blo to make it heat resistant; made experimental gold ruby and Tiffany-type dope glass; made the first

Cambridge commercial selenium ruby; developed Cambridge Alexandrite using the rare-earth neodymium, a very expensive glass ingredient that causes the color to change from pink in artificial light to blue in sunlight; and developed the opal glass named Crown Tuscan. New colors introduced in the pressed and blown vase lines while Hellmers was in Cambridge included Mulberry, Willow Blue, Forest Celadon Green, Golden Shower, and Cherry Gold Red.

Hellmers brought home samples of the glass items he helped to create. Over the years and after many household moves, however, only a small collection survived. A few items were used, while most were neatly stored away on shelves in the kitchen cabinets. Blue was Hellmers's favorite color for dishes, but the color may not have become popular because, as his daughter Ann once said, "Have you ever seen a fried egg on a blue plate?"

1932—Akro Agate, Clarksburg, West Virginia. Hellmers was rehired at Akro Agate to develop glass for the emerging toy dish business. He said that marbles had been a seasonal item and that toy dishes, developed to fill the production gap, became a very large volume item.

According to Hellmers, "Most of the Akro presswares, especially vases, were made after I left, with one or two exceptions. I personally helped to design and make the children's ware. Originally the sets. . .were made only in transparent amber, green and blue. These sets were sold in 7-piece sets and 16-piece sets and sold mostly to Woolworths. . . .You probably will notice the closed handles. . .as compared to open handles on cups and such. These [closed handles] were made to use block molds instead of the more expensive open and shut molds."

I have a black pot that was the original of this line, made without bas-relief, as shown in Figure 19 of Appleton's *Akro Agate* book. This was a tryout and bas-relief was cut into the mold later. (Figure 19 is Pattern No. 300 according to Appleton, and Banded Dart according to Florence, 1975.) I also have the ashtray (Figure 62, Appleton), first made with no Akro mark on the bottom.

1935—Aladdin Industries, Alexandria, Indiana. For the second time, Hellmers was hired away from Akro, this time by Aladdin Industries to make colored glass for the company. He became glass-house superintendent and was responsible for batch

Fig. 72. Henry Hellmers, glass-house superintendent, photographed in 1973.

mixing, colors, production, and work assignments. Until then, clear, amber, and green crystals had been made satisfactorily, along with moonstones of variable quality.

Hellmers helped design a continuous tank for clear crystal chimney glass when he arrived. Built larger than usual, the tank design resulted in a reduction in rejects of at least 25 percent because of improved uniformity and elimination of seedy glass. This was a significant savings, as some 10,000 lamp chimneys were produced daily, eight months during the year, from this tank. Hellmers supervised a maximum of 110 people in the glass-house operations. There were three turns (shifts), usually with forty glassworkers during the day, thirty during the afternoon, and twenty to twenty-five at night.

One of his foremen said, "Henry was a brilliant glass chemist. He knew exactly how everything that he put together would react and what color it would be." Needless to say, the records agree that "he got the job done" to make white, pink, and green moonstones during his first year at Aladdin. Other colors of glass for lamps followed later on at the request of the marketing department.

Hellmers provided the expertise needed at

Aladdin, and during the nine years he worked there, he formulated the glass colors that helped make Aladdin lamps so widely collectible today. His opal glass, named Alacite, is collected solely for its beauty in kerosene lamps, electric lamps, finials, and dishware. Alacite was the only colored glass made for lamps after Hellmers left Aladdin.

Hellmers especially liked the black and white moonstone combinations, but "nobody else did, so we did not make much in black." The covered cigarette trays made in black with a clear cover and clear ashtrays were other favorite items of his made at Aladdin.

1942—Lancaster Lens Company, Lancaster, Ohio. During World War II, Hellmers made special glass for signal lenses and wing lights for the military. While still employed by Lancaster, he served with the U.S. Tariff Commission in Washington, D.C., for one year. He helped allocate equipment and supplies to domestic manufacturers during the war. While serving in this position, Hellmers had lunch with his close friend V. S. Johnson, Sr., at the Willard Hotel in Washington on the day Johnson died.

1946—Owens-Corning Fiberglass, Newark, Ohio. During the next twenty years or so, Hellmers worked for companies that specialized in fiberglass, glass fibers for insulation, mats, and glass blocks. He consulted with other companies and continued his interest in colored glass.

1949—Glass Fibers Company, Waterville, Ohio.

1949—Pittsburgh-Corning, Port Allegany, Pennsylvania. During this tenure, Hellmers helped design and build glass furnaces for Pittsburgh-Corning. After his retirement in 1962, Pittsburgh-Corning sent him to Belgium to build a furnace at Tessenderlo near Brussels. In 1972 he returned to see the completed plant in operation. Hellmers consulted for the Research Department at Monroeville, Pennsylvania, on foam glass and glass insulation products from 1964 to 1966.

Over the years, Hellmers consulted with many companies. He spoke highly of his relationships with Fred Carder, Steuben Glass, and Carl Erickson. Praising Heisey, Cambridge, and Fostoria for their fine glassware, he consulted with these and other companies to help solve their production problems with special glass or glass colors.

Heisey Glass Company, Newark, Ohio. Hellmers made Alexandrite at Heisey after his production at Cambridge. He stated that Heisey made a relatively large amount of Alexandrite while he was there.

Erickson Glass Company, Bremen, Ohio. Hellmers worked with Carl Erickson on many occasions, helping to match colors of early American glass that Erickson reproduced for the Metropolitan Museum in New York. A favorite ashtray of his was one that Carl Erickson made especially for him. It was typically Erickson with spaced bubbles in the glass, but it had a raised center so that Hellmers could tap out his pipe.

L. J. Houze Convex Glass Company, Point Marion, Pennsylvania. Hellmers helped perfect glass for marbleized steering wheel knobs and vaseline glass that contained uranium as a coloring agent.

Hellmers also said that he worked with the following companies on a consulting basis: Alley Agate Company, Sisterville, West Virginia; Louie Glass Company, Weston, West Virginia; Fostoria Glass Company, Moundsville, West Virginia; and Federal Glass Company, Columbus, Ohio.

Throughout their married life, Henry and Mary Hellmers moved many times. Mary took it good-naturedly. In an interview I had with her in Port Allegany, she said they had lived there twenty-seven years, the longest period in any town. "I have moved nineteen times since marriage," she said. Then in a joking manner she added, "I would rather move than dust the house." The Hellmers usually rented in their new town, "always looking for a better house or location."

Although Hellmers was a company manager while working for Aladdin, he was considered "one of the boys" and had excellent rapport with the glassworkers. One of Aladdin's foremen said that "Henry was a real gentleman, one of the nicest bosses I ever worked for." One day Mary Hellmers called on the telephone and asked to speak to Mr. Hellmers. The guard answered that he did not know a Mr. Hellmers. When she asked for Henry Hellmers, he replied, "Oh yes, I know Henry."

While it is appropriate to single out Eugene Schwarz and Henry Hellmers for their accomplishments, I do not want to overlook all those who played important roles to help develop, manufacture, and sell Aladdin electric lamps.

Aladdin factory superintendents following S. D. Goodwin at Alexandria were Tom Blain and Harry Flint. Glass-house superintendents were Jesse Said, Floyd Pruden, Henry Hellmers, and Albert Ingram. Charles W. Clemens was chief designer after Schwarz, and he moved to Nashville. Clemens received many design patents for his electric lamps during the later years. Additional management people are listed in Appendix C. See *A-ladd-in SerVice* newsletters for stories and names of factory workers.

Fig. 73. Retirement party for "Shock" Hughes in 1950 *(left to right):* Floyd Pruden, glass-house superintendent; "Shock" Hughes, shift foreman; Bennie DiRuzza, shift foreman; Izzie Ryan, shift foreman.

Table 4. Guide to Dating Aladdin Electric, Table, Boudoir and Pin-up Lamps, 1930-1956

Year	Sales number[a]	Kind	Year	Sales number[a]	Kind
1930	E-200 to E-205	table	1947	G-280 to G-294	table
	E 300 to E-305	table		M-279	table
1931	Unknown (783 vase)	table	1948	G-294 to G-308	table
	Unknown (785 vase)	table		G-34 to G-38	boudoir
....	Unknown (789A vase)	table		W-300	table
1932	E-310 to E-390	table	1949	G-309 to G-321	table
	E-410	boudoir		G-40 to G-43	boudoir
1933	G-1 to G-19	table		G-202	desk
	G-10	boudoir		M-250 to M-252	table
1934	G-20 to G-30	table		G-354	pin-up
	G-23	boudoir		G-377	urn
1935	G-31 to G-70	table	1950	G-322 to G-334	table
	G-33, G-48, G-50	boudoir		G-44 to G-46	boudoir
	M-1 to M-5	table	1951	G-335C to G-348	table
	MM-6, MM-7	table		G-355C, G-378C	Hoppy
1936	G-71 to G-90	table		G-47C, G-48, G-203R	boudoir
	M-80	table		G-379	urn
1937	G-92 to G-163	table		P-401 to P-408	table
	M-91, M-93, M-122,			W-346, W-347	table
	M-123, M-143, M-146,		1952	G-349 to G-367	table
	M-150, M-158 to			G-49, G-50	boudoir
	M-160, M-164	table		P-409 to P-423	table
	W-147, W-148, W-151,			P-51 to P-53	bedroom
	W-161	table		TV-380	television
1938	G-165 to G-181	table		M-367	urn
	G-15 to G-17	boudoir	1953	P-424 to P-471	table
	M-164, M-174 to			P-54 to P-61, M-59	bedroom
	M-176, M-180, M-182	table		TV-381, TV-382,	
	M-350	pin-up		TV-426	television
1939	G-183 to G-203	table		M-381, M-445 to	
	G-18 to G-21	boudoir		M-458, M-463, M-468,	
	G-351	pin-up		M-469	table
1940	G-206 to G-223	table	1954	P-473 to P-517	table
	G-22 to G-27	boudoir	to	P-64 to P-74	bedroom
	M-218	table	1955	M-62, M-70	bedroom
	G-352	pin-up		D-5, D-6	table
1941	G-224 to G-250	table		TV-383 to TV 387	television
	G-28 to G-34	boudoir		M-475, M-476, M-480,	
	M-238	table		M-494, M-495, M-505,	
	G-213A, G-232A	urns		M-513, M-519 to M-521	table
	G-353	pin-up		W-501 to M-503, W-515	table
1942	G-251 to G-258	table		MT-507 to MT-509	Magic-
	G-35	boudoir		MT-518	Touch
	G-375	urn			
1946	G-259 to G-278	table			
	G-36	boudoir			
	M-275 to M-277	table			
	G-376	urn			

aWe do not know if all sales numbers were assigned in the glass (G) and pottery (P) series.

4. Identification of Aladdin Electric Lamps

Aladdin created more than 500 different designs of table lamps and 250 different floor lamps. If one considers different kinds of glass and different glass and metal color decorations, the total number of Aladdin electric lamps approaches 2,000. This chapter will help collectors to identify their lamps and tell when they were made.

Table Lamp Design Numbers

Aladdin numbered its electric lamps by referring to them as "Stock No." or "Design Number" until 1942 and as "Lamp No." or "Design Number" from 1946 to 1955. These numbers were used in the catalogues and advertisements and they are listed by year in Table 4.

From 1930 to 1933 the design numbers were preceded by the letter *E* to distinquish electric lamps from the predominant kerosene lamp inventory. For example, the following stock numbers designate the style and finish color of the Vogue lamps:

Pedestals	Colors	Vases
E-200	green	E-300
E-201	blue	E-301
E-202	peach	E-302
E-203	orange	E-303
E-204	red	E-304
E-205	ebony	E-305

The *E* numbers were used for new designs sold for the 1932 season, but the lamps were not given separate numbers for each color (see Appendix D, catalogue for 1933).

The use of *G* to designate glass electric lamps began in 1933. Initially the series of *M* numbers (metal lamps) and *G* numbers were two distinct sets consecutively numbered. When these two relatively simple systems were combined, the numbering system became a little more complicated. In 1936 each new lamp design, whether glass or metal, was assigned a number in a single consecutive number series. The lamp composition was designated by the prefix letter *G* for glass and *M* for metal. (See Appendix B for other designations.)

Wholesale price lists and illustrated catalogues were published in January and July (or August) to correspond with show dates for new lamp designs. Lamps were made to supply the orders received. The introduction of new lamps generally followed the sequence given in Table 4. On occasion, however, a particular design might be withheld and not released until the next "season." If not ordered and produced, these one-of-a-kind lamps were often sold to employees. The numbers of each lamp manufactured are not known.

In 1938 the small boudoir lamps were assigned numbers beginning with G-15 to start a boudoir series along with the table lamps.

Fig. 74. G-36 boudoir lamp, 1946.

G-36 boudoir lamp, 1948.

Boudoir lamps were usually smaller and did not have finials. At this point, the numbers of some obsolete lamps were duplicated. Collectors will therefore find that the same number was assigned to different lamp designs in different years. The situation can easily be remedied if collectors distinguish lamps by kind (for example, G-17 boudoir versus G-17 table) or by the year sold (G-17, 1933, versus G-17, 1938).

To make matters more confusing today, new design numbers, usually in consecutive order, were assigned to lamps that (a) differed only in the size of shade offered, (b) had illuminated and nonilluminated lamp bases, (c) had different decoration colors, or (d) were made of different kinds of glass. This numbering system means that a few identical base designs have two or more design numbers.

Although most lamps were sold for only one or two years, some proved so popular that they were sold over a period of several years. For example, the floral design (G-186, same as G-187 except for the harp and shade) was sold from 1939 through 1942 and from 1946 through 1951.

Floor Lamp Design Numbers

Aladdin standardized its numbering system for floor lamps about 1936. Each lamp carried a four-digit sales number. The first two digits identified the type of lamp or light fixture. The last two digits identified the ornamental design of the lamp base and spindle.

As an example, using 60 as the last two digits for the design, the following number system would establish the sales number for each floor lamp:

1060	Junior or Juniorette floor lamps, later called Lounge lamps
2060	Bridge lamp
3360	Single top light, standard socket, with reflector
3460	Cast three-light cluster, all standard sockets
3560	Single Mogul top light with reflector
3660	Three candle arms, with Mogul socket and reflector
3960	Three candle arms with Mogul socket and reflector, and night light.
4560	Torchere floor lamp
4760	Single Mogul top light with three-way switch
4860	Circuline fluorescent floor lamp
5060	Three candle arms with harp and standard socket for reflector bulb
6060	Bridge lamp with reflector, single standard socket
7060	Combination table and Bridge lamp, or swing arm Bridge lamp

Fig. 75. Floor lamps, 1935 *(left to right)*: Bridge 2064, Reflector 3464.

Names of Lamps

With only a few exceptions, Aladdin did not give names to its electric lamps. All lamps were sold by their stock numbers or lamp design numbers. In some instances, collectors have given them names such as cupid (G-46), double nudes (G-163), candelabra (G-211), golden pheasant (G-234), and lady with dog (G-343). The exceptions where Aladdin supplied names were:

1932	Vogue Pedestal	E-200 series
	Vogue Vase	E-300 series
1935	Susie	G-77
	Lulu	G-130
1949	Allegro	G-42
	Celeste	G-186
	Bolero	G-314
	Classic	G-315
	Princess	G-318
1954	Magic Touch	MT-507, MT-508, MT-509, MT-518

How Lamps Were Signed

Although design numbers were not marked on Aladdin electric lamps, most, but not all, were signed with the company name or code. The signature differed depending on the kind of lamp and period when it was made. Sometimes the name Aladdin was misspelled.

Until the time Schwarz set up pattern and white-metal shops at Alexandria, all the white-metal and bronze lamp components were purchased. Cast floor lamp bases were purchased from the Woodruff & Edwards Foundry in Elgin, Illinois, and from the Swayne Robinson Foundry in Richmond, Indiana. These bases had no markings unless they were applied after manufacture. We do not know the significance of numbers that appear on lamp bases, especially on floor lamps. Some may have different numbers on the same lamp.

Fig. 76. Signatures molded into metal bases of floor lamps.

Molded in metal bases. The signatures were usually molded in the base of white-metal or bronze lamps as raised letters and numbers on the underside. Sometimes the letters were incised. Some lamps have more than one signature. A few early lamps were signed by raised letters on a metal band that was glued or riveted on the bottom, usually of bronze bases. On some white-metal bases the signatures may be very faint and difficult to find. Often they are located along the outer edge or rim.

The following are examples of signatures:

MANTLE LAMP CO

MANTLE LAMP CO
OF AMERICA

THE
MANTLE LAMP COMPANY
OF AMERICA

THE
MANTLE LAMP
COMPANY OF AMERICA 3531

THE MANTLE LAMP COMPANY OF AMERICA
INC

ALADDIN

ALADDIN 5289

ML 40611
ALADDIN 40611

ML 40607 D [raised]
ALADDON 40607-D [raised]
ML 40607 D [incised]

ALADDIN 41002
ALADDIN 41182

ALLADIN
40706

Molded in glass bases. The Alacite glass lamp bases were usually marked with raised letters along the bottom edge:

ALADDIN

PAT. APP. FOR

Paper labels. Small paper labels, which were applied on the underside of the base or foot, are usually found on early glass lamps. Sometimes the labels have dropped off, leaving an outline in the painted surface.

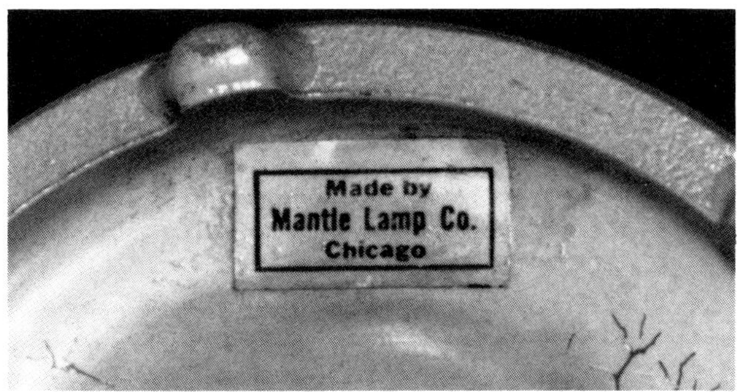

Fig. 77. Signatures printed on small paper labels glued under table lamp bases.

Silver and black labels. These labels may be found on the exterior of some lamps (G-201, G-202, G-229, and G-375, for example).

Fig. 78. This black and silver "Alacite by Aladdin" label is found on some lamps.

Fig. 79. Paper stickers found inside or outside electrical fixtures of Aladdin lamps.

Stickers on electrical fixtures. Paper stickers may be found on the outside or the inside of the electrical fixture of glass, metal, pottery, or wood lamps.

Letters stamped in black ink. These signatures are usually found on the felt or cloth pad under pottery table lamps. Sometimes the lettering is on the pottery base, hidden under the pad.

ALADDIN

ALADDIN INDUSTRIES INC

Fig. 80. Signature stamped in black ink under pottery lamps.

Paper disc. A paper information disc containing information may be found under some table lamps such as G-144.

Fig. 81. Paper disc under some illuminated base glass lamps.

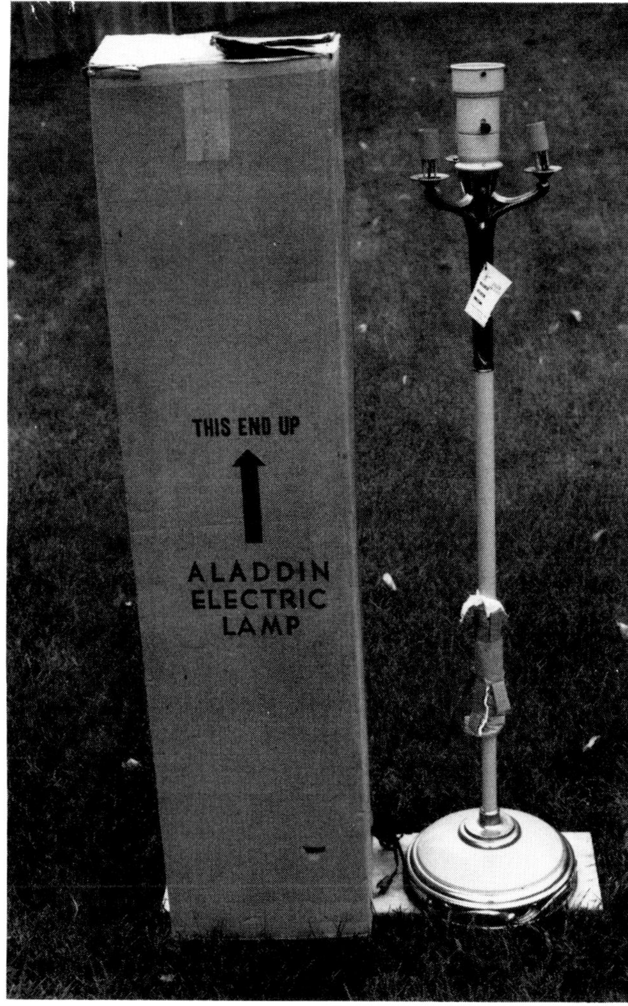

Fig. 82. Aladdin lamps may have an identifying tag and may be boxed for shipment.

the drawings. These names are used with the finials illustrated here. Collectors have also named finials, and those names are included in parentheses.

Most Aladdin finials were made to fit $^1/_4$-inch 27-thread tap size. Some of the early finials, however, were made for $^1/_8$-inch I.P.S.; these were more common on floor lamp finials. Some were made to fit both sizes.

Three variations of brass ferrules can be found on the glass finials. Ferrules are shown with correct finials in the drawings; however, some finials may have more than one ferrule if they were made over several years.

A finial may be made in different kinds of glass, finishes, or colors. In addition, there may be mold variations in the design. There are noticeable differences in the size or design of some Aladdin finials. Wreath comes in two sizes, one thick and the other much thinner. The thick wreath is found in three different ferrules. Cadillac also has a thick and a thin version. Others probably exist as a result of the modification of molds or making new ones. Study and cataloguing of all these possibilities have been left to collectors.

Some glass finials were imperfectly formed during manufacture when the glass did not fill the mold. A good example is the "open wreath" finial, which was not sold as a new design as far as we know.

There are numerous variations of brass, wood, and plastic finials similar to the ones Aladdin purchased. No doubt some of these were substituted and sold on Aladdin electric lamps, but we cannot verify them all.

Finials: Dating and Variations

The finials shown in this book were sold on Aladdin lamps. Based on original drawings and catalogue illustrations, the date given is the first year sold. Some finials were used over many years and others were not. In many instances, a lamp was fitted with one of a choice of finials, even though only one is illustrated in company literature. More than one finial may therefore be appropriate for authenticity.

The Mantle Lamp Company did not sell finials by name. Each had a part number or sales number. However, many of the original drawings studied for this book were named on

Fig. 83. Precision finials before cracking off the cullet. The molten glass was forced into the molds to fill each finial, making ten at one time.

(Worlds Fair)
1932

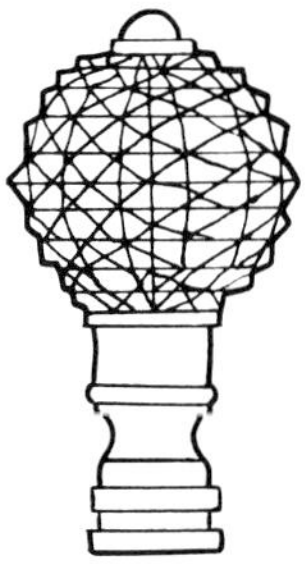

Optic Ball
(Miss Ophelia)
1934

(Mystic Ball)
1934

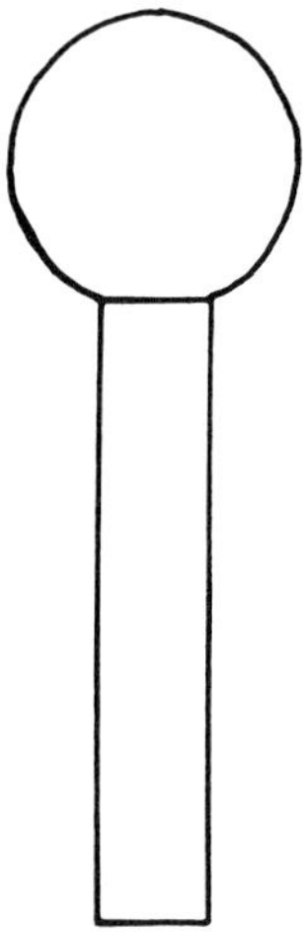

(Mystic Staff)
1934

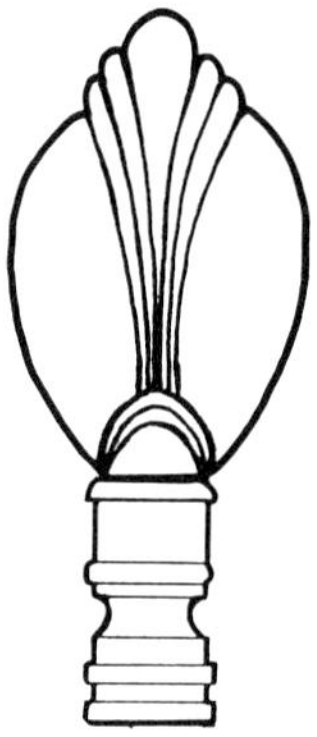

Pear
(Princess)
1935

Rosette
(Gracette)
1935

Palmette
(Fanciful)
1935

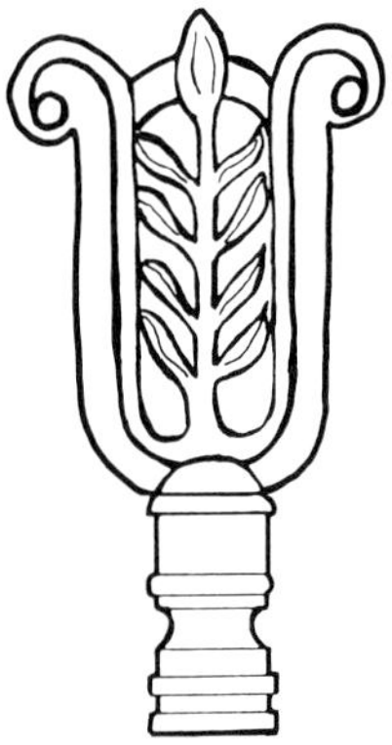

Lyre
(Lorelei)
1936

Leaf Medallion
(Dahlia)
1936

Reeded Fan
(Fantasia)
1936

Floral
(Wild Flower)
1936

Wreath
(Wreath)
1936

Fig. 84. Glass finials made by Aladdin. Names in parentheses have been given to the finials by collectors.

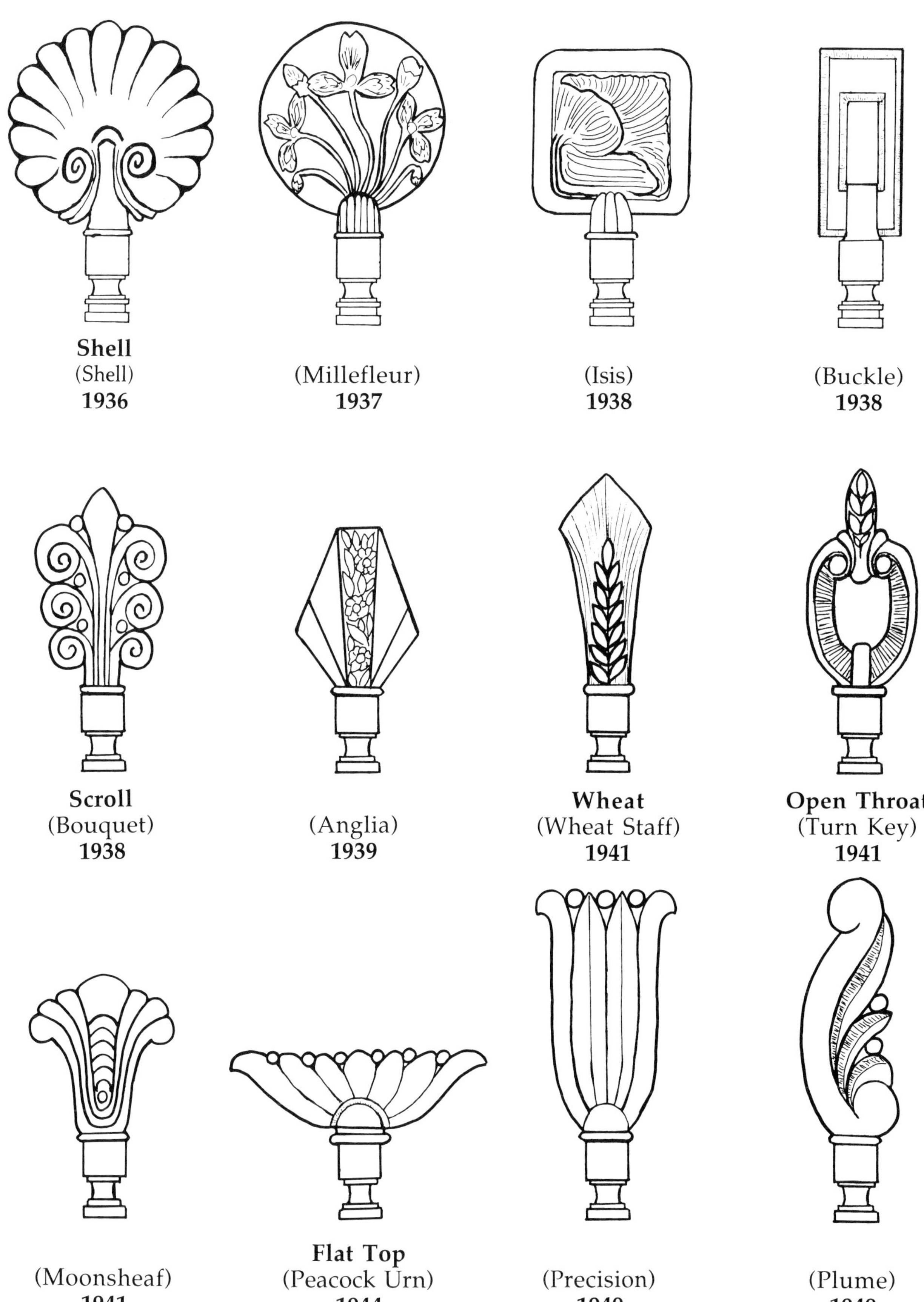

Fig. 84 *continued.* Glass finials made by Aladdin.

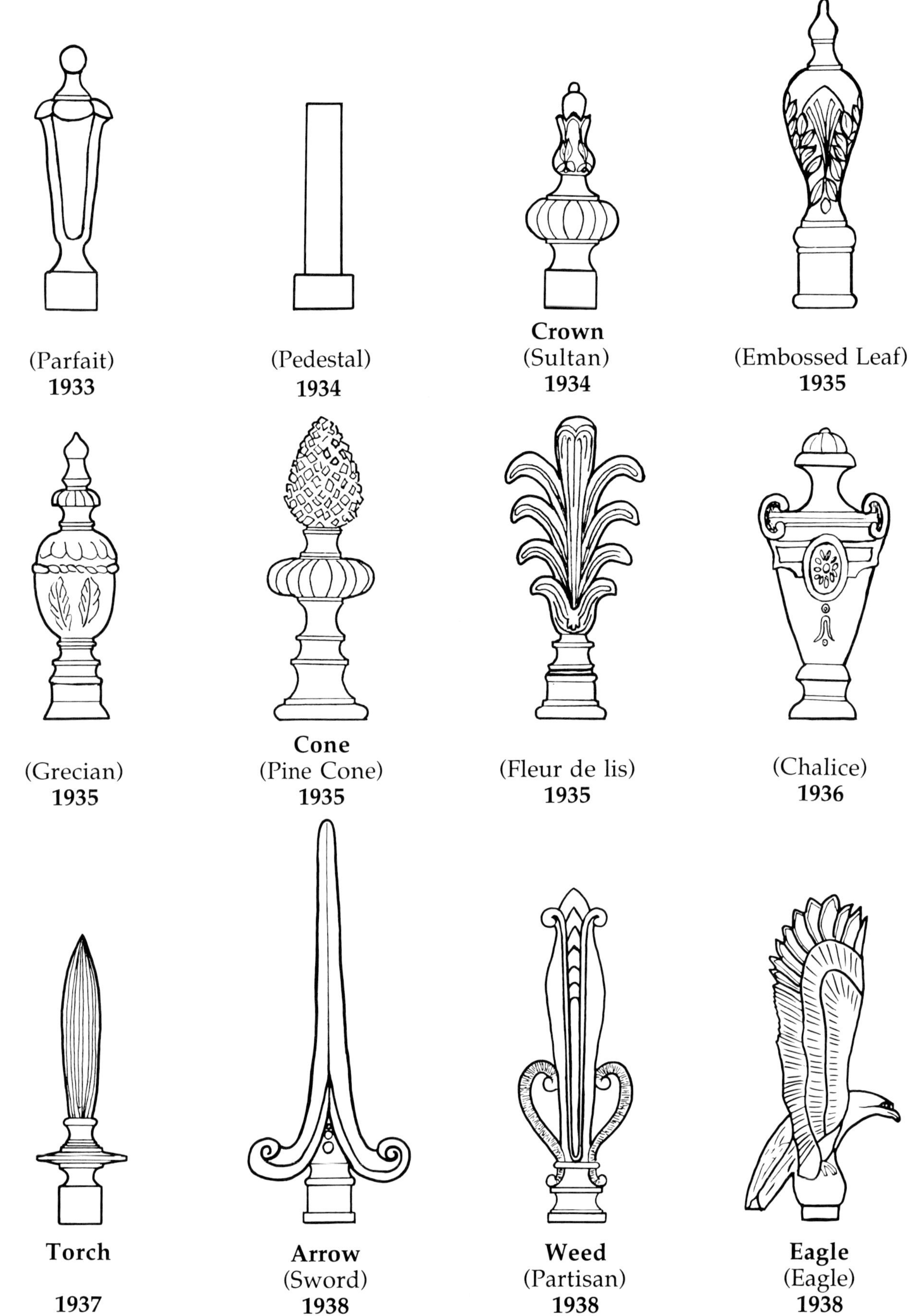

Fig. 85. Metal finials made by Aladdin. Names in parentheses have been given to the finials by collectors. The bottom row of finials is reduced slightly more than the top two rows.

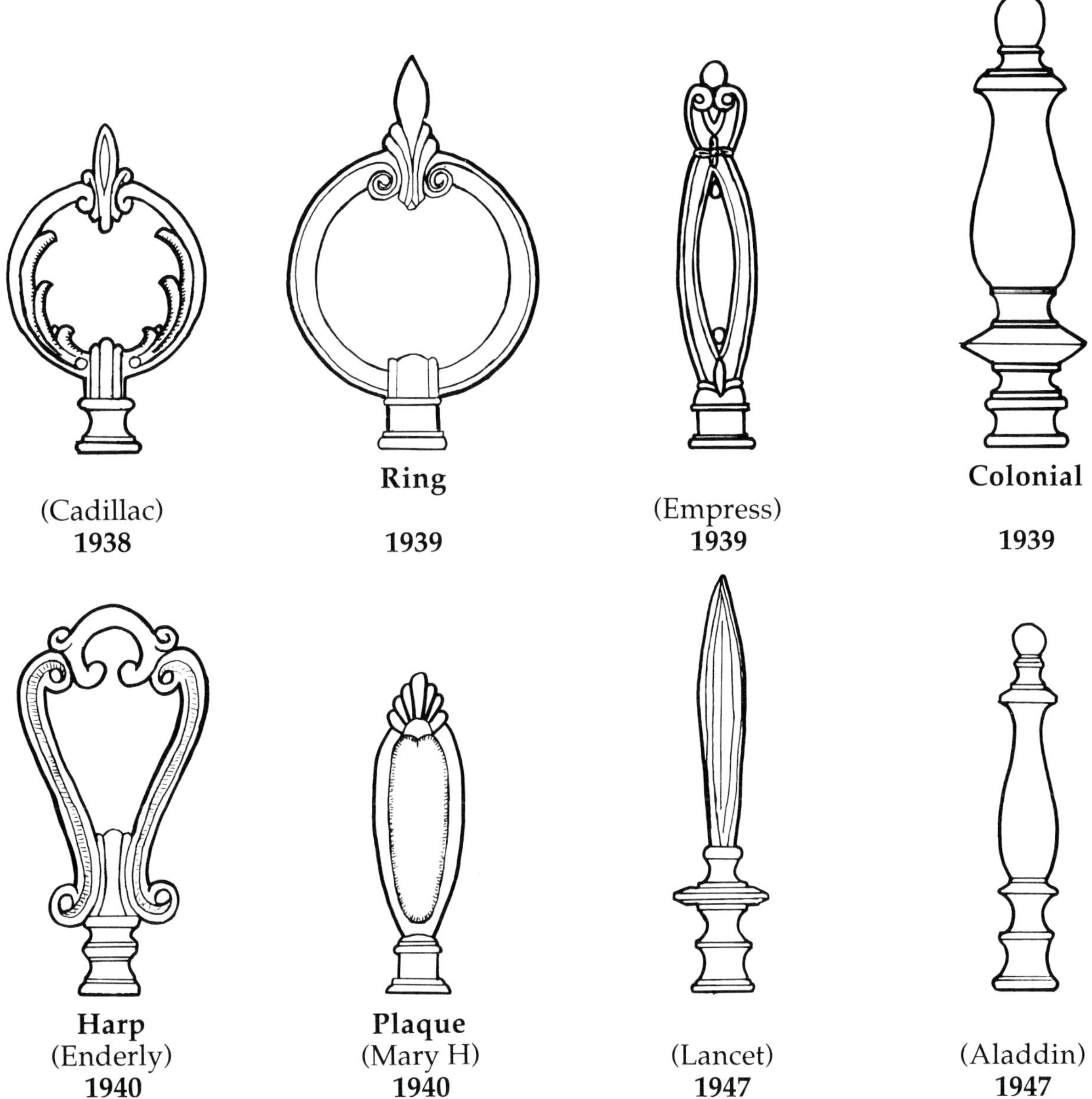

Fig. 85 *continued.* Metal finials made by Aladdin.

Fig. 86. Metal finials purchased by Aladdin. Names in parentheses have been given to the finials by collectors.

(Colony II)
1938

(Aristocrat)
1947

(Olympic)
1947

(Post)
1950

(Chilo S)
1951

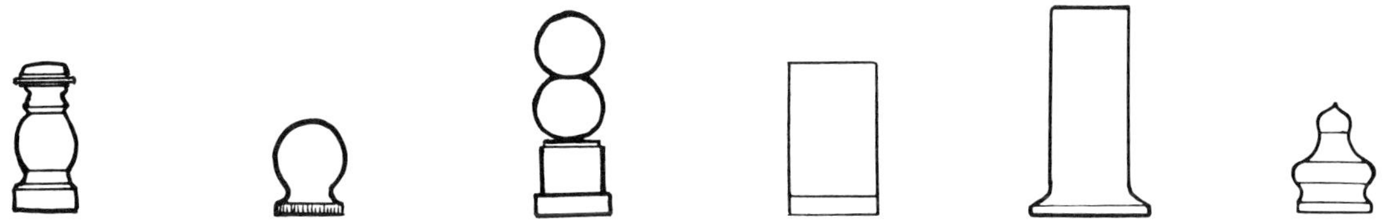

(Pawn)
1952

(Bald Knob)
1952

(Metomic)
1952

(Berger)
1954

(Top Hat)
1954

(Caplet)
1954

Fig. 86 *continued*. Metal finials purchased by Aladdin.

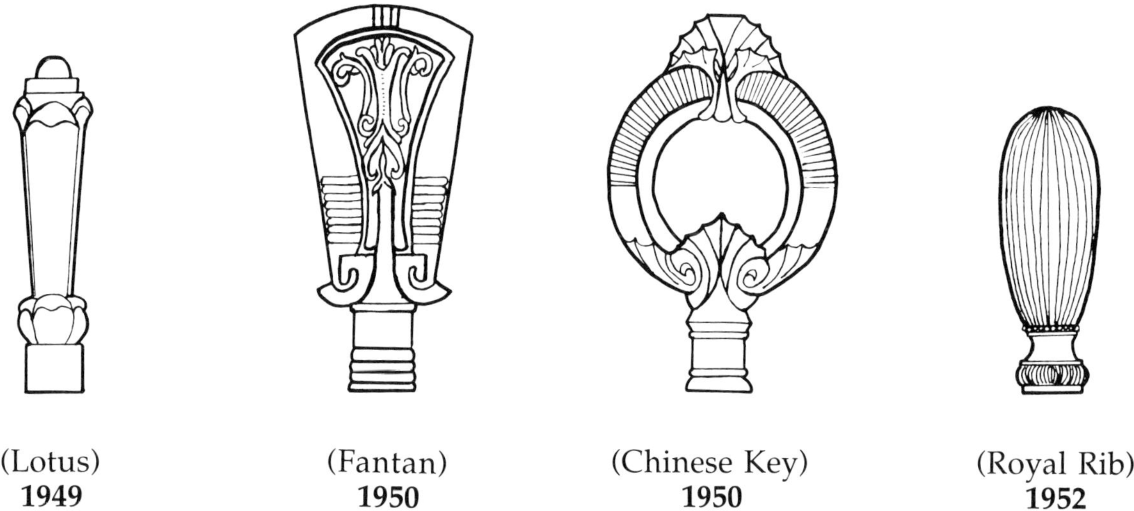

(Lotus)
1949

(Fantan)
1950

(Chinese Key)
1950

(Royal Rib)
1952

Fig. 87. Plastic finials purchased by Aladdin. Names in parentheses have been given to the finials by collectors.

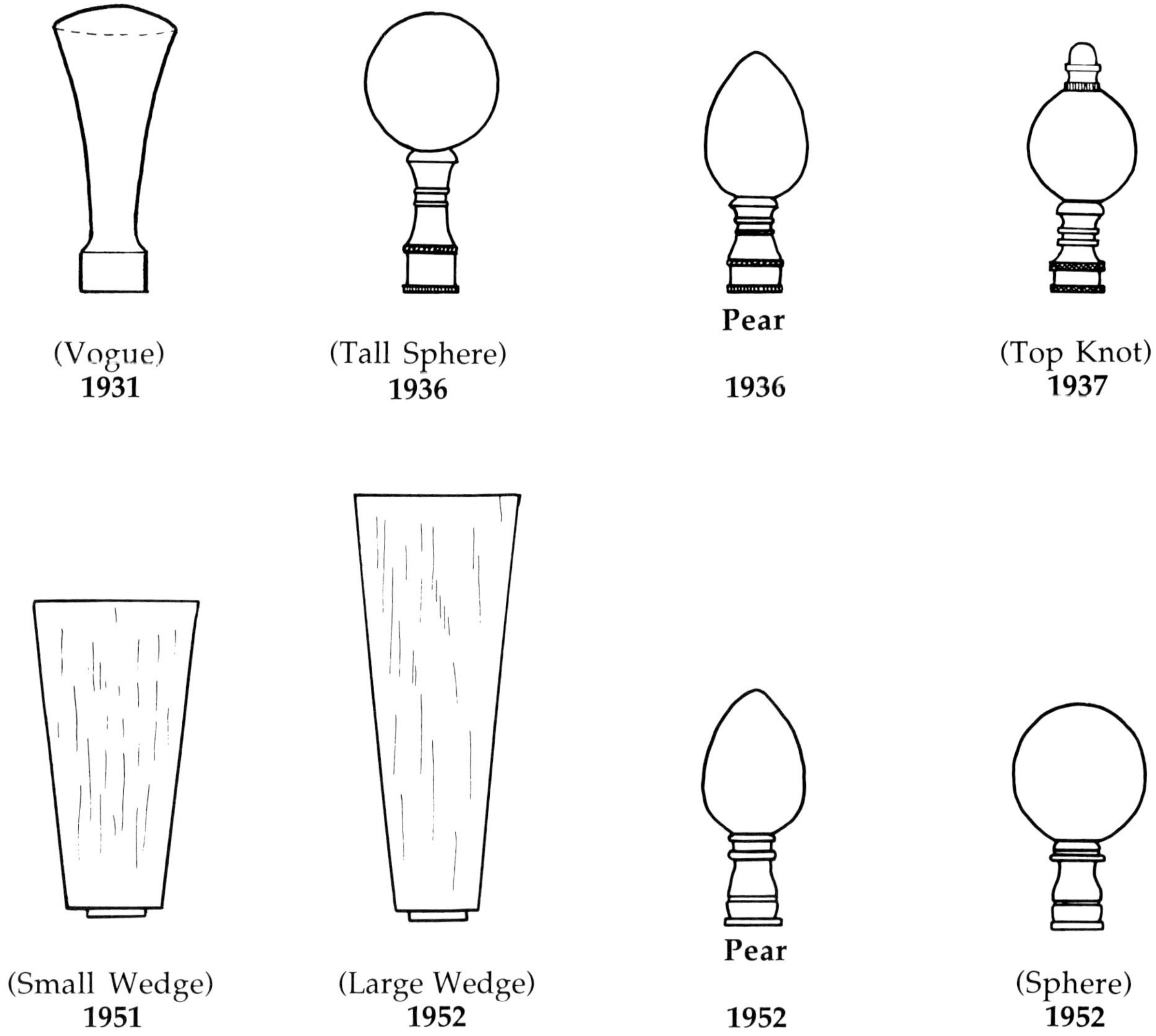

(Vogue)
1931

(Tall Sphere)
1936

Pear
1936

(Top Knot)
1937

(Small Wedge)
1951

(Large Wedge)
1952

Pear
1952

(Sphere)
1952

Fig. 88. Wood finials purchased by Aladdin. Names in parentheses have been given to the finials by collectors.

(Chilo Marble)
1951

(Chilo Marble)
1952

(Marblehead)
1952

Fig. 89. Glass finials purchased by Aladdin. Names in parentheses have been given to the finials by collectors.

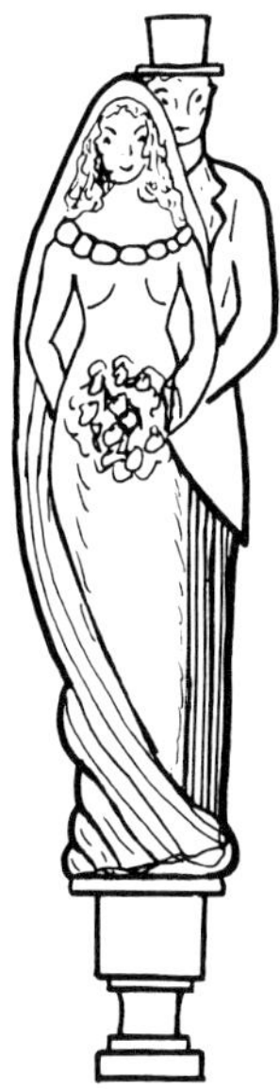

Fig. 90. Bride and Groom glass finial made by Aladdin, 1949. The groom's coat is usually painted black.

Fig. 91. Pottery finial purchased by Aladdin.

Fig. 92. Examples of purchased plastic finials found on Aladdin and other electric lamps.

Fig. 93. Aladdin lamp finial assortment, 1941.

Aladdin Lamps Sold
by Another Company

Aladdin electric portable lamps were made in a wide range of styles, prices, and quality of workmanship by the Aladdin Manufacturing Company in Muncie, Indiana. These lamps are often mistaken as products of Aladdin Industries, maker of Aladdin kerosene mantle lamps and Aladdin electric lamps, in nearby Alexandria. The two companies were completely separate competitors.

Founded in 1919 by O. Sacksteder, Jr., the Aladdin Manufacturing Company was located at 2500 South Hackley (18th and Hackley) in Muncie, Indiana. The lamps made there are referred to as "Aladdin-Muncie Lamps" to avoid confusion with those made in Alexandria. Muncie was called "Magic City" in reference to the Aladdin Manufacturing Company operations.

At least three different kinds of markings identify Aladdin-Muncie Lamps: (a) paper tags attached by a string, (b) decal-type stickers that display one of the company's logos affixed on or near the bulb sockets, and (c) embossed identification on the underside of the castiron bases. The embossed letters usually say "Aladdin Mfg. Co., Muncie, Ind." Not all lamps were marked, however. The tag and decal may be missing on the lamps found today, and not all of the lamps have embossed names in the base. Few if any of the shades are marked.

The Mantle Lamp Company was awarded the Aladdin trademark after a long period of litigation through the U.S. Patent Office, the District Court, Circuit Court of Appeals, and the Supreme Court. The final decision, which came in November 1935, gave the Mantle Lamp Company the sole right to use the name "Aladdin" on lamps and shades of any kind. It also required the Aladdin Manufacturing Company to discontinue using the word "Aladdin" in its firm name. Contrary to a statement in *Aladdin—The Magic Name in Lamps,* the company did not go out of business in the late 1930s. Instead, the name was changed to General Lamps Company in 1936. The company finally went out of business in 1959.

Fig. 96. Examples of "Aladdin" lamps sold by Aladdin Mfg. Co., Muncie, Indiana. These lamps are sometimes confused with those made by Aladdin Industries, Alexandria, Indiana.

Fig. 94. W-300 bowlers Aladdin lamp, 1948.

Fig. 95. Aladdin Service Awards, Nashville, Tennessee, 1959 *(left to right):* V. S. Johnson, Jr., president, Aladdin Industries, Inc.; W. H. F. Millar, attorney; F. W. Spangler, chemist and technical adviser, mantles and wicks; T. A. Blain, vice president, traffic and purchasing; S. B. Huse, purchasing and production control, kerosene lamps and heaters; E. Bittner, technical advisor, glass bottles; William Hollis, draftsman, research and development; C. G. Morgan, assistant to vice president, purchasing and traffic; Ralph High, production control manager; Ann C. Schultz, personal secretary to V. S. Johnson, Jr., and previously to V. S. Johnson, Sr.

Bibliography

Aladdin Electric Lamps Fall-Winter Catalog. 1951. Reprint by J. W. Courter, Route 1, Simpson, IL 62985.

Aladdin Electric Portable Lamps and Value Guide. 1935. Catalog No. 33, "Aladdin-Muncie lamps." Reprint by J. W. Courter, R. 1, Simpson, IL 62985.

A-Ladd-in SerVice. 1943-1945. Newsletters published in book form, 1985, by J. W. Courter, Route 1, Simpson, IL 62985.

Appleton, Dr. Budd. 1972. *Akro Agate.* Privately printed.

Courter, J. W. 1971. *Aladdin—The Magic Name in Lamps.* Published by author, Route 1, Simpson, IL 62985.

Courter, J. W. 1975. Aladdin blue flame heat from kerosene. *The Mystic Light of the Aladdin Knights* 3(5):1, 8-10.

Courter, J. W. 1975. The Aladdin ski-stove. *The Mystic Light of the Aladdin Knights* 3(6):1, 4-5.

Courter, J. W. 1976. Aladdin's fabulous figurine lamps. *The Mystic Light of the Aladdin Knights* 4(1):1, 3, 6-9.

Courter, J. W. 1978. Aladdin deco figurine lamps. *Hobbies* 83(1):115-116.

Courter, J. W. 1984. Aladdin: The last holdout in an era of electric power. *The Rushlight* 50(2):16-18.

Florence, Gene. 1975. *The Collectors Encyclopedia of Akro Agate Glassware.* Paducah: Collector Books.

Gillinder, James. 1920. Glass. In *Manual of Industrial Chemistry* (3d ed.). Ed. Allen Rogers. New York: D. Van Nostrand. 336-359.

Glassware rejects cut 25% by building longer tank. 1941 (June). *Ceramic Industry.* 43-44.

Hastings, Robert J. 1972. *A Nickel's Worth of Skim Milk.* Carbondale: Southern Illinois University Press.

Hellmers, Henry T. 1970-1978. Personal correspondence and papers: J. W. Courter private collection.

Hodkin, F. W., and A. Cousen. 1925. *A Textbook of Glass Technology.* New York: D. Van Nostrand.

Keating, Paul W. 1954. *Lamps for a Brighter America— A History of the General Electric Lamp Business.* New York: McGraw Hill.

Lamps (magazine). 1932-1933.

Lighting and Lamps (magazine). 1934-1952 (formerly *Lamps*, 1932-1933).

McClinton, Katharine Morrison. 1972. *Art Deco—A Guide for Collectors.* New York: Clarkson N. Potter.

Small Town, U.S.A. 1944. U.S. Goverment publication reprinted by the Alexandria Chamber of Commerce. 36 pp.

Thuro, Catherine M. V. 1983. *Oil Lamps II: Glass Kerosene Lamps.* Paducah: Collector Books.

Welker, John and Elizabeth. 1985. *Pressed Glass in America.* Ivyland, PA: Antique Acres Press.

Appendix A

Chronology of Aladdin Electric Lamps

1930
- Eugene Schwarz moved to Alexandria from Chicago.
- The first electric lamp styles were a 786 vase and a 781A pedestal, designed in July and September. The lamps were sold without the Aladdin name.
- A boudoir lamp was also designed, but there is no information on its production.

1931
- Table lamps 786 and 781A were named Vogue and sold through 1932, possibly longer.
- The paper shades were called Aladdinite parchment.
- New vase lamps 783, 785, and 789A were designed. These lamps were designated with an *E* number for retail sales.

1932
- All electric lamps and shades were sold under the name Aladdin, beginning in July.
- Floor lamps were introduced.
- All lamps sold from 1930 to 1932 used a screwtype plug.

1933
- The *G* number system was started with G-1 to G-19 lamps.
- The two-pronged plug was used hereafter.
- The glass for G-16 and G-17 was described as semi-opal in white, rose, amber, and green. These lamps were also made in a copper green crystal.
- Bridge and Junior floor lamps were introduced.
- The fluted paper shade was developed by Eugene Schwarz.
- Whip-o-lite shades were introduced in national lamp shows for the 1934 lighting season.

1934
- Moonstone electric lamps were introduced and named in sales literature.
- Whip-o-lite parchment was named in the literature.

1935
- Henry Hellmers was hired as glass-house superintendent.
- Velvex vases were named and introduced. Table lamps made of glass similar to the vases were introduced.
- The first metal table lamp, M-1, was introduced.
- Etched moonstone lamp bases with a lighted base were said to resemble alabaster glass.
- Lamps approved by the Illuminating Engineering Society (I.E.S.) were sold.
- First Torchere floor lamps were introduced.
- First bed lamps were introduced with design numbers similar to the numbers for shade. They were shades only with an electric socket in them.

1936
- Henry Hellmers developed "special glass" for Susie and Lulu figures.
- Eugene Schwarz perfected the process to slush-cast white-metal floor lamp spindles in one piece.

1937
- Glass vase GV-162 and bookends BE-10 were offered.
- First wood lamps W-147, W-148, and W-151 were introduced.
- Parvelour shades were introduced in national lamp shows.

1938
- First hang-up lamp, M-350.
- Moonstone lamps were named Aladex.
- Opalique was introduced. The first specifically named in the sales literature were G-17, G-173, G-178, G-179, and G-181E.
- Parvelour shades were named in sales catalogues.
- The glass-molding process to make hollow stem glass lamps was improved by Eugene Schwarz.

1939
- Alacite was introduced. The first ones specifically identified in the sales literature were G-18, G-19, G-20, G-172, G-177, G-183, G-185, G-186, G-187, and G-188. G-351 was the first Alacite hang-up lamp.
- Whip-o-lite was called "the parchment eternal."

1941
- Lighted urns G-213A and G-232A were introduced.

1942
- Henry Hellmers left Aladdin.

1943
- V. S. Johnson, Sr., died suddenly and V. S. Johnson, Jr., was elected president.
- The production of electric lamps was curtailed by the War Production Board.

1945
- V. S. Johnson, Jr., completed military service and took over as president.

1946
- The electric line was quickly reinstated after the war.
- Alacite lamps G-222, G-267, G-268, and G-260 were featured by John Wanamaker in New York.

1947
- Certified lamps were introduced (G-285C and G-287C).

1948
- Construction of a new plant to manufacture vacuum bottles was begun in Nashville, Tennessee.

1949
- The Mantle Lamp Company of America changed its name to Aladdin Industries, Inc. The Nashville plant was opened and the Chicago general offices were closed.

1950
- Hoppy lamps were introduced.

1951
- Chicago designer Robert Burton helped design electric lamps and wrote a "Decorator Guide" for the new electric Aladdin line.
- Recipe lamps were introduced.
- First pottery lamps were introduced.
- Boudoir lamps were now called Bedroom lamps.

1952
- Alexandria plant was closed. All lamp manufacturing was consolidated in Nashville.

1953
- Charles Clemens, who had worked with Schwarz, became chief designer of electric lamps in Nashville.

1954
- Magic Touch lamps were introduced.

1955
- The last electric catalogue was published.

1956
- The last electric lamps were sold.

Appendix B

Letter Designations for Aladdin Electric Lamps

A   Suffix   No light inside vase table lamp (1930-1931)

A   Suffix   Designates conversion of G-213 and G-232 to urn lamps G-213A and G-232A in 1941. Also designates nonilluminated bases for G-186, G-257, G-263, and G-267 in 1946 (G-186A etc.)

B   Prefix   Bridge floor lamp (1934) and later bed lamp (1950-1951)

BE   Prefix   Book ends (1937)

C   Prefix   Colonial floor lamp (1934)

C   Suffix   Certified lamp (1947-1951) except the Hopalong Cassidy Ranch House lamps, which are also marked with a suffix "C"

CD   Suffix   Certified lamp with decal (see D suffix)

CLM   . . .   Certified Lamp Maker. CLM lamps all have exclusive glass and metal reflectors (1947-1951)

D   Prefix   Discontinued lamps made from obsolete parts (1955)

D   Suffix   Applied decal, 1947-1951. Aladdin began decorating table lamps with floral decals in 1947. They were fired on the lamp base. Some "D" lamps were also available in other finishes, usually gold luster.

E   Prefix   Electric Aladdin lamp (1931-1933)

E   Suffix   Etched lamp base or vase

F   Prefix   Floor lamp (1955)

G   Prefix   Glass lamp (1933-1952)

GV   Prefix   Glass vase (1937)

IES   Prefix   Designated a "Study and Reading Lamp or Shade" that complied with specifications of the Illuminating Engineering Society. All used glass reflectors and were made in both floor and table styles (1935-1936)

J   Prefix   Junior floor lamps (1934)

M   Prefix   Metal lamp (1935-1956)

M   Suffix   Copper-trimmed Whip-o-lite shade (1938-1939)

ML   Prefix   Found with a number on the underside of floor lamps; some floor lamps with ML on the base may not be Aladdin

MM   Prefix   Metal and moonstone lamp (1935)

MT   Prefix   Magic Touch lamp (1954-1956)

P   Prefix   Pottery lamp (1951-1956)

R   Suffix   Reflector floor lamp (1933-1934)

R   Suffix   Recipe lamps designated in cooperation with General Electric Company promotion to improve home lighting. Some had 3-way fixtures for new 2-filament bulbs (1951-1952)

S   Prefix   Smoker floor lamp (1932)

SS   Suffix   Designates bed lamp to match boudoir shade pattern (1938-1939)

T   Prefix   Indicates Torchere

T   Suffix   Indicates 2-light cluster (1935)

TV   Prefix   Television lamp (1952-1956)

W   Prefix   Wood lamp (1937-1938, 1951-1952)

Appendix C

Management, Aladdin's Alexandria Works, 1948 to 1949

Located at the home offices in Nashville, Tennessee:
V. S. Johnson, Jr., president
A. J. Carlson, director of operations
T. A. Blain, vice president for purchasing and traffic
George Hastings, public relations director
Fred Hinton, comptroller

Located in Alexandria, Indiana:
W. B. Engh, director of research
E. Schwarz, director of design
Harry Flint, factory manager
F. W. Spangler, engineer special assignment
Herman Durr, production superintendent
Ralph High, production control manager
S. D. Goodwin, service department manager
P. McAllister, chief chemist
C. R. Cox, chief engineer
Earl Mock, chief inspector
J. Wallsmith, purchasing agent
E. Kriel, personnel manager
R. Dickinson, office manager
R. Bassett, assistant chief engineer
E. Williams, foreman, plating and finishing department
R. Clegg, foreman, white-metal and buffing department
Charles Hunt, foreman, shade department
Earl Durr, foreman, mantle and wick department
J. Magee, gum manufacturing department
G. A. Ingram, foreman, glass blowing department
R. Clegg, foreman, punch press and kerosene assembly department
R. Hieatt, foreman, electric lamp department
R. Allen, process stores
A. Trout, production and material control supervisor
S. B. Huse, shipping supervisor
H. Hines, time study supervisor
M. Holmes, foreman, mold making and machine shop
B. Meyers, process engineer
F. Smith, assistant chief inspector
E. O. Phillips, assistant chief inspector (stoves and lanterns)
M. Lewis, foreman, receiving and internal transport
B. M. Morgan, foreman, warehouse and shipping
Rosanna Duffitt, nurse
Irene Watcher, personnel clerk

Appendix D

Trade Catalogues, 1933 to 1955

Year	Pages
1933	70-71
1934	72-73
1935	74-77
1935	78-80
1937	81-83
1938	84-85
1939	86-97
1940	98-109
1940	110-122
1941	123-133
1942	134-135
1946	136-142
1947	143-151
1948	152-155
1948	156
1949	157-171
1950	172-182
1951	183-193
1952	194-204
1952	205-208
1953	209-212
1953	213-216
1955	217-224

Decorative Glass Aladdin Electric Table Lamps

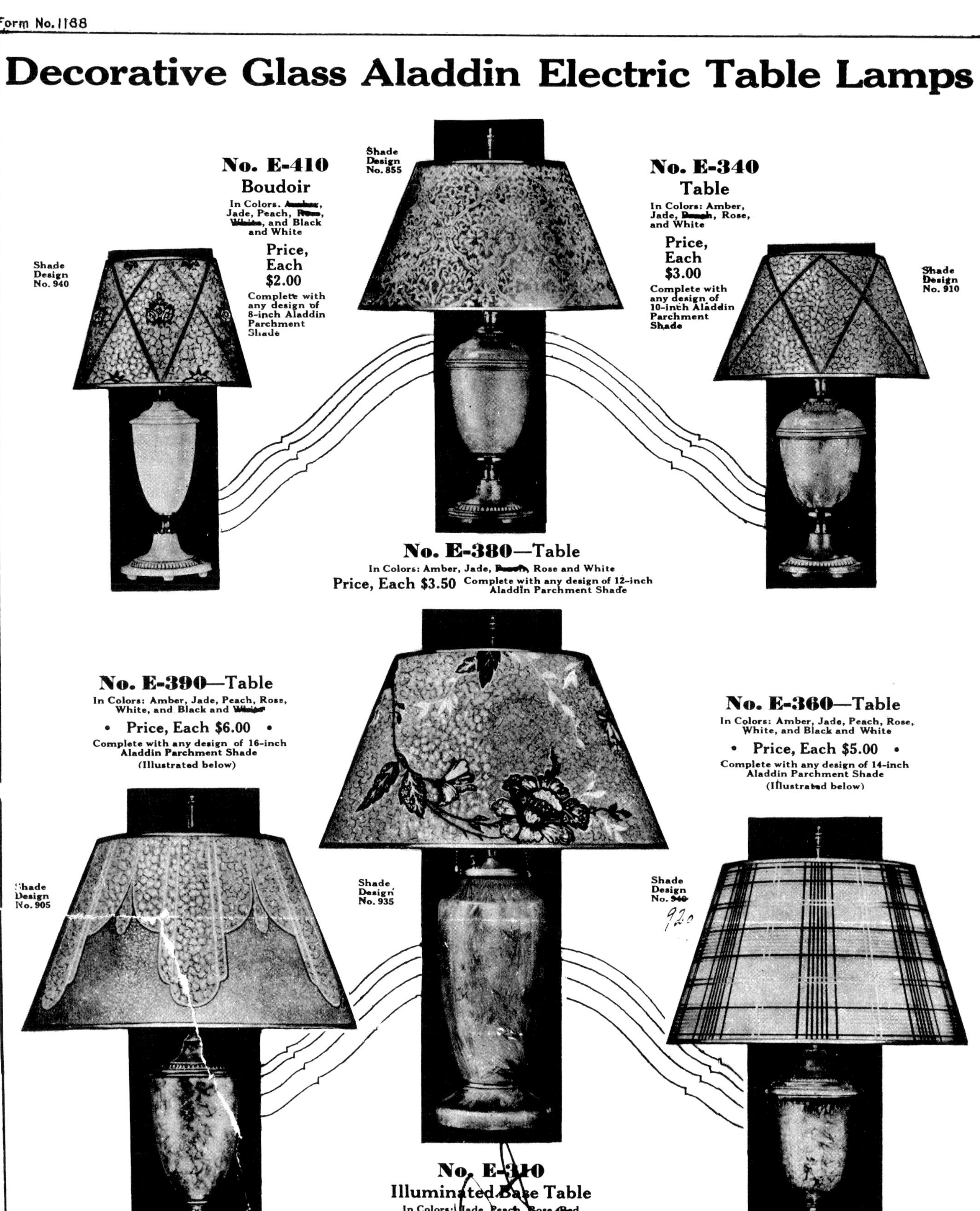

The Mantle Lamp Company of America, Inc.
609 W. Lake Street, Chicago, Illinois

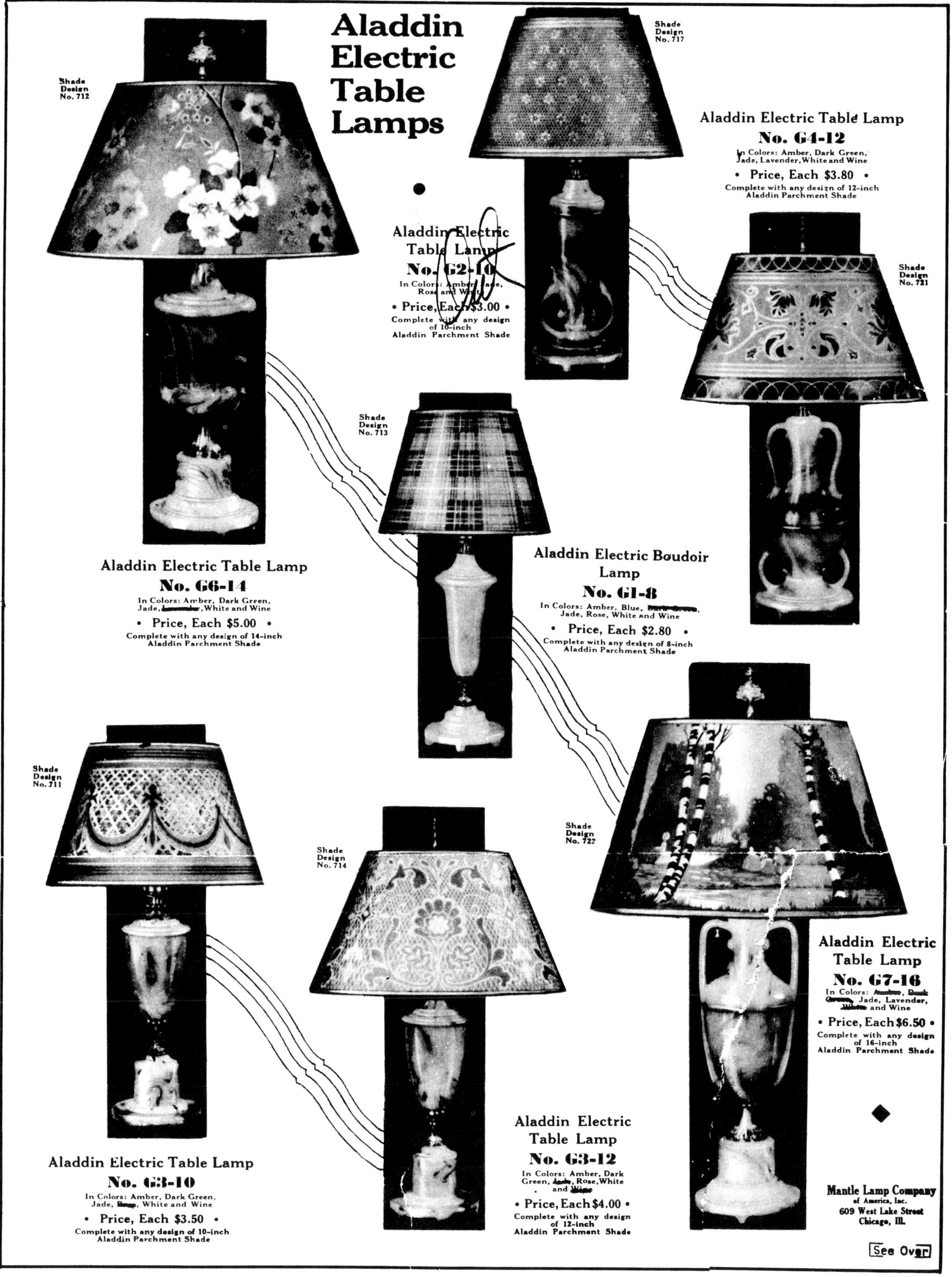
Shade
Design
No. 712

Shade
Design
No. 717

Aladdin
Electric
Table
Lamps

Aladdin Electric Table Lamp
No. G4-12
In Colors: Amber, Dark Green,
Jade, Lavender, White and Wine
• Price, Each $3.80 •
Complete with any design of 12-inch
Aladdin Parchment Shade

Aladdin Electric
Table Lamp
No. G2-10
In Colors: Amber, Jade,
Rose and Wine
• Price, Each $3.00 •
Complete with any design
of 10-inch
Aladdin Parchment Shade

Shade
Design
No. 721

Shade
Design
No. 713

Aladdin Electric Table Lamp
No. G6-14
In Colors: Amber, Dark Green,
Jade, Lavender, White and Wine
• Price, Each $5.00 •
Complete with any design of 14-inch
Aladdin Parchment Shade

Aladdin Electric Boudoir
Lamp
No. G1-8
In Colors: Amber, Blue, Dark Green,
Jade, Rose, White and Wine
• Price, Each $2.80 •
Complete with any design of 8-inch
Aladdin Parchment Shade

Shade
Design
No. 711

Shade
Design
No. 722

Shade
Design
No. 714

Aladdin Electric
Table Lamp
No. G7-16
In Colors: Amber, Dark
Green, Jade, Lavender,
White and Wine
• Price, Each $6.50 •
Complete with any design
of 16-inch
Aladdin Parchment Shade

Aladdin Electric Table Lamp
No. G3-10
In Colors: Amber, Dark Green,
Jade, Rose, White and Wine
• Price, Each $3.50 •
Complete with any design of 10-inch
Aladdin Parchment Shade

Aladdin Electric
Table Lamp
No. G3-12
In Colors: Amber, Dark
Green, Rose, White
and Wine
• Price, Each $4.00 •
Complete with any design
of 12-inch
Aladdin Parchment Shade

Mantle Lamp Company
of America, Inc.
609 West Lake Street
Chicago, Ill.

See Over

LOOK AT THESE AMAZ
They Won't Last Long at These Low

ORDER QUICK ...
First Come   First Served

14" SHADE
No. 752

15" SHADE
No. 763

8" SHADE
No. 714

Table Lamp
G28-14
Amber
Green
Rose
White

$338 Now $275

Table Lamp
G30-15
Amber
Green
Rose
White

$275 Now $195

Boudoir Lamp
G10-8
Amber
Blue
Green
Orchid
Rose
White

$145 Now $110

$250 Now $235

18" SHADE
No. 747

14" SHADE
No. 754

16" SHADE
No. 732

8" SH
No. 7

Table Lamp
G26-14
Amber
Green
Rose
White

$263 Now $250

Table Lamp
G17-16
Rose
Copper-
Green

$322 Now $250

$360 Now $275

$360 Now $250

16" SHADE
No. 758

14" SHADE
No. 741

Table Lamp
G29-16
Amber
Green
Rose
White

$423 Now $365

Table Lamp
G18-14
Amber
Green
Rose
White
Blue
Black-
Gold
Black-
Chromium

$423 Now $350

J-120
Junior
Gold and
Bronze with
Amber
Bowl
or

J-121
Junior
Gold and
Bronze with
Green Bowl

C130
Colonial
Gold and
Bronze with
Green Bowl

SEE REVERSE SIDE FOR A

ZING VALUES
Prices
12" SHADE
No. 768
16" SHADE
No. 741L
14" SHADE
No. 751
16" SHADE
No. 736L
16" SHADE
No. 736L
Table Lamp
G25-12
Amber
Green
Rose
White
Crystal
$3.00 Now $2.75
Table Lamp
G20-16
Amber
Blue
Green
Rose
White
$3.13 Now $2.75
Table Lamp
G27-14
Amber
Green
Rose
White
Crystal
$4.25 Now $2.50
Table Lamp
G19-16
Amber
Green
White
18" SHADE
No. 753
16" SHADE
No. 776
ADE
42
18" SHADE
No. 757
$5.50 Now $3.50
$5.50 Now $4.00
12" SHADE
No. 753
$5.75 Now $3.75
$6.50 Now $4.50
11" SHADE
No. 776
$6.25 Now $4.25
J-132
Gold and
Bronze
B-131
Gold and
Bronze
J-131
Gold and
Bronze
B-134
Bronze and
Brushed
Nickel
J-134
Bronze and
Brushed
Nickel
DDITIONAL FLOOR LAMPS ALSO AT REDUCED PRICES

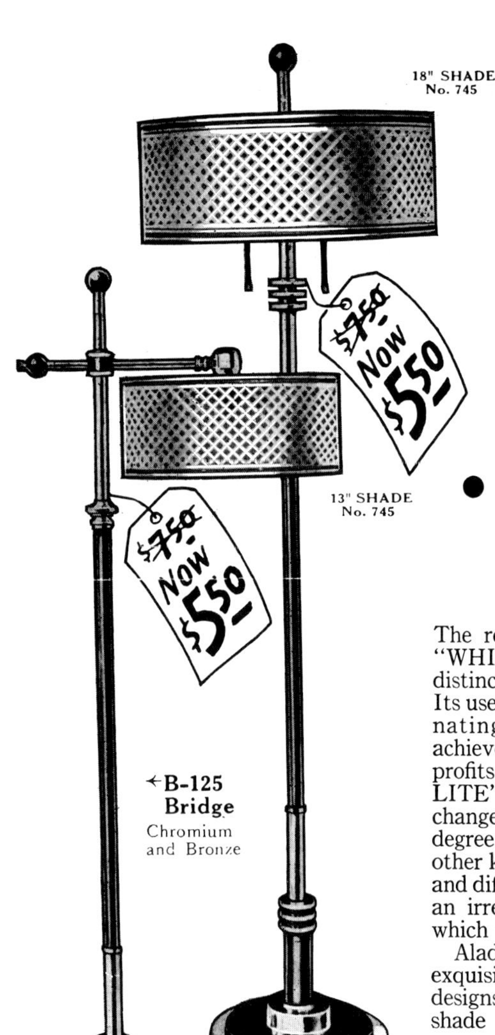

Stock an Assortment
of Aladdin
Whip·o·lite Shades

These Exquisite Shades Will Stimulate Your Lamp Shade Sales and Show You What Real Profit-Taking Means

The recent development and perfection of "WHIP-O-LITE" — the shade material of distinction—has and is creating a sensation. Its use in Aladdin Shades produces an illuminating effect long sought, never before achieved, and is producing most gratifying profits for its dealers everywhere. "WHIP-O-LITE" is absolutely oil-less, will neither change color nor warp or buckle. It has a degree of transparency that far exceeds all other known shade materials, while softening and diffusing the light beneath and imparting an irresistible eye appeal to any shade of which it is made.

Aladdin "WHIP-O-LITE" shades are most exquisitely decorated in "fast" oil colors, in designs created by the country's foremost shade designer, and are generally accepted everywhere as standards of comparison and leaders in vogue.

Aladdin "WHIP-O-LITE" shades are made in the standard Empire shapes; in a delightful new fluted type, both in sizes of 8″, 10″, 12″, 14″, 16″ and 18″, and also in drum and special cone shapes. A complete illustrated list of designs, sizes, colors and shapes gladly sent upon request.

In order not to lose time in getting your share of the quick profits these shades will give you, send us your order for only 12, and let us fill your order with the most popular designs, colors and shapes in our line, or if preferred, you may make selections from designs shown in this folder.

Net Wholesale Prices Each:

12″ Size (Empire)	$ .75	16″ Size (Empire)	$1.15	18″ Size (Empire)	$1.25
12″ Size (Fluted)	1.10	16″ Size (Fluted)	1.50	18″ Size (Fluted)	1.75

Read What These Dealers Say:

J. C. CLOWER FURNITURE CO.
GULFPORT, MISSISSIPPI

"Early in the year we received the first shipment of lamps and shades from you. As soon as they were unpacked, we concluded that their beauty and lighting effectiveness were more nearly perfect than anything we had seen. Our customers confirmed this, for even though we do not do a large business, the principle of selectiveness is just as complete as though ours were a large business. The quality in your lamps and shades is absolute, not comparative."

E. LEO HARRIS
126 No. Lawrence, WICHITA, KANS.

"The Aladdin Lamps and Shades arrived late yesterday and we unpacked the shipment and placed same on sale immediately and we want to write you to express our appreciation for making prompt shipment and the condition of the merchandise when it arrived.

We can truthfully say that it was the best packed, neatest and cleanest merchandise that we have ever unpacked. Really we think your merchandise wonderful and today have had several compliments and have sold four bridge lamp shades."

THE EMPORIUM
ST. PAUL, MINNESOTA

"We have had unusual success on your Aladdin Whip-o-lite shades and find we overlooked buying the 16-inch size. These have been selling so rapidly that we have broken the units and sold the shades in the 16-inch size separately, therefore, kindly rush to us thirty-six 16-inch shades, as per order enclosed."

The 1935 *SPRING* *Line of Beautiful Fast-Selling*
Aladdin
ELECTRIC LAMPS *and* Whip-O-Lite SHADES

IN presenting the new 1935 spring line of Aladdin Electric Lamps and Whip-o-lite shades to a large and constantly growing number of dealers, we do so with the knowledge already clearly demonstrated and proved that these beautiful new medium and low-priced units represent the outstanding values in their field.

Ever since their formal presentation at the recent national lamp shows, and later their presentation by hundreds of dealers to the consumer, this line has moved with an ever increasing rapidity, and has and is daily putting more and more quick and substantial profits into their dealers' pockets.

You will find the entire Aladdin line for Spring 1935 illustrated on the center spread of this broadside in black and white, which medium conveys only a small part of their exceptional beauty and charm, much of which lies in the delicacy of the soft pastel tones in which both lamps and shades are decorated. The beauty of design is, of course, readily apparent, but only personal inspection can reveal the excellent material and craftsmanship employed in their production. The finish of metal parts in these lamps, whether plated or lacquered is comparable only with lamps of much higher price. Withal, these lamps possess the Nth degree of eye appeal.

The Aladdin Whip-o-lite shades with which all Aladdin lamps are equipped deserve your special attention. They, while illustrated as are ordinary parchment shades, are nevertheless vastly different in lighting effect and appearance. Whip-o-lite, the material of which Aladdin shades are exclusively made, is the most amazing development in shade material ever made. It is highly transparent, diffuses light more pleasingly than any known glass, and is so much like genuine sheep-skin in appearance as to confuse even the expert. It is exceedingly durable, is washable, does not discolor, warp or buckle. It is absolutely oil-less. All Whip-o-lite shades are decorated in fadeless oil colors in a wide variety of designs and in the most popular colors. They may be purchased separately if desired.

Aladdin lamps are presented in boudoir, table styles and also in floor lamps in junior, bridge and reflector types, in a wide range of medium and low prices. They will meet the present day demands for value, in a manner that will prove exceedingly satisfactory in quick turnover and profits for all dealers who stock them.

Beauty and Utility Marvelously Combined In
Aladdin I. E. S. Lamps

No lamp department is complete these days unless offering a line of I.E.S. lamps with which to meet the tremendous demand created by the vast sums of money being spent to advertise this new scientific type of lighting device. All Aladdin I.E.S. lamps, of course, bear the official certificate of approval, evidence of full compliance with exacting specifications. Aladdin I.E.S. lamps however are more than just highly efficient lighting devices, they are also highly artistic in design and finish, possessing irresistible eye appeal, affording dealers the necessary element to make them move readily. Aladdin I.E.S. lamps represent a value far beyond what can usually be secured at their moderate prices.

When in
Chicago
Visit our permanent display room, 1524 Merchandise Mart.

609 W. Lake St., Chicago, Ill. • **721 E. Yamhill St., Portland, Ore.**

THE MANTLE LAMP COMPANY OF AMERICA, INC.

For SURE and QUICK PROFITS-STOCK
and Table Lamps
Bed Lamp No. 875SS
10" at Bottom
See Inside Pages For Other Designs
14" Square Shade Design 865
8" Shade Design 792
8" Shade Design 751
With 2-Lt. Cluster G49T
Table Lamp G49—14"
Amber Green Rose White
Height Overall 21"
14" Shade Design 831
Table Lamp G18—14"
Amber Green Rose White Blue Black
Base Gold on all Colors. Black-Chromium or Gold
Height Overall 23"
14" Shade Design 828
Table Lamp G42—14"
Amber Green Rose White
Height Overall 22¾"
14" Shade Design 68
Table Lamp G26—14"
Amber Green Rose White
Height Overall 21¼"
16" Shade Design 829
14" Shade Design 825
Table Lamp G43—14"
Amber Green Rose White
Height Overall 23"
14" Shade Design 875
Boudoir Lamp G48—8"
Amber Green Rose White Blue Orchid
Height Overall 13¼"
Boudoir Lamp G23—8"
Amber Green Rose White Blue Orchid
Height Overall 14"
12" Shade Design 753
Table Lamp G34—12"
Amber Green Rose White
Height Overall 18½"
14" Shade Design 782
14" Shade Design 876
14" Square Shade Design 866
Table Lamp M4—14"
Gold
Gold and Green Ivory and Gold
Height Overall 23"
Table Lamp G44—14"
Amber Green Rose White
Height Overall 20"
With 2-Lt. Cluster G46T
Table Lamp G46—16"
Amber Green Rose White
Height Overall 23¾"
Table Lamp G31—14"
Amber Green Rose White
Height Overall 20½"
12" Shade Design 830
16" Shade Design 827
Table Lamp G38—16"
Crystal only
Height Overall 23¼"
Table Lamp G37—14"
Crystal only
Height Overall 22½"
16" Shade Design 852
14" Shade Design 833
Table Lamp M2—16"
Oxidized Brass High-Lighted
Height Overall 23¾"
Table Lamp M1—14"
Oxidized Brass High-Lighted
Height Overall 21"
Table Lamp G41—12"
Amber Green Rose White
Height Overall 19½"
6" Shade Design 762
Boudoir Lamp G33—6"
Green Rose White Yellow
Height Overall 15½"
4½" Shade Design 878
Boudoir Lamp G50—4½"
Amber Green Rose White Blue Orchid
Height Overall 16"
10" Shade Design 761
Table Lamp G24—10"
Green Rose White Yellow
Height Overall 22"

THE five beautiful new Aladdin Electric Floor lamps of the Reflector type Nos. 3348, 3349, 3352, 3354, and 3356 illustrated at right and left of this panel, may be secured in four different combinations of head and socket equipment. In order, however, to simplify the ordering of these different lamps, each lamp has been given an individual number according to type of head and socket equipment.

Order Under the Following Numbers:

If you desire Reflector lamps illustrated equipped with type "A" head, and one-light 250 volt standard bulb Porcelain socket with 10-inch Glass Reflector.	If you desire Reflector lamps illustrated equipped with Type "A" head and one-Light Mogul Porcelain socket for large 250V standard bulb, center, and 3 standard bulb, and 3-2-1 switch, and 10-inch Glass Reflector.	If you desire Reflector lamps illustrated equipped with Type "B" head fitted with one-light 250V standard bulb socket in center and 3 standard bulb porcelain side sockets with proper control switch and 10-inch Glass Reflector.	If you desire Reflector lamps illustrated equipped with Type "B" head fitted with one-light Mogul Porcelain socket for large shanked, 300-200-100 watt bulb in center, and 3 standard bulb porcelain side sockets with proper control switch and 10-inch glass Reflector.
No. 3348	No. 3548	No. 3448	No. 3648
No. 3349	No. 3549	No. 3449	No. 3649
(Design 51 not made in this arrangement)	(Design 51 not made in this arrangement)	No. 3451	(Design 51 not made in this arrangement)
No. 3352	No. 3552	No. 3452	No. 3652
No. 3354	No. 3554	No. 3454	No. 3654
No. 3356	No. 3556	No. 3456	No. 3656

Be sure to specify your choice of finish as well as the number of the lamp desired. Although illustrated with certain designs of shades, shades of other designs and shapes may be specified. Give number, color and size. Consult shade chart for sizes, shapes and colors available, and Floor Lamp price list for prices of complete lamps in the various shade combinations. Aladdin Slip-Neck Glass Reflectors are standard and are supplied unless metal reflectors are specifically requested.

See Opposite Side for
Aladdin
I.E.S. Table and Floor Study and Reading Lamps and Shades.

Stock these NEW Aladdin Electric TABLE & FLOOR Lamps

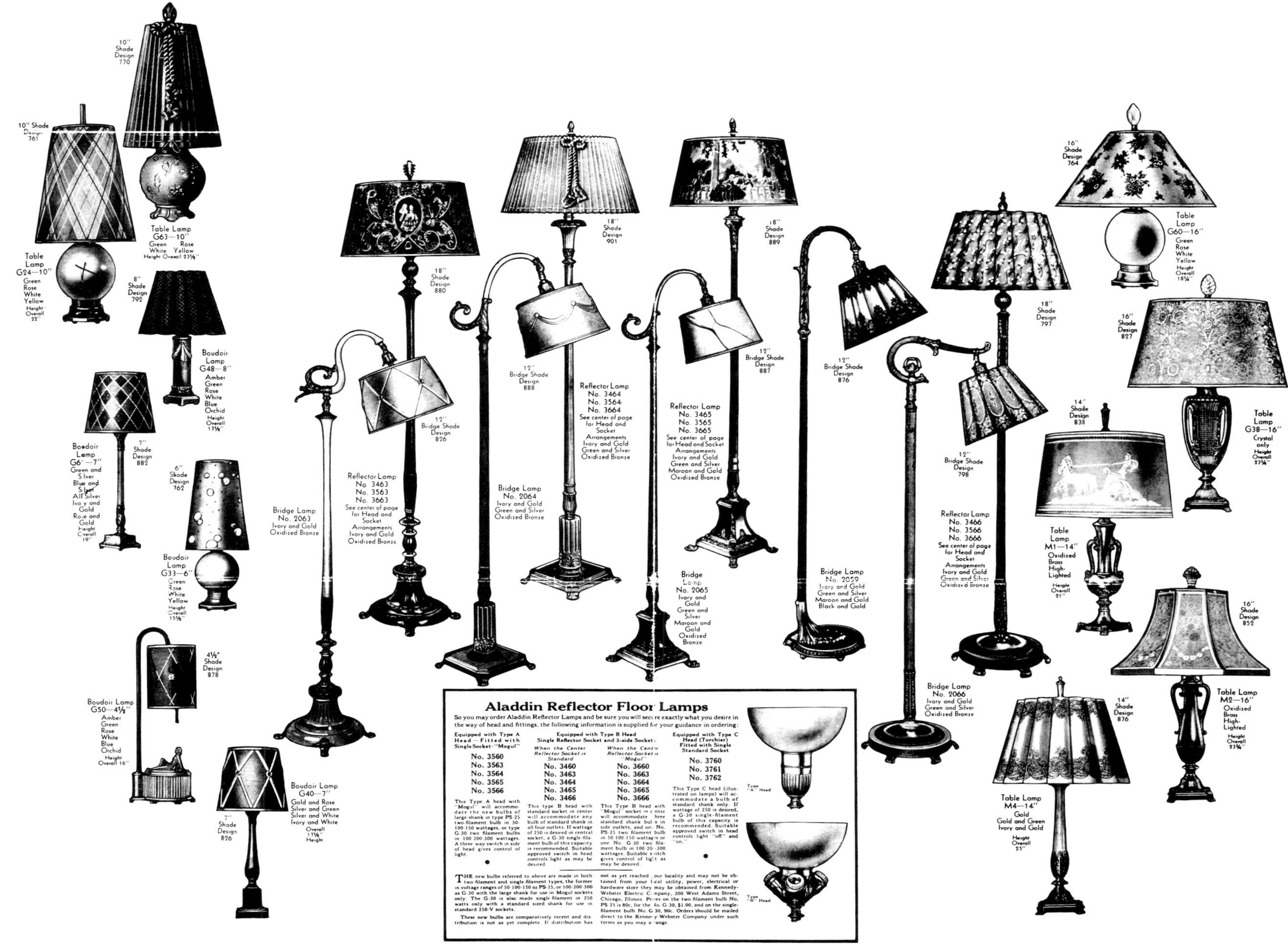

Aladdin Reflector Floor Lamps

So you may order Aladdin Reflector Lamps and be sure you will secure exactly what you desire in the way of head and fittings, the following information is supplied for your guidance in ordering:

Equipped with Type A Head—Fitted with Single Socket-"Mogul"

No. 3560
No. 3563
No. 3564
No. 3565
No. 3566

Equipped with Type B Head Single Reflector Socket and 3-side Socket:

When the Center Reflector Socket is Standard

No. 3460
No. 3463
No. 3464
No. 3465
No. 3466

When the Center Reflector Socket is "Mogul"

No. 3660
No. 3663
No. 3664
No. 3665
No. 3666

Equipped with Type C Head (Torchier) Fitted with Single Standard Socket

No. 3760
No. 3761
No. 3762

This Type A head with "Mogul" will accommodate the new bulbs of large shank in type PS-25 two-filament bulb in 50-100-150 wattages, or type G-30 two filament bulbs in 100-200-300 wattages. A three-way switch in side of head gives control of light.

This type B head with standard socket in center will accommodate any bulb of standard shank in all four outlets. If wattage of 250 is desired in central socket, a G-30 single-filament bulb of this capacity is recommended. Suitable approved switch in head controls light as may be desired.

This Type B head with "Mogul" socket in center will accommodate three standard shank bulbs in side outlets, and one No. PS-25 two filament bulb in 50-100-150 wattages or one No. G-30 two filament bulb in 100-20.-300 wattages. Suitable switch gives control of light as may be desired.

This Type C head (illustrated on lamps) will accommodate a bulb of standard shank only. If wattage of 250 is desired, a G-30 single-filament bulb of this capacity is recommended. Suitable approved switch in head controls light "off" and "on."

THE new bulbs referred to above are made in both two-filament and single-filament types, the former in voltage ranges of 50-100-150 as PS-25, or 100-200-300 as G-30 with the large shank for use in Mogul sockets only. The G-30 is also made single-filament in 250 watts only with a standard sized shank for use in standard 250-V sockets.

These new bulbs are comparatively recent and distribution is not as yet complete. If distribution has not as yet reached your locality and may not be obtained from your local utility, power, electrical or hardware store they may be obtained from Kennedy-Webster Electric Company, 300 West Adams Street, Chicago, Illinois. Prices on the two-filament bulb No. PS-25 is 80c, for the 4o. G-30, $1.00, and on the single-filament bulb No. G-30, 90c. Orders should be mailed direct to the Kennedy-Webster Company under such terms as you may arrange.

Aladdin
I·E·S· LAMPS
Better Light Better Sight

THESE new creations in Aladdin I. E. S. table and floor, study and reading lamp styles are designed to meet the growing demand for lamps of this type which not only comply fully and completely with the exacting specifications of this type of lighting device, but also have eye-appeal and decorative effect as well.

Aladdin I. E. S. lamps have several structural innovations which admit of greater latitude in these features. For instance, the columns, instead of the usual thin metal-tube ordinarily used, are of cast white-metal in one single piece, which may be made to take any size or outside form of decoration desired. This construction also secures greater strength and solidity, and gives the artist almost unlimited scope for the exercise of his talent. This distinctive new lamp structure is undoubtedly the greatest advance in lamp manufacture in many, many years, and makes Aladdin I. E. S. lamps outstanding values.

Giving value far in excess of that usually represented by their price is what makes Aladdin I. E. S. lamps far outstrip others in sales and profits for those fortunate dealers who can secure a sufficient number to be kept constantly in stock.

All Aladdin I. E. S. Lamps are well within the moderate price class, although their appearance, workmanship, materials and finish would lead one to believe them of much higher price. Note the illustrations and descriptions below.

Aladdin I. E. S. Table Type Study and Reading Lamp No. M-5. Illustrated fitted with 19" Aladdin I. E. S. Shade Design No. 12. Made in two finishes —Gold (Illustrated) or Ivory and Gold. Equipped with single socket for Standard 100 Watt bulb and 8" Aladdin Glass Reflector. Switch in ornamental shell at top.

Aladdin I. E. S. Table Type Study and Reading Lamp No. M-5. Illustrated fitted with 19" Aladdin I. E. S. Shade Design No. 25. Made in two finishes— Gold or Ivory and Gold (illustrated). Single Socket for standard 100 Watt bulb and with 8" Aladdin Glass Reflector. Switch in ornamental shell at top.

Aladdin I. E. S. Study and Reading Lamp—floor type No. 3368. Illustrated with 19" Aladdin I. E. S. Shade Design No. 27. Available in three finishes: Ivory and Gold, Maroon and Gold, and Oxidized Bronze. Fitted with single socket in head for standard 100 Watt bulb, and with a 9⅜" Aladdin Glass Reflector.

Aladdin I. E. S. Study and Reading Lamp—floor type No. 3367. Illustrated with 19" Aladdin I. E. S. Shade Design No. 25. Available in four finishes: Ivory and Gold, Green and Silver, Bronze and Gold, or Oxidized Bronze. Fitted with single socket in head for standard 100 Watt bulb, and with 9⅜" Aladdin Glass Reflector.

Aladdin I. E. S. Study and Reading Lamp—floor type No. 3567. Illustrated with 19" Aladdin I. E. S. Shade Design No. 26. Available in four finishes: Ivory and Gold, Green and Silver, Bronze and Gold, or Oxidized Bronze. Fitted with Mogul socket and canopy switch for 50-100-150 Watt bulb. 9⅜" Aladdin Glass Reflector.

Aladdin I. E. S. Study and Reading Lamp—floor type No. 3568. Illustrated with 19" Aladdin I. E. S. Shade Design No. 27. Available in three finishes: Ivory and Gold, Maroon and Gold, and Oxidized Bronze. Fitted with Mogul socket and canopy switch for 50-100-150 Watt bulb. 9⅜" Aladdin Glass Reflector.

BETTER LIGHT BETTER SIGHT

ALADDIN I. E. S. SHADES

All the different designs of Aladdin I. E. S. Shades illustrated on this page are 19" diameter at bottom, 9½" at top, and 8½" in vertical height, a proportion exactly suited for balance and for the proper and effective distribution of light. Designs No. 25, 26 and 27 illustrated are available in choice of three color effects— Ivory, Tan, and Green.

Aladdin I. E. S. Table Type Study and Reading Lamp No. MM-6. Combination spindle Metal and Moonstone Glass Base, in choice of Silver plated spindle and Green Moonstone Base (illustrated) or Ivory and Gold plated spindle and White Moonstone Base. Equipped with single Mogul Socket and canopy switch for 50-100-150 Watt bulb. 9⅜" Aladdin Glass Reflector.

Aladdin I. E. S. Table Type Study and Reading Lamp No. MM-7. All metal spindle and base. In choice of three finishes: Ivory and Gold, Green and Silver, and Bronze (illustrated). Equipped with single Mogul socket and canopy switch for 50-100-150 Watt bulb. 9⅜" Aladdin Glass Reflector.

The Mantle Lamp Company of America, Inc.
609 West Lake Street   721 East Yamhill Street
Chicago, Illinois   Portland, Oregon

TORONTO   LONDON   PARIS   SYDNEY   MELBOURNE   BUENOS AIRES

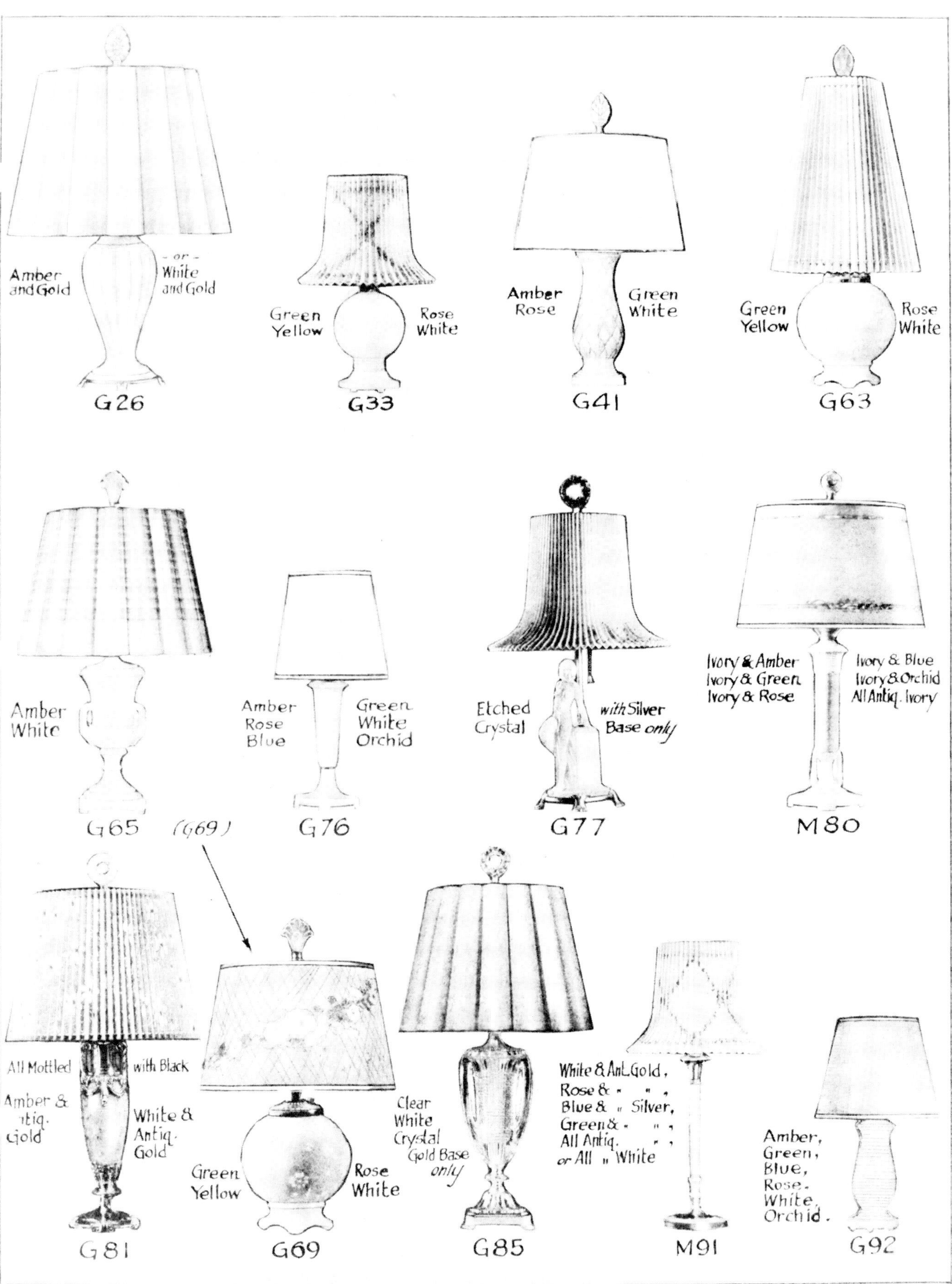

Amber and Gold
- or -
White and Gold
G 26
Green Yellow
Rose White
G 33
Amber Rose
Green White
G 41
Green Yellow
Rose White
G 63
Amber White
G 65
(G69)
Amber Rose Blue
Green White Orchid
G 76
Etched Crystal
with Silver Base only
G 77
Ivory & Amber
Ivory & Green
Ivory & Rose
Ivory & Blue
Ivory & Orchid
All Antiq. Ivory
M 80
All Mottled
with Black
Amber & Antiq. Gold
White & Antiq. Gold
G 81
Green Yellow
Rose White
G 69
Clear White Crystal Gold Base only
G 85
White & Ant. Gold,
Rose & " ",
Blue & " Silver,
Green & " ",
All Antiq. " ",
or All " White
M 91
Amber, Green, Blue, Rose. White. Orchid.
G 92

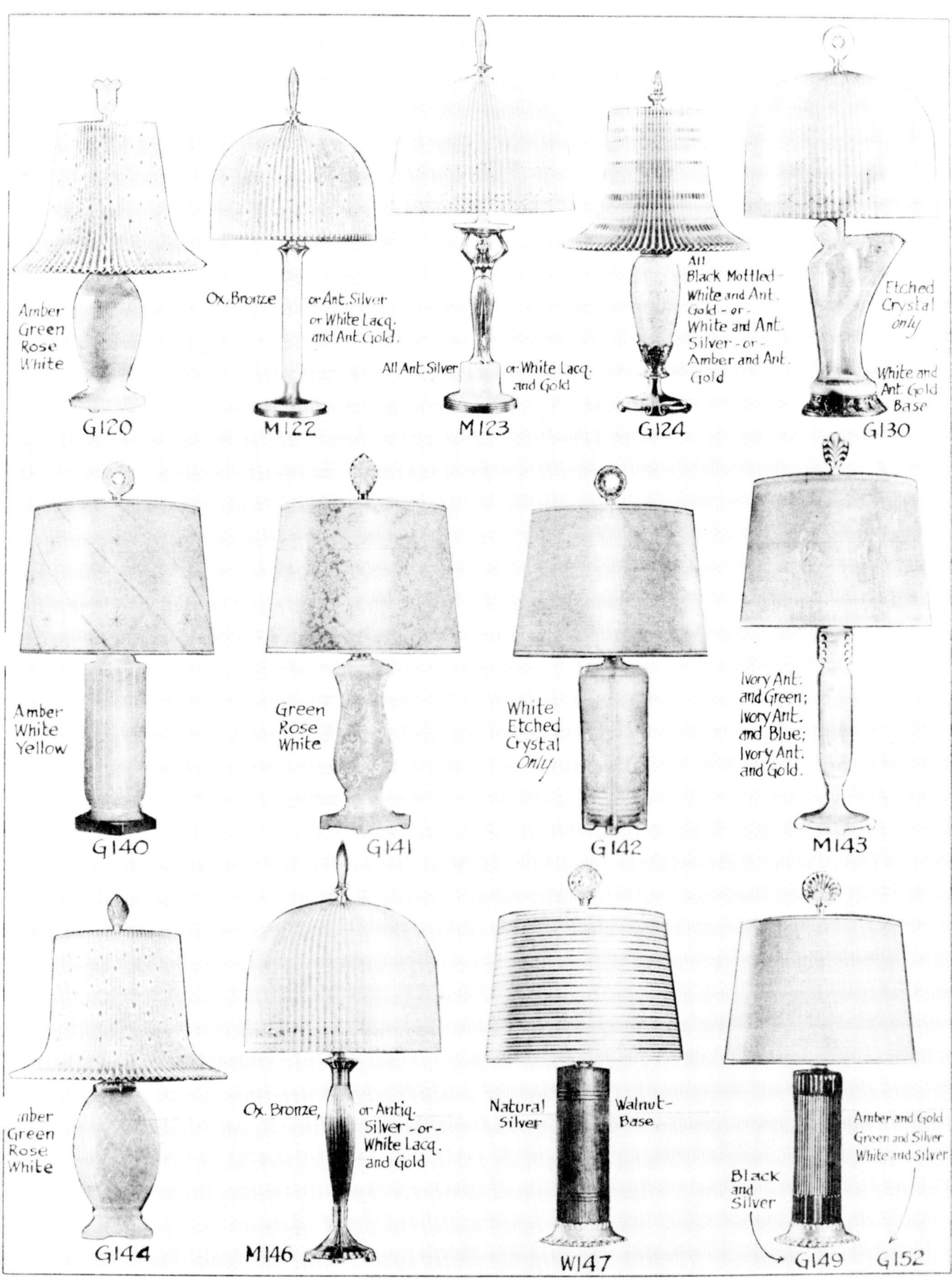

Amber
Green
Rose
White

G120

Ox. Bronze   or Ant. Silver
or White Lacq.
and Ant. Gold.

M122

All Ant. Silver   or White Lacq.
and Gold

M123

All
Black Mottled -
White and Ant.
Gold - or -
White and Ant.
Silver - or -
Amber and Ant.
Gold

G124

Etched
Crystal
only

White and
Ant. Gold
Base

G130

Amber
White
Yellow

G140

Green
Rose
White

G141

White
Etched
Crystal
Only

G142

Ivory Ant.
and Green;
Ivory Ant.
and Blue;
Ivory Ant.
and Gold.

M143

Amber
Green
Rose
White

G144

Ox. Bronze,   or Antiq.
Silver - or -
White Lacq.
and Gold

M146

Natural
Silver   Walnut
Base

W147

Amber and Gold
Green and Silver
White and Silver

Black
and
Silver

G149   G152

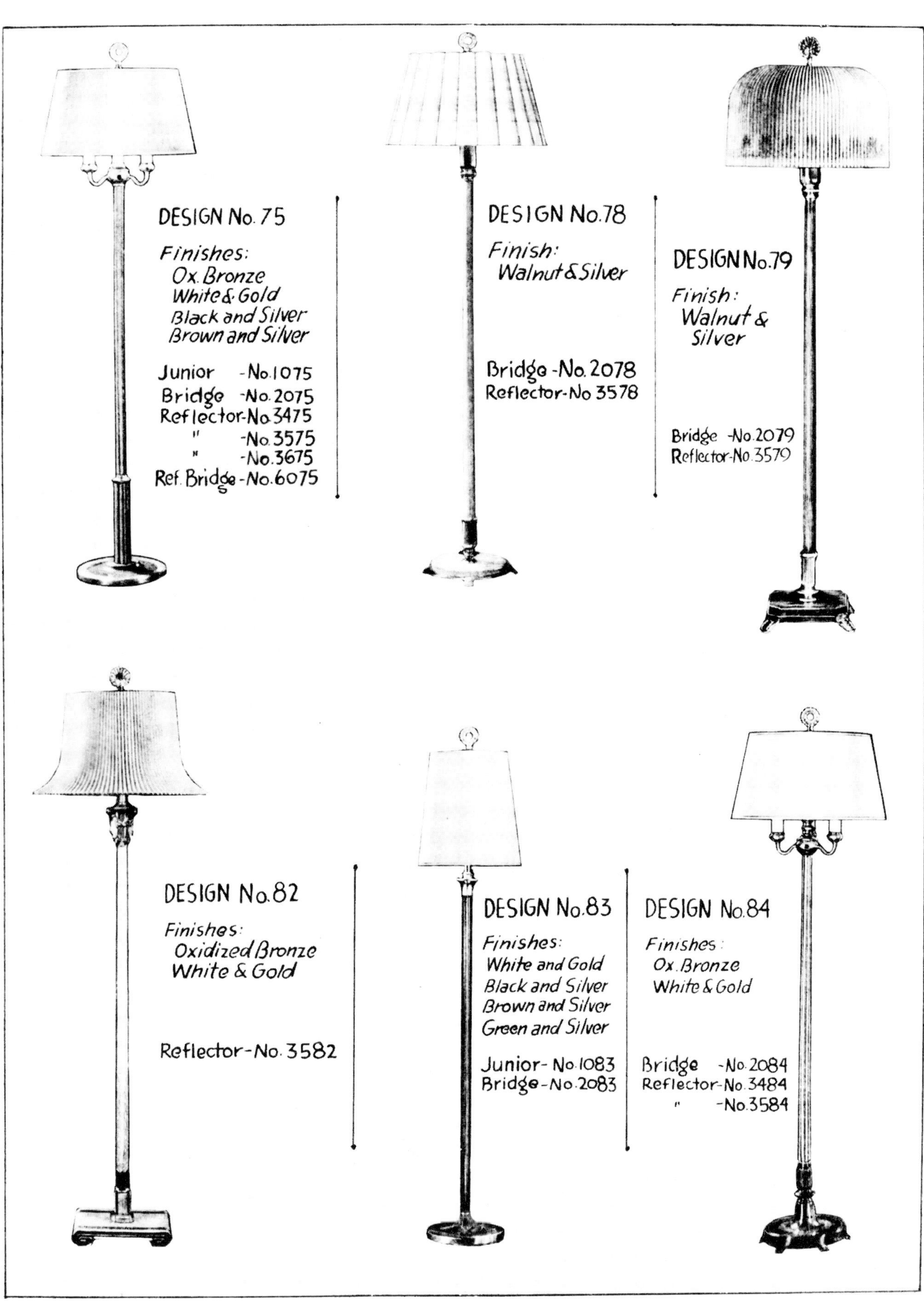

DESIGN No. 75

Finishes:
Ox. Bronze
White & Gold
Black and Silver
Brown and Silver

Junior   -No.1075
Bridge   -No.2075
Reflector-No.3475
   "   -No.3575
   "   -No.3675
Ref. Bridge -No.6075

DESIGN No. 78

Finish:
Walnut & Silver

Bridge -No.2078
Reflector-No.3578

DESIGN No. 79

Finish:
Walnut &
Silver

Bridge -No.2079
Reflector-No.3579

DESIGN No. 82

Finishes:
Oxidized Bronze
White & Gold

Reflector-No. 3582

DESIGN No. 83

Finishes:
White and Gold
Black and Silver
Brown and Silver
Green and Silver

Junior- No.1083
Bridge -No.2083

DESIGN No. 84

Finishes:
Ox. Bronze
White & Gold

Bridge   -No.2084
Reflector-No.3484
   "   -No.3584

Quan-tity	Lamp No.	Choice of Finish or Color	Shade Size
1	G-144	A-G-R-W	14"
1	G-155	White & Black, White & Amber White & Green, All White	13"
1	G-94	Green & Silver Black & Silver	13"
1	M-159	Ivory & Gold Oxidized Bronze, All Silver	12"
1	M-146	All Silver White & Gold	16
1	G-173	Ivory & Green Clear or Blue	12"
1	G-166	W-G-P-B-Y	10
1	G-171	W-G-P-Y	12"
2	G-17	Crystal Glass Opalique Glass	7"
1	G-124	White & Antiq. Gold, White & Antiq. Silver, Amber and Antiq. Gold	14
2	M-158	Ivory & Gold, Copper & Silver Oxidized Bronze, All Silver	7"
1	G-165	W-T-G	12"
1	G-178	G-I-B-T	14"
1	G-177	Ruby or Amber	16
1	G-157	Ivory & Gold, Crystal & Gold, Amber & Bronze	13"

THE MANTLE LAMP COMPANY OF AMERICA, INC., 223

Aladdin
ELECTRIC LAMPS
AND SHADES

Foreword
1939 DESIGNS

*L*amps and Shades of quality *that sell at a profit* for the dealer are to be found on the following pages of this catalog of Aladdin Electric Lamps and Aladdin Whip-o-lite Shades in Standard Decoration and in the sensational new Parvelour.

Aladdin also presents herein for the first time a select group of Pure Dye Silk Hand Sewn Shades in response to a demand of many Aladdin dealers for a quality shade of this type at reasonable prices.

All of the various models and designs in Boudoir, Table and Floor lamps as well as the many new designs in Shades have been carefully inspected by the most discriminating of buyers during nation-wide lamp shows, and have been pronounced the "tops" in their respective class and price range.

The most flattering compliments paid this line are the generous orders placed for this merchandise. Reorders already received indicate an eager consumer acceptance, and further substantiate the fact (if any is needed) that Aladdin Electric Lamps and Shades, *do sell* readily and *at a profit* for our dealers.

With your first order you can prove this statement most convincingly.

THE MANTLE LAMP COMPANY OF AMERICA
Incorporated

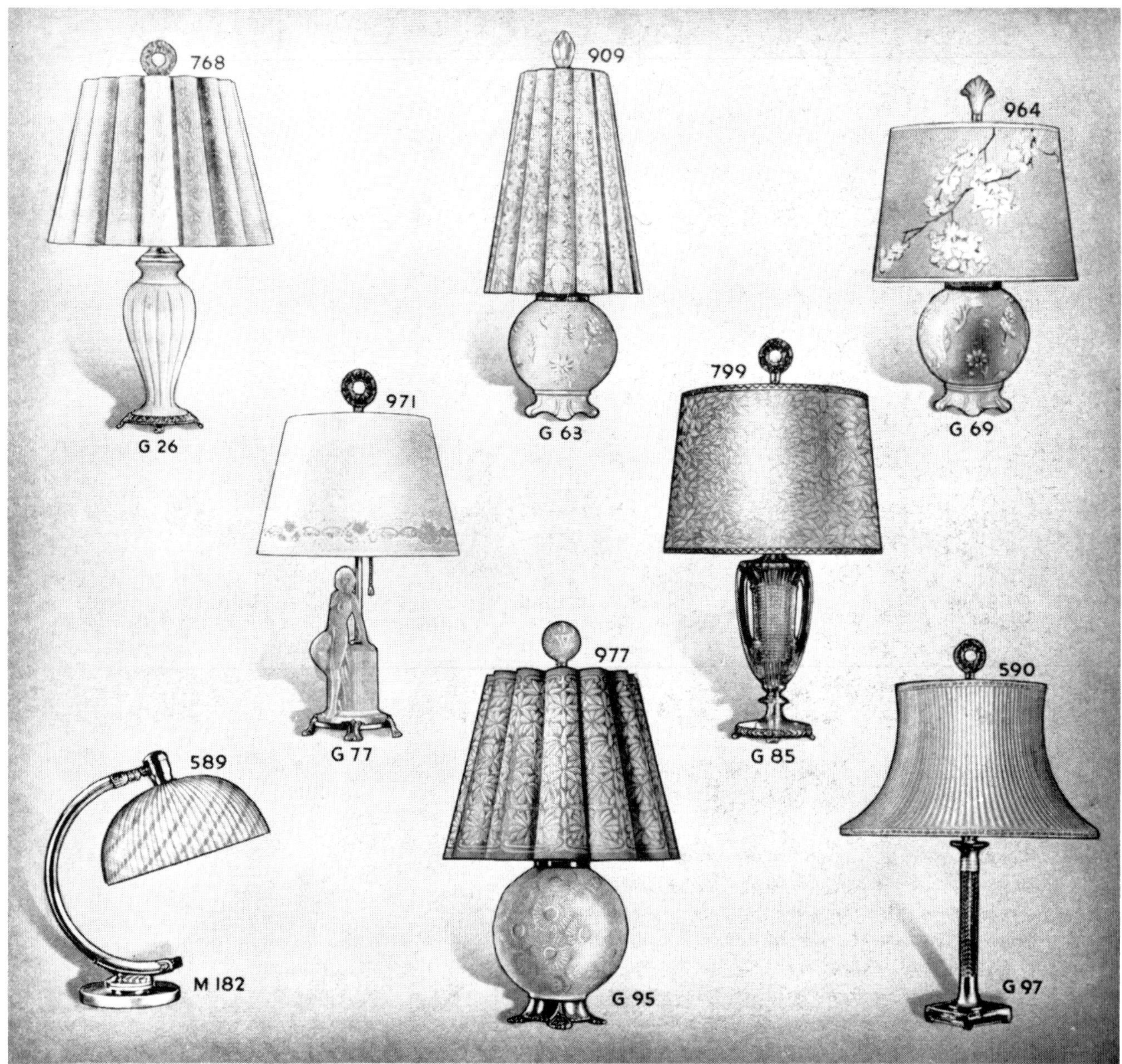

ALADDIN *Electric* TABLE LAMPS

G26—As illustrated at left above, is in the extremely popular fluted vase design and is of Aladex glass with a graceful metal base. Height, 21¼" overall. Supplied in combination of Amber vase and Gold base or White vase and Gold base. Fitted with a single-light push-thru socket, harp and finial. Shown equipped with 14" Fluted Whip-o-lite Shade No. 768. Any 13" or 14" fluted shade adaptable.

G63—Shown at center above, is of the popular illuminated base, ball type. Created in Aladex glass. Height, 22½" overall. In all-white, Peach, Green or Yellow. Single chain-pull socket, with cover switch for base light. Shown with No. 909 10" Fluted Whip-o-lite Shade.

G69—Shown at right above, another popular illuminated base, ball-type lamp in Aladex glass. Height, 18½" overall. In all-white, Peach, Green or Yellow. Single push-thru socket, harp and finial, and cover switch for base light. Shown with Aladdin Whip-o-lite Shade, Parvelour trimmed, 12" Shade No. 964. Any 12" empire, fluted or bell pleated shade suitable.

G77—Shown in center above, is a most artistic figure lamp, created in etched Crystal glass, with metal base Silver plated. Available in this combination only. Height, 24" overall. Fitted with single-light chain-pull socket, harp and finial. Shown with 12" Aladdin Empire Parvelour Shade, Design No. 971.

G85—As illustrated at right center, is of armed vase design and created in combination of Clear, Sparkling Crystal and metal base. Furnished in Crystal and Gold Antiqued base only. Height, 23½". Fitted with single-light push-thru socket, harp and finial. Shown with 13" Aladdin Parvelour Shade, Design No. 799. Any 13" fluted, 13" empire or 14" bell pleated shade adaptable.

G95—In the ever popular ball shape. Of etched Aladex glass with stone flower decoration in relief. Base is of metal. Harp and glass finial. In Amber and Gold, Green and Silver, White and Gold. Overall, 24". Shade, 16" Whip-o-lite Fluted and Flocked Shade of Design No. 977.

G97—To meet the growing demand for a table lamp in Clear Crystal, Aladdin offers this unusually attractive creation. Metal breaks at base and top are finished in Silver. Equipped with single light socket, push-thru switch, harp and Crystal finial. Shown with 14" Aladdin Pleated and Flocked Whip-o-lite Shade, Design No. 590. Overall, 23¾".

M182—A graceful 1-piece cast metal lamp creation which may be used for table or desk lighting. Has single standard swivel socket with control switch in base. Overall, 15½". In Ivory and Gold, Oxidized Bronze, or Black and Silver. Special 10" Whip-o-lite Pleated Shade No. 589, available in White or Tan. Metal Shade 958 optional.

DISTINCTIVE ALADDIN *Electric*

G130—As illustrated at upper left, the draped figure is in Etched Crystal on a beautiful ornamental base. This most artistic lamp is fitted with single, chain-pull socket. Harp and etched Crystal finial. Height overall, 24½". Base is White Lacquer and Antiqued Gold. Shown here equipped with a 15" Aladdin Pure Dye Silk Shade No. S310.

G154—Illustrated at top left is a very charming small table lamp in modern design. Either entirely in Clear Sparkling Crystal or in combinations of Crystal with Amber, Green or Ruby. Equipped with one-light socket with push-thru switch. Height, 15". Shown with 6½" diameter Parvelour Shade No. 585 with clamp fitter.

G155—Illustrated at top center is an unusually attractive vase design in Moonstone, beautifully etched. Offered in all white and three, two-color combinations: White and Black, White and Amber, or White and Green. Equipped with one-light standard socket, push thru switch, harp and finial. Height, 25". Shown equipped with 13" Empire Whip-o-lite Shade No. 967.

G156—Shown at top right center is a most pleasing creation in a mounted urn type lamp. Base is cast metal, and urn is etched fluted Moonstone. Offered in White and Silver, Green and Silver and Tan and Bronze. Height, 23". Single socket, harp and finial. Shown fitted with 14" Aladdin Whip-o-lite Shade Design No. 969.

M160—Illustrated above, a most unique, novel and attractive designed table lamp, of All Metal. Offered in three finishes: Silver and Gold, Silver and Black, or all Oxidized Bronze. Has knob switch control in base for single socket. Height, 15½". Shown fitted with special rotating 10" Pleated Whip-o-lite Shade No. 583.

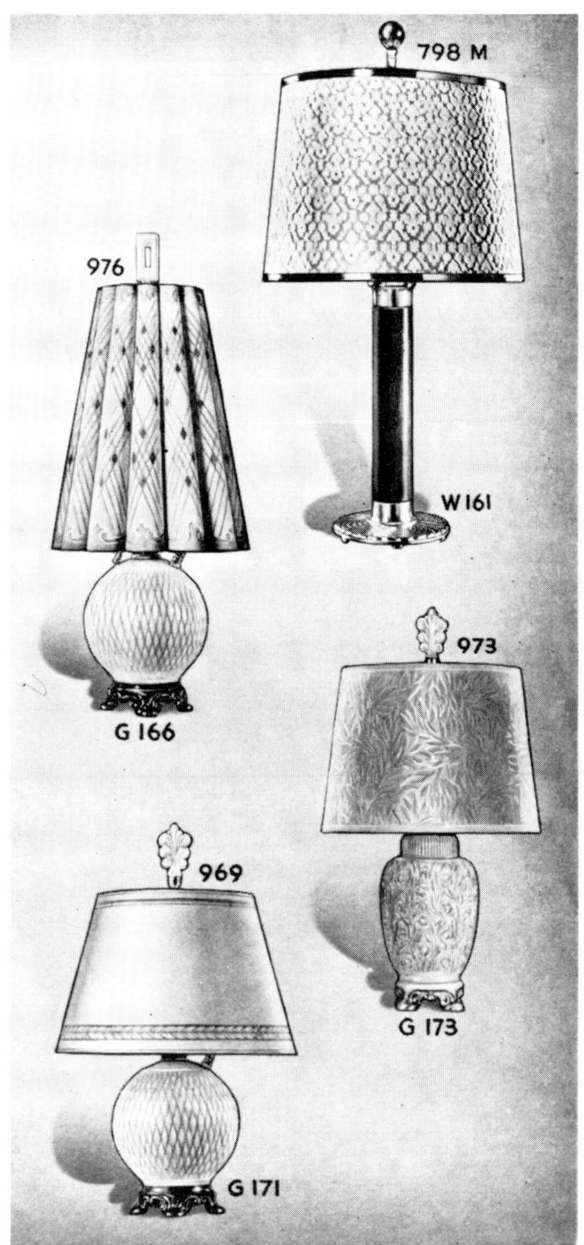

G167—Illustrated at extreme left on opposite page, is a very unique example of the expert glass makers art in floral vase design. In all Moonstone glass. Available in all White etched, or White (not etched) Amber decorated, or White (not etched) Rose decorated. 23" high. One-light socket. Shown fitted with 14" Aladdin Fluted flock decorated Shade No. 977.

G168—Illustrated at bottom of panel on opposite page, is an especially attractive urn design lamp in decorated Moonstone glass. Fitted with one-light socket, harp and finial and with illuminated base socket and separate switch. 22½" high. In Amber, Green or Ivory. Shown fitted with 13" Aladdin Whip-o-lite Shade No. 966.

G169—Illustrated on opposite page at lower right, is in column design in prismatic crystal glass with metal base Antiqued Gold and Silver plated—Somewhat colonial in character, it is proving very popular in its quiet dignity and charm. It is fitted with a single light socket, harp and finial. Shown equipped with 13" Aladdin Empire Parvelour Shade design No. 799.

G171—Illustrated at left, is of the exceedingly popular ball design in decorated Moonstone glass. Illuminated base with separate switch. Also 1-light socket, harp and finial. Available in White, Green, Peach or Yellow. With harmonizing decorated base and feet. 18½" high. Shown here with 12" Aladdin Whip-o-lite Shade, Design No. 969.

G173—Aladdin Table Lamp illustrated at left is a charming small lamp, created in the new Opalique glass in ornamental urn design. Supplied in four colors: Clear Opalique, or Opalique decorated Blue, Ivory or Green. One-light push-thru socket, harp and finial. 12" Shade—Aladdin Embossed Parvelour No. 973. Height 20" overall.

TABLE LAMPS

W161—Shown at right above is a combination wood and pedestal design lamp in the modern mode—of strong eye-appeal. Base and cap of metal with spindle of selected walnut finished in natural color. Metal is bright Copper plate. Height, 25". With 6" plastic reflector, 3-way switch, socket, harp and walnut finial. Shown with 13" Empire Parvelour Shade No. 798M. (Metal trimmed to match base).

G163—Illustrated at left center, is a most alluring creation in all glass figure work of a character found only in the highest class and costliest of foreign importations. Of the metal mounted urn type. In Amber or Green tinted etched Crystal glass urn with metal plated base. Equipped with single socket, harp and finial. Height, 23". Shown fitted with 13" Embossed Parvelour Shade No. 972.

M164—Illustrated in center of grouping on opposite page is an all metal pedestal lamp of plain practical design for homes, offices or hotels. Offered in three finishes: Oxidized Bronze, Silver and Copper, or All-Silver. Supplied only with All Metal 12" Shade No. 950 in finishes to match base. Height, 21".

G165—Illustrated at right center, opposite page, is of a beautiful urn design with decoration in relief. Mounted on a graceful metal base. Urn is of Moonstone glass. Available in White with Silver and Gold base; Tan with Oxidized Bronze base, or Green with Silver and Gold base. One-light socket, harp and finial. 21" high. Shown fitted with 12" Aladdin Whip-o-lite Shade, No. 964.

G166—Illustrated at left in panel above, is of the exceedingly popular modern ball design in decorated Moonstone. Illuminated base. Available in White, Green, Peach, Blue or Yellow. 22½" high. Shown fitted with 10" tall Aladdin Flock decorated Whip-o-lite Shade No. 976.

TABLE *and* BOUDOIR

Design M174

Illustrated at right below, is an all-metal table lamp very graceful and beautifully proportioned. Handsomely plated in semi-dull Silver with Gold trim—one finish only. One-light socket, harp and finial. Shown with 13" Aladdin Silk Shade No. S310. Any 12" Empire shade adaptable. Twenty-one inches high overall.

Design M175

As shown on adjoining page, is a very dignified and rich appearing table lamp in all metal of Georgian design. Supplied in one heavily plated finish only in Satin Silver. Equipped with one-light push-thru socket, harp and finial. Shown with 15" Aladdin Satin Silk stretched Shade No. S310. 14" Bell Pleated Whip-o-lite Shade No. 590 adaptable. Height overall, 24½".

Design M176

Illustrated in panel below, is the same in all respects to the dignified and pleasing M175 described above, except it is fitted with one-light canopied socket with turn switch and 6" plastic reflector. Shown with 14" Bell Pleated Whip-o-lite Shade No. 590. Satin Silk 15" Shade No. S310 adaptable. Height overall, 24¾".

Design G177

As is illustrated on adjoining page, is a vase type table lamp with Colonial atmosphere executed in sparkling colored Crystal glass. Choice of Ruby glass with Gold plated base, or Amber glass and Oxidized Bronze base. One-light push-thru socket, harp and finial. Shown with Aladdin Whip-o-lite Shade No. 963. Height overall, 22".

Design G178

As is pictured at the bottom of panel below, is of a classic mounted urn design, with petal pattern in relief. Executed in new and distinctive Aladdin Opalique glass. Available in Green with Silver and Gold base; Ivory with Silver and Gold base; Blue with Silver base or Tan with Oxidized Bronze base. One-light push-thru socket, harp and finial. Shade shown is No. 966 of 14" size in Empire Whip-o-lite. Height 24".

Design M181

Illustrated at bottom left of next page, is an exceptionally fine example of the glass workers skill executed in Opalique glass. It is available in Ivory with Silver, Gold trimmed, base; or in Amber with an Oxidized Bronze base. One-light socket, push-thru switch, harp and finial. Height 23½" overall. Shown fitted with 18" Bell Pleated Whip-o-lite Shade of design No. 587.

Design G179

Illustrated at lower left of opposite page, is of a modified vase design, in combination of etched Opalique glass and metal. Striking in effect. Available in White with Silver, Gold trim base and head; and in Tan with Oxidized Bronze base and head. One-light socket, harp and finial. Shown with 14" Whip-o-lite Shade No. 965. Height 24½".

Design M180

As shown at bottom of panel, is another very artistically designed all-metal table lamp which has struck popular fancy. Available in choice of Silver plate—Gold trimmed, or in Oxidized Bronze plate highlighted. One-light socket, harp and finial. Shown here fitted with 15" Aladdin Silk Shade No. S302.

Aladdin Bed Lamp
Design 909SS

As illustrated center opposite page, in Fluted Whip-o-lite, 10" at bottom. Fitted with 1-light socket, bed hooks, cord and plug. Available in White, Green, Rose, Amber and Blue. Made to match table lamps fitted with Shade Design 909.

Aladdin Hang-Up Lamp
Design M350

As is illustrated in lower right hand corner, opposite page, is the complete answer to the demand for this type of lamp. Of all-metal construction, beautifully plated in Silver and Gold, or Oxidized Bronze highlighted. One-light socket—push-thru switch. Shown fitted with 7" Whip-o-lite Shade No. 967.

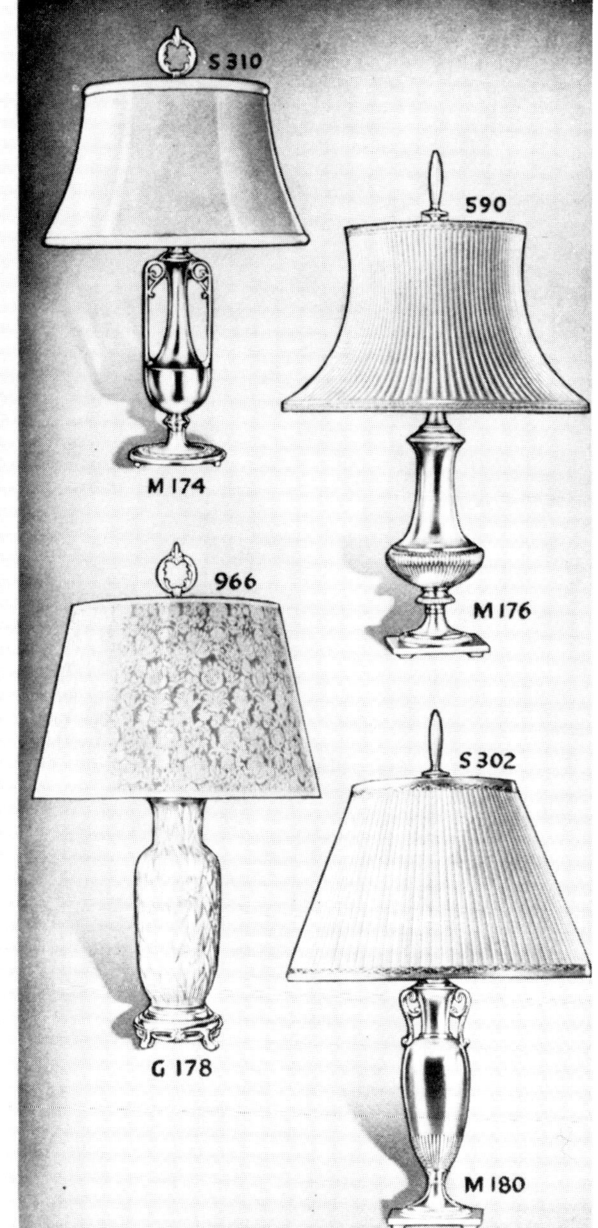

LAMPS OF BEAUTY

ALADDIN
Boudoirs
Dainty-Decorative Delightful

•
Design G15

As shown below, in combination of Clear Crystal and Amber and color decoration; Clear Crystal and White; Crystal and Green; Crystal and Rose; Crystal and Blue. One-light push-thru socket. 15" overall. 7" Parvelour Shade No. 794 shown.

Design G16

As illustrated below, an exquisitely dainty figure boudoir lamp. Available in Etched Crystal in choice of Clear, Brown or Ivory Base, or in all Opalique glass. One-light socket — push-thru switch. 16" high. 7" Parvelour Shade No. 798 shown.

Design G17

As illustrated below, is of the new and beautiful Opalique glass of one-piece pattern, or if preferred supplied in Clear Crystal as well. One-light socket and push-thru switch. 7" Whip-o-lite Shade No. 967 shown.

Design G33

As shown below, is in the ever popular ball design. Satisfyingly simple. In decorated Aladex glass—in White, Rose, Green or Yellow. Is 15½" high. One-light push-thru socket. Shown fitted with 8" fluted Whip-o-lite Shade No. 909.

Design G96

As shown below, of clear sparkling Crystal only. Colonial design one-piece spindle. A very popular number. Height 15½" overall. One-light socket with push-thru switch. Shown with 7" Whip-o-lite Shade No. 964.

Design G153

As illustrated below, is a delightful boudoir lamp, made in a multi fluted vase pattern of Aladex glass. In six colors: Amber, Green, Rose, White, Blue or Orchid. One-light socket, push-thru switch. 14" high. Shown with 7" Whip-o-lite Shade No. 964.

Design M158

As illustrated below, an all-metal, one-piece boudoir, answering a popular demand for a lamp of the tall spindle type. Available in choice of 4 platings: Ivory and Gold; Copper and Silver; Oxidized Bronze or all Silver. One-light push-thru socket. 19" high. 7" Parvelour Shade No. 798 shown.

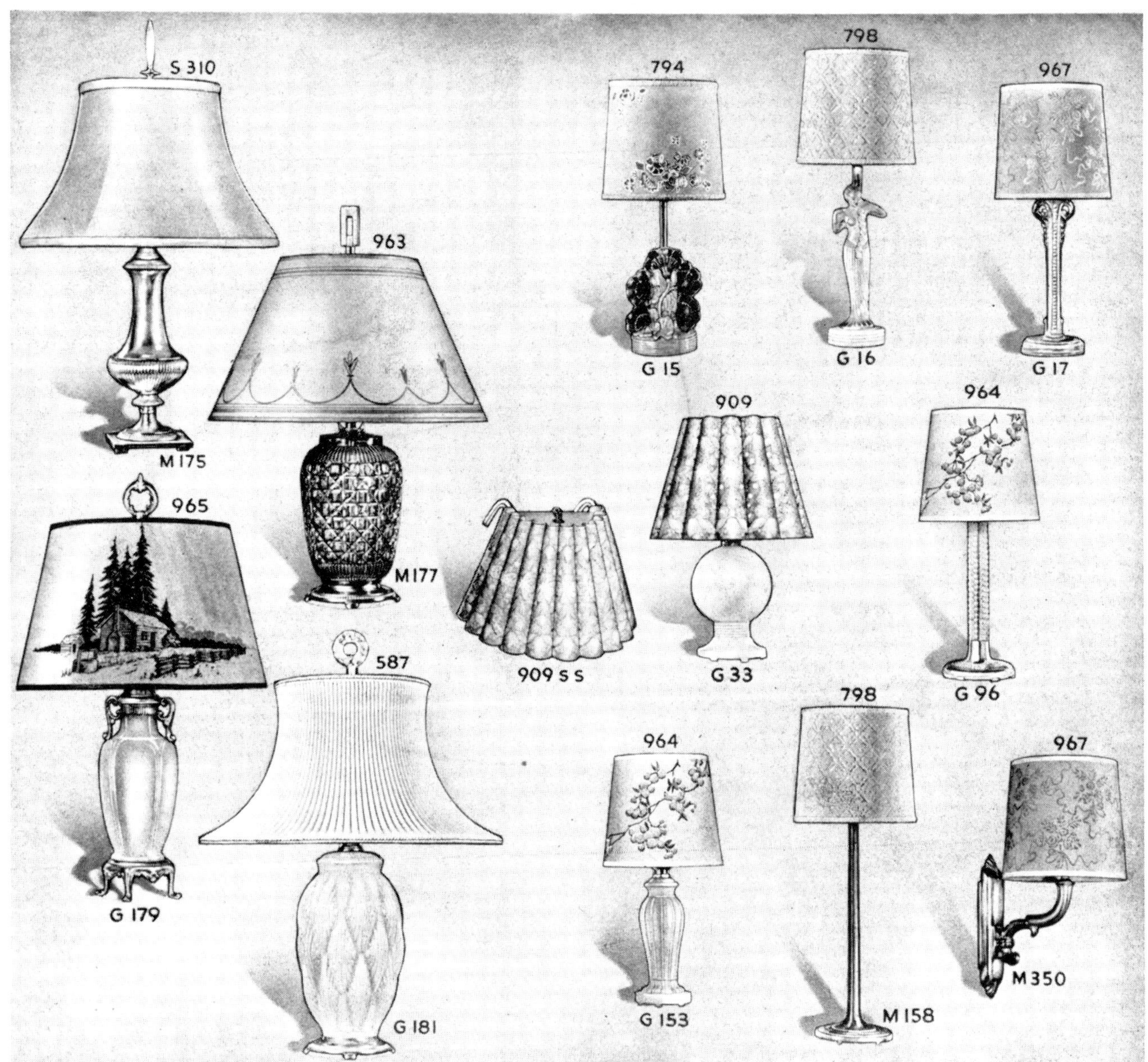

Charming **ALADDIN**

WHILE quality is readily apparent in all Aladdin Electric Lamps, there is no other division in the line where it is more pronounced than in Aladdin floor lamps. Each floor lamp is an individualized unit, practically every part being designed, and made in our own factory especially for it with skilful hands, and artistic minds, setting the completed Aladdin above and apart from the usual "stock part" or "assembled" unit. Finishes are of the highest order, and all wiring, switches and sockets are approved.

ALADDIN REFLECTOR
Design 3501

Illustrated at extreme lower left, is a beautiful example of the sub-base type of floor lamp, so popular and increasingly so at present. The attractive spindle plain, tapered, and lower break in this lamp is of Aladdin's exclusive one-piece cast metal construction. Has Single Mogul Socket and control switch for 50-100-150 or 100-200-300 Watt bulb. 10" Glass Reflector. Available in 3 finishes—Oxidized Bronze, Ivory and Gold, or Silver-Gold trimmed. Shown with 18" Whip-o-lite Shade No. 961.

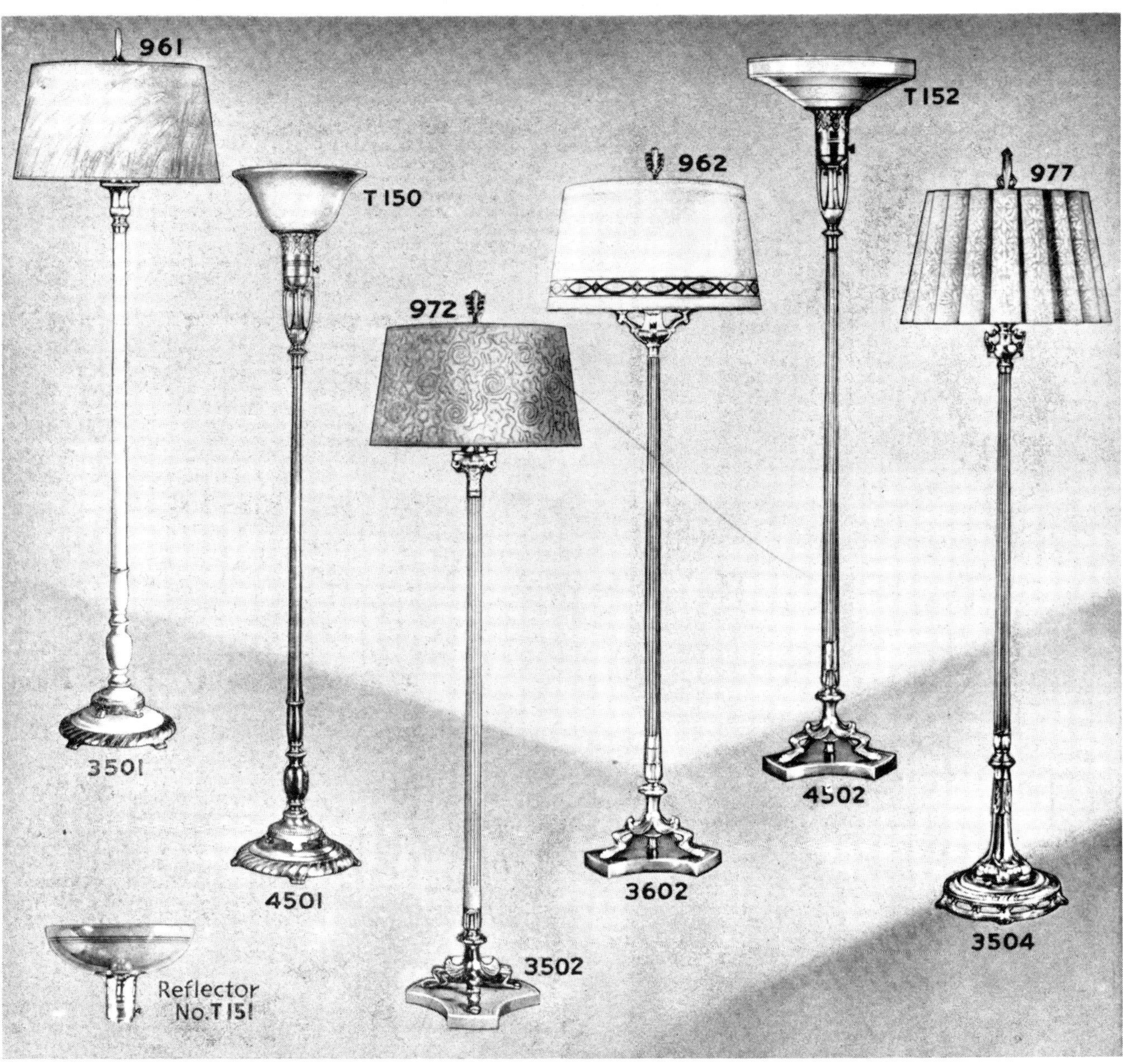

ELECTRIC FLOOR LAMPS

ALADDIN TORCHIERE
Design 4501

As illustrated at lower left of opposite page, is Aladdin interpretation of what a lamp of this type should be and wherever presented has met with universal acclaim. Like its companion No. 3501, it is of the new sub-base, cast spindle and break type and the illustration shows how handsome and well proportioned for artistic harmony it is. Has 1-Light Mogul Socket, and canopy switch for control of 50-100-150 or 100-200-300 Watt bulb. Shown equipped with Inverted Bell Glass Reflector 12" diameter. No. T-150 or may be supplied with No. T-151-2 or 3 Reflector if desired.

Available in Oxidixed Bronze finish only.

ALADDIN REFLECTOR
Design 3502

Illustrated at lower left, is another exclusive Aladdin creation of the one-piece cast metal spindle construction. Base is plain and of a modified triangular type surmounted with a footed and winged tripod break of beautiful design. Spindle is tapered and fluted, with Ionic break at Top. Fitted with 1-light Mogul Socket with canopy control switch for 50-100-150 or 100-200-300 Watt bulb. Approved wiring, switches and sockets. Available in Ivory and Gold or Oxidized Bronze finishes. Shown fitted with 18" Aladdin Parvelour Embossed Shade No. 972.

ALADDIN Junior REFLECTOR
Design 3602

Illustrated at lower left, is similar in design to the No. 3502 Aladdin Reflector described at left, except it has not alone a 1-light Mogul Socket for 50-100-150 or 100-200-300 Watt bulb, but also has 3 candle arms fitted with standard sockets. Two three-way switches are in canopy for separate control of the Mogul or candle arm lamps, providing 6-way control. Candle arms are of exclusive design in cast metal — very attractive. This beautiful Aladdin may be secured in Oxidized Bronze or Ivory and Gold finishes. Shade is 18" Aladdin Whip-o-lite Design No. 962.

ALADDIN TORCHIERE—Design 4502

The Aladdin torchiere lamp in this beautiful design of base and fluted spindle is here because of its especial attractiveness and fitness in this popular type of floor lamp. The simplicity of its design permits its use in a great variety of situations. Available in Oxidized Bronze Finish only. Provided with Mogul socket, proper switch for control of 50-100-150 or 100-200-300 Watt bulb, with approved wiring and cord. Shown equipped with Mottled and striped glass reflector No. T-152 in Tan.

ALADDIN REFLECTOR—Design 3504

This new Aladdin reflector lamp is presented with especial pride in its exceptional beauty. Its base is massive yet because of its open work pattern it appears light and delicate. It is surmounted with a cast metal spindle with sub-base and fluted shaft in Aladdins famous one-piece construction. As shown, is fitted with Mogul socket and canopy switch for control of 50-100-150 or 100-200-300 Watt bulb, and approved wiring and cord. Available in Oxidized Bronze, Ivory and Gold, or Silver-Gold trimmed. Shown with Aladdin 18" Fluted Shade Design No. 977.

ALADDIN Junior REFLECTOR–Design 3604

This Aladdin Junior Reflector is, as may be readily seen, an adaptation from the No. 3504 described, and is substantially the same except in its head. In this Junior Reflector 1-Light Mogul socket, and switch for control of 50-100-150 or 100-200-300 Watt bulb is supplemented with 3 candle arms for standard bulbs with progressive switch making it a 6-way lamp. Available in 3 finishes—Oxidized Bronze, Ivory and Gold, or Silver-Gold trimmed. Illustrated with 18" Aladdin Whip-o-lite Shade No. 963.

ALADDIN REFLECTOR BRIDGE—Design 6004

The popularity of this type of lamp continues and with this beautiful new Aladdin in this model it will find ready consumer acceptance. Substantially the same in base and one-piece spindle as its companion lamps Nos. 3504 and 3604. As illustrated, is fitted with a most attractive bridge arm, canopy, canopy switch and 1-light standard socket with 8" Plastic reflector. Available in Oxidized Bronze, Ivory and Gold or Silver-Gold trimmed. Shade shown is 12" Aladdin Embossed Parvelour No. 973.

ALADDIN TORCHIERE—Design 4504

At the insistent demand of buyers, we have found it necessary to add this type of lamp in this most popular series of floor lamps. Base and fluted spindle is same as used in Nos. 3504-3604 and 6004 lamps described above. Reflector head as shown is provided with a Mogul Socket and 3-way canopy switch for control of 50-100-150 or 100-200-300 Watt bulb. Available in Oxidized Bronze, Ivory and Gold or Silver-Gold trimmed. Metal crowned reflector is 13¾" in diameter in Mottled and leaf decorated glass in tan and brown No. T-153. (T-150-1 or 2 if preferred).

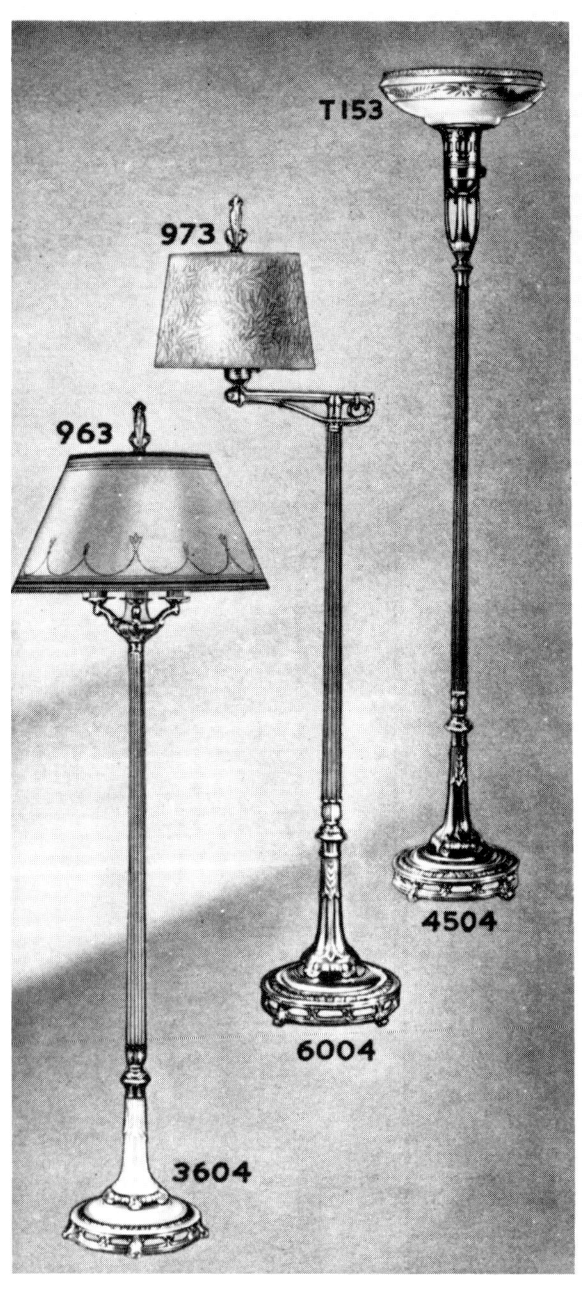

ALADDIN FLOOR LAMPS
of Loveliness and Grace

The prime factor of course for a quick consumer acceptance of home lighting devices is their attractiveness and on that basis alone Aladdin Floor Lamps are exceptional. But in Aladdins just attractiveness alone is not enough—it must be inbuilt and lasting, not merely skin-deep. That's why only the best materials and master craftmanship go into each and every one. A policy of this kind is what we believe to be the only foundation upon which we, as manufacturers, and our dealers can safely build. Lasting consumer satisfaction is what builds the most enviable reputations.

Juniorette Floor Lamp, Design 1005

Illustrated at right, is a novelty floor lamp which because of its unusualness, its utility and its charm, has swept the field. Modernistic in motif. Fitted with a single, pull-chain socket, harp and finial. Available in white and Gold or on Oxidized Bronze Lacquer. Shown equipped with 18" Aladdin Bell Pleated Whip-o-lite Shade, Design No. 588.

Juniorette Floor Lamp, Design 1093

Illustrated at right, an eye-arresting Junior floor lamp of striking design in combination Crystal glass spindle and metal base. Offered only in Clear White Crystal with Silver-plated base and head. Single chain-pull socket, with harp and finial. Shown equipped with Aladdin 16" Fluted, flock-decorated shade, of Design 977.

Juniorette Floor Lamp, Design 1094

Illustrated at right, here is a very attractive novelty floor lamp of unusual design, entirely of metal, and most handsomely finished. Choice of two combinations: Ivory and Gold or in Copper and Silver. Shown fitted with 18" Aladdin Bell Pleated Whip-o-lite Shade of Design No. 588.

Bridge Lamp, Design 2083

Illustrated at right on adjoining page, is a companion Bridge to the Juniorette lamp 1005 and of same design in base and spindle. Bridge Arm is one-piece metal of graceful curvature, fitted with standard turn-knob socket and shell. Available in White and Gold or in Oxidized Bronze Lacquer. Shown fitted with 12" Pleated Whip-o-lite Bell Shade No. 576.

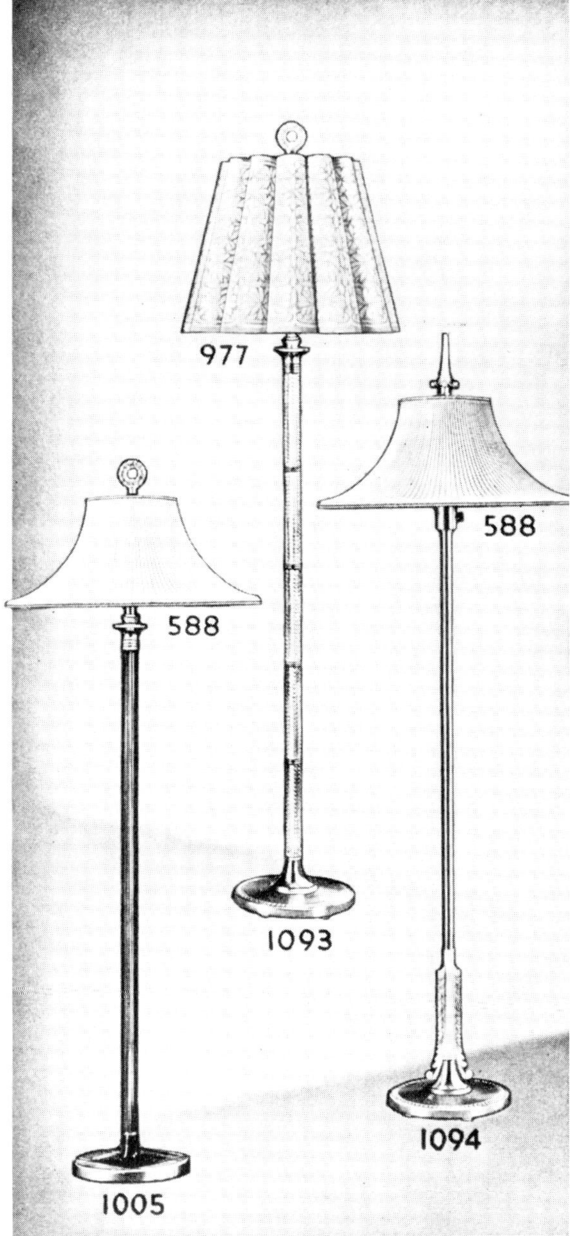

Aladdin Reflector, Design 3503

Illustrated below, is what it has already proved to be, a very popular Floor Reflector lamp with a square base and break of simple design. Spindle is beautifully fluted and of Aladdin's patented, 1-piece, cast metal construction. Head fitted with a Mogul socket with 3-way switch for 50-100-150 or 100-200-300 watt bulb. In 3 finishes: Oxidized Bronze, Ivory and Gold or Silver and Gold. Shown fitted with 18" Aladdin Whip-o-lite Shade, Design No. 965.

Aladdin Reflector, Design 3595

Illustrated below, is of the popular reflector type. Beautiful tapered spindle is cast of metal in one-piece—a form of construction patented by Aladdin and recognized as the outstanding progressive step in floor lamp manufacture. Has single Mogul Socket for two-filament bulbs of 50-100-150 or 100-200-300 watts. Switch in head. Offered in Oxidized Bronze, Ivory and Gold or Silver and Gold. Shown with 18" Empire Whip-o-lite Shade No. 962.

Aladdin Reflector, Design 3596

As illustrated below, is floor lamp of unusual charm because of its simplicity of line and decoration. Base and head of metal, beautifully finished in polished copper, and spindle of selected grain walnut, natural finish. Has single Mogul socket for two-filament, three-intensity bulbs with knob switch in canopy. 10" glass reflector. Shown equipped with Copper trimmed 18" Parvelour Shade, No. 798M.

Aladdin Reflector Bridge, Design 6096

As illustrated, a reflector bridge of same design as its companion Reflector Lamp No. 3596. Base and bridge arm of metal, polished copper plated, and spindle of selected grain walnut. Equipped with canopied one-light socket for 40-60-100 watt bulb, and three-way switch for control. 8" plastic reflector. Shown fitted with Copper trimmed 12" Parvelour Shade No. 798M.

Aladdin Reflector Bridge, Design 6013

As illustrated below—a reflector bridge lamp of very charming, dignified and simple design. Is fitted with one standard socket, and 3-way canopy switch to control 40-60-100 watt bulb. Has 8" diameter Plastic reflector. Beautifully finished in Ivory and Gold or in Brown lacquer base and finished Copper spindle. Shade shown—12" Empire Whip-o-lite of design No. 967.

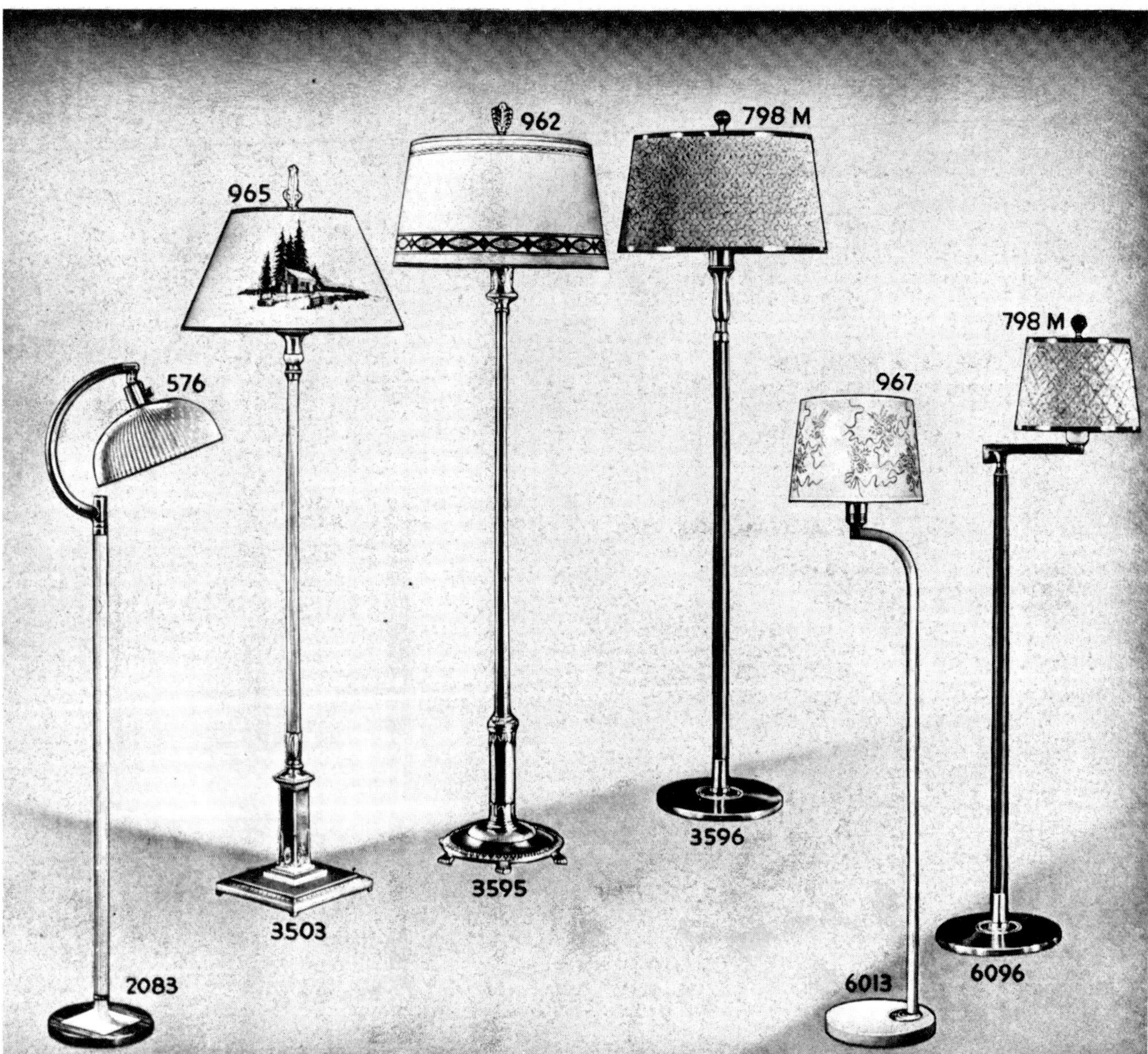

NOVELTY FLOOR LAMPS

Design 7088

As is illustrated at left, is a combination bridge lamp and table, of combination wood and metal construction. Base as well as spindles, and table top are in beautiful walnut finish with metal silver plated. Single swivel canopied push-thru switch socket. Shown fitted with 12" Dome Pleated Shade No. 820.

Design 7089

As is illustrated at left, is of the same general design as 7088 at left, except it is of all-metal construction except table top and base are of laminated wood. Furnished in one finish only: White and Gold. Single, swivel, canopied, push-thru switch socket. Shown fitted with 12" Dome Pleated Shade No. 820.

Design 7014

As may be observed from illustration at left, this lamp is of a simple modern design, in all metal except its table top of selected grain laminated wood. Fitted with 1 standard socket and 3-way switch in canopy for 40-60-100 watt bulb. 8" Plastic reflector. In two finishes: Ivory and Gold with table top in White lacquer; or in Brown and Copper with top in Walnut finish. Shade shown—12" Empire Whip-o-lite of design No. 618.

Design 7090

As illustrated at left, is a very popular novelty bridge lamp in combination of metal and wood. Offered in metal Silver plated with Walnut finished base and shelves. Single rotating socket with control switch in finial. Shade shown 9" Pleated Bell No. 578.

Design 7091

As illustrated at left, is a unique combination of reflector bridge lamp and end table. Supplied in one finish only—Walnut and Silver. Has single socket with 3-way canopy switch for 40-60-100 watt bulb. 8" Plastic reflector. Shade shown—12" Empire Parvelour of design No. 797.

Aladdin Electric Lamps and Shades

★ In this catalog of Aladdin built Boudoir, Table and Floor Lamps and Whip-o-Lite Shades, you will find a line of merchandise which has an established reputation for exceptional excellence in design, materials, finish and craftsmanship. Merchandise which is power packed with that elusive, indefinable quality which excites and stimulates desire for ownership to a remarkable degree, and reduces sales resistance to a minimum. This element combined with their high "I.Q." (inherent quality) and their reasonable prices is the open sesame that has opened and is continuing to open the door to sales and profits to Aladdin dealers everywhere.

Alacite, the amazing new lamp base material produced exclusively by Aladdin has so thoroughly demonstrated its ever increasing popularity that dealers generally have demanded a larger variety and number of lamps in this material be added to the line. So you'll find many new and pleasing numbers in Alacite as well as in other materials shown in these pages.

You will also notice the greatly increased number of designs and styles which are now included in the Aladdin Electric Floor Lamp Line. Ever since Aladdin first introduced the first revolutionary, long, one-piece cast-metal spindle, it was ordained that eventually it would be the standard of comparison by which others must be judged whether it be for charm and beauty, for finish or value.

For lamps that sell quickly and sell at a profit, that assure long-lasting consumer service and satisfaction, and make friends for your store, be sure they bear the trade-mark ALADDIN.

THE MANTLE LAMP COMPANY OF AMERICA
Incorporated

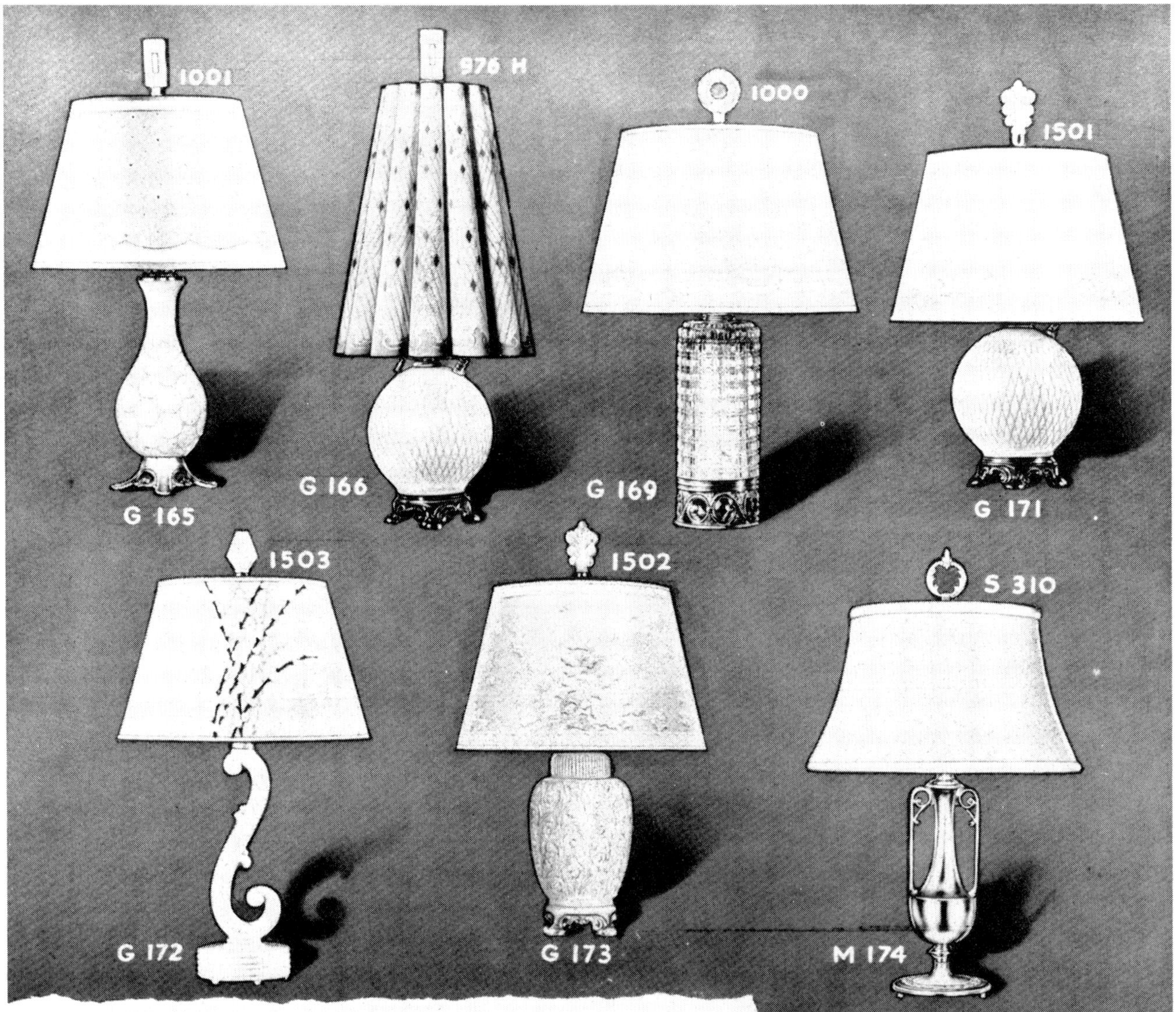

Aladdin *Electric* Table Lamps

DELIGHTFUL ★ CHARMING

Design No. G 165

In upper row above, a graceful urn of decorated Opalique glass with design in relief, mounted on attractive metal base. In white with Antiqued Gold base or Tan with Oxidized Bronze base. Harp, Finial and 1-Lt. Socket. 21" high. Shown with 12" Whip-o-lite Shade No. 1001.

Design No. G 166

In upper row above, in the ever popular ball and diamond relief design, of decorated Opalique glass. 1-Lt. in Bowl with separate switch, and fitted with 1-Lt. Socket, Harp and Finial. In White, Green, Blue, Peach or Yellow. 22½" high. Shown here with 10" tall Whip-o-lite Shade No. 976 H.

Design No. G 169

In upper row above, of Colonial column design, in clear sparkling prismatic crystal glass, with a handsome harmonizing cast metal base. Base is beautifully finished in Antiqued gold plate. Very popular. It is fitted with 1-Lt. Socket, Harp and harmonizing crystal Finial. 23" high. Shown with 14" Whip-o-lite Shade No. 1000.

Design No. G 171

In upper row above, in the modern ball pattern, with diamond relief design, in decorated Opalique glass. Has illuminated base with separate switch. Also 1-Lt. Socket, low Harp and Finial. 18½" high. Available in Green, Peach, White or Yellow. Shown here with decorated 12" Whip-o-lite Shade No. 1501.

Design No. G 172

In row directly above, is in a very unique serpentine, hollow-blown pedestal design in Ivory Alacite only. Pedestal is integral with base. Concealed cord from base to 1-Lt. push-thru socket. Harp and Alacite Finial. 23¾" high. Illustrated here with 12" Whip-o-lite Shade No. 1503.

Design No. G 173

In row directly above, is a charming, small relief-decorated vase design lamp, in Aladdin's new Opalique glass. A popular number. Available in Clear Opalique or decorated in Ivory, Green or Blue. 20" high. Has 1-Lt. Socket push-thru switch, Harp and Finial. Illustrated above with 12" Whip-o-lite Shade of design No. 1502.

Design No. M 174

At right in row above, in all-cast metal of a delightful, armed urn design. Graceful — well proportioned. Available only in a handsomely and heavily plated Satin Silver, and Antiqued. 1-Lt. Socket, Harp and Finial. Height 21" overall. Shown here with 13" Aladdin Silk Shade of Design No. S 310.

Design No. M 175

Illustrated at right, is of a dignified urn design in Georgian decoration and is very rich in appearance. 24¼" high. In one finish only — Satin Silver Plate and highlighted. Fitted with 1-Lt. push-thru Switch Socket, Harp and Finial. Shown here fitted with 15" Aladdin Stretched Silk Shade of Design No. S 310.

[3]

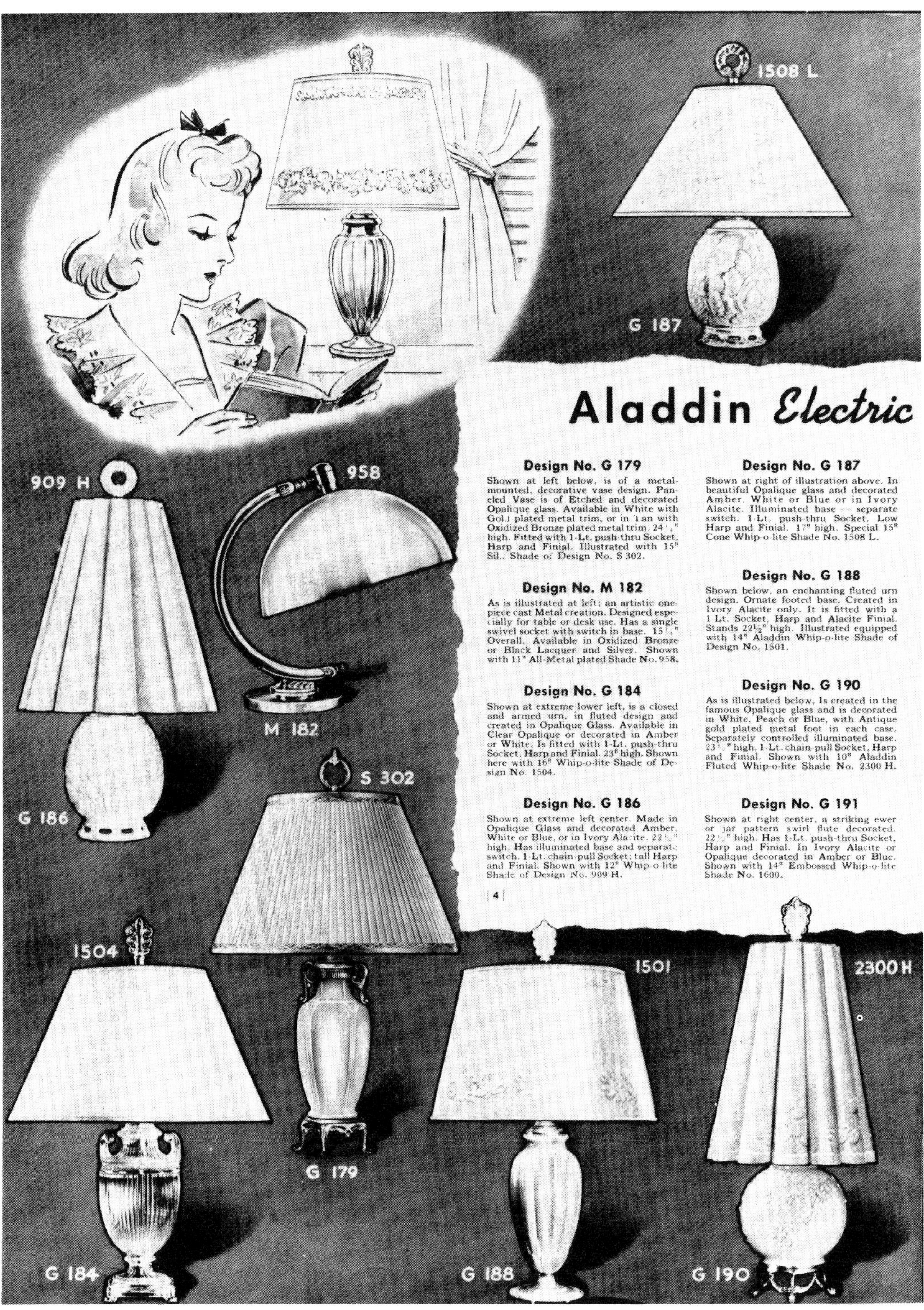

Aladdin *Electric*

Design No. G 179

Shown at left below, is of a metal-mounted, decorative vase design. Paneled Vase is of Etched and decorated Opalique glass. Available in White with Gold plated metal trim, or in Tan with Oxidized Bronze plated metal trim. 24½" high. Fitted with 1-Lt. push-thru Socket, Harp and Finial. Illustrated with 15" Sil. Shade of Design No. S 302.

Design No. M 182

As is illustrated at left; an artistic one-piece cast Metal creation. Designed especially for table or desk use. Has a single swivel socket with switch in base. 15½" Overall. Available in Oxidized Bronze or Black Lacquer and Silver. Shown with 11" All-Metal plated Shade No. 958.

Design No. G 184

Shown at extreme lower left, is a closed and armed urn, in fluted design and created in Opalique Glass. Available in Clear Opalique or decorated in Amber or White. Is fitted with 1-Lt. push-thru Socket, Harp and Finial. 23" high. Shown here with 16" Whip-o-lite Shade of Design No. 1504.

Design No. G 186

Shown at extreme left center. Made in Opalique Glass and decorated Amber, White or Blue, or in Ivory Alacite. 22½" high. Has illuminated base and separate switch. 1-Lt. chain-pull Socket; tall Harp and Finial. Shown with 12" Whip-o-lite Shade of Design No. 909 H.

Design No. G 187

Shown at right of illustration above. In beautiful Opalique glass and decorated Amber, White or Blue or in Ivory Alacite. Illuminated base — separate switch. 1-Lt. push-thru Socket. Low Harp and Finial. 17" high. Special 15" Cone Whip-o-lite Shade No. 1508 L.

Design No. G 188

Shown below, an enchanting fluted urn design. Ornate footed base. Created in Ivory Alacite only. It is fitted with a 1 Lt. Socket, Harp and Alacite Finial. Stands 22½" high. Illustrated equipped with 14" Aladdin Whip-o-lite Shade of Design No. 1501.

Design No. G 190

As is illustrated below, Is created in the famous Opalique glass and is decorated in White, Peach or Blue, with Antique gold plated metal foot in each case. Separately controlled illuminated base. 23½" high. 1-Lt. chain-pull Socket, Harp and Finial. Shown with 10" Aladdin Fluted Whip-o-lite Shade No. 2300 H.

Design No. G 191

Shown at right center, a striking ewer or jar pattern swirl flute decorated. 22½" high. Has 1-Lt. push-thru Socket, Harp and Finial. In Ivory Alacite or Opalique decorated in Amber or Blue. Shown with 14" Embossed Whip-o-lite Shade No. 1600.

[4]

Table Lamps

(Continued)

Design No. G 192

Illustrated directly above, is in Ivory Alacite only, mounted on a cast metal Antiqued Gold base. Fitted with 1-Lt. push-thru Socket, low Harp and Alacite Finial. Shown with 15" Cone Whip-o-lite Shade No. 1508 L. 19¼" high.

Design No. G 193

Same as G 192 but is also fitted with 1-Lt. Socket and switch for illuminating base.

Design No. G 194

Illustrated at center above. Is the same as G 192 described above but is fitted with a high harp to accommodate a tall shade. Shown here fitted with 13" Fluted Parvelour Whip-o-lite Shade No. 2300.

Design No. G 195

Same as G 194 but is also fitted with 1-Lt. Socket and switch for illuminating base. 20¼" high.

Design No. G 196

Shown at top right. In Ivory Alacite only with a cast metal Antique Gold finish base. Shown with 14" Whip-o-lite Shade No. 1003. 23½" high.

Design No. G 197

Same as G 196 but is also fitted with socket and switch for illuminating base.

Design No. G 198

Shown at right center, is in Ivory Alacite, or in decorated Alacite in Blue, Tan, Maroon or Green. 1-Lt. Socket, Harp and Finial. 23¾" high. Shown with 14" Whip-o-lite Shade No. 1000.

Design No. G 199

Same as G 198, but is also fitted with 1-Lt. socket and switch for illuminating base.

Design No. G 200

Shown at bottom right, supplied in Clear Crystal, or in Antiqued Ivory Alacite. 1-Lt. Socket, Harp and Finial. 21" high. Shown with 12" Whip-o-lite Shade No. 1001.

Design No. G 201

Shown at right, supplied in Ivory Alacite or in etched Crystal decorated in White, Green or Rose. Swiveled, turn-knob switch socket. Concealed wiring. Shade shown — 9" Cone Whip-o-lite No. 1004. 13" high.

Design No. G 202

Shown at center below, in Ivory Alacite, or in etched Crystal decorated White, Amber, Green or Rose. 1-Lt. Socket, Harp and Finial. Shade shown — 12" Whip-o-lite No. 2003. 21¾" high.

Design No. G 203

Shown at left below, in Ivory Alacite only. 1-Lt. Socket, Harp and Finial. 21¼" high. Shade shown—12" Whip-o-lite No. 1002.

[5]

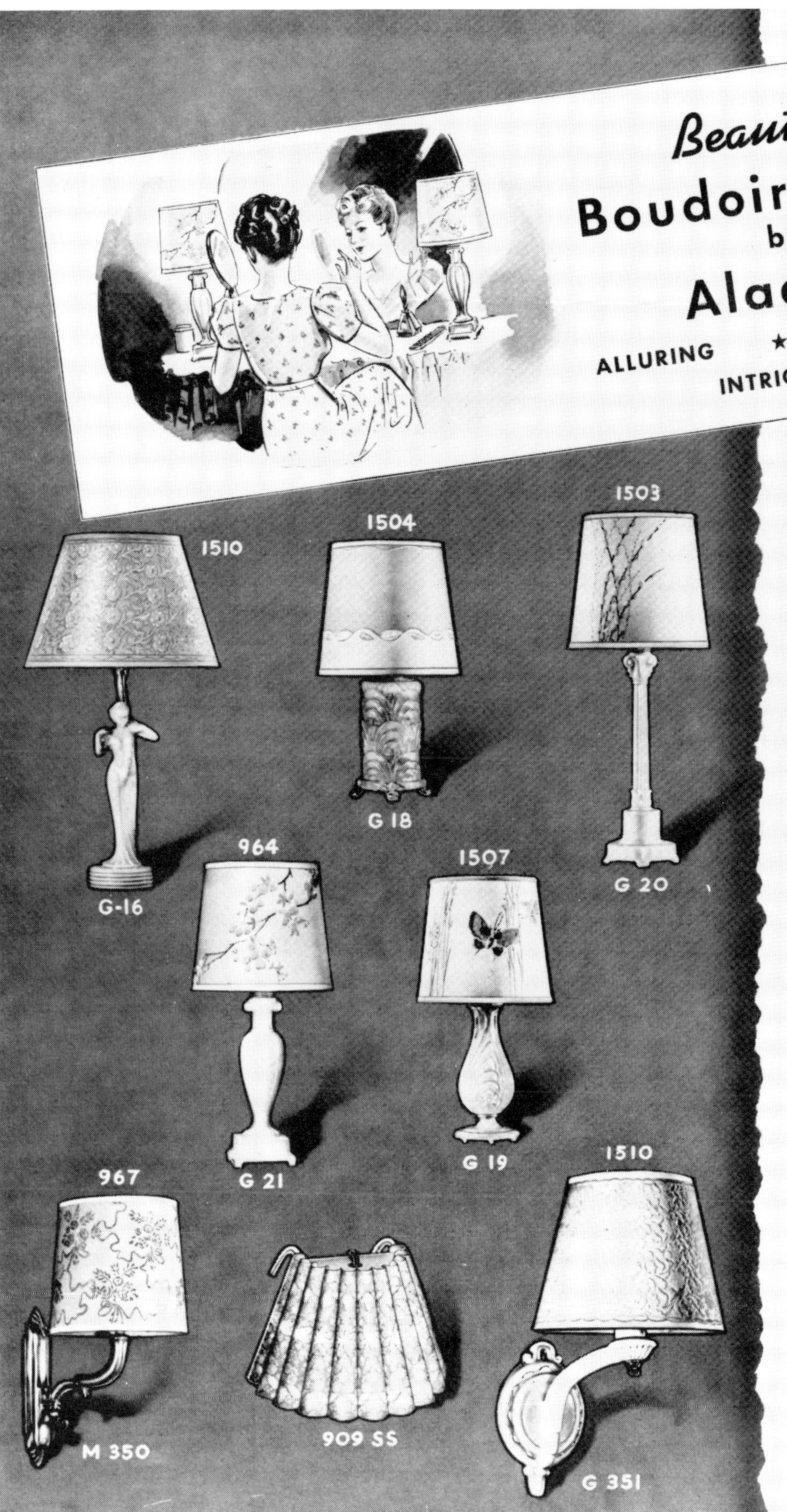

Beautiful Boudoir Lamps
by Aladdin

ALLURING ★ FASCINATING
INTRIGUING

Design No. G 16

Shown at top left, is an unusually fine example of moulded figure work. It is created in alluring Ivory Alacite. Has 1-Lt. push-thru switch socket, and concealed wiring thru base. All metal parts Gold plated and lacquered. Base is hand antiqued. In Ivory Alacite only. 17" high. Is illustrated here equipped with 10" Whip-o-lite Shade of Design No. 1510.

Design No. G 18

Shown at top center, is handsome low-type boudoir lamp of unique style. It is created in sunburst relief design—very modern. Available in decorated Opalique glass in Green, Rose or Blue, in sparkling clear Crystal, or in Ivory Alacite. 13" high. Fitted with 1-Lt. push-thru socket with cord thru base. Shown here with 7" Whip-o-lite Shade of Design No. 1504.

Design No. G 19

Shown at right center, is another new, low, glass urn pedestal boudoir lamp of modern type. It is executed in the increasing popular, beautiful and intriguing Ivory Alacite only. 14" high. It is fitted with 1-Lt. push-thru socket with concealed cord. Shown here with 7" Whip-o-lite Shade No. 1507.

Design No. G 20

Shown at top right, is a most unusual example of the beautiful designing and glass makers art. In One-piece moulded Ivory Alacite, or in decorated Etched Crystal in White, Green, Rose or Blue. Hollow pedestal carries cord thru base to 1-Lt. push-thru socket. 17" high. Shown here with 7" Aladdin Whip-o-lite Shade of Design No. 1503.

Design No. G 21

For this new vogue type of boudoir illustrated at left center, both Ivory Alacite, and Etched and decorated Crystal in White, Rose, Green or Blue were chosen to carry out the delicacy and daintiness of its simple artistic design. 15" high. It is fitted with 1-Lt. push-thru socket with concealed cord. It is shown here equipped with 7" Whip-o-lite Shade of Design No. 964.

★

Aladdin Hang Up Lamps
In Metal • In Glass

Design No. M 350

As is illustrated at lower left hand corner is a complete answer to the demand for this type of lamp. Of all metal one-piece cast construction. It is supplied in choice of two plated finishes: Silver and Gold, or in Oxidized Bronze artistically highlighted. 1-Lt. push-thru socket. Illustrated with 7" Aladdin Whip-o-lite Shade No. 967.

Design No. G 351

Shown at right at bottom of page, is of the wall medallion pattern. Is created in Ivory Alacite only. Fitted with single candle and 1-Lt. socket with twin-knob switch in hollow arm. Design is dignified and simple and will harmonize nicely in most any surroundings. Shown here equipped with 10" Shade Design No. 1510.

★

Aladdin Bed Lamps
In Fluted Whip-o-lite

As is illustrated at bottom center, is made of Fluted Whip-o-lite and is decorated in a beautiful design No. 909SS. It is provided with socket, long length cord and rubber covered hooks. 10" wide at bottom. In design it matches Shade No. 909 so that it will harmonize with boudoir or night table lamps so equipped. Available in Amber, White, Green, Rose or Blue.

| 6 |

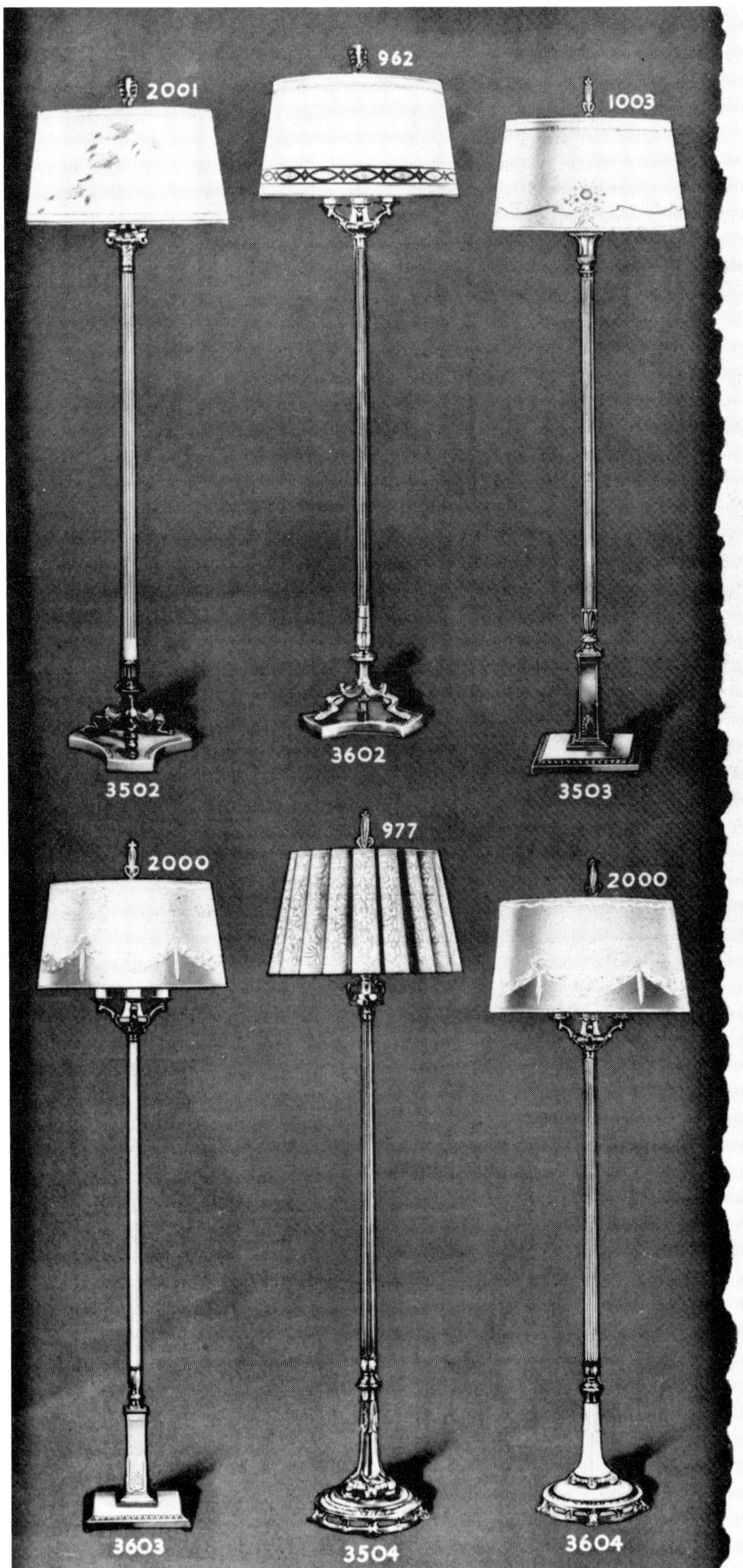

Aladdin
Electric FLOOR LAMPS
A True Expression of the Artistry of Fine Lamp Making

THE quickness with which consumers accept home lighting devices is determined quite often by eye-appeal, and this important element is most apparent in every Aladdin Floor Lamp. In Aladdins however just temporary attractiveness is not enough —it must be inbuilt and lasting—not merely surface beauty. That's why only the best materials and master craftsmanship goes into each and every one. It is our belief that it is only by following a fixed policy of this kind that lasting consumer service and satisfaction may be obtained, and create a firm foundation on which dealers may safely build.

In line with this policy Aladdin has developed its beautiful exclusive, long, one-piece, cast and hand-chased spindles and breaks—the first major improvement in lamp construction in many years. All Aladdin Floor Lamps shown herein have this feature.

Aladdin Reflector—No. 3502
3-Way Lighting (See Note)
Oxidized Bronze or Silver and Gold Plated
10" Glass Reflector
18" Whip-o-lite Shade No. 2001 Shown

Aladdin Reflector—No. 3602
6-Way Lighting (See Note)
Oxidized Bronze or Silver and Gold Plated
10" Glass Reflector
18" Whip-o-lite Shade No. 962 Shown

Aladdin Reflector—No. 3503
3-Way Lighting (See Note)
Oxidized Bronze, Ivory and Gold or Silver
and Gold Plated
10" Glass Reflector
18" Whip-o-lite Shade No. 1003 Shown

Aladdin Reflector—No. 3603
6-Way Lighting (See Note)
Oxidized Bronze, Ivory and Gold or Silver
and Gold Plated
10" Glass Reflector
18" Whip-o-lite Shade No. 2000 Shown

Aladdin Reflector—No. 3504
3-Way Lighting (See Note)
Oxidized Bronze, Ivory and Gold or Silver
and Gold Plated
10" Glass Reflector
18" Whip-o-lite Shade No. 977 Shown

Aladdin Reflector—No. 3604
6-Way Lighting (See Note)
Oxidized Bronze, Ivory and Gold or Silver
and Gold Plated
10" Glass Reflector
18" Whip-o-lite Shade No. 2000 Shown

NOTE:

Aladdin's 3-Way Lamps are equipped with 1-Mogul Socket wired for 3-way control of 50-100-150 or 100-200-300 Watt bulbs. Aladdin 6-Way Lamps are equipped with 1-Mogul Socket wired for 3-Way control of 50-100-150 or 100-200-300 Watt bulbs, and also fitted with ornamental 3-armed head with 3 candles and Sockets for Standard bulbs and wired for 3-Way separate control. Bulbs are not included with lamps.

[7]

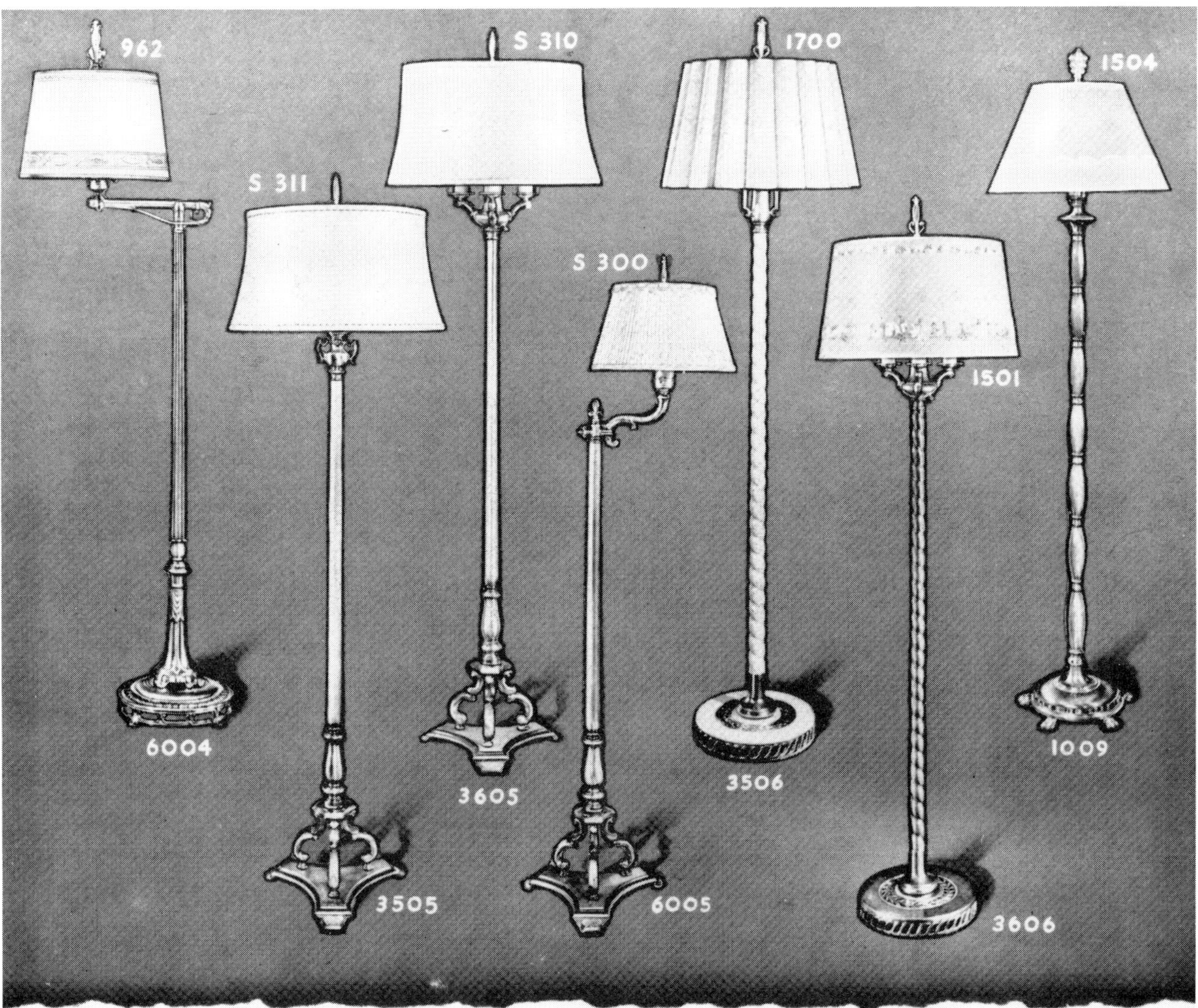

Aladdin *Electric* Floor

RICH ENDURING FINISHES

Aladdin Reflector Bridge No. 6004
One Light Canopied Socket with Turn Knob
Switch — 8" Glass Reflector
Oxidized Bronze, Ivory and Gold or Silver
and Gold Finishes
12" Whip-o-lite Shade No. 962 Shown

Aladdin Reflector—No. 3505
3-Way Lighting (See Note)
Oxidized Bronze or China Bronze Finishes
10" Glass Reflector
19" Silk Shade Design S 311 Shown

Aladdin Reflector—No. 3605
6-Way Lighting (See Note)
Oxidized Bronze or China Bronze Finishes
10" Glass Reflector
19" Silk Shade Design S 310 Shown

Aladdin Reflector Bridge No. 6005
One Light Canopied Socket with Turn Knob
Switch — 8" Glass Reflector
Oxidized Bronze or China Bronze Finishes
13" Silk Shade Design S 300 Shown

Aladdin Reflector—No. 3506
3-Way Lighting (See Note)
Oxidized Bronze, Ivory and Gold or Silver
and Gold Finishes
10" Glass Reflector
18" Fluted Whip-o-lite Shade No. 1700 Shown

Aladdin Reflector—No. 3606
6-Way Lighting (See Note)
Oxidized Bronze, Ivory and Gold or Silver
and Gold Finishes
10" Glass Reflector
18" Whip-o-lite Shade No. 1501 Shown

Aladdin Reflector—No. 1009
One-Light Chain-Pull Socket
Oxidized Bronze, Silver and Gold or
Two-Tone Gold Finishes
6" Plastic Reflector
16" Whip-o-lite Cone Shade No. 1504 Shown

Aladdin Reflector—No. 3519
3-Way Lighting (See Note)
Oxidized Bronze, Antiqued Ivory or
Gold Finishes
10" Glass Reflector
18" Whip-o-lite Shade No. 999 Shown

Aladdin Reflector—No. 3619
6-Way Lighting (See Note)
Oxidized Bronze, Antiqued Ivory or
Gold Finishes
10" Glass Reflector
18" Whip-o-lite Shade No. 2003 Shown

Aladdin Reflector—No. 3620
6-Way Lighting (See Note)
Antiqued Ivory Lacquer Finish Only
8" Glass Reflector
18" Whip-o-lite Shade No. 1503 Shown

Aladdin Reflector—No. 3521
3-Way Lighting (See Note)
Antiqued Ivory Lacquer Finish Only
8" Glass Reflector
18" Whip-o-lite Shade No. 1001 Shown

Aladdin Reflector—No. 3621
6-Way Lighting (See Note)
Antiqued Ivory Lacquer Finish Only
8" Glass Reflector
19" Silk-Rayon Shade No. R 377 Shown

Lamps ★ PATENTED FEATURES

(Continued)

Aladdin Reflector—No. 3622
6-Way Lighting (See Note)
Oxidized Bronze or Antique Ivory or Gold
10" Glass Reflector
19" Whip-o-lite Shade No. 1508 Shown

Aladdin Reflector—No. 3523
3-Way Lighting (See Note)
Oxidized Bronze, Antique Ivory or
Gold Finishes
10" Glass Reflector
19" Cone Whip-o-lite Shade No. 1002 Shown

★

NOTE:

Aladdin's 3-way Lamps are equipped with 1-Mogul
Socket wired for 3-way control of 50-100-150 or
100-200-300 Watt bulbs. Aladdin 6-Way Lamps are
equipped with 1-Mogul Socket wired for 3-Way control of 50-100-150 or 100-200-300 Watt bulbs, and
also fitted with ornamental 3-armed head with 3
candles and sockets for standard bulbs and wired
for 2-way separate control. Bulbs are not included
with lamps.

Aladdin Reflector—No. 3623

6-Way Lighting (See Note)
Oxidized Bronze, Antique Ivory or Gold
10" Glass Reflector
19" Silk-Rayon Shade No. R 377 Shown

**Aladdin Reflector Bridge
No. 6023**

One Light Canopied Socket with Turn Knob
Switch — 8" Glass Reflector
Oxidized Bronze, Antique Ivory or Gold
12" Whip-o-lite Shade No. 999 Shown

Aladdin Regular Bridge—No. 2023

One Light Swivel Canopied Socket
with Turn Knob Switch
Oxidized Bronze, Antique Ivory or Gold
Special Plastic Reflector and Diffuser
12" Whip-o-lite Shade No. 1501 Shown

Aladdin Reflector—No. 3624

6-Way Lighting (See Note)
Oxidized Bronze, Antique Ivory or Gold
10" Glass Reflector
18" Whip-o-lite Shade No. 2000 Shown

Aladdin Reflector—No. 3625

6-Way Lighting (See Note)
Oxidized Bronze, Silver and Gold or
Two-Tone Gold
10" Glass Reflector
20" Silk-Rayon Shade No. R 381 Shown

Aladdin Reflector—No. 3626

6-Way Lighting (See Note)
Oxidized Bronze, China Bronze, or
Two-Tone Silver
10" Glass Reflector
19" Silk-Rayon Shade No. R 380 Shown

IN selling Aladdin Electric Floor Lamps dealers will for the first time have the decided advantage of offering a product that has outstanding features never before found in floor lamp construction, and also at the same time enjoy the benefits of the irresistible eye-appeal to which this new construction contributes so much.

Most dealers are familiar with the ordinary type of construction which consists of a base and a multiplicity of parts varying from a few to fifty or more, strung vertically upon a pipe. They may consist of light, flimsy tubing, shells, pressings, and short cast breaks, in most cases stock parts picked up at random and assembled in various ways to form various indifferent designs. Aladdin Floor Lamps are constructed upon an entirely different basis. Each lamp is specifically designed for its purpose and

NOTE: Aladdin's 3-way Lamps are equipped with 1-Mogul Socket wired for 3-way control of 50-100-150 or 100-200-300 Watt bulbs. Aladdin 6-Way Lamps are equipped with 1-Mogul Socket wired for 3-Way

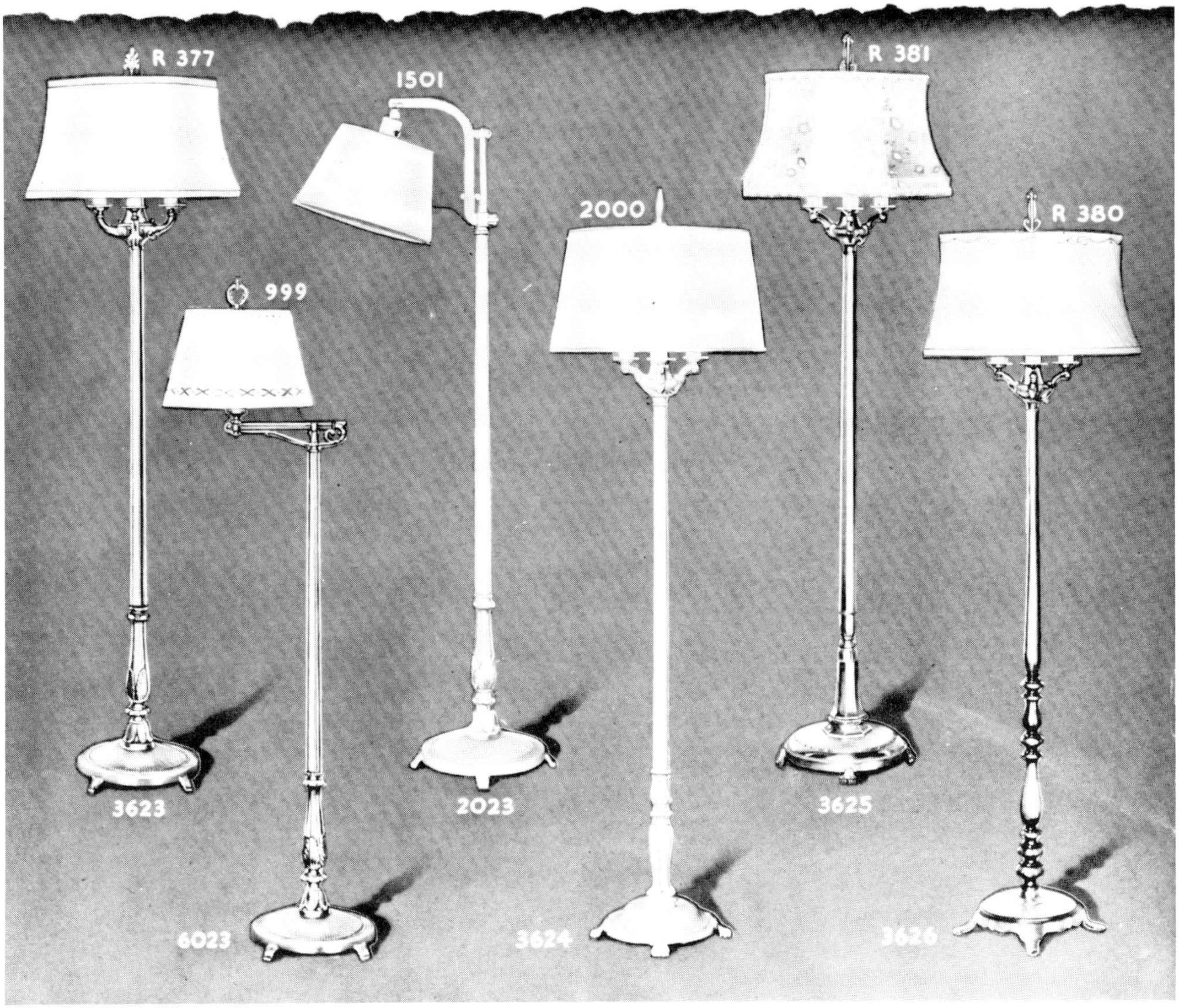

Floor Lamps ★ ★ ★

for the effect the corps of expert Aladdin designers wish to attain. Aladdin's new type of patented construction consisting of a long, especially designed, one-piece, metal spindle cast integral with the break, reduces the number of parts to a minimum, and adds desirable weight and permanent solidity.

Most purchasers of floor lamps will see the value in and appreciate this new construction, and Aladdin dealers should not fail to capitalize upon it in their sales presentation of Aladdin lamps to their profit.

All Aladdin Floor Lamps are handsomely finished in heavy plate or top-quality lacquer or the two in combination with especial attention to long-life and durability. These beautiful enduring finishes are applied by the most skilled craftsmen by the latest modern methods, and make for long continued consumer service and satisfaction.

control of 50-100-150 or 100-200-300 Watt bulbs, and also fitted with ornamental 3-armed head with 3 candles and sockets for standard bulbs and wired for 3-way separate control. Bulbs are not included with lamps.

Aladdin Reflector—No. 3627
6 Way Lighting (See Note)
Oxidized Bronze or Silver and Gold
Green Onyx Trimmed
10" Glass Reflector
19" Silk-Rayon Shade No. R 378 Shown

Aladdin Reflector—No. 3628
6 Way Lighting (See Note)
Oxidized Bronze Only
Green Onyx Trimmed
10" Glass Reflector
19" Pure Dye Silk Shade No. S 300

Aladdin Reflector—No. 3533
3 Way Lighting (See Note)
Oxidized Bronze or Two-Tone Gold
Pedrara Onyx Trimmed
10" Glass Reflector
18" Whip-o-lite Shade No. 2001 Shown

Aladdin Novelty Reflector No. 7016
One Light Canopied Socket and Turn Knob Switch
Swinging Arm 8" Glass Reflector
Oxidized Bronze, Ivory and Gold or Silver and Gold
18" Silk-Rayon Shade No. R 379 Shown

Aladdin Novelty Reflector No. 7017
One Light Canopied Socket and Turn Knob Switch
Swinging Arm 8" Glass Reflector
Oxidized Bronze or Silver and Gold
18" Silk-Rayon Shade No. R 379 Shown

Aladdin Novelty Reflector No. 7029
One Light Canopied Socket and Turn Knob Switch 8" Glass Reflector
15" Diameter Table
Oxidized Bronze and Walnut Finish or All Silver and Red Maple
18" Silk-Rayon Shade No. R 379 Shown

11

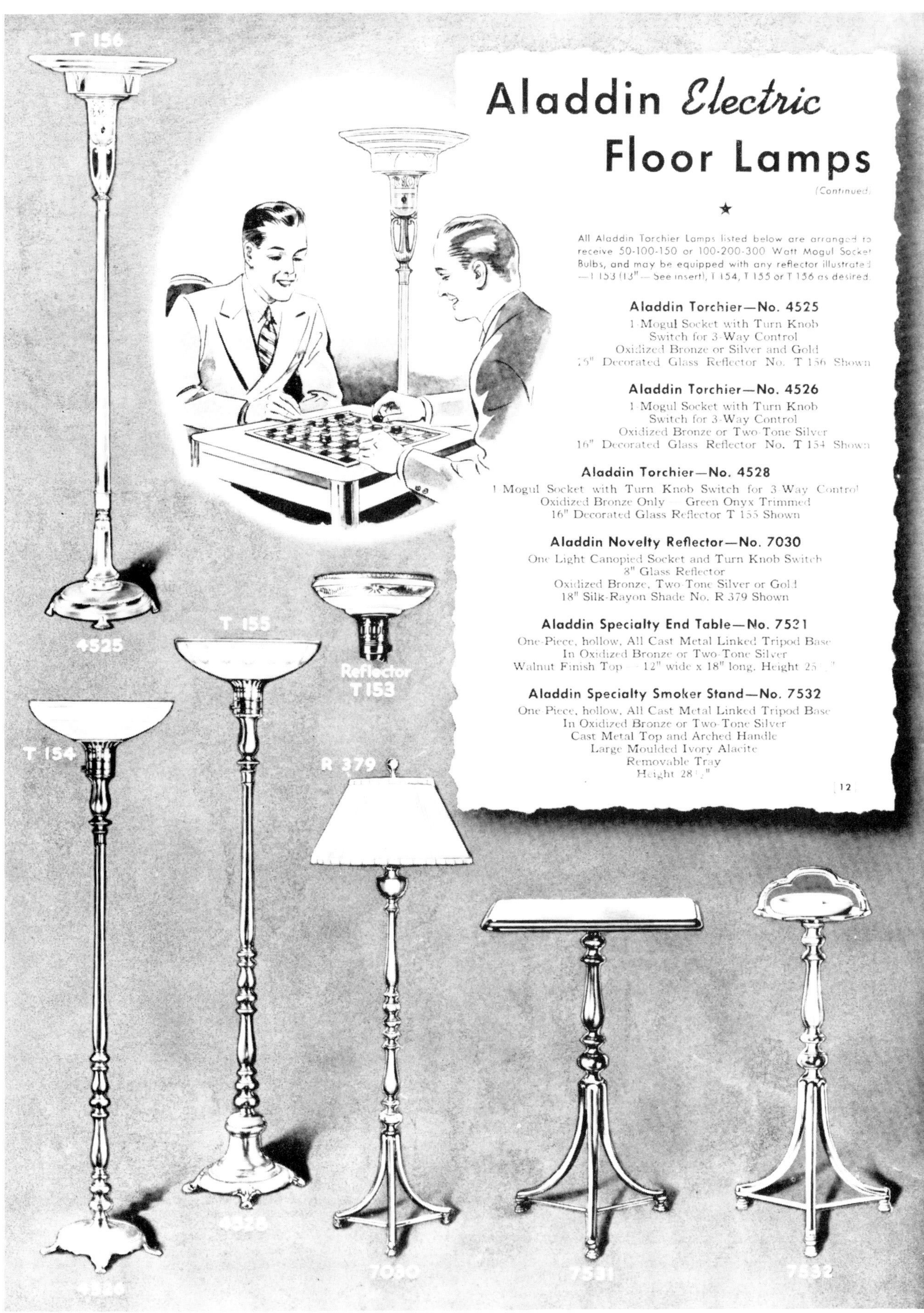

Aladdin *Electric* Floor Lamps

(Continued)

★

All Aladdin Torchier Lamps listed below are arranged to receive 50-100-150 or 100-200-300 Watt Mogul Socket Bulbs, and may be equipped with any reflector illustrated —T 153 (13" — See insert), T 154, T 155 or T 156 as desired.

Aladdin Torchier—No. 4525
1 Mogul Socket with Turn Knob
Switch for 3-Way Control
Oxidized Bronze or Silver and Gold
16" Decorated Glass Reflector No. T 156 Shown

Aladdin Torchier—No. 4526
1 Mogul Socket with Turn Knob
Switch for 3-Way Control
Oxidized Bronze or Two-Tone Silver
16" Decorated Glass Reflector No. T 154 Shown

Aladdin Torchier—No. 4528
1 Mogul Socket with Turn Knob Switch for 3 Way Control
Oxidized Bronze Only — Green Onyx Trimmed
16" Decorated Glass Reflector T 155 Shown

Aladdin Novelty Reflector—No. 7030
One Light Canopied Socket and Turn Knob Switch
8" Glass Reflector
Oxidized Bronze, Two-Tone Silver or Gold
18" Silk-Rayon Shade No. R 379 Shown

Aladdin Specialty End Table—No. 7521
One-Piece, hollow, All Cast Metal Linked Tripod Base
In Oxidized Bronze or Two-Tone Silver
Walnut Finish Top — 12" wide x 18" long. Height 25"

Aladdin Specialty Smoker Stand—No. 7532
One-Piece, hollow, All Cast Metal Linked Tripod Base
In Oxidized Bronze or Two-Tone Silver
Cast Metal Top and Arched Handle
Large Moulded Ivory Alacite
Removable Tray
Height 28½"

12

Aladdin
Electric Lamps and Shades
"ALADDIN" Reg. U. S. Pat. Off. and Canada

Foreword:

Discriminating lamp buyers, we believe, will find much to interest them within these pages. Dominating eye-appeal combined with excellence of material and superior craftsmanship marks this new 1940-41 fall and winter line of Aladdin Electric Lamps and Whip-o-lite and Fabric Shades.

The greatly augmented Aladdin floor lamp line merits especial attention, not alone because of its increased numbers and variety, but for the distinctly new and better method of construction employed in their making, such as is found in some numbers in which the entire unit except head is cast in a single unit.

There are few lines, if any, in which the public will as readily recognize real values. This fact undoubtedly accounts in a large measure for the eager consumer acceptance of it, and the corresponding rapid turnover and profit Aladdin dealers everywhere enjoy.

The Mantle Lamp Company of America, Inc.

223 West Jackson Boulevard
Chicago, Illinois

721 East Yamhill Street
Portland, Oregon

Permanent Display Rooms: At Chicago, Ill., 1224 Merchandise Mart; at High Point, N. C., 6th Floor Southern Furniture Exposition Bldg.; at San Francisco, Calif., Western Furniture Exchange Bldg.

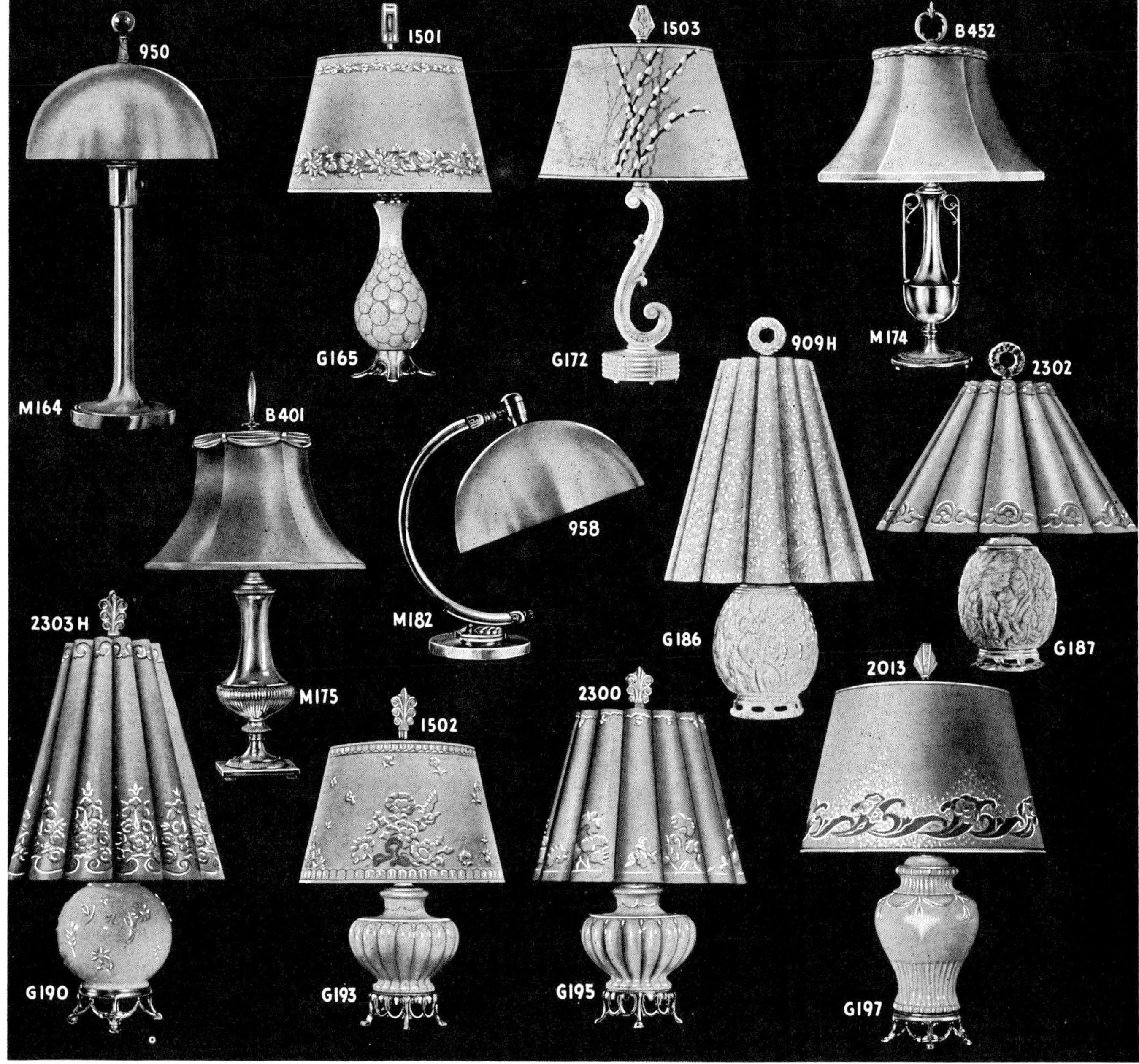

Aladdin *Electric* Table Lamps

M164

An all-metal, practical modern design, pedestal lamp for homes, offices and hotels. In Satin Silver or Oxidized Bronze plate. 10½″ metal matching shade, No. 950. 1-Lt. socket, turn knob switch, harp and finial. 21″ high.

G165

Of relief-decorated urn design in Antiqued Ivory Alacite only. Attractive metal base finished in Antique Satin Gold. 1-Lt. socket with push-thru switch, harp and finial. 21″ high. Shown with 12″ Whip-o-lite Shade No. 1501.

G172

A very attractive and unusual design. Hollow, cord-concealing, serpentine pedestal integral with base. 1-Lt. push-thru socket, harp and finial. In Ivory *Alacite only. 21¾″ high. Shown with 12″ Whip-o-lite Shade No. 1503.

M174

In all cast metal of armed urn design, graceful, well proportioned. Finished in Antiqued 2-tone Silver plate only. 1-Lt. push-thru socket, harp and finial. 21″ high. Shown with 13″ Silk Shade B-452.

M175

Of classic Georgian urn design in all cast metal. Dignified and rich in appearance. 24¾″ high. In plated polished Silver finish only 1-Lt. push-thru socket, harp and finial. Shown with 14″ Celanese and Rayon Shade No. B-401.

*Alacite—Reg. U.S. Pat. Off.

FOREMOST IN

Artistic Design
Craftsmanship • Utility

•

M182

A one-piece cast metal creation for desk or table. Artistic—practical. Single swivel socket and turn-knob base switch. 15¼″ high. In Oxidized Bronze or Silver, black lacquer trimmed. Shown with matching finish 10½″ metal dome Shade No. 958.

G186

In leaf embossed, acorn shaped design in one-piece Ivory Alacite, or in decorated Amber, White or Blue. 22½″ high. Switch controlled light in base. 1-Lt. chain-pull socket, tall harp and finial. Shown with 12″ Fluted Whip-o-lite Shade No. 909-H.

G187

Of same base design as G-186 described above. In one-piece Ivory Alacite or decorated Amber, White or Blue. Switch controlled light in base. 17″ high. 1-Lt. chain-pull socket, short harp and finial. Shown with 15″ cone Fluted Whip-o-lite Shade No. 2302.

G190

Of the ever popular ball motif in floral spray relief. Ornate cast metal base. In Opalique glass decorated White, Peach or Blue. Gold finish base. Switch controlled light in base. 1-Lt. chain-pull socket, harp and finial. 23½″ high. 12″ Fluted Whip-o-lite Shade No. 2303-H.

G193

Of deep fluted, low-urn, design created in Ivory Alacite **only,** on cast metal base in Antique Gold plate finish. Switch controlled light in bowl. 1-Lt. push-thru socket, short harp and finial. 19¼″ high. Shown with 12″ Whip-o-lite Shade No. 1502. Any 15″ cone Whip-o-lite Shade, Empire or Fluted adaptable.

G195

Of deep fluted, low-urn design, created in Ivory Alacite **only** with cast metal base finished Antique Gold plate. Switch controlled light in base. 1-Lt. push-thru socket, medium harp and finial. 20¼″ high. Shown with 13″ semi-tall Fluted Whip-o-lite Shade No. 2300.

G197

In a striking reverse-flute vase design, mounted on all-metal base. In Ivory Alacite vase, or Alacite vase decorated in Tan with bases in Satin-Gold plate. Switch controlled light in base. 1-Lt. push-thru socket, harp and finial. 23½″ high. 14″ Whip-o-lite Shade No. 2013 shown.

Aladdin
Electric Table Lamps
of Charm and Distinction

(Continued from page 3)

G202
A beautiful one-piece armed vase and square base lamp in Ivory Alacite or Etched decorated crystal in Rose or Tan. 1-Lt. push-thru socket, harp and finial. Shade shown, 12″ Whip-o-lite No. 2003. 21¾″ high.

G203
A unique and different one-piece, hollow, cord-concealing spindle and oval base lamp in Ivory Alacite only. 1-Lt. push-thru socket, harp and finial. Shade shown, 12″ Whip-o-lite No. 1502. 21¼″ high.

G206
In floral and leaf design in relief on metal mounted urn. In Ivory Alacite, or Alacite decorated in Tan, Blue, or Maroon with Gold plate base. Candelabra socket and switch for light in base. 1-Lt. push-thru socket, harp and finial. Shade, 13″ Whip-o-lite, No. 1005; 22″ high.

G207
In bottle-neck fluted urn and graceful side-arm design, mounted on cast metal base. In Ivory Alacite, or Alacite decorated Tan; base —Gold plate. 1-Lt. push-thru socket, harp and finial. Shade, 12″ Whip-o-lite No. 2007. 21½″ high.

G208
Same as No. G-207 described above except in addition is provided with candelabra socket and concealed base switch for light in base. 21½″ high. Suggested alternate shade—13″ R-383.

G209
A most attractive, square-base, pedestal and fluted bowl design lamp in a single piece. In Ivory Alacite, or clear or Blue decorated Crystal. 21½″ high. 1-Lt. push-thru socket, harp and finial. Shade 15″ cone Fluted Whip-o-lite No. 2302.

G210
In an ever-popular vase design with round base in one-piece. In Ivory Alacite, or decorated Alacite in Tan. 21½″ high. 1-Lt. push-thru socket, harp and finial. Shade, 13″ Whip-o-lite, No. 2010.

G211
A candelabra as illustrated, of ornate twin-arm, oval base, and tall candle design. In Ivory Alacite only—Ivory metal parts. Two candelabra lamp sockets for candles and turn-knob switch in base. 18½″ high. Not arranged for shades.

G212
A segmented or deep fluted vase mounted on a cast metal base. In Ivory Alacite, or Alacite decorated Tan. 23½″ high. 1-Lt. push-thru socket, tall harp and finial. Also concealed switch and standard socket for light in base. Shade, 12″ fluted Whip-o-lite No. 2300-H

G213
Of a striking and unusual mounted and leaf-armed bottle design. Ornate cast metal base. In Ivory Alacite, or decorated Alacite in Blue or Tan. Antique Gold plated base. Concealed switch for light-in-base. 1-Lt. push-thru socket, harp and finial. Shade, 13″ Whip-o-lite, No. 2015.

(Continued on page 5)

G199
Of relief and reverse-flute bottle design with all cast metal base. In Ivory Alacite, or decorated Alacite in Blue, Tan, Maroon or Green. Base Antique Gold. Switch controlled light in base. 1-Lt. push-thru socket, harp and finial. 23¾″ high. Shade shown 14″ Whip-o-lite No. 1000.

G201
A small one-piece, hollow arm, desk or radio lamp. Of Ivory Alacite, or decorated Alacite in Blue, Green or Rose. 1-Lt. swivel socket and turn-knob switch. Concealed cord. 9″ cone bridge fitter Whip-o-lite shade No. 1004 shown.

Aladdin *Electric* Table Lamps – *Continued*

•

G214

Of a most popular and fascinating oriental design with decagon base in one-piece. Hollow blown pedestal to conceal cord. In Ivory Alacite, or Alacite base and Tan decorated pedestal, or Alacite base and Blue decorated pedestal. 22″ high. 1-Lt. push-thru socket, harp and finial. Shade, 12″ Whip-o-lite, No. 2020.

G215

In an intriguing Early American design with a cast metal base and spindle with a mounted fluted bowl. Choice of Gold plated base and Alacite bowl, or Silver plated base and Blue Crystal Bowl. 23¾″ high. 1-Lt. push-thru socket, harp and finial. Bell shade, 14″ Celanese and Rayon, No. B-403.

G216

Of same details as No. G-215 above, except equipped with 1 3-way, turn-knob standard size socket canopy, and 6″ light-diffusing glass bowl. Designed for use of G. E., type D, 30-70-100 watt bulb. Shade, 14″ Celanese Flounce and Rayon, No. B-402.

G217

A graceful, charming vase design with leaf spray in high relief. In Ivory Alacite, or decorated Tan or Green. Low cast metal Gold plated base, concealed base switch and socket for light in bowl. 1-Lt. push-thru socket, harp and finial. 20¾″ high. Shade, 13″ Whip-o-lite, No. 2018.

M218

An interesting swirl design vase of an antique jar pattern in one-piece cast metal. In Silver and Gold, or in Oxidized Bronze plate. 20¾″ high. 1-Lt. push-thru socket, harp and finial. Shade, 14″ Celanese and Rayon Bell, No. B-401.

G219

A delightful combination of a blown segmented design vase and cast metal base. Vase of Alacite only with Gold plated base. 1-Lt. push-thru socket, harp and finial. 22½″ high. Shade, 14″ Whip-o-lite, No. 2026.

G220

A charming long necked and winged vase creation, mounted on a cast metal base. In Ivory Alacite or decorated Alacite in Tan or Blue. Has 1-Lt. push-thru socket, harp and finial. 22½″ high. Shade, 14″ Whip-o-lite, No. 2017.

G221

The effect of this exceptionally fine pressed and blown vase is most alluring. Ornate cast metal base. In Ivory Alacite or decorated Alacite in Tan—both bases Oxidized Bronze highlighted. 1-Lt. push-thru socket, harp and finial. 22″ high. Shade, 13″ Whip-o-lite, No. 2023.

G222

A simple, yet most artistic armed vase with integral base. In Ivory Alacite, or decorated Alacite in Tan, Blue, or Green. 22½″ high. 1-Lt. push-thru socket, harp and finial. Shade shown, 14″ Whip-o-lite, No. 2022.

G223

For quiet charm and dignity, few lamps surpass this spiral and capped column and square base creation. In Ivory Alacite, or decorated Alacite in Tan or Blue. 22″ high. 1-Lt. push-thru socket, harp and finial. Shade, 12″ Whip-o-lite, No. 2016.

(Continued on Page 6)

The Trade Mark

Aladdin

is a recognized

EMBLEM

of

QUALITY

Aladdin *Electric* Bed Lamps

Designs Nos. 2010SS, 2021SS, 2027SS and 2302SS, as illustrated are of Whip-o-lite, and have 1-Lt. chain-pull sockets and generous length approved cords with rubber covered hooks. Made to match Shades of similar numbers. No. 2010SS in Variegated only; others in White, Blue, Green, Rose or Tan.

Aladdin *Electric* Boudoir Lamps
Delightful • Dainty • Different

G16

An unusually fine example of molded figure work. It is created in alluring Ivory Alacite only. 1-Lt. push-thru switch socket with concealed wiring thru base. All metal parts Gold Plated and lacquered. Base is hand antiqued. 17″ high. Shade, 10″ Whip-o-lite, No. 1510.

G20

A most unusual and beautiful artistic designing and glass makers art. In one-piece Ivory Alacite or decorated Green, Rose or Blue. Hollow pedestal carries cord thru base to 1-Lt. push-thru socket. 17″ high. Shown here with 7″ Aladdin Whip-o-lite Shade of Design No. 1503.

G21

Both Ivory Alacite and decorated Rose, Green or Blue were chosen to carry out the delicacy and daintiness of this artistic design. 15″ high. 1-Lt. push-thru socket with concealed cord. Shade, 7″ Whip-o-lite, No. 964.

G22

In a delightful hollow scroll pedestal design, integral with base. In Ivory Alacite or decorated Alacite in Blue, Rose or Tan. Concealed cord. 1-Lt. push-thru socket. 15⅛″ high. Shade, 8″ Whip-o-lite, No. 2004.

G23

Of delicate, round, and capitaled pedestal and square base design. Very handsome. In Ivory Alacite or decorated Alacite in Blue, Rose or Tan; Gold plated Metal parts. 1-Lt. push-thru socket. Concealed cord. 14½″ high. Shade, 8″ Whip-o-lite, No. 2007.

G24

Is an unusually fine one-piece molded figure design of cherub on a fluted base. In Ivory Alacite, Gold plated metal parts. 1-Lt. push-thru socket. Concealed cord. 15″ high. Shown with 8″ Whip-o-lite Shade No. 2012.

G25

A delicate, slender, ornate, hollow, one-piece pedestal on a curved-flute base. Concealed Cord. 16½″ high. In Ivory Alacite or decorated Alacite in Blue, Rose or Green. 1-Lt. push-thru socket. Shade, 7″ Whip-o-lite, No. 2021.

G27

An artistic spiral vase, eared, with round, footed integral base. Concealed cord. Ivory Alacite or decorated in Alacite in Blue, Rose or Tan. 1-Lt. push-thru socket. Shade 7″ Whip-o-lite, No. 2027. 14″ high.

Aladdin *Electric* Hang-Up Lamps

G351

Of an attractive wall medallion pattern. In Ivory Alacite only. Single candle and 1-Lt. socket with turn-knob switch in hollow arm. Dignified and simple and will harmonize nicely in most surroundings. Shade, 8″ Whip-o-lite, No. 1510.

G352

Of ornate vertical panel and scroll Arm design. Single socket candle with wall turn-knob switch. In Ivory Alacite, or decorated Alacite in pastel Tan, Blue or Rose. Very decorative. 1-Lt. candle and socket. Turn-knob switch in placque. Shade, 7″ Whip-o-lite, No. 2010.

Aladdin Reflector No. 3334

As shown at top right center. Equipped with one standard Socket and Turn-Knob One-way Switch for standard bulb. 8″ Glass Reflector. Available in choice of 2 finishes: Oxidized Bronze or Antiqued Ivory Lacquer and Gold. Shown with 18″ Whip-o-lite Parvelour Shade No. 2009.

Aladdin Reflector No. 3605

Illustrated at upper left. Equipped for 6-way lighting—1 Mogul reflector socket and 3-way switch and 3 candle arm standard sockets and switch. 10″ Glass Reflector. Two finishes: Oxidized Bronze or Flemish Bronze. Shown with 18″ Fluted Whip-o-lite Parvelour Shade No. 2301.

Aladdin Reflector No. 3625

Shown at upper left center. Equipped for 6-way lighting—1 Mogul reflector Socket and 3-way switch and 3 Candle Arm Standard Sockets and Switch. 10″ Glass Reflector. Three finishes: Oxidized Bronze, or Colonial Brass or Two-Tone Silver and Gold. Shown with 18″ Fluted Whip-o-lite Parvelour Shade No. 2303.

Aladdin Reflector No. 3636

In middle row at left. Equipped for 6-way lighting—1 Mogul reflector socket and 3-way switch with 3 Candle Arm Standard Sockets and switch. 10″ Glass Reflector. Two finishes: Ivory and Gold Antiqued, and Two-Tone Silver and Gold. Shown with 18″ Whip-o-lite Parvelour Shade No. 2008.

Aladdin Reflector No. 3637

Illustrated, middle row center. Equipped with 1-Light Mogul Socket with 3-way canopy switch, and 3 Standard Socket Candle Arms with switch. 10″ Glass Reflector. Three finishes: Oxidized Bronze or Ivory and Gold Antiqued, or Silver and Gold. Shown with 18″ Whip-o-lite Parvelour Shade No. 2011.

Aladdin Reflector No. 3638

Shown in center row at right. Equipped with 1-Light Mogul Socket and 3-way canopy switch, with 3 Standard Socket Candle Arms with switch. 10″ Glass Reflector. Two finishes: Ivory and Gold Antiqued, or Gold Antiqued. Shown with 18″ Whip-o-lite Parvelour Shade No. 1006.

Aladdin Reflector No. 3935

As illustrated at upper right. Equipped with 1-Light Mogul Socket with 3-way canopy switch, and 3 Standard Socket Candle Arms with switch. Also has base switch controlled Night Light in base. 10″ Glass Reflector. Three finishes: Oxidized Bronze, Ivory and Gold Antiqued, or Gold Antiqued. Shown with 19″ Celanese and Rayon Shade No. R-382.

Aladdin Reflector No. 3938

As illustrated directly at right. Equipped with 1-Light Mogul Socket with 3-way Canopy Switch and 3 Standard Socket Candle Arms and switch. Also has canopy switch for Night Light in head. 10″ Glass Reflector. Two finishes: Ivory and Gold Antiqued or Gold Antiqued. Shown with 18″ Whip-o-lite Parvelour Shade No. 2009.

Aladdin *Electric* Floor Lamps Continued

Aladdin Reflector No. 3639

Shown in top row left. Equipped with 1-Light Mogul Socket and 3-way canopy switch, and 3 Standard Socket Candle Arms with switch. 8″ Glass Reflector. Two finishes: Oxidized Bronze or Gold Antiqued. Shown with 18″ Whip-o-Lite Shade No. 2001.

Aladdin Reflector No. 3640

Illustrated in center top row. Equipped with 1-Light Mogul Socket and 3-way canopy switch, and 3 Standard Socket Candle Arms with switch. 10″ Glass Reflector. Two finishes: Colonial Brass or Flemish Bronze. Shown with 18″ Whip-o-lite Shade No. 2006.

Aladdin Reflector No. 3641

Illustrated in top row center. Equipped with 1-Light Mogul Socket and 3-way canopy switch, and 3 Standard Socket Candle Arms with switch. 10″ Glass Reflector. Two finishes: Flemish Bronze or Two-Tone Silver and Gold. Shown with 18″ Whip-o-lite Parvelour Shade No. 2005.

Aladdin Reflector No. 3642

Shown in top row at right. Equipped with 1-Light Mogul Socket and 3-way canopy switch, and 3 Standard Socket Candle Arms with switch. 10″ Glass Reflector. Two finishes: Oxidized Bronze or Two-Tone Silver and Gold. Shade shown, 19″ Silk and Rayon, No. S312.

Aladdin Reflector No. 3943
with Beam Night Light

Illustrated at lower left. Equipped with 1-Light Mogul Socket and 3-way canopy switch, and 3 Standard Socket Candle Arms with switch. Also has Beam Night Light in head, with switch. 10″ Glass reflector. Three finishes: Oxidized Bronze, or Ivory and Gold Antiqued, or Two-Tone Silver and Gold. Shade shown, 18″ Whip-o-lite Parvelour, No. 2009.

Aladdin Reflector No. 3644

Shown at left middle row. Equipped with 1-Light Mogul reflector Socket and 3-way canopy switch, and 3 Standard Socket Candle Arms with switch. 10″ Glass Reflector. Three finishes: Oxidized Bronze, Ivory and Gold Antiqued, or Gold Antiqued. Shade, 18″ Whip-o-lite Parvelour, No. 2006.

Aladdin Reflector No. 3645

Illustrated at center. Equipped with 1-Light Mogul Socket and 3-way canopy switch, and 3 Standard Socket Candle Arms and Switch. 10″ Glass Reflector. Two finishes: Oxidized Bronze. or Gold Antiqued. Shown with 18″ Whip-o-Lite Shade No. 2014.

Aladdin Relector No. 3945
with Beam Night Light

Illustrated at right center. Equipped with 1-Light Mogul Socket and 3-way canopy switch, and 3 Standard Socket Candle Arms. 10″ Glass Reflector. Two finishes: Oxidized Bronze or Gold Antiqued. Shown with 18″ Whip-o-lite Parvelour Shade No. 2025.

Aladdin *Electric* Floor Lamp — *Continued*

★

Sensationally New Aladdin Floor Lamp Construction

First to develop its now famous one-piece cast spindles Aladdin has now gone forward by introducing Floor Lamps in which the base as well as the spindle is cast in a single unit. This revolutionary construction permanently eliminates the possibility of weak, tilting, wabbly spindles, which is an inherent weakness where many parts such as base, breaks, seating rings and tubes are strung on pipe and held in position under compression only, as in the ordinary method. The solidity and permanency of this new construction will appeal to all lamp purchasers and is employed in Aladdin Floor Lamps, Nos. 3646, 3646S, 3946, 2050, 3650, 3650S, 3950, 3354, 3555, 2055.

Aladdin Reflector No. 3646

Illustrated in top row left. Of the sensational new two-piece Aladdin Construction. (See Right.) Equipped with 1-Light Mogul Socket and 3-way canopy switch, and 3 standard socket candle arms and switch. 10″ glass Reflector. Three finishes: Oxidized Bronze, or Ivory and Gold Antiqued, or Gold Antiqued. Shade shown, 18″ Whip-o-lite Parvelour No. 2020.

Aladdin Reflector No. 3946
with Beam Night Light

Shown in top row left center. Same in all equipment and finishes as No. 3646 above, except head construction, which provides for Beam Night Light and control switch for same and easily removable bulb and globe. Shade shown, 18″ Whip-o-Lite Parvelour, No. 2014.

Aladdin Reflector No. 3647

Illustrated in top row right center. Equipped with 1-Light Mogul Socket and 3-way canopy switch, and 3 Standard Socket Candle Arms with switch. 10″ Glass Reflector. Two finishes: Oxidized Bronze, or Ivory and Gold Antiqued. Shade shown, 18″ Whip-o-lite Parvelour No. 2025.

Aladdin Reflector No. 3649

Shown in top row right. Equipped with 1-Light Mogul Socket and 3-way canopy switch, and 3 Standard Socket Candle Arms with switch. 10″ Glass Reflector. Two finishes: Oxidized Bronze, or Ivory and Gold Antiqued. Shade shown, 18″ Whip-o-lite Parvelour and Fluted, No. 2303.

Aladdin Reflector No. 3949
with Beam Night Light

Illustrated center row right. Same in all equipment and finishes as No. 3649 described at bottom of left column, except head construction provides for Beam Night Light and control switch with easily removable bulb and globe. Shade shown, 19″ Celanese and Rayon, No. R-382.

Aladdin Diffusing Bridge No. 2050

Shown directly at right. Of the sensational new 2-piece Aladdin construction (see right). Equipped with 1-Light, canopied, swivel, turn-knob, Standard Socket, and 8″ detachable plastic diffuser which covers the bulb. Two finishes: Oxidized Bronze, or Ivory and Gold Antiqued. Shade, 12″ Whip-o-lite Parvelour, No. 2016.

Aladdin Reflector No. 3650

Illustrated in middle row left. Of the sensational new two-piece Aladdin construction (see right). Equipped with 1-Light Mogul Socket and 3-way canopy switch, and 3 Standard Socket Candle Arms with switch. 10″ Glass Reflector. Three finishes: Oxidized Bronze, or Ivory and Gold Antiqued, or Gold Antiqued. Shade, 18″ Whip-o-lite Parvelour, No. 2024.

Aladdin Reflector No. 3950
with Beam Night Light

Shown at center. Same in all equipment, and finishes as No. 3650, above, except head construction provides for Beam Night Light and control switch, with easily renewable bulb and globe. Shade shown, 18″ Whip-o-lite Parvelour, No. 2016.

Aladdin Reflector No. 3651

Shown directly at right. Has a beautiful round and tri-footed one-piece cast spindle, mounted on dome base with open work feet. Equipped with 1-Light Mogul socket and 3-way canopy switch, and 3 standard socket candle arms with switch in one-piece metal casting. 10″ Glass Reflector. Two finishes: Oxidized Bronze or Two-Tone Silver and Gold. Shade shown. 18″ Whip-o-lite Parvelour, No. 2020.

Aladdin Reflector No. 3951

with Beam Night Light

Illustrated at center top row. Same in design and construction as the No. 3651 described above, but in addition it is fitted with a Beam Night Light with separate switch in candle arm cluster head. 10″ Glass Reflector. Two finishes: Oxidized Bronze, or Two-Tone Silver and Gold. Shown with Celanese and Rayon 19″ Shade, No. S-312.

Aladdin Reflector No. 3952

with Beam Night Light

Shown at right in top row. Constructed with a heavy, one-piece fluted cast metal spindle with integral ornate tri-finned and footed break, mounted on deep large diameter base with open work feet. Equipped with 1-Light Mogul socket with 3-way switch, and 3 Standard socket candle arms and switch. Also has Beam Night Light and switch in candle arm cluster. Easily renewable bulb and globe. 10″ Glass Reflector. Two finishes: Oxidized Bronze, or Two-Tone Silver and Gold. Shown with 19″ Celanese and Rayon Shade, No. B-451.

Aladdin Reflector No. 3653

Illustrated in lower row at center. Consists of an intrigueing ox-tail design, one-piece cast metal footed spindle. Large diameter heavy deep base with open work feet. Fitted with 1-Light Mogul socket with 3-way canopy switch, and 3 standard socket candle arms with switch. 10″ Glass Reflector. Two finishes: Oxidized Bronze, or Two-Tone Silver and Gold. Shown with 19″ Celanese and Rayon Shade No. B-450.

Aladdin Diffuser No. 3354

Lounge Type—56″ High

Shown directly at lower right. In the latest vogue of medium low floor lamp, with an octagon base and fluted spindle of Aladdin's sensationally new one-piece construction (see page 9), topped with a fluted glass bowl. Equipped with 1-Light medium bulb-size socket with 3-way canopy switch for G. E. Type D, 30-70-100 Watt Bulb, and 6″ glass diffuser globe. Two combinations: Colonial Brass with Alacite bowl, or Silver and Gold with Blue Crystal Bowl. Shade, 18″ cone Whip-o-lite, No. 2027.

Aladdin Reflector No. 3555

Lounge Type—57″ High

Illustrated in lower row at right. In the modern trend of lower floor lamps, and Aladdin's sensational development of one-piece base and spindle (see page 9) construction. Equipped with 1-Light Mogul socket and 3-way switch, and 8″ Glass Reflector. Two finishes: Colonial Brass, or Two-Tone Silver and Gold, shown with 18″ cone Celanese and Rayon Shade No. R-379.

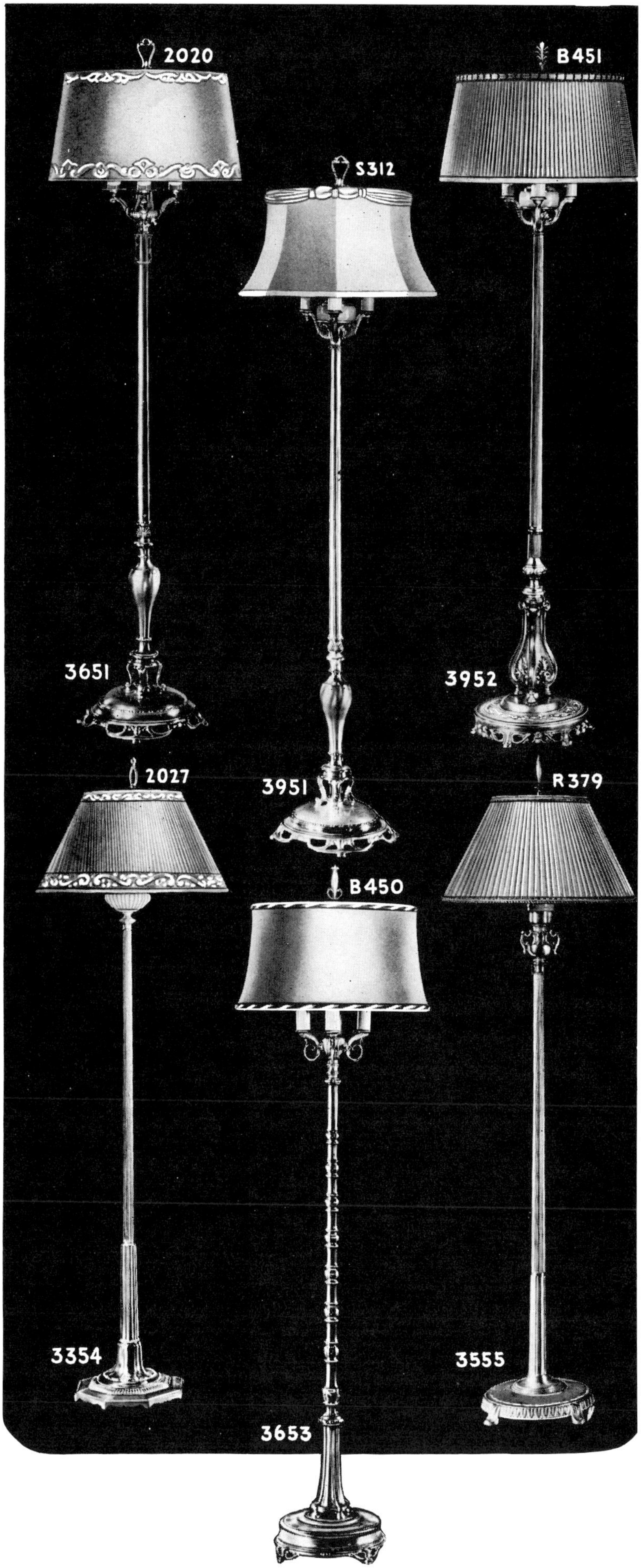

Aladdin *Electric* Floor Lamps— Continued

Aladdin Bridge No. 2055

Shown at left above. Of Aladdin's new, revolutionary, unit base and spindle construction (see page 9). Fitted with 1-Light canopied standard socket with swivel and turn-knob switch. Especially designed for small homes and hotel rooms. Two finishes: Oxidized Bronze or Silver, Black Lacquer trimmed. Shown with 10½" all-metal Shade No. 958.

Aladdin Reflector No. 3556
Lounge Type—58¼" High

Illustrated in top row above. Another handsomely designed new, low, modern reflector lamp in one-piece base and spindle construction. Has 1-Light Mogul socket with 3-way turn-knob canopy switch. 8" glass reflector. Two finishes: Oxidized Bronze or Ivory and Gold. Shown with 16" Whip-o-lite Parvelour Shade No. 1501.

Aladdin Swing-Arm Bridge No. 7017
(Reflector Type)

Shown in bottom row above. Has one-piece hexagon cast spindle and large diameter circular base for stability. Big arc double-acting bridge arm. Fitted with 1-Light Mogul socket with 3-way switch in canopy. 8" glass Reflector. Two finishes: Oxidized Bronze, or silver and Gold. Shade shown, 18" cone Celanese and Rayon, No. R-379.

Aladdin Reflector No. 7030
Lounge Type—51½" High

Shown in top row center. Of Aladdin two-piece tied tripod base, and spindle construction in Colonial design. Fitted with 1-Light 3-way medium base, turn knob canopied socket. 8" Glass Reflector. Three finishes: Oxidized Bronze, Two-Tone Silver, or Two-Tone Gold. Shade, 18" cone, Celanese and Rayon, No. R-379.

Aladdin Multi-Adjustable Bridge or Reflector No. 7057

Shown lower row extreme right. An entirely new and different type adjustable bridge or reflector lamp. Large diameter base and spindle on cast metal of two-piece only. Light adjustable horizontally or vertically with shade held vertical in any position. Fitted with 1-Light Mogul socket and 3-way canopy switch. Two finishes: Oxidized Bronze or Silver and Gold Antiqued. Shown with 18" cone Whip-o-lite Shade, No. 2006.

Aladdin Swing-Arm Bridge No. 7042
(Reflector Type)

Illustrated in bottom row above. Of a beautiful Ox-tail design with large diameter base, of two-piece construction. Fitted with medium arc, double-acting swing arm, and 1 3-way canopied standard socket with turn-knob switch. 6" plastic reflector. Two finishes: Oxidized Bronze, or Two-Tone Silver and Gold. Shade, 12" Whip-o-lite Parvelour, No. 2007.

Aladdin Swing-Arm Bridge No. 7044
(Reflector Type)

Shown in top row at right. Of hexagon spindle and base design, two-piece construction. Fitted with medium arc, double-acting swing arm, and 1 3-way canopied standard socket with turn knob switch. 6" plastic reflector. Three finishes: Oxidized Bronze, or Ivory and Gold, or Gold Antique. Shade, 12" Whip-o-lite Parvelour, No. 2005.

Better Light · *Better* Sight
LAMPS OF QUALITY

Aladdin I.E.S. Reflector No. 3625S

Shown at upper left. In strict conformity to I.E.S. specifications and equipped for 6-way lighting—1 Mogul reflector Socket and 3-way switch and 3 Candle Arm Standard Sockets and Switch. 10″ Glass Reflector. Three finishes: Oxidized Bronze, or Colonial Brass or Two-Tone Silver and Gold. Shown with I.E.S. 19″ Celanese and Rayon shade No. B-451.

Aladdin I.E.S. Reflector No. 3641S

Illustrated in upper left. In strict conformity to I.E.S. specifications and equipped with 1-Light Mogul Socket and 3-way canopy switch, and 3 Standard Socket Candle Arms with switch. 10″ Glass Reflector. Two finishes: Flemish Bronze or Two-Tone Silver and Gold. Shown with I.E.S. Celanese and Rayon Shade No. R-377.

Aladdin I.E.S. Reflector No. 3646S

Illustrated in top row right. In strict conformity to I.E.S. specifications and of the sensational new two-piece Aladdin Construction. (See Page 9.) Equipped with 1-Light Mogul Socket and 3-way canopy switch, and 3 standard socket candle arms and switch. 10″ glass Reflector. Three finishes: Oxidized Bronze, or Ivory and Gold Antiqued, or Gold Antiqued. Shade shown, 19″ I.E.S. Celanese and Rayon, No. R-375.

Aladdin I.E.S. Reflector No. 3649S

Shown in lower row left. In strict conformity to I.E.S. specifications and equipped with 1-Light Mogul Socket and 3-way canopy switch, and 3 Standard Socket Candle Arms with switch. 10″ Glass Reflector. Two finishes: Oxidized Bronze, or Ivory and Gold Antiqued. Shade shown, 19″ I.E.S. Celanese and Rayon, No. R-382.

Aladdin I.E.S. Reflector No. 3650S

Illustrated in lower row center. In strict conformity to I.E.S. specifications and of the sensational new two-piece Aladdin construction (See Page 9). Equipped with 1-Light Mogul Socket and 3-way canopy switch, and 3 Standard Socket Candle Arms with switch. 10″ Glass Reflector. Three finishes: Oxidized Bronze, or Ivory and Gold Antiqued, or Gold Antiqued. Shade 19″ I.E.S. Celanese and Rayon No. S-312.

Aladdin I.E.S. Reflector No. 3653S

Illustrated in lower row at right. In strict conformity to I.E.S. specifications and consists of one-piece cast metal footed spindle with large diameter heavy deep base with open work feet. Fitted with 1-Light Mogul socket with 3-way canopy switch, and 3 standard socket candle arms with switch. 10″ Glass Reflector. Two finishes: Oxidized Bronze, or Two-Tone Silver and Gold. Shown with 19″ Celanese and Rayon Shade No. B-450.

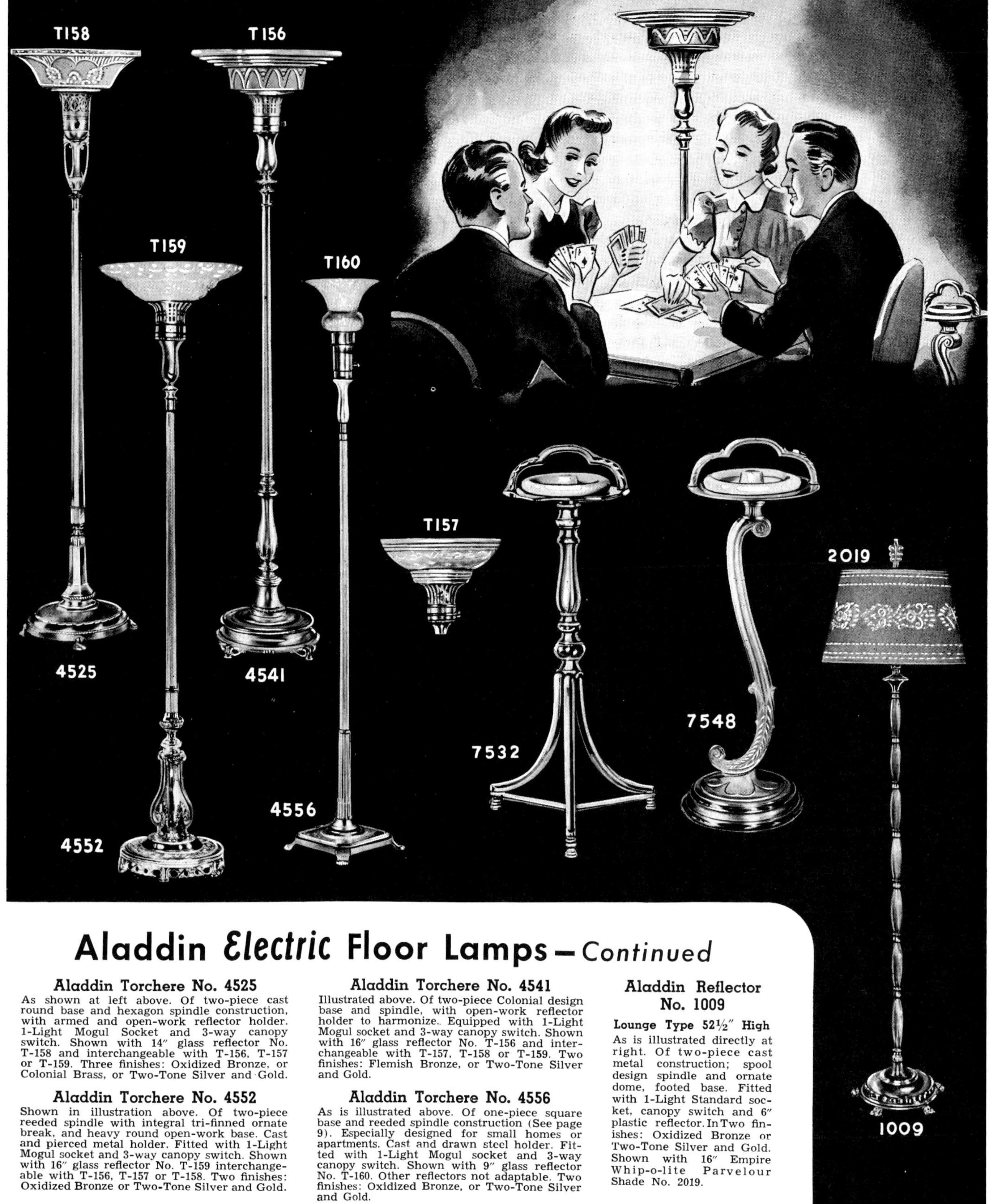

Aladdin *Electric* Floor Lamps — Continued

Aladdin Torchere No. 4525

As shown at left above. Of two-piece cast round base and hexagon spindle construction, with armed and open-work reflector holder. 1-Light Mogul Socket and 3-way canopy switch. Shown with 14″ glass reflector No. T-158 and interchangeable with T-156, T-157 or T-159. Three finishes: Oxidized Bronze, or Colonial Brass, or Two-Tone Silver and Gold.

Aladdin Torchere No. 4552

Shown in illustration above. Of two-piece reeded spindle with integral tri-finned ornate break, and heavy round open-work base. Cast and pierced metal holder. Fitted with 1-Light Mogul socket and 3-way canopy switch. Shown with 16″ glass reflector No. T-159 interchangeable with T-156, T-157 or T-158. Two finishes: Oxidized Bronze or Two-Tone Silver and Gold.

Aladdin Torchere No. 4541

Illustrated above. Of two-piece Colonial design base and spindle, with open-work reflector holder to harmonize.. Equipped with 1-Light Mogul socket and 3-way canopy switch. Shown with 16″ glass reflector No. T-156 and interchangeable with T-157, T-158 or T-159. Two finishes: Flemish Bronze, or Two-Tone Silver and Gold.

Aladdin Torchere No. 4556

As is illustrated above. Of one-piece square base and reeded spindle construction (See page 9). Especially designed for small homes or apartments. Cast and drawn steel holder. Fitted with 1-Light Mogul socket and 3-way canopy switch. Shown with 9″ glass reflector No. T-160. Other reflectors not adaptable. Two finishes: Oxidized Bronze, or Two-Tone Silver and Gold.

Aladdin Reflector No. 1009

Lounge Type 52½″ High

As is illustrated directly at right. Of two-piece cast metal construction; spool design spindle and ornate dome, footed base. Fitted with 1-Light Standard socket, canopy switch and 6″ plastic reflector. In Two finishes: Oxidized Bronze or Two-Tone Silver and Gold. Shown with 16″ Empire Whip-o-lite Parvelour Shade No. 2019.

Aladdin *All-Metal* Smoking Stands

Aladdin Smoking Stand No. 7532

As shown above. In Colonial design, with graceful linked, tripod base. Heavy pressed-steel plate and cast metal handle. Deep flanged 8″ Ivory Alacite removable tray. Two finishes: Oxidized Bronze, or Two-Tone Silver. 25½″ high.

Aladdin Smoking Stand No. 7548

As illustrated above. In serpentine design of one-piece cast metal spindle and base. Heavy pressed steel plate and ornate handle. Deep flanged 8″ Ivory Alacite removable tray. Two finishes: Colonial Brass or Two-Tone Silver and Gold. 25½″ high.

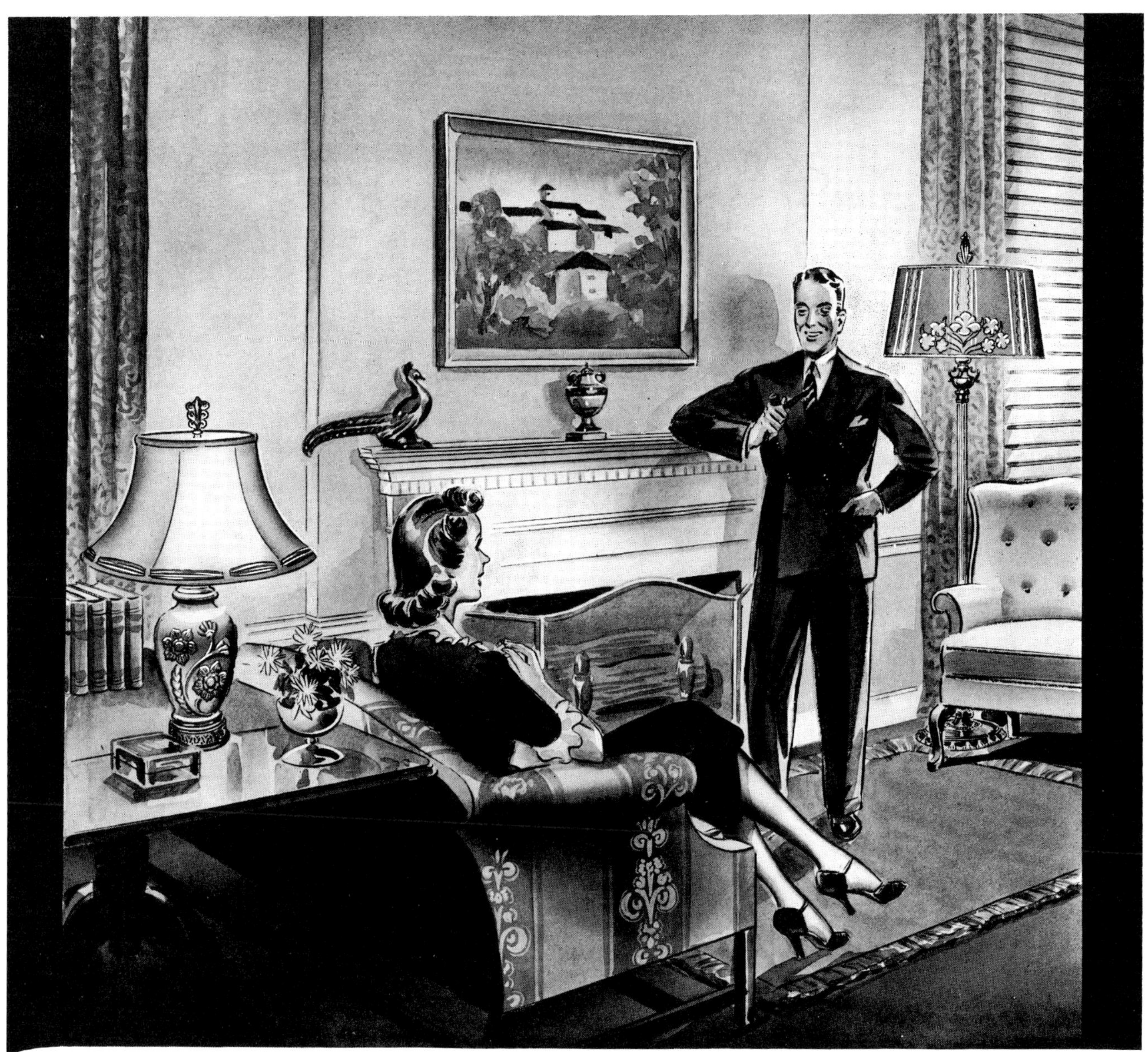

Foreword

It is with pleasure and pride that we present Aladdin dealers with this graphic representation of our new 1941-42 Fall and Winter line of Aladdin Quality Electric Lamps and Aladdin Quality Whip-o-lite and Fabric Shades. Painstaking effort, exceptional artistry, careful craftsmanship and select materials has made each and every one of these units an exceptional value. Strong irresistible inbuilt eye-appeal assure dealers of a quick and ready consumer acceptance and a surprisingly rapid turnover.

To all our present and prospective Aladdin dealers we dedicate this booklet, solicit their orders for this exceptional-value merchandise in the firm conviction that it will greatly assist in building a most pleasant and profitable lamp business for each and every one of them.

The Mantle Lamp Company of America, Inc.

223 West Jackson Boulevard, Chicago, Ill.   721 East Yamhill Street, Portland, Oregon

Form No. 1181 — July 1, 1941 — Printed in U. S. A.

Aladdin *Electric* Table Lamps

Unusual Creations of Artistic Design, Possessing Outstanding Merit for Value,
Eye-Appeal and Craftsmanship Extraordinary

No. M-164

An all-metal, practical modern design, pedestal lamp for homes, offices and hotels. In Satin Silver or Oxidized Bronze Plate. 10½" metal matching shade No. 950. 1-Light socket, Turn-Knob Switch, Swivel Harp and Ball Finial. 21" High.

No. G-201

A small one-piece, hollow arm, desk or radio lamp. Of Ivory Alacite, or decorated Alacite in Blue, Green or Rose. 1-Light Swivel Socket and Turn-Knob switch. Concealed cord. 9" cone bridge fitter Whip-o-lite shade No. 2044.

No. G-213—Illuminated Base

Of a striking and unusual mounted and leaf-armed bottle design. Ornate cast metal base. In Ivory Alacite, or decorated Alacite in Tan or Blue. Blue has silver plated Base—others Gold. Concealed switch for illuminating base. 1-Light Push-Thru Socket, Harp and Finial. Shade, 13" Whip-o-lite No. 2015 shown.

No. G-186—Illuminated Base

In leaf embossed, acorn shape design in one-piece Ivory Alacite, or Alacite decorated Tan or Blue. 22½" high. 1-Light open socket—1-Light Socket in base to illuminate it—3-Way Switch in open socket controls both. Tall Swivel Harp—Alacite Finial. 12" Fluted Whip-o-lite Shade No. 909H shown.

No. G-202 or G-245

A beautiful one-piece armed vase and square base lamp in Ivory Alacite or Alacite decorated In Rose or Blue. 1-Light Push-Thru socket, Swivel Harp and Alacite Finial. Shade shown 12" Whip-o-lite No. 2049. 21¾" high. Also as Indirect type with 6" Plastic Reflector as No. G-245.

No. G-214 or G-248

Of a most popular oriental design with decagon base in one-piece. Hollow blown pedestal conceals cord. In Ivory Alacite, or Alacite decorated Tan or Blue. 22" High. 1-Light Push-Thru socket, Swivel Harp and Alacite Finial. Shade, 12" Whip-o-lite No. 2054. Also as Indirect Type with 6" Plastic Reflector as No. G-248.

No. G-195—Illuminated Base

Of deep fluted, low-urn design, created in Ivory Alacite only with cast metal base in Antique Gold Plate. 1-Light open socket—1-Light socket in base to illuminate it—3-Way Switch in open socket controls both. Swivel Harp and Alacite Finial. 20¼" high. Shown with 13" Fluted Whip-o-lite Shade No. 2300.

No. G-212—Illuminated Base

A segmented or deep fluted vase mounted on a cast metal Gold-Plated base. In Ivory Alacite, or Alacite decorated Tan. 23½" high. 1-Light open socket—1-Light socket in base to illuminate it—3-Way switch in open socket controls both. Swivel Harp and Alacite Finial. Shade, 12" Fluted Whip-o-lite No. 2300-H shown.

No. G-217—Illuminated Base

A graceful, charming vase design with leaf spray in high relief. In Ivory Alacite, or decorated Tan or Green. Gold Plated Base. 1-Light Open Socket—1-Light Socket in Base to illuminate it—3-Way Switch in open socket controls both. 1-Light Push-Thru Socket, Swivel Harp and Alacite Finial. 20¾" High. Shade, 13" Whip-o-lite No. 2018 shown.

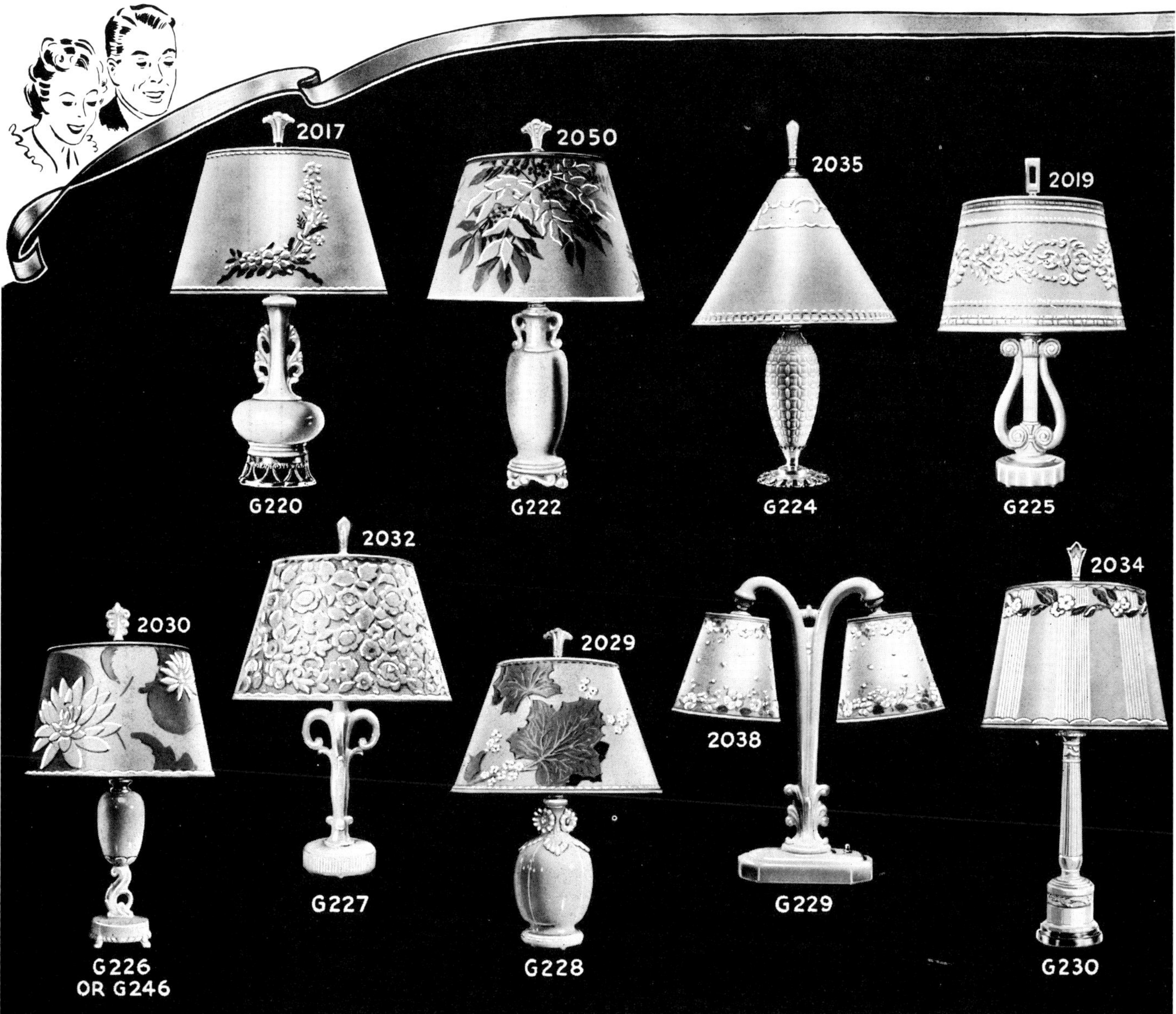

Aladdin *Electric* Table Lamps

• CONTINUED •

No. G-220—Illuminated Base

A charming long necked and winged vase creation, mounted on a gold-plated metal base. In Ivory Alacite or decorated Alacite in Tan or Blue. 1-Light open socket. 1-Light Socket in base 3-way switch controls both. Swivel harp—Alacite finial. 22½″ high. Shade, 14″ Whip-o-lite, No. 2017.

No. G-225

In the Regency vogue, and created with Lyre and reverse-fluted base in one unit. Hidden cord thru base to 1-Light push-thru socket, with swivel harp and Alacite finial. In all Ivory Alacite, or decorated Rose, Gold or Blue. Shade shown 12″ Parvelour decorated Whip-o-lite No. 2019. 20¼″ high.

No. G-228

A fascinating medium-sized lamp of fluted urn and pressed flower design, and base in one unit. Cord thru base to 1-Light push-thru socket, swivel harp and Alacite finial. In All Ivory Alacite, Alacite decorated Rose or Blue. 13″ Shade —No. 2029 in Parvelour Whip-o-lite shown. 21½″ high.

No. G-222

A simple, yet most artistic armed vase with integral base. In Ivory Alacite, or decorated Alacite in Tan, Blue, or Green. 22½″ high. 1-Light push-thru socket, Swivel harp and Alacite finial. Shade shown, 14″ Whip-o-lite. No. 2050.

No. G-226 or G-246

A most delightful design created in one-piece Alacite, with secreted cord. Graceful scroll unites footed base and ovate urn. Has 1-Light push-thru socket, swivel harp and Alacite finial. In all Ivory Alacite, or decorated in Green or Brown. Shown with 12″ Parvelour decorated Whip-o-lite shade No. 2030. 20¾″ high. Also as Indirect type with 6″ Plastic Reflector as No. G-246.

No. G-229

An ingenious "between bed" lamp of one-piece construction. Oblong base, with 2 graceful and ornate arms which conduct hidden cord to 2 standard sockets from switch in base. In All Ivory Alacite, or decorated Alacite in Rose or Blue. 16½″ high. Shown with 2 special 6″ reverse clamp fitter Parvelour Whip-o-lite shades No. 2038.

No. G-224

A beautiful combination Alacite and metal lamp with all-over embossed urn, and graceful openwork, cast, gold-plated metal base. Has 1-Light push-thru socket, swivel harp and Alacite finial. In Ivory Alacite, or in Gold or Rose. 13″ Special Cone Parvelour decorated Whip-o-lite Shade No. 2035 shown; especially made and fitted to this lamp, 21½″ high.

No. G-227

An artistic modern interpretation of the Prince's feathers of Regency era. Hollow blown spindle conceals cord. Created in All Ivory Alacite or Ivory Alacite decorated in Brown. Has 1-Light push-thru socket, swivel harp and Alacite finial. 14″ Parvelour Whip-o-lite shade No. 2032 shown. 22¾″ high.

No. G-230

A strictly authentic Regency creation of dignity and refinement, in Alacite with cast Gold-plated metal sub-base. Has 1-Light push-thru socket, swivel harp and Alacite finial. 24″ high. In All Ivory Alacite or Alacite decorated in Brown or Blue. Shown with 12″ Special Parvelour decorated Shade No. 2034.

Aladdin *Electric* Table Lamps

• CONTINUED •

No. G-231

An exquisite example of harmony in line and design. Beautiful embossed urn surmounts open-work metal base—gold plated. Has 1-Light push-thru socket, swivel harp and Alacite finial. In All Ivory Alacite, or Alacite decorated in Rose or Gold. 21″ high. Shade 12″ Parvelour decorated Whip-o-lite No. 2034, Special for G-230, G-231 and G-234.

No. G-234

A tall, modern, pedestal design with Golden Crowned Pheasant figure mounted on an oval base. In one-piece Ivory Alacite, or in Alacite decorated in Rose or Blue. Hollow blown spindle secretes cord. Has 1-Light standard push-thru socket. Harp and Alacite finial. Height 22½″ overall. Shown with Special 12″ Parvelour Whip-o-lite Shade No. 2045. Alternate Shade No. 2034.

No. G-237

A combination glass and metal lamp, reminiscent of the Colonial period. In two different combinations:—Alacite Ivory Bowl or Ruby Crystal Bowl, both with Gold Pedestal. 25½″ high. Has 1-Light push-thru socket, bowl-matching Finial, and Harp. Illustrated here with 15″ Bell Shaped Fabric Shade No. B-456.

No. G-232—Illuminated Base

Of delicately winged, long-neck fluted urn design, mounted on Gold-Plated metal base. Has 1-Light standard push-thru open socket and standard socket for 7W bulb, and 3-way switch on open socket to control both. In All Ivory Alacite, or decorated Alacite in Rose or Blue. 14″ Shade—Parvelour fluted Whip-o-lite No. 2304 shown. 22½″ high.

No. G-235

In a very graceful serpentine and floral design with round footed base, of one-piece construction. Available in Ivory Alacite, or decorated Alacite in Rose or Brown. Hollow spindle hides cord. Has 1-Light standard push-thru socket. Harp and Alacite finial. Height 21¼″ overall. Shade shown, 12″ No. 1007, in decorated Whip-o-lite.

No. M-238

A medium sized, all-metal, all purpose inverted type desk or table lamp for hotels or homes; of one piece base and hollow arm construction. In Black and Silver or Oxidized Bronze and Gold. Has 1-Light socket in canopy with turn-knob switch. Fitted with 6″ ornamented Plastic Shade No. P-94 in Tan or White. Height of lamp overall—15½″.

No. G-233—Illuminated Base

A delightful ball-type lamp with deep embossed stone flower design bowl, gold plated open-work metal base. Has 1-Light open socket, and socket in base for illuminating it—3-way switch in shade socket controls both. In All Ivory Alacite or Alacite decorated Tan. Shown with 17″ Fabric Shade No. B-453, 23¼″ high. 17″ Fabric Shade No. B-457 or 17″ Whip-o-lite Shade No. 2300 as alternates. (B-457 shade shown on G-236.)

No. G-236—Illuminated Base

This outstanding artistic lamp is in urn design with surface highly embossed in stone flowers and leaf spray. Mounted on Gold-Plated base. Has 1-Light open socket, and 1 in base for illumination—a 3-way switch in open socket controls both. In Ivory Alacite, or decorated Alacite in Rose, Blue or Tan. 23″ high. Harp and Alacite finial. Shade shown Fabric No. B-457. (Alternates 17″—Fabric B-453 shown on G-233 or Whip-o-lite Shade No. 2300.)

No. G-239 or G-250

An interesting, intriguing one-piece lamp of much artistic merit and charm. Embossed floral design in bowl. In Ivory Alacite, or decorated Alacite in Tan or Rose. Has 1-Light push-thru socket, swivel harp and Alacite finial. Its height overall is 22″. Shown in illustration above with 14″ Parvelour Whip-o-lite Shade No. 2046. Also available in Indirect type with 6″ Plastic reflector as No. G-250.

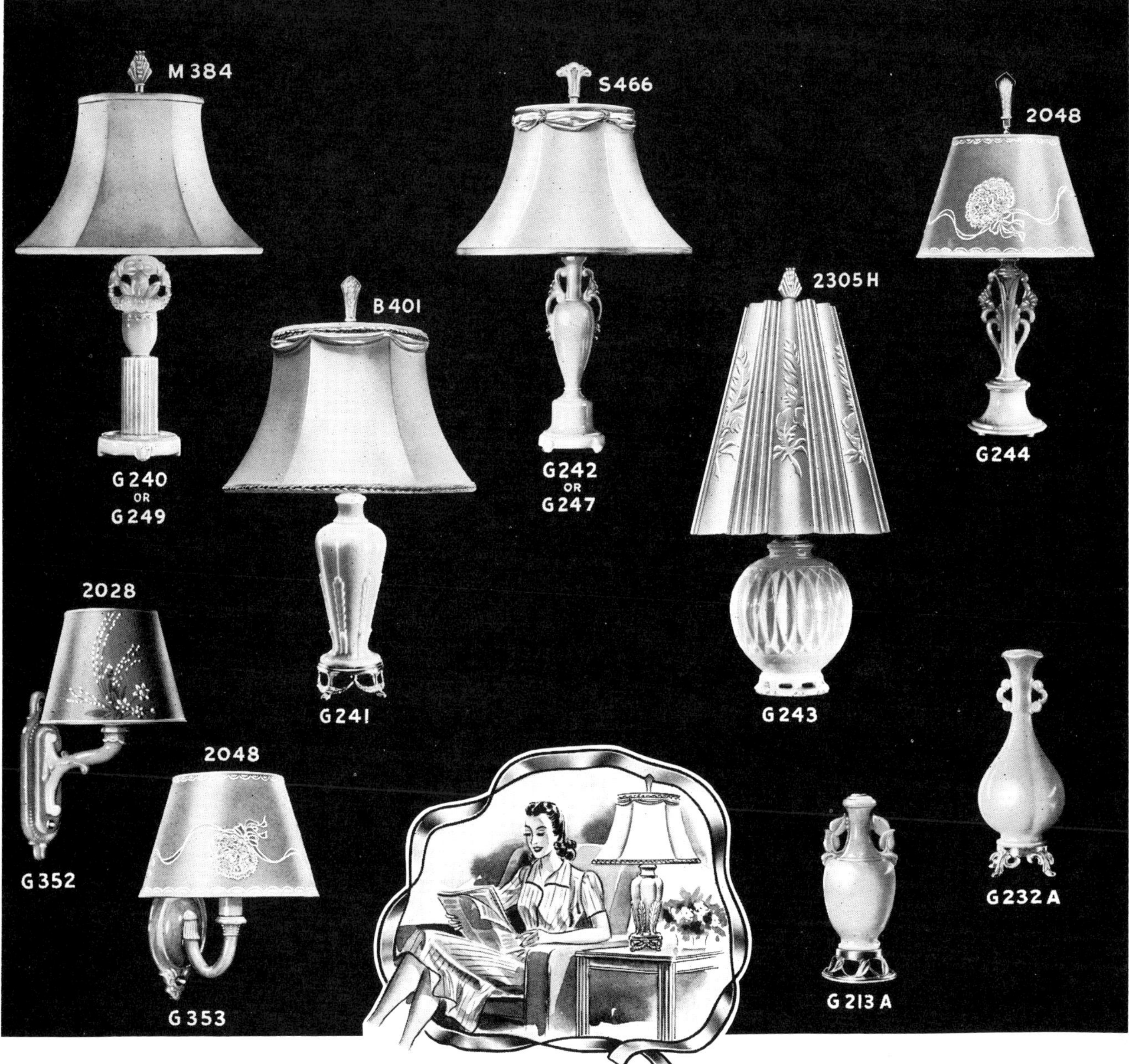

Aladdin *Electric* Table Lamps
• CONTINUED •

No. G-240 or G-249
Base of this lamp simulates a column surmounted with a bowl of flowers. Very subtle and alluring. Of one-piece construction. Available in Ivory Alacite, or decorated Alacite in Green or Brown. Has 1-Light socket, push-thru switch, Alacite Finial and Swivel Harp. Height 22½″. Shown with 14″ Bell Fabric Shade No. M-384. Also in Indirect Type with 6″ Plastic Reflector, as No. G-249.

No. G-243—Illuminated Base
A new Aladdin creation in the ever popular ball type of lamp with 7″ diameter embossed bowl. Of one-piece pattern, and supplied in Antiqued Ivory Alacite, or decorated Alacite in Rose or Blue. 18½″ high. 1-Light socket in base for illuminating it, and 1 open socket; 3-way switch controls both. Tall Harp and Alacite Finial. Designed for 12″ tall shade. No. 2305H in Fluted Parvelour Whip-o-lite shade shown.

No. G-241—Illuminated Base
A graceful ornamented and fluted urn mounted on a footed metal base. Available in 4 colors; Ivory Alacite, or Alacite decorated in Tan, Rose or Blue. Is equipped with 1-Light open socket in base for illuminating it; 3-way switch controls both lights. Harp and Finial. Height 23″. Shown here with 14″ Bell Fabric Shade No. B-401.

No. G-244
A delicate, dainty, small lamp of unusual charm and beauty. Has wing-like scrolls on opposite sides of slender hollow pedestal on round footed base. In Ivory Alacite, or decorated Alacite in Rose or Blue. 18½″ high. 1-Light socket, swivel harp and Alacite finial 10″ washer fitter. Parvelour Whip-o-lite Shade No. 2048 shown.

No. G-242 or G-247
A charming, slender, cylindrical, one-piece lamp of the vase type with neck ornamented with scroll arms at sides. Made in Ivory Alacite, or decorated Alacite in Rose and Blue. Fitted with 1-Light push-thru socket, Harp and Finial. Height 20¾″ overall. Illustrated with 13″ Bell Stretched Fabric Shade No. S-466. Also in Indirect Type with 6″ Plastic Reflector, as No. G-247.

Aladdin Electric Hang-Up Lamps
No. G-352
Of one-piece ornate vertical panel and scroll arm design. Has single candle and socket with push-knob switch in wall plate. In Ivory Alacite, or decorated Alacite in Rose, Blue or Tan. 7″, 8″ or 10″ Parvelour Whip-o-lite clamp-fitter shades adaptable. Shown here with 8″ Shade No. 2028.

No. G-353
Of a most pleasing and restful design with oval wall plate and semi-circle projecting arm. Has a single candle and socket with push-knob switch in wall plate. In Ivory Alacite, or decorated Alacite in Blue or Rose. 7″, 8″ or 10″ Parvelour Whip-o-lite Clamp-fitter shades are adaptable. Shade shown here is 10″ of Design No. 2048.

Aladdin Decorative Illuminated Urns
No. G-213A
This delicate dainty urn with its graceful leaf design arms and open-work Gold-Plated metal base is exceedingly popular as a radio, buffet or mantle-piece ornament. Has 1-Light socket in base for illuminating it, with push switch in base. In Ivory Alacite, or decorated Alacite in Blue or Tan.

No. G-232A
This attractive, two-piece, illuminated unit with its slender necked, fluted and eared urn, and its Gold-Plated metal base makes an ideal ornament for radio, buffet or mantle. Has 1-Light socket in base for illumination, with push-switch in base. In Ivory Alacite, or decorated Alacite in Rose or Blue.

Delightful Aladdin *Electric* Boudoir Lamps of *Charm*

[With the exception of Boudoir Lamp G-16, All Boudoirs shown have hollow blown spindles]
[to secrete cord, and allows its entrance thru base and spindle;—a most desirable, exclusive]
[and patented Aladdin feature. All have long Approved cord and Single Push-Thru Socket.]

No. G-16
As illustrated, In Ivory Alacite only with Gold Plated metal spindle. 17″ high. Shown with 10″ clamp fitter. Parvelour Whip-o-lite Shade No. 2048.

No. G-25
Shown top row right. Available in Ivory Alacite, or Alacite decorated Rose, Blue or Green. 16½″ high. 7″ Shade Parvelour Whip-o-lite No. 2021.

No. G-30
Pictured in lower row left. Available in Ivory Alacite, or Alacite decorated in Rose or Blue. 15¾″ high. 8″ Parvelour Whip-o-lite Shade No. 2052 shown.

No. G-21
As is shown above in Ivory Alacite or Alacite decorated Rose, Blue or Green. 15″ high. Shade shown—7″ Parvelour Whip-o-Lite No. 964.

No. G-27
Illustrated at left center. Supplied in Ivory Alacite or Alacite decorated Rose, Blue or Tan. 14″ high. 8″ Parvelour Whip-o-lite Shade No. 2033 shown.

No. G-31
Shown in Picture in lower right. In Ivory Alacite, or Alacite decorated Rose or Blue. 13¾″ high. Shade illustrated 7″ Parvelour Whip-o-Lite Shade No. 2049 shown.

No. G-33
Illustrated in lower row left. Supplied in Ivory Alacite, or Alacite decorated in Rose or Blue. 8″ Juvenile Parvelour Whip-o-Lite Shade No. 2055 shown.

No. G-22
Illustrated above, available in Ivory Alacite or Alacite decorated Blue, Rose or Tan. 15⅛″ high. Shade shown— 8″ Fluted Parvelour Whip-o-lite No. 2305.

No. G-28
Shown at right center. Available in Ivory Alacite or Alacite decorated Rose, Blue or Green. 16½″ high. Parvelour Whip-o-lite Shade No. 2036 Shown.

No. G-24
As in above illustration, available only in Ivory Alacite. Delicately Antiqued. 14½″ high. Shown with 7″ Juvenile Whip-o-lite Shade No. 2059 Variegated.

No. G-29
Illustrated lower left. Supplied in Ivory Alacite, or Alacite decorated Rose, Blue or Green. 14½″ high. 7″ Parvelour Whip-o-Lite Shade No. 2037 shown.

Delicate · **Aladdin Bed Lamps** · Colorful
IN PARVELOUR DECORATED WHIP-O-LITE
All Aladdin Bed Lamps are equipped with generous Approved Cords 1-Light Chain-pull socket, and rubber covered hooks.
No. 2036SS—(9″ high x 9″ wide x 6″ deep). In Parvelour Decorated Whip-o-lite in White, Rose, Blue or Green. (Matches Shade No. 2036).
No. 2037SS—(9″ high x 9″ wide x 6″ deep). In Parvelour Decorated Whip-o-lite in Variegated colors. (Matches Shade No. 2036.)
No. 2305SS—(6″ high x 10½″ wide x 7″ deep). In Fluted Parvelour Decorated Whip-o-lite in Rose, White, Blue or Tan. (Matches Shade No. 2305.)

Aladdin
Electric
Floor
Lamps

•

Aladdin Reflector
No. 3649

One-Light Mogul Sockets with 3-Way Switch. and 3-Candle Arm Sockets and 3-Way Switch. 61″ High to Top of 10″ Glass Reflector.
Oxidized Bronze or Ivory and Gold Finish
18″ Fluted Parvelour Whip-o-lite Shade No. 2303 Shown.

Aladdin Reflector and Night
Light No. 3949

One-Light Mogul Socket and 3-Way Canopy Switch, and 3-Candle Arm Sockets and 3-Way Switch to control Candle Sockets and 7-Watt Bulb installed in Night Light Globe. 61″ High to Top of 10″ Glass Reflector.
Oxidized Bronze or Ivory and Gold Finish
19″ Empire Fabric Shade No. R-382 Shown.

Aladdin Regular Bridge
No. 2058

One-Light Standard, Turn-Knob, Swivel Socket; and Socket Cover. 56″ in Height to Top of Bridge Arm.
In Bronze (Plate Lustre) and Ivory and Gold Finish
12″ Whip-o-lite Shade No. 2053 Shown.

Aladdin Reflector
No. 3658

One-Light Mogul Socket with 3-Way Switch, and 3-Candle Arm Sockets and 3-Way Switch.
59″ High to Top of 10″ Glass Reflector.
In Bronze (Plate Lustre) and Ivory and Gold Finish
(Two of like finish to a Carton only)
18″ Parvelour Whip-o-lite Shade No. 2040 Shown.

Aladdin Reflector and Night
Light No. 3958

One-Light Mogul Socket and 3-Way Canopy Switch, and 3-Candle Arm Sockets and 3-Way Switch to control Candle Sockets and 7-Watt Bulb installed in Night Light Globe.
59½″ High to Top of 10″ Glass Reflector.
In Bronze (Plate Lustre) and Ivory and Gold Finish
(Two of Like Finish to Carton Only.)
19″ Bell Fabric Shade No. R-375 Shown.

Aladdin Reflector
No. 3662

One-Light Mogul Socket with 3-Way Switch, and 3-Candle Arm Sockets and 3-Way Switch.
59″ High to Top of 10″ Glass Reflector.
In Bronze (Plate Lustre) and Ivory and Gold Finish
(Two of like finish to a carton only)
18″ Parvelour Whip-o-lite Shade No. 2039 Shown.

Aladdin Reflector and Night
Light No. 3962

One-Light Mogul Socket and 3-Way Canopy Switch, and 3-Candle Arm Sockets and 3-Way Switch to control Candle Sockets and 7-Watt Bulb installed in Night Light Globe.
59½″ High to Top of 10″ Glass Reflector.
In Bronze (Plate Lustre) and Ivory and Gold Finish
(Two of a Like Finish to a Carton Only)
19″ Empire Fabric Shade No. M-388 Shown.

Aladdin Swing Arm
Reflector Bridge No. 7062

Fitted with 1-Light Mogul Socket with 3-Way Turn-Knob Switch in Canopy. 6″ Offset Double Swing Arm. Canopy arranged for and supplied with 8″ Glass Reflector.
57½″ High to Top of 8″ Glass Reflector
In Bronze (Plate Lustre) and Ivory and Gold Finish
14″ Parvelour Whip-o-lite Shade No. 2053 Shown.

Aladdin *Electric*
Floor Lamps · CONTINUED ·

Aladdin Reflector No. 3666

One-Light Mogul Socket with 3-Way Switch, and 3-Candle Arm Sockets and 3-Way Switch. 61⅝″ High to Top of 10″ Glass Reflector.
Oxidixed Bronze, Ivory and Gold or Silver and Gold Finish
18″ Parvelour Whip-o-lite Shade No. 2038 Shown.

Aladdin Fluorescent and Reflector No. 3767

Equipped with new improved type holder for 2-parallel, 15″ Fluorescent Tubes, wiring accessories and Switch; also with 1-Light Mogul Socket and 3-Way Switch. Switches operate separately. 60⅜″ High to Top of 10″ Glass Reflector.
In Oxidized Bronze, Ivory and Gold, or Silver and Gold Finishes.
18″ Parvelour Whip-o-lite Shade No. 2057 Shown.

Aladdin Reflector and Night Light No. 3967

One-Light Mogul Socket and 3-Way Canopy Switch, and 3-Candle Arm Sockets and 3-Way Switch to control Candle Sockets and 7-Watt Bulb installed in Night Light Globe. 60½″ High to Top of 10″ Glass Reflector.
Oxidized Bronze or Silver and Gold Finish
19″ Bell Fabric Shade No. M-385 Shown.

Aladdin Torchere No. 4567

Equipped with 1-Light Mogul Socket with 3-Way Turn-Knob Switch located in Flaring Ornamental, Torchere Reflector Holder. Aladdin Torchere Reflectors Nos. T-158, T-159, T-162 to T-164 Adaptable—See page 18 for illustration. 58½″ High to Top of Torchere Holder.
In Oxidized Bronze, Silver and Gold, or Ivory and Gold Finish
16″ Torchere Reflector No. T-164 Shown.

Aladdin Reflector and Night Light No. 3969

One-Light Mogul Socket and 3-Way Canopy Switch, and 3-Candle Arm Sockets and 3-Way Switch to control Candle Sockets and 7-Watt Bulb installed in Night Light Globe. 60½″ High to Top of 10″ Glass Reflector.
Oxidized Bronze or Ivory and Gold Finish
18″ Parvelour Whip-o-lite Shade No. 2043 Shown.

Aladdin Reflector No. 3668

One-Light Mogul Socket with 3-Way Switch, and 3-Candle Arm Sockets and 3-Way Switch. 60½″ High to Top of 10″ Glass Reflector.
Oxidized Bronze or Silver and Gold Finish
18″ Parvelour Whip-o-lite Shade No. 2054 Shown.

Aladdin Reflector No. 3669

One-Light Mogul Socket with 3-Way Switch and 3-Candle Arm Sockets and 3-Way Switch. 60¾″ High to Top of 10″ Glass Reflector.
Oxidized Bronze or Ivory and Gold Finish
19″ Bell Fabric Shade No. B-458 Shown.

Aladdin Reflector No. 3670

One-Light Mogul Socket with 3-Way Switch, and 3-Candle Arm Sockets and 3-Way Switch. 61¾″ High to Top of 10″ Glass Reflector.
Oxidized Bronze, Silver and Gold or Ivory and Gold Finish
19″ Empire Fabric Shade No. S-468 Shown.

Aladdin *Electric* Floor Lamps
• CONTINUED •

Aladdin Reflector
No. 3671
One-Light Mogul Socket With 3-Way Switch, and 3-Candle Arm Sockets and 3-Way Switch. 61¼″ High to Top of 10″ Glass Reflector.
Oxidized Bronze or Silver and Gold Finish
19″ Empire Fabric Shade No. S-467 Shown.

Aladdin Fluorescent and
Reflector No. 3771
Equipped with new improved type holder for 2-parallel, 15″, Fluorescent Tubes, wiring accessories and switch; also with 1-Light Mogul Socket and 3-Way Switch. Switches operate separately. 61¼″ High to Top of 10″ Glass Reflector.
Oxidized Bronze or Silver and Gold Finish
18″ Parvelour Whip-o-lite Shade No. 2049 Shown.

Aladdin Reflector and
Night Light No. 3971
One-Light Mogul Socket and 3-Way Canopy Switch, and 3-Candle Arm Sockets and 3-Way Switch to control Candle Sockets and 7-Watt Bulb installed in Night Light Globe. 60½″ High to Top of 10″ Glass Reflector.
Oxidized Bronze or Silver and Gold Finish
18″ Parvelour Whip-o-lite Shade No. 2046 Shown.

Aladdin Reflector
No. 3672
One-Light Mogul Socket with 3-Way Switch and 3-Candle Arm Sockets and 3-Way Switch. 61″ High to Top of 10″ Glass Reflector.
In Oxidized Bronze, Gold, or Silver and Gold Finish.
18″ Parvelour Whip-o-lite Shade No. 2056 Shown.

Aladdin Torchere
No. 4572
Equipped with 1-Light Mogul Socket with 3-Way Turn-Knob Switch located in Flaring Ornamental, Torchere Reflector Holder.
Aladdin Torchere Reflectors Nos. T-158, T-159, T-162 to T-164 Adaptable—Shown on Page 18. 58½″ High to Top of Torchere Reflector Holder.
Oxidized Bronze or Silver and Gold Finish
Torchere Reflector No. T-163 Shown.

Aladdin Swing Arm
Reflector Bridge No. 7072
Fitted with 1-Light Mogul Socket with 3-Way Turn-Knob Switch in Canopy. Canopy arranged for and supplied with 8″ Glass Reflector. 7½″ Offset Double Swing Arm. 57½″ High to Top of 8″ Glass Reflector.
In Oxidized Bronze, Gold, or Silver and Gold Finish.
18″ Cone Fabric Shade No. R-379 Shown.

Aladdin Reflector
No. 3673
One-Light Mogul Socket with 3-Way Switch, and 3-Candle Arm Sockets and 3-Way Switch. 61″ High to Top of 10″ Glass Reflector.
Oxidized Bronze or Ivory and Gold Finish
19″ Empire Fabric Shade No. R-382 Shown.

Aladdin Reflector and
Night Light No. 3973
One-Light Mogul Socket and 3-Way Canopy Switch, and 3-Candle Arm Sockets and 3-Way Switch to control Candle Sockets and 7-Watt Bulb installed in Night Light Globe. 61″ High to Top of 10″ Glass Reflector.
Oxidized Bronze or Ivory and Gold Finish
18″ Parvelour Whip-o-lite Shade No. 2025 Shown.

(10)

Aladdin *Electric* Floor Lamps

• CONTINUED •

Aladdin Swing Arm Reflector Bridge No. 7073

Fitted with 1-Light Mogul Socket with 3-Way Turn-Knob Switch in Canopy. Canopy arranged for and supplied with 8" Glass Reflector. 7½" Offset Double Swing Arm.
57" High to Top of 8" Glass Reflector.
Oxidized Bronze or Ivory and Gold Finish
16" Cone Fabric Shade No. M-387 Shown.

Aladdin Multi-Adjustable Reflector-Bridge No. 7073-A

Fitted with a jointed arm that rotates thru a complete circle, and also permits the raising or lowering of the arm from a horizontal to a vertical position at any point on circle. Has 1-Light Mogul Socket and 3-Way Canopy Switch.
Height to top of 8" Glass Reflector in low position—53¾"; in top position 63½".
Oxidized Bronze or Ivory and Gold Finish
18" Cone Parvelour Whip-o-lite Shade No.2040 Shown.

Aladdin Reflector No. 3674

One-Light Mogul Socket with 3-Way Switch, and 3-Candle Arm Sockets and 3-Way Switch.
61" High to Top of 10" Glass Reflector.
In Gold, or Silver and Gold Finish
18" Parvelour Whip-o-lite Shade No. 2033 Shown.

Aladdin Reflector No. 3675

One-Light Mogul Socket with 3-Way Switch, and 3-Candle Arm Sockets and 3-Way Switch.
60¾" High to Top of 10" Glass Reflector
Oxidized Bronze or Silver and Gold Finish
18" Parvelour Whip-o-lite Shade No. 2051 Shown.

Aladdin Reflector and Night Light No. 3976

One-Light Mogul Socket and 3-Way Canopy Switch, and 3-Candle Arm Sockets and 3-Way Switch to control Candle Sockets and 7-Watt Bulb installed in Night Light Globe.
60½" High to Top of 10" Glass Reflector.
In Ivory and Gold or Silver and Gold Finish.
18" Parvelour Whip-o-lite Shade No. 2042 Shown.

Aladdin Reflector No. 3577

One-Light Mogul Socket 3-Way Turn-Knob Switch-in-Canopy—8" Glass Reflector.
Oxidized Bronze or Silver and Gold Finish
18" Empire Fabric Shade No. R-376 Shown.

Aladdin Torchere No. 4577

Equipped with 1-Light Mogul Socket with 3-Way Turn-Knob Switch located in Flaring Ornamental, Torchere Reflector Holder. Aladdin Torchere Reflector No. T-161 only, Adaptable.
54½" High to Top of Torchere Reflector Holder.
Oxidized Bronze or Silver and Gold Finish
10" Ornamental Torchere Reflector No. T-161 Shown.

Aladdin All-Metal Smoking Stand No. 7548

As illustrated above. In Serpentine Design of one-piece cast metal spindle and base. Heavy pressed steel plate and ornate handle. Deep flanged 7" Ivory Alacite removable tray. Three finishes: Oxidized Bronze, Colonial Brass or Two-Tone Silver and Gold
25½" High.

Aladdin *Electric* Lamp Shades

Whip-o-lite • Parvelour

• CONTINUED •

No. 2057

Illustrated above, of Parvelour decorated Whip-o-lite. In 2 sizes— 12″ (9″x12″x8″ high) bridge fitter, and 18″ (15⅝″x18½″x10″) washer fitter in 2 colors—White or Tan.

No. 2058

As shown in above illustration, of Parvelour decorated Whip-o-lite. In one size only, viz: 14″ (9″x14″x8¾″) washer fitter, in 3 colors—White, Blue or Tan.

No. 2059

Shown in illustration above. A Mother Goose Juvenile on decorated Whip-o-lite. In one size only, 8″ (5″x8″x6¼″ high) clamp fitter, in Variegated colors.

Aladdin Ornamental Torchere Reflectors

No. T-158

An ornamental glass reflector in embossed design as pictured above. Has decorative top metal ring. 14″ diam. top. In mottled NuGold only. Fits all standard size holders.

No. T-159

A beautiful and different reflector in a decorative moulded design. 16″ diameter top. In mottled NuGold only. Fits all standard size holders.

No. T-161

A very graceful, tall bell-shaped reflector in moulded design as pictured. 10″ diameter at top. Designed for and fits Torchere Lamp No. 4577 only.

No. T-162

A most striking reflector with design in clear glass with white frosted background. Bowl shape—16″ diameter top. Designed to fit all standard size torchere holders.

No. T-163

A very late and popular reflector, with a grape and leaf design in Ivory Antique, or Highlighted NuGold. 16″ diameter at top. Fits all standard size torchere holders.

No. T-164

Another popular and favorite reflector in Flower Basket design. Design in White on NuGold background. 16″ diameter at top. Fits all standard size torchere holders.

All Torchere Reflectors above, except T-161 are interchangeable on Torchere Reflector Lamps Nos. 4567 and 4572.

Aladdin *Electric* LAMPS

The FIRST LINE OF DEFENSE against dull, lifeless homes

THIS folder presents only the latest additions to the famous line of Aladdin Electric Lamps and Shades. Many other very artistic numbers in both lamps and shades are still included in the line, and are illustrated in our complete catalog No. 1181— July 1, 1941 and to which this folder is supplemental. Price List accompanying this folder covers all merchandise illustrated herein as well as all those items shown in our catalog No. 1181 which are still available. A copy of this catalog will be gladly furnished upon request as long as limited supply lasts.

NEW 1942 ALADDIN *Electric* FLOOR LAMPS
OF RARE BEAUTY AND CHARM

ALADDIN REFLECTOR — No. 3678
Of Design as illustrated at left above. Has One-Light Mogul socket with 3-way switch, and 3-candle arm sockets and 3-way switch. 10" Glass reflector. In Bronze Plate Luster, or Ivory and Gold finish. Shown here with 19" Fabric Shade No. R-377.

ALADDIN REFLECTOR WITH NIGHT LIGHT — No. 3978
Of Design shown at left above. Has One-Light Mogul socket and 3-way switch, and 3-candle arm sockets and 3-way switch to control candle sockets and 7-watt night light in globe. In Bronze Plate Luster or Ivory and Gold finishes. 18" Whip-o-lite Shade No. 2062.

ALADDIN SWING ARM REFLECTOR BRIDGE — No. 7078
Illustrated above at left. Has One-Light Mogul socket with 3-way turn-knob switch. 7" Off-set Double Swing Arm. 8" glass reflector. In Bronze Plate Luster or Ivory and Gold finishes. 18" Cone Whip-o-lite Shade No. 2054.

ALADDIN REFLECTOR — No. 3679
As illustrated at left. Has One-Light Mogul Socket with 3-way switch, and 3-candle arm sockets and 3-way switch. 10" glass reflector. In Bronze Plate Luster, or Ivory and Gold finish. Shown here with 19" Fabric Shade No. R-375.

ALADDIN REFLECTOR WITH NIGHT LIGHT — No. 3979
As illustrated at left. Has One-Light Mogul socket and 3-way switch and 3-candle arm sockets and 3-way switch to control candle sockets and 7-watt night light in globe. In Bronze Plate Luster or Ivory and Gold finishes. 18" Whip-o-lite Shade No. 2065.

GIVE YOUR HOME A "Lift"

2063
2064
2068
2065
G375
G34
G35
G251
2060
B469
G252
2062
2061
G253
G256
G254
G255
S465
2306H
G257
G258

New 1942 Aladdin Electric Table Lamps
In Characteristic Beauty and Refinement

DESIGN No. G-251
As illustrated, in Genuine Alacite in Ivory or Alacite decorated in Rose or Blue. 1-Light push-thru Socket, harp and finial. 18" high. 10" Whip-o-lite Shade No. 2068 shown.

DESIGN No. G-252
Shown above, in Genuine Alacite in Ivory or Alacite decorated in Rose, Blue or Tan. 1-Light push-thru socket, harp and finial. 22" high. 12" Whip-o-lite Shade No. 2065 shown.

DESIGN No. G-253
As illustrated, in Genuine Alacite in Ivory or Alacite decorated in Rose or Blue. 1-Light push-thru socket, harp and finial. 20¼" high. 12" Whip-o-lite Shade No. 2060 shown.

DESIGN No. G-254
ILLUMINATED BASE
As shown in Genuine Alacite in Ivory, or Alacite decorated Blue or Tan. One 3-way turn-knob switch socket, harp and finial. 23¾" high. 16" Fabric Shade No. B-469 shown.

DESIGN No. G-255
ILLUMINATED BASE
Shown above, in Genuine Ivory Alacite or Alacite decorated Blue or Tan. One 3-way turn-knob switch socket, harp and finial. 20¼" high. 14" Whip-o-lite Shade No. 2061 shown.

DESIGN No. G-256
As shown above, in Genuine Alacite in Ivory, or decorated Alacite in Rose or Tan. One Light push-thru socket, harp and finial. 21½" high. 14" Shade No. 2062 in Whip-o-lite shown.

DESIGN No. G-257
ILLUMINATED BASE
Illustrated at left, in Genuine Alacite in Ivory, or decorated Alacite in Blue or Tan. One 3-way turn-knob switch socket, harp and finial. 17½" high. 14" Fabric Shade No. S-465 shown.

DESIGN No. G-258
ILLUMINATED BASE
As shown at left. Same as G-257 above, except with high harp to accommodate No. 2306H high fluted Whip-o-lite Shade. 22¾" high.

ALADDIN BOUDOIR LAMPS
DESIGN No. G-34
Illustrated upper left. In one-piece with patented hollow blown pedestal in Genuine Alacite in Ivory, or decorated Alacite in Rose, Blue or Tan. One-Light push-thru socket. 15½" high. Shown with 8" Empire Whip-o-lite Shade Design No. 2063.

DESIGN No. G-35
As is shown at upper left. In one-piece, with patented hollow blown pedestal in Genuine Alacite in Ivory or decorated Ivory in Rose or Blue. 15" high. Illustrated with 7" Empire Whip-o-lite Shade No. 2064.

Aladdin Decorative Lighted Urn
DESIGN No. G-375
In a most artistic and realistic representation of dancing figures. In Genuine Alacite in Ivory only with Gold plated metal base. One Light socket and push-in switch in base.

Aladdin *Electric* FLOOR LAMPS

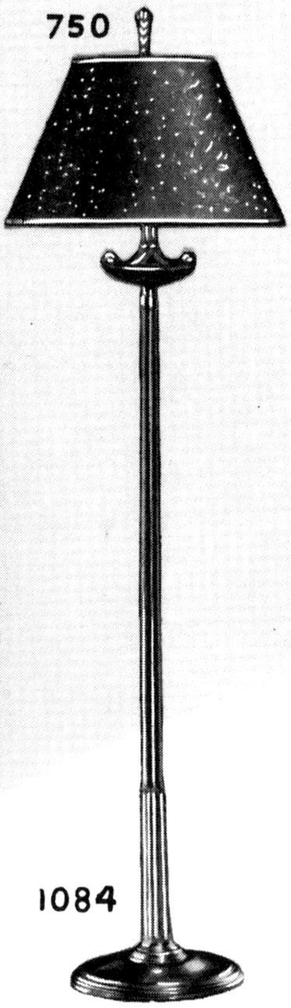

2061

2067

1526

750

JUNIOR FLOOR LAMP
No. 1084

Height 54"

In Oxidized Bronze or Polished Brass

16" Satin-lite Shade
No. 750

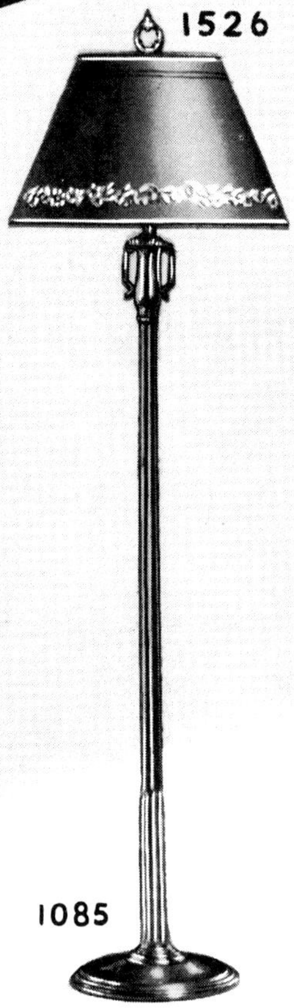

1084

JUNIOR FLOOR LAMP
No. 1085

Height 54"

In Oxidized Bronze or Polished Brass

16" Whip-o-lite Shade
No. 1526, Variegated

1085

NOTE—Both Junior Floor Lamps No. 1084 and 1085 Fitted with single 1-Light Socket with self-contained Switch.

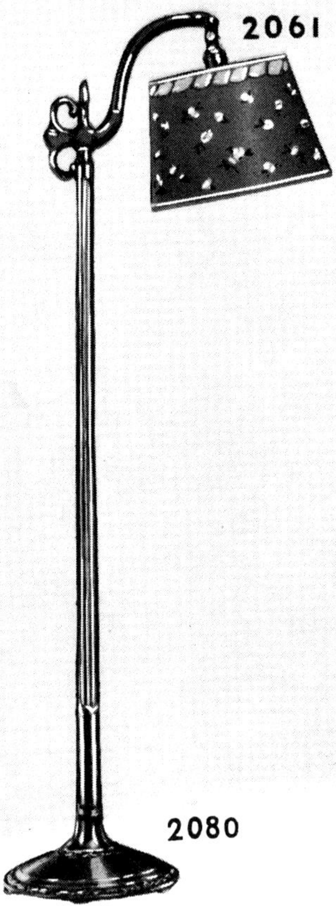

BRIDGE LAMP
No. 2080

In Oxidized Bronze or Ivory and Gold

12" Whip-o-lite Shade
No. 2061, Tan

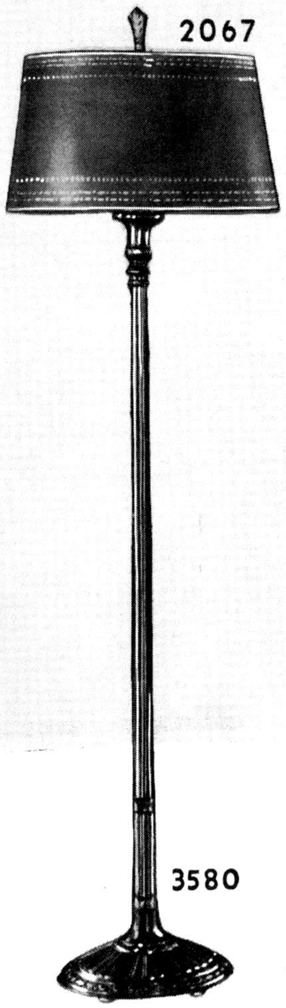

2080

REFLECTOR FLOOR LAMP
No. 3580

Single 3-way Mogul Socket

In Ivory and Gold or Oxidized Bronze

18" Whip-o-lite Shade
No. 2067, Variegated

3580

GLASS REPLACEMENT REFLECTORS

12 Unit - Alacite FINIAL ASSORTMENT

No. 81, White Mazed Glass, 8" dia. top, 5¾" high; neck 2¼" dia.

No. 101, White Mazed Glass, 10" dia. top, 5½" high; neck 2⅞" dia.

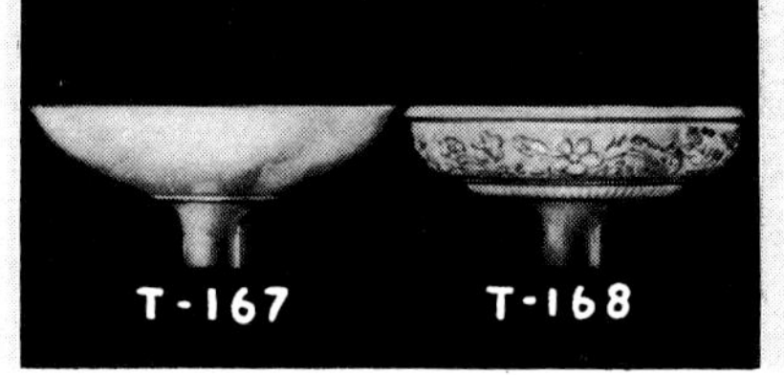

No. 167, Plain White Glass, 16" dia. top; neck 2⅝" O. D.

No. 168, Embossed Glass Decorated Tan; 14" dia. top, neck 2⅝" O. D.

BEAUTIFUL DISPLAY STAND
shown, included Free with First Order for 12 Units.

2054

2074

1528

2033

REFLECTOR
FLOOR LAMP
No. 3582

Single 3-way Mogul
Socket

In Ivory and Gold
or Oxidized Bronze

18" Whip-o-lite Shade
No. 2074, Variegated

REFLECTOR
FLOOR LAMP
No. 3681

Single 3-way Mogul
Socket and 3
Candle Arm
Sockets

In Ivory and Gold
or Oxidized Bronze

18" Whip-o-lite
Shade No. 2033
Variegated

REFLECTOR
FLOOR LAMP
No. 3680

Single 3-way Mogul
Socket, and 3 Candle
Arm Sockets

In Ivory and Gold
or Oxidized Bronze

18" Whip-o-lite Shade
No. 2054, Variegated

REFLECTOR
FLOOR LAMP
No. 3682

Single 3-way Mogul
Socket, and 3
Candle Arm
Sockets

In Ivory and Gold
or Oxidized Bronze

18" Whip-o-lite Shade
No. 1528, Variegated

3680

3582

3682

3681

750

750

750

M-277

M-275

M-276

376

Beautiful
SILVERED METAL
TABLE LAMPS

THE three, all-metal, table lamps shown
at left are all of classic design. Each
including finial, is heavily plated in silver
and highly polished. All have single one-
light sockets with self-contained switch.
M-276 and M-277 are 25" in height and
fitted with 14", No. 750 Satin-lite shade
in Champagne or Wine as desired. The
M-275 is 23" in height and is equipped
with 12" Satin-lite Champagne or Wine
Shade No. 750.

These charming No. 376 urns will find a warm welcome in many, many homes. As mantle, radio,
buffet decoration they are almost a "must." You're
sure to find a ready acceptance for these unusual
creations. In Ivory Alacite only.

See enclosed leaflet for Dealer's Wholesale Prices on all items shown herein.

These New Artistic
Aladdin URNS

Of stately Grecian design are available in
pairs only. They are equipped with a
single, standard, one-light socket,
cord and plug with push down
switch in base for control.

12-Lamp & Shade Selection No. 21C

(For Details of Each Lamp See Back Page)

No. of Lamps	Lamp No.	Alacite In	Design of Shade	Size	Color	Whole-sale Price*
2	G-186A	Alacite	909H	12"	White	
2	G-267A	Tan	2072	14"	Tan	
2	G-270	Blue	1526	14"	Vari.	
2	G-271	Ala. Antiq.	1528	14"	Vari.	
2	G-272	Ala. Antiq.	1527	14"	Vari.	
2	G-274	Rose	2033	14"	Vari.	

For Individual Lamp, and Total Wholesale Price of above selection, see separate price list enclosed.

12-Lamp & Shade Selection No. 22C

(For Details of Each Lamp See Back Page)

No. of Lamps	Lamp No.	Alacite In	Design of Shade	Size	Color	Whole-sale Price*
2	G-222	Alacite	2063	14"	Vari.	
1	G-257A	Tan	2306	13"	Tan	
2	G-259	Tan	2061	12"	Tan	
2	G-263A	Alacite	2306H	12"	Tan	
1	G-265	Tan	2071	14"	Tan	
2	G-270	Rose	1525	14"	Rose	
2	G-274	Alacite	2074	14"	Vari.	

*For Individual Lamp, and Total Wholesale Price of above selection, see separate price list enclosed.

12-Lamp & Shade Selection No. 24C

(For Details of Each Lamp See Back Page)

No. of Lamps	Lamp No.	Alacite In	Design of Shade	Size	Color	Wholesale Price*
1	G-257A	Alacite	2306	13"	White	
1	G-278	Alacite	1527	12"	Vari.	
2	G-263A	Alacite	2306H	12"	Tan	
1	G-265	Alacite	2071	14"	White	
1	G-266	Alacite	2070	14"	White	
1	G-266	Tan	2070	14"	Tan	
1	G-267A	Tan	2072	14"	Tan	
2	G-268	Rose	1525	12"	Rose	
1	G-270	Ala. Antiq.	1525	14"	White	
1	G-274	Tan	2061	14"	Tan	

For Individual Lamp, and Total Wholesale Price of above selection, see separate price list enclosed.

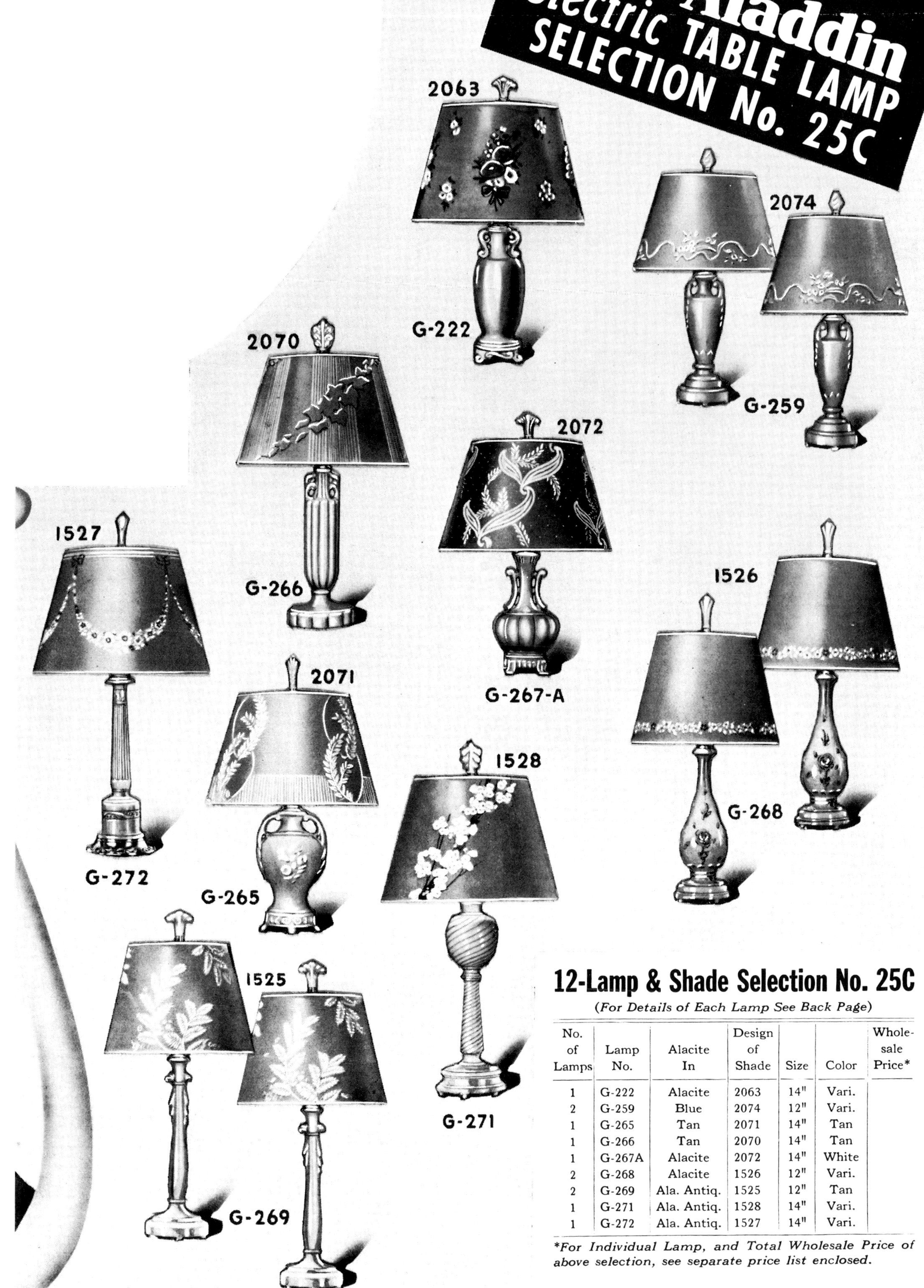

12-Lamp & Shade Selection No. 25C

(For Details of Each Lamp See Back Page)

No. of Lamps	Lamp No.	Alacite In	Design of Shade	Size	Color	Whole-sale Price*
1	G-222	Alacite	2063	14"	Vari.	
2	G-259	Blue	2074	12"	Vari.	
1	G-265	Tan	2071	14"	Tan	
1	G-266	Tan	2070	14"	Tan	
1	G-267A	Alacite	2072	14"	White	
2	G-268	Alacite	1526	12"	Vari.	
2	G-269	Ala. Antiq.	1525	12"	Tan	
1	G-271	Ala. Antiq.	1528	14"	Vari.	
1	G-272	Ala. Antiq.	1527	14"	Vari.	

For Individual Lamp, and Total Wholesale Price of above selection, see separate price list enclosed.

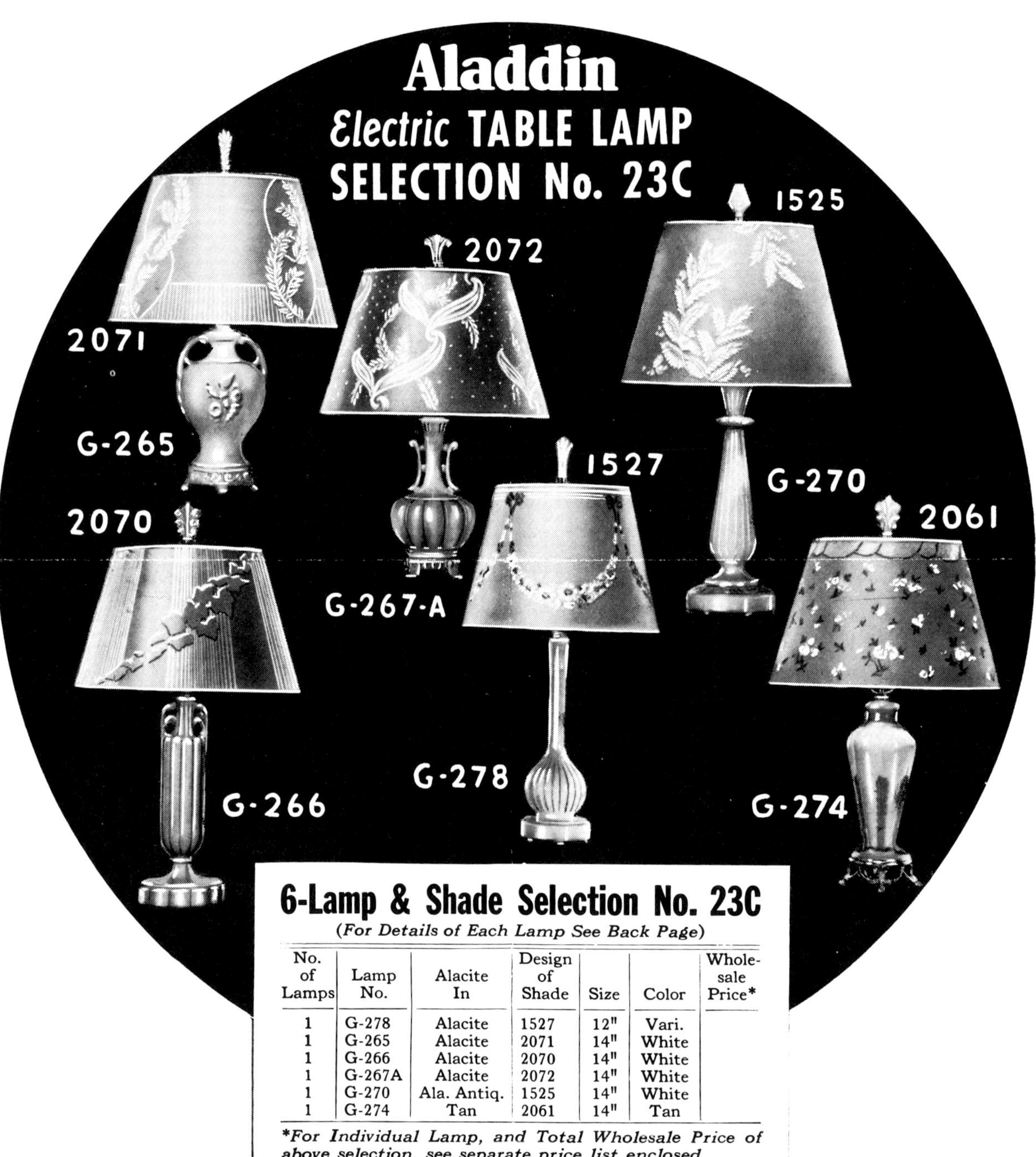

6-Lamp & Shade Selection No. 23C
(For Details of Each Lamp See Back Page)

No. of Lamps	Lamp No.	Alacite In	Design of Shade	Size	Color	Whole-sale Price*
1	G-278	Alacite	1527	12"	Vari.	
1	G-265	Alacite	2071	14"	White	
1	G-266	Alacite	2070	14"	White	
1	G-267A	Alacite	2072	14"	White	
1	G-270	Ala. Antiq.	1525	14"	White	
1	G-274	Tan	2061	14"	Tan	

For Individual Lamp, and Total Wholesale Price of above selection, see separate price list enclosed.

URNS

G-376: Charming lighted urns in Ivory Alacite will find a warm welcome in any home. They fit so well in so many places that they are almost a decorator's "must." Each urn is equipped with a standard light socket and a push-down type electric switch. 8¼" high.

G-377: Lighted Ivory Alacite Urns will add charm and dignity to the dining room or bedroom; they are exceptionally pleasing when placed on a radio or mantle. We suggest you feature these lovely table lights for profit, for satisfied customers. 11" high overall.

Aladdin*

TABLE LAMPS

G-268
G-268
G-186
G-269
G-269

INDEX

PAGES
TABLE LAMPS   4, 5, 6, 7
FLOOR LAMPS   8, 9, 10, 11
REFLECTORS   11
LAMP SHADES, URNS 12, 13
DEALER MAT SERVICE 14, 15
FINIALS 14

G-268: Graceful decorated urn-type table lamp. Comes in Ivory Alacite or Ivory Alacite Decorated Rose. Equipped with Push-Thru type electric switch in a standard socket. 24" high overall. Shade, 12" Whip-o-lite No. 1534, Variegated; 13" Fabric No. R-475, Rose or Blue Decorated.

G-186: This charming ball-type table lamp is richly decorated and has an attractive illuminated base. Comes in Ivory Alacite. Equipped with 3-way turn-knob electric switch in a standard socket. 23" high overall. Shade, 12" No. 909-H, White.

G-269: The tall slender base is delicately formed and beautifully decorated. Comes in Ivory Alacite. The standard light socket has a push-thru type electric switch. 27" high overall. Shade, 12" Whip-o-lite No. 1525, Tan; 13" Fabric No. R-475, Blue or Rose.

* Reg. U.S. Pat. Off.

G-272: This unusually attractive column is delicately ornamented. Comes in Antiqued Ivory Alacite only. The standard light socket is equipped with a push-thru type electric switch. 26¾" high overall. Shade, 14" Whip-o-lite No. 1527, Variegated.

G-270: Slender fluted base simulates a column. Ivory Alacite, Ivory Alacite Decorated Rose, Ivory Alacite Decorated Blue. The standard light socket has push-thru type electric switch. 27" high overall. Shade, 14" Whip-o-lite No. 1525, White or Rose; No. 1530, Variegated.

G-281: Dainty column of this lamp adds charm to any room. Ivory Alacite, Ivory Alacite Decorated Rose, Ivory Alacite Decorated Blue. Standard socket has push-thru type switch. 24" high overall. Shade, 12" Whip-o-lite No. 1532, Variegated; 13" Fabric No R-475 Rose or Blue.

G-282: Vase type column with arms makes very artistic table lamp. Ivory Alacite or Ivory Alacite Decorated Tan. The Standard light socket has push-thru type switch. 24" high overall. Shade, 14" Whip-o-lite No. 1533, Variegated; 15" Fabric No. B-474, White.

G-285: Beautiful spiral-fluted base has a lighted bowl. In Ivory Alacite (Bolite). The standard socket has a 3-way turn-knob switch. 29" high overall. Shade, 16" Whip-o-lite No. 1532, Variegated; 16" Fabric No. B-477, White.

G-285-C: Graceful, dignified Certified table lamp. Comes in Ivory Alacite. Comes equipped with a Certified Glass and Metal Reflector. 26" high overall. Shade, 16" Fabric No. R-477, White.

G-290-D: This graceful decalcomania decorated base lamp is mounted on a metal footing. Base is illuminated. Comes in Ivory Alacite. Equipped with a 3-way turn-knob socket. 24″ high overall. Shade, 15″ Fabric No. B-474, White.

G-288: The ornamented base is illuminated. Ivory Alacite, Ivory Alacite Decorated Rose, Ivory Alacite Decorated Tan. The standard socket has a 3-way turn-knob switch. 24½″ high overall. Shade, 17″ Fabric No. B-478, Tan or Rose.

G-289: Vase type base with metal footing. Ivory Alacite, Ivory Alacite Decorated Rose, Ivory Alacite Decorated Tan. Illuminated Base. Standard socket has 3-way turn-knob electric switch. 24″ high overall. Shade, 14″ Whip-o-lite No. 1531, Variegated; 15″ Fabric No. B-474, White.

G-291-D: A pleasing decalcomania decorated base, mounted on metal footing and illuminated. The standard socket has a 3-way turn-knob electric switch. In Ivory Alacite. 27″ high overall. Shade, 16″ Fabric No. B-477, White.

***Reg. U. S. Pat. Off.**

M-277: An all-metal base simulates a graceful old-world vase. Finished in polished silver plate. Comes equipped with a standard light socket which has a push-thru type electric switch. 25″ high overall. Shade, 14″ Empire Satinlite No. 750, Wine.

M-279: The column of this lamp is made of metal and finished in polished brass. Comes equipped with a standard light socket and push-thru type electric switch. 24½″ high overall. Shade 12″, Whip-o-lite No. 1532, Variegated.

G-292: Bowl type lamp with illuminated base and metal footing. In Ivory Alacite or Ivory Alacite Decorated Tan. 3-way turn-knob electric switch in a standard socket. 20″ high overall. Shade, 13″ Fluted Whip-o-lite No. 2307, Variegated or Tan.

G-293: This table lamp comes equipped with an illuminated base. In Ivory Alacite or Ivory Alacite Decorated Tan. The standard light socket is equipped with a 3-way turn-knob switch. 23″ high overall. Shade, 12″ Fluted Whip-o-lite No. 2307H, Variegated or Tan.

M-275: The unusually attractive base of this table lamp is made entirely of metal and is finished in polished silver plate. Standard light socket has a push-thru type switch. 23″ high overall. Shade, 12″ Empire Satinlite No. 750, Wine.

M-276: This charming base is delicately fluted and made entirely of metal and is finished in polished silver plate. The standard light socket is equipped with a push-thru type electric switch. 25″ high overall. Shade, 14″ Empire Satinlite No. 750, Wine.

G-280: Base of this lamp is combination polished brass finish and Ivory Alacite. Comes equipped with a standard light socket and push-thru type switch. 27½″ high overall. Shade, 16″ Whip-o-lite No. 1532, Variegated.

G-287-C: Beautiful Certified light table lamp. Comes in Ivory Alacite. Is equipped with a Certified Glass and Metal Reflector. 26″ high overall. Shade, 16″ Fabric No. R-477, White.

Aladdin*

FLOOR LAMPS

3680: Ornamented base, fluted column floor lamp. Ivory and gold or oxidized bronze finish. Equipped with a 3-way Mogul base socket and 3 candle arm sockets. 60" high overall. Shade, 18" Whip-o-lite No. 2074, Variegated.

3682: Delicately ornamented base, tapering flute column floor lamp. Ivory and gold or oxidized bronze finish. Equipped with a 3-way Mogul base socket and 3 candle arm sockets. 60" high overall. Shade, 18" Whip-o-lite No. 1528, Variegated.

3686: Dignified floor lamp with highly ornamented base. Deep bronze or silver and gold finish. Equipped with a 3-way Mogul base socket and 3 candle arm sockets. 60" high overall. Shade, 18" Whip-o-lite No. 1533, Tan; 19" Fabric No. R-471, White.

3688: Tall, dignified very graceful floor lamp. Golden bronze finish. Equipped with Mogul Socket 3-way switch for 3-candle arms. 60" high overall. Shade, 19" Fabric No. R-472, White; 19" Fabric No. B-476, Tan.

3689: Turned and ornamented base with attractive fluted column and ornamented candle arms. Ivory and gold or oxidized bronze finish. Equipped with a 3-way Mogul base socket and 3 candle arm sockets. 60" high overall. Shade, 19" Fabric No. B-476, White; 18" Whip-o-lite No. 1534, Variegated.

3690: Beautifully ornamented base floor lamp. Ivory and gold or oxidized bronze finish. Equipped with a 3-way Mogul base socket and 3 candle arm sockets. 60" high overall. Shade, 18" Whip-o-lite No. 1535T; 19" Fabric No. R-472, White.

4791-C: "Certified" Type Floor Lamp. In oxidized bronze finish only. Comes equipped with a 3-way Mogul Socket. Certified Glass and Metal Reflector. 60" high overall. Shade, 19" Fabric No. R-472, Tan.

4886-C: Certified Circline Floor Lamp delicately made and beautifully finished in either oxidized bronze or highly polished silver plate. Equipped with a 3-way Mogul Socket. Certified Glass and Metal Reflector and Circline Fluorescent tube. 60" high overall. Shade, 19" Fabric No. B-476, Tan.

3685: Delicately ornamented base, tapering column Floor Lamp. In Ivory and Gold or Oxidized Bronze Finish. Equipped with a 3-way Mogul socket and 3 candle arm sockets. 60" high overall. Shade, 18" Whip-o-lite No. 2067, Tan.

*Reg. U. S. Pat. Off.

3688
3689
3690
3689
3690
3685
3688
4791C
4886C

7089
7092
7092
T170
4584
3982
1084
1085
3982
5088
5088
*Reg. U.S. Pat. Off

Aladdin*

FLOOR LAMPS

4584: Torchere floor lamp. In oxidized bronze finish only. Comes equipped with a 16" Nu-Gold Reflector and 3-way Mogul base socket with turn-knob electric switch. Illustrated is No. T-170 Glass Reflector. 62" high overall.

No. 81: White Glass Replacement Reflector. 8" top diameter; 2¼" neck diameter; 5¼" high overall.

No. 101: White Glass Replacement Reflector. 10" top diameter; 2⅞" neck Diameter; 5½" high overall.

No. T-167: Plain Glass Replacement Reflector. 16" top diameter, 2⅝" neck diameter O. D.

No. T-168: Embossed Glass Replacement Reflector decorated Tan. 14" top diameter; 2⅝" neck diameter O. D.

2080: Curved arm Bridge Type Floor Lamp. Comes in Ivory and Gold or Oxidized Bronze Finish. Equipped with a standard 1-light swivel socket and push-thru type electric switch. 56" high overall. Shade, 12" Bridge Whip-o-lite No. 1526, Variegated.

3687: Very graceful, highly ornamented column and beautiful base. In deep bronze or 2-tone silver finish. Equipped with a 3-way Mogul base socket and 3 candle arm sockets. 60" high overall. Shade, 19" Fabric, No. R-470, Tan or White.

3692: Dainty floor lamp with ornamented candle arms. Ivory and gold or oxidized bronze finish. Equipped with a 3-way Mogul base socket and 3 candle arm sockets. 60" high overall. Shade, 18" Whip-o-lite No. 1528, Variegated; 19" Fabric No. R-472, Tan.

3982: Exceptionally dainty base floor lamp. Ivory and gold or oxidized bronze finish. Equipped with 3-way Mogul base socket, 3 candle arm sockets and night light. 60" high overall. Shade, 18" Whip-o-lite No. 1525, White; 19" Fabric No. R-472, White.

1084: Attractive, decorative Floor Lamp. Comes in Oxidized Bronze finish with fluted metal base. Equipped with a standard socket and push-thru type electric switch. 54" high overall. Shade, 16" Whip-o-lite No. 1526, Variegated.

1085: Beautifully finished and trimmed base floor lamp. In oxidized bronze. Comes equipped with a 1-light socket and push-thru type electric switch. 54" high overall. Shade, 16" Whip-o-lite No. 1526, Variegated.

5088: Tall, graceful floor lamp. Ivory and gold or Golden Bronze finish. Equipped with turn-knob switch for Bolite reflector type 200 watt bulb and 3-way switch for 3-candle arms. 60" high overall. Shade, 19" Fabric No. R-472, White; 19" Fabric No. B-476, Tan.

7089: Swing-Arm Bridge Lamp. Comes in Oxidized Bronze Finish or Ivory and Gold. Equipped with a standard light socket and turn-knob switch, 8" glass reflector and swing arm. 56" high overall. Shade, 16" Fabric No. R-472, Tan or White.

7092: Bridge-type floor lamp with double swing-arm. Choice of ivory and gold or oxidized bronze finish. Equipped with a 3-way Mogul type-light socket, 8" glass reflector and swing arm. 56" high overall. Shade, 16" Fabric No. R-472, White or Tan or 16" Whip-o-lite No. 1526 Variegated.

Base G296-D—Classic figure design on lighted Ivory Alacite base. Overall height 25″, with standard socket and 3-way turn knob switch. **Shade B-477**—16″ white fabric. Also available in Shade #1541—16″ Empire Whip-O-Lite.

Base G282—Attractive table lamp in Ivory Alacite or Tan Decorated base, standard socket and push thru switch. Overall height 24″. **Shade 2308**—11″ White fluted Whip-O-Lite as shown. Also available in any standard 14″ Empire Whip-O-Lite shade or B474 white 15″ fabric.

Base G294-D—Colonial scene on lighted Ivory Alacite base makes this a perfect table lamp for rooms decorated in Early American, 24″ high. **Shade 1541**—14″ Whip-O-Lite Empire as shown. Also available with 2308—14″ fluted Whip-O-Lite shade.

Base G298D—The handsome floral design on lighted Ivory Alacite base helps this lamp dress up the appearance of any room. Has standard socket, 3-way turn knob switch. 27½″ high. **Shade 1542**—16″ Empire Whip-O-Lite as shown.

Base G290D—Gold finish metal mounting, beautiful floral design on lighted Ivory Alacite base. One of the loveliest lamps in our line. 24″ high, standard socket, 3-way turn knob switch. **Shade 2308**—14″ White fluted Whip-O-Lite. Also available with regular 14″ Empire Whip-O-Lite shade.

Base G282—A steady favorite with lamp prospects. Ivory Alacite or Tan Decorated base with standard socket and push thru switch. Stands 24″ high. **Shade 1538**—14″ Empire Whip-O-Lite as shown.

Base G296-D—Golden lustre finish lighted Ivory Alacite base, lovely 25″ high table lamp. Standard socket, 3-way turn knob switch. **Shade 1541**—16″ Empire Whip-O-Lite. Also available with B477 fabric 16″ white.

Base G294-D—Lighted Ivory Alacite base richly finished with a golden lustre for a luxurious table lamp that appeals to every customer. 24″ high, standard socket, 3-way turn knob switch. **Shade 2308**—14″ Fluted Whip-O-Lite as shown. Also available with 1541—14″ Empire Whip-O-Lite shade.

Base G284—Made in Ivory Alacite or Tan decorated. Base is lighted, has standard socket, and 3-way turn knob switch, 23″ high. **Shade 2307H**—12″ Whip-O-Lite fluted shade as shown.

Base G283—Handsome Ivory Alacite or tan decorated, lighted base table lamp, 20" high with 3-way turn knob switch. **Shade 2307**— 13" Fluted Whip-O-Lite as shown.

Aladdin *

This is a view of the glass and metal reflector exclusive on Certified lamps. Features the new G. E. trigger ring socket and switch.

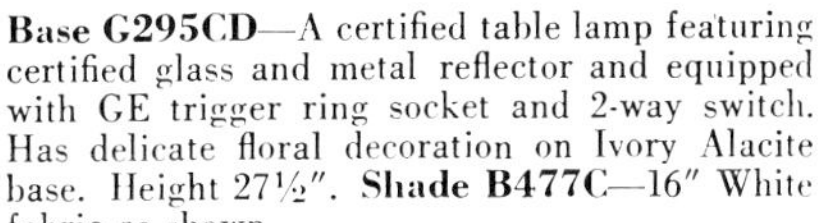

Base G295CD—A certified table lamp featuring certified glass and metal reflector and equipped with GE trigger ring socket and 2-way switch. Has delicate floral decoration on Ivory Alacite base. Height 27½". **Shade B477C**—16" White fabric as shown.

The beauty and original design of these Aladdin Electric Table Lamps is an indication of the fine Aladdin craftsmanship that assures you extra years of satisfying service. Each lamp is made to exacting specifications according to exclusive Aladdin styles to give you more light . . . more beautiful lighting . . . more lighting value. There's an Aladdin Electric Table Lamp for your every need.

Base G291-D—Gold finish metal mounting, beautiful floral design adds rich beauty to lighted Ivory Alacite base. Standard socket, 3-way turn knob switch, 27" high. **Shade 2308**—16" Fluted Whip-O-Lite as shown. Also available with B477—16" white fabric shade.

Base 3688—Attractive 3 candle arm lamp equipped with mogul socket. 10" glass reflector. 60" high. Has unusual combination ivory and gold, or golden bronze finish. Cast head and spindle construction. **Shade 1539**—19" Whip-O-Lite.

Base 3993—A most attractive and practical floor lamp. One piece base and spindle construction. Your choice of ivory and gold, or oxidized bronze finish. 60" high. Equipped with mogul socket and 3 standard socket candle arms. Also has beam night light in head. 10" glass reflector. **Shade 1538**—19" Whip-O-Lite.

Base 4584—Rich looking Torchere floor lamp in luxurious silver and gold, or rich oxidized bronze finish. Cast spindle construction. Has 3-way mogul socket. Shown with T170—16" Nu-Gold reflector. Also available with T167 or T168 Reflectors.

Base 3693—Slim tapered column and 3 candle arms give this lamp an exceptionally dignified and attractive appearance. Luxurious ivory and gold or oxidized bronze finish helps make this a truly unusual lamp in style, appearance and value. One piece base and spindle construction. Mogul socket, 10" glass reflector. 60" high. **Shade 1534**—19" Whip-O-Lite.

Aladdin *

Nothing adds as much to the bright, cheerful,
liveability of a room as a well designed floor lamp.
Aladdin Electric Floor Lamps are available in a wide
range of decorator styles to blend with the interior
of your room. Look for the single unit base and
spindle, an important construction feature in many
Aladdin lamps; prevents weak, wobbly, unsafe lamps.
The Aladdin spindle is permanently rigid to give
you a safer, better-looking floor lamp. You'll find
Aladdin Lamps distinctive in appearance, high
in quality, outstanding in value.

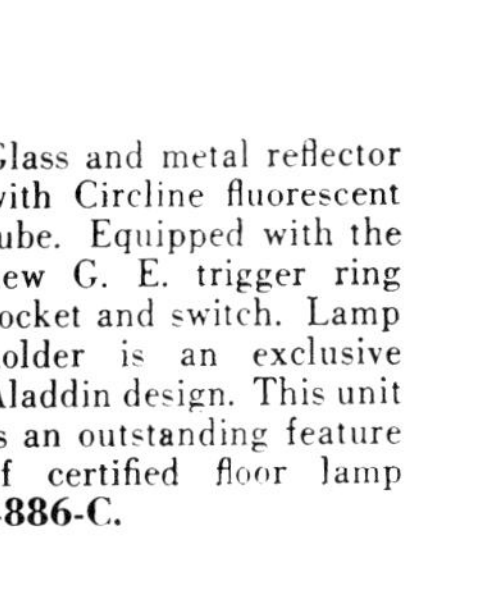

Glass and metal reflector
with Circline fluorescent
tube. Equipped with the
new G. E. trigger ring
socket and switch. Lamp
holder is an exclusive
Aladdin design. This
unit is an outstanding feature
of certified floor lamp
4886-C.

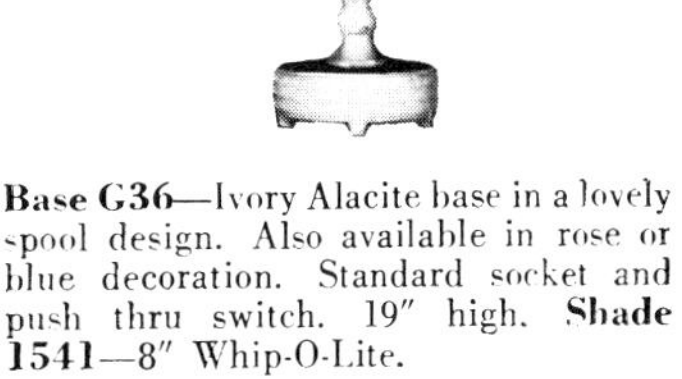

BOUDOIR LAMPS

Base G36—Ivory Alacite base in a lovely
spool design. Also available in rose or
blue decoration. Standard socket and
push thru switch. 19" high. **Shade
1541**—8" Whip-O-Lite.

Base G34—A delicately designed boudoir lamp with Ivory Alacite base. Also
available in rose or blue decoration to
blend with almost any interior. Has
standard socket, push thru switch. 19"
high. **Shade 1539**—8" Whip-O-Lite.

Base 4886C—Certified Circline floor lamp. Rich, highly
polished silver plate or handsome oxidized bronze finish.
Features Circline fluorescent tube, certified glass and metal
reflector, mogul socket, GE trigger ring switch. Cast head
and cast spindle construction. 60" high. **Shade R479C**—
Matching tan or white design on stretched rayon, rayon
lined, braid trim. 19" diameter.

*Reg. U. S. Pat. Off.

NO. G296-D Illuminated base. Top illustration shows classic figure design on Ivory Alacite base, gold banded. Lower right photo shows Golden Lustre base. Height: 25″. Turn knob 3-way switch.

NO. G38 Same design as G30 but taller. Height: 19″. In Ivory Alacite, Rose or Blue. Standard socket and push-thru switch. Shown with Whip-O-Lite Shade No. 1544, clamp fitter, 8″ bottom diameter. Also available with any 8″ shade.

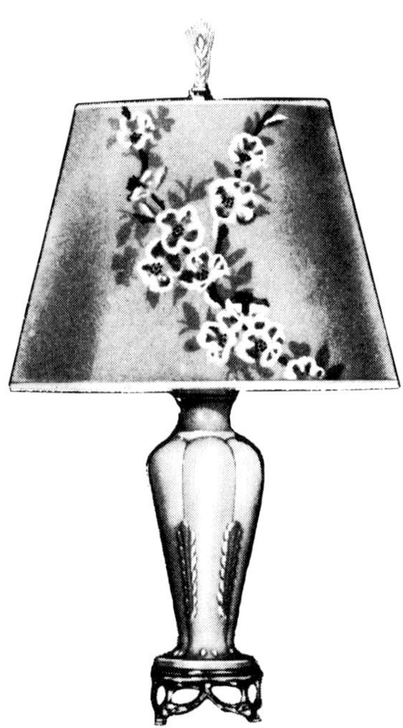

NO. G289 Illuminated base. Beautiful vase type lamp with golden finish, delicately designed metal base. Comes in Ivory Alacite, Tan or Rose. Has 3-way turn knob switch and standard socket. Height: 24″.

NO. G36 Lovely spool design in all Ivory Alacite, Rose or Blue. Standard socket with push-thru switch. Height: 19″. With Shade No. 1541, Whip-O-Lite, 8″ diameter, clamp fitter, as shown. Or any 8″ Whip-O-Lite shade can be used.

made up of Aladdin's Design Staff headed by Mr. Eugene Schwarz, and Independent Designer Consultants led by Mr. Robert Burton, carefully analyzed the continuous Preference Research conducted among homemakers and retail lamp specialists. Interpreted through the drawing board to the finished product, Aladdin styling is a joining together of *your* personal desires *and* the creative talents of these renowned designers.

A DESIGN ACHIEVEMENT

On these pages, shown in full color, are the table lamps Mrs. American Homemaker has asked for. Aladdin Industries, Incorporated, for almost half a century creators of the famous Aladdin Lamps, sent interviewers into communities from coast to coast asking women everywhere what they would like in new lamp designs. From the thousands of answers and suggestions received, Aladdin stylists and well-known Designer-Consultants evolved the creations we now set before you. Milady . . . these are *your* lovely lamps. Make your selection from them, fully assured of their correctness!

Aladdin® A LEADER FOR FORTY YEARS

A famous Lamp Magazine points out that of the thousands of lamps offered for sale in the United States, the public recognizes only two brand names. One, is *Aladdin!* Such recognition can only come to a manufacturer when, throughout the years, that company has served the public honestly and well. For more than forty years the makers of Aladdin Lamps have offered to the public, only the very best in materials, workmanship and design. The name Aladdin is your guarantee of Quality!

MODERN MANUFACTURING FACILITIES

Aladdin Industries, Incorporated, with its 40 years of experience in the field, its many manufacturing plants and its highly skilled technical staff, is in a unique position to make better, more attractive lamps with manufacturing economies that are passed on to homemakers. This, because Aladdin designers and engineers constantly seek for better methods of making lamps—methods that will result in high styled lamps of finest quality at moderate prices.

G314 Here's a luxurious lamp that lends elegance and beauty to any room in the home. Illuminated base casts a gentle glow when viewing television. Fired-on ceramic finish. Lamp comes in Chinese Red, Chartreuse and Ivory Alacite and has extra-wide harp to accommodate standard or reflector-type bulb . . . SHADE ·551—16″ or SHADE ·803—17″ for above lamp. Described in shade section.

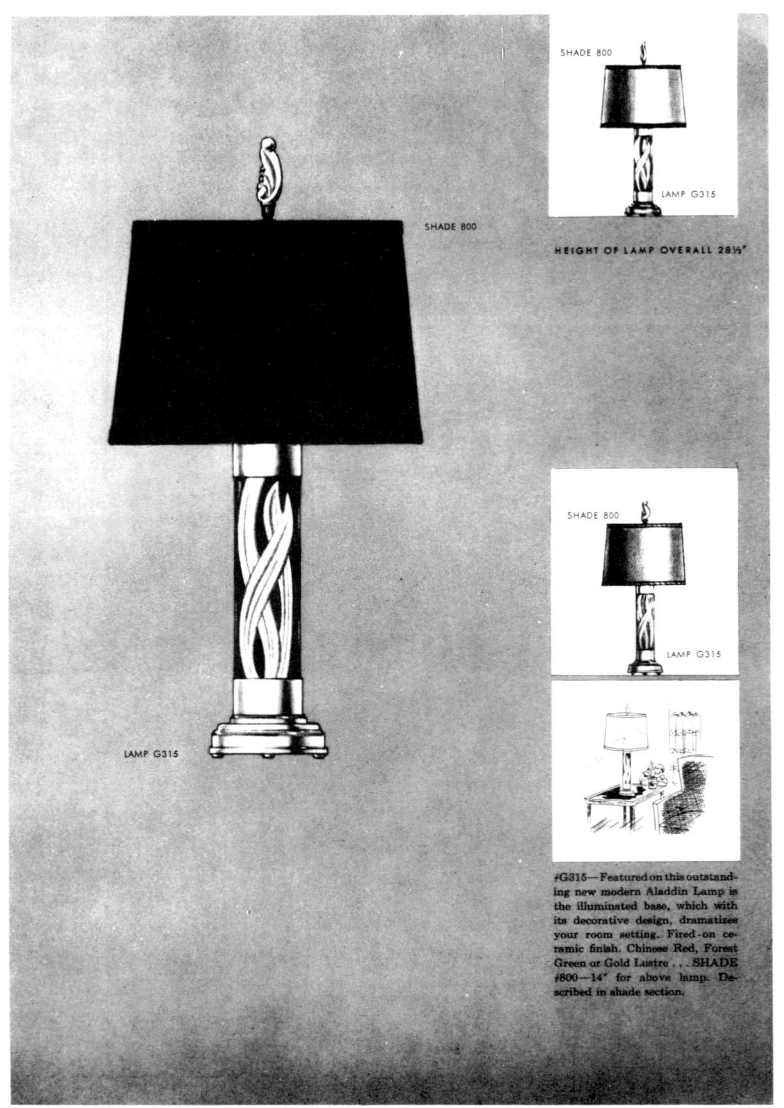

#G315—Featured on this outstanding new modern Aladdin Lamp is the illuminated base, which with its decorative design, dramatizes your room setting. Fired-on ceramic finish. Chinese Red, Forest Green or Gold Lustre . . . SHADE #800—14″ for above lamp. Described in shade section.

#G316—16″ Illuminated base lamp. Accommodates standard or reflector-type bulb. Its graceful classic style will arouse enthusiastic approval from every visitor. Two-tone base has simple vertical lines pleasingly contrasted with the curved vase form. Fired-on ceramic finish. Available in Dubonnet, Smoke Grey and Forest Green . . . SHADE #802—16″ Deep Drum style as shown above. Described in shade section.

#G318—Smart styling and the graceful simplicity of this model gives it a charm seldom found in table lamps. The illuminated base is perfect in period or modern setting. Fired-on ceramic finish. Comes in Rust, Forest Green and Chinese Red with wide harp to accommodate standard or reflector-type bulb . . . SHADE #551—16″ Flared Bell in colors to match. Described in shade section.

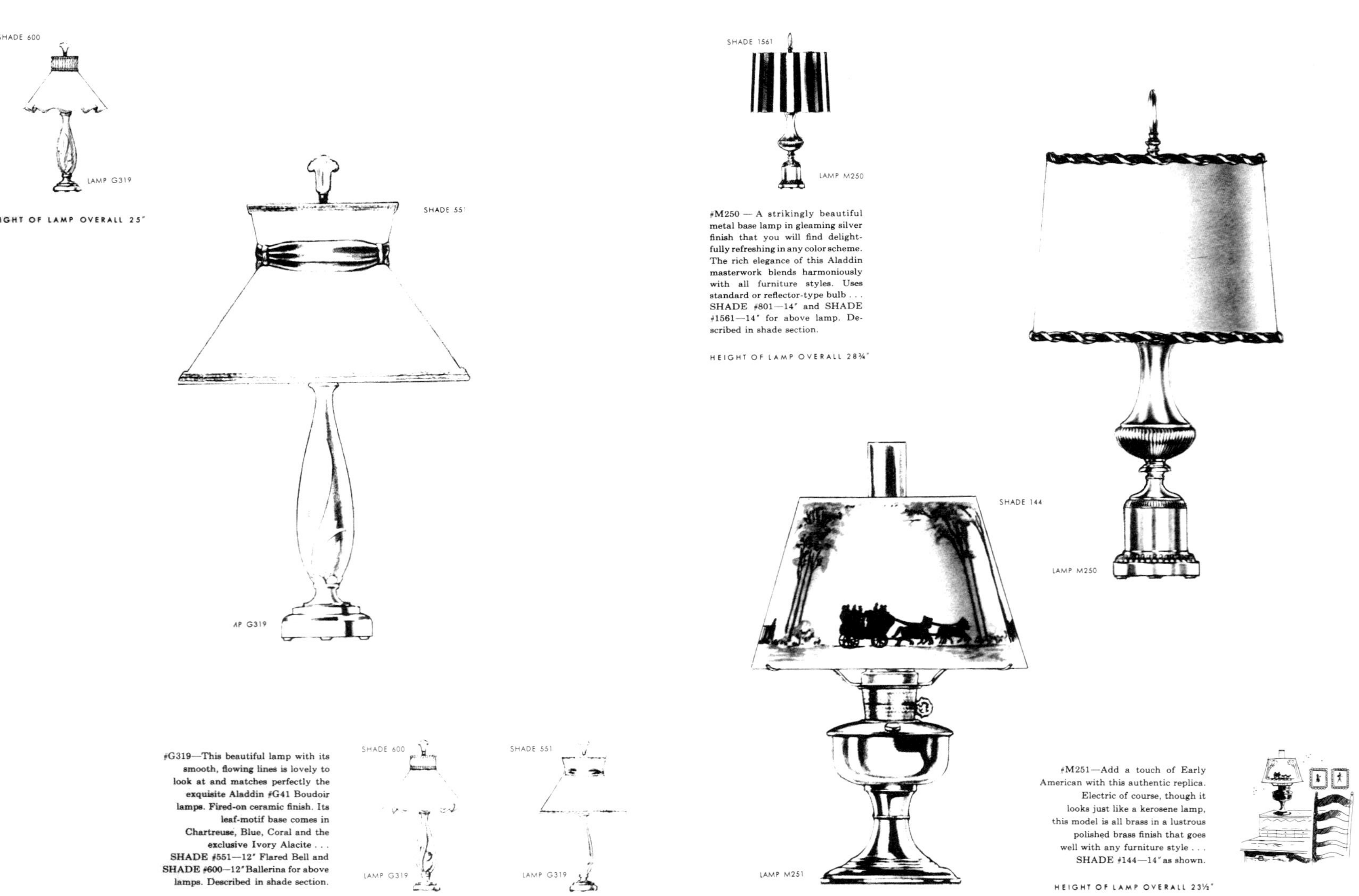

#G319—This beautiful lamp with its smooth, flowing lines is lovely to look at and matches perfectly the exquisite Aladdin #G41 Boudoir lamps. Fired-on ceramic finish. Its leaf-motif base comes in Chartreuse, Blue, Coral and the exclusive Ivory Alacite . . . SHADE #551—12″ Flared Bell and SHADE #600—12″ Ballerina for above lamps. Described in shade section.

#M250 — A strikingly beautiful metal base lamp in gleaming silver finish that you will find delightfully refreshing in any color scheme. The rich elegance of this Aladdin masterwork blends harmoniously with all furniture styles. Uses standard or reflector-type bulb . . . SHADE #801—14″ and SHADE #1561—14″ for above lamp. Described in shade section.

HEIGHT OF LAMP OVERALL 28¾″

#M251—Add a touch of Early American with this authentic replica. Electric of course, though it looks just like a kerosene lamp, this model is all brass in a lustrous polished brass finish that goes well with any furniture style . . . SHADE #144—14″ as shown.

HEIGHT OF LAMP OVERALL 23½″

This year Aladdin offers the most attractive line of table lamps in its more than 40 years of service to the American home-maker. Lovely combinations of exclusive Alacite lamp bases and the famous washable Whip-O-Lite Shades. A feature on all lamps (except boudoir styles) is the glowing radiance of Aladdin's "Illuminated" bases (many with 3-way switch control) adding softness and charm wherever they are used. With just the bases lighted, a gentle illumination makes television viewing more restful . . . easier on the eyes and as night lamps in halls or the children's room, they're ideal. Aladdin Lamps are permanently fired in Aladdin's unique Alacite.

Aladdin ®

SHADE 2309H

LAMP G300

SHADE 2309

LAMP G301

#G300—Illuminated base. A beautiful and interesting combination of a ball type base with tall fluted shade. Make your choice of Green or Golden Lustre. Both have the Ivory Alacite daisy decoration. Comes with 3-way turn-knob switch. Height: 25½"... SHADE #2309H—Tall Fluted Whip-O-Lite shade, 12" bottom diameter.

#G301—This lamp has same base and colors as #G300, but height is 20½"...SHADE #2309 Fluted Whip-O-Lite shade, 13" bottom diameter.

#G302 — An attractive urn-type lamp designed with graceful flowing lines. Comes in deep Dubonnet, pastel Green or warm Coral, gold banded with beautiful floral design in Ivory Alacite. Standard socket with push-thru switch. Height: 25¾"... SHADE #1551—Whip-O-Lite, 14" bottom diameter in colors to match base.

SHADE 1551

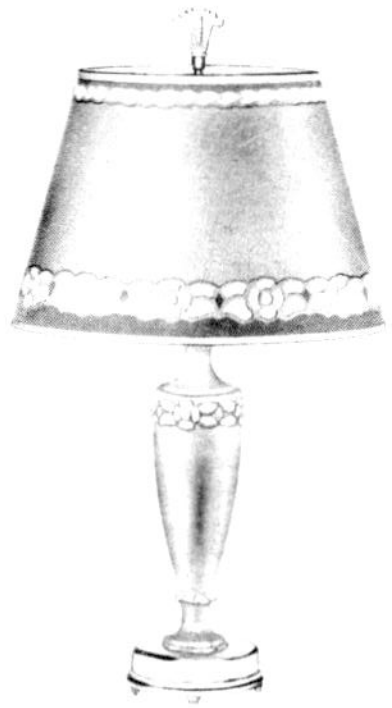

LAMP G302

#G302—An attractive urn-type lamp designed with graceful flowing lines. Comes in deep Dubonnet, pastel Green or warm Coral, gold banded with beautiful floral design in Ivory Alacite. Standard socket with push-thru switch. Height: 25¾"... SHADE #2310—14" bottom diameter in colors to match base. Fluted Whip-O-Lite.

SHADE 2310

LAMP G302

#G304—Illuminated base. Harp designed for use with standard or Bolite bulb. A tall, stately lamp in warm Coral or beautiful Maize set off by Ivory Alacite, rich golden finish metal base. Height: 27½". Has 3-way turn-knob switch ...SHADE #500—A lovely Whip-O-Lite shade with fabric top trim. 16" bottom diameter.

SHADE 500

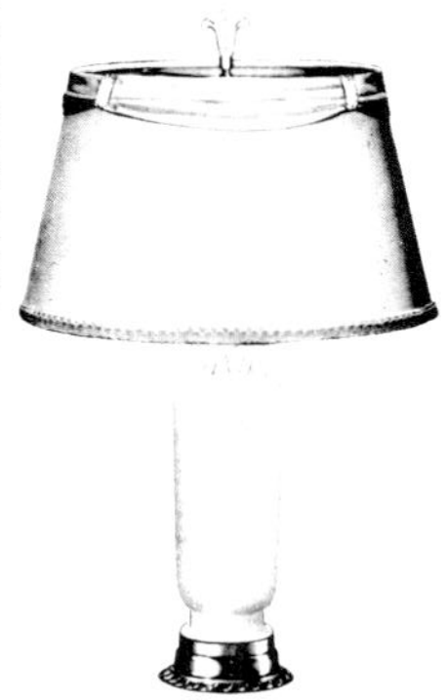

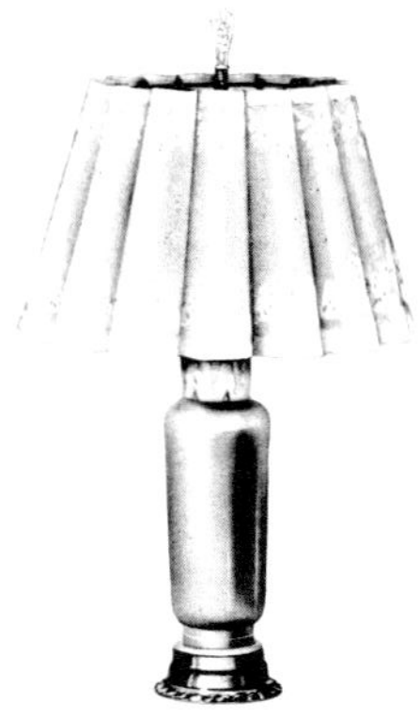

LAMP G304

#G304—Illuminated base. Harp designed for use with standard or Bolite bulb. A tall, stately lamp in warm Coral or beautiful Maize set off by Ivory Alacite, rich golden finish metal base. Height: 27½". Has 3-way turn-knob switch ...SHADE #2309— Fluted Whip-O-Lite shade, 16" bottom diameter.

SHADE 2309

LAMP G304

table   lamps

SHADE 600

LAMP G305

#G305—A lovely lamp with smoothly designed urn-type base. A night stand table lamp matching Boudoir Lamp G40, shown in boudoir section. Made in Ivory Alacite, Coral, Green and Blue. Standard socket with push-thru switch. Height: 23½". Shown with SHADE #600—12", described in shade section.

SHADE B480

LAMP G303

#G303—Columnar styled with beautiful illuminated base, this graceful table lamp is a charming addition to any home. It comes equipped with a 3-way turn-knob switch. Height is 27" and the lamp is available in smoke Grey or pastel Green, set off by Ivory Alacite with rich Gold banding . . . SHADE #2309 is the fluted Whip-O-Lite style with 16" bottom diameter. Described in shade section.

SHADE 2309

LAMP G303

SHADE 500

LAMP G303

#G303—Here is another beautiful columnar-type, illuminated base model table lamp to grace the living rooms of Mrs. America. It comes equipped with a 3-way turn-knob switch. Height is 27" and lamp is available in smoke Grey or pastel Green, set off by Ivory Alacite richly Gold banded . . . SHADE #B480—Hand sewn fabric, in Eggshell with Dubonnet or Green trim, 16" bottom diameter. Also available with 16" SHADE #500, described in shade section.

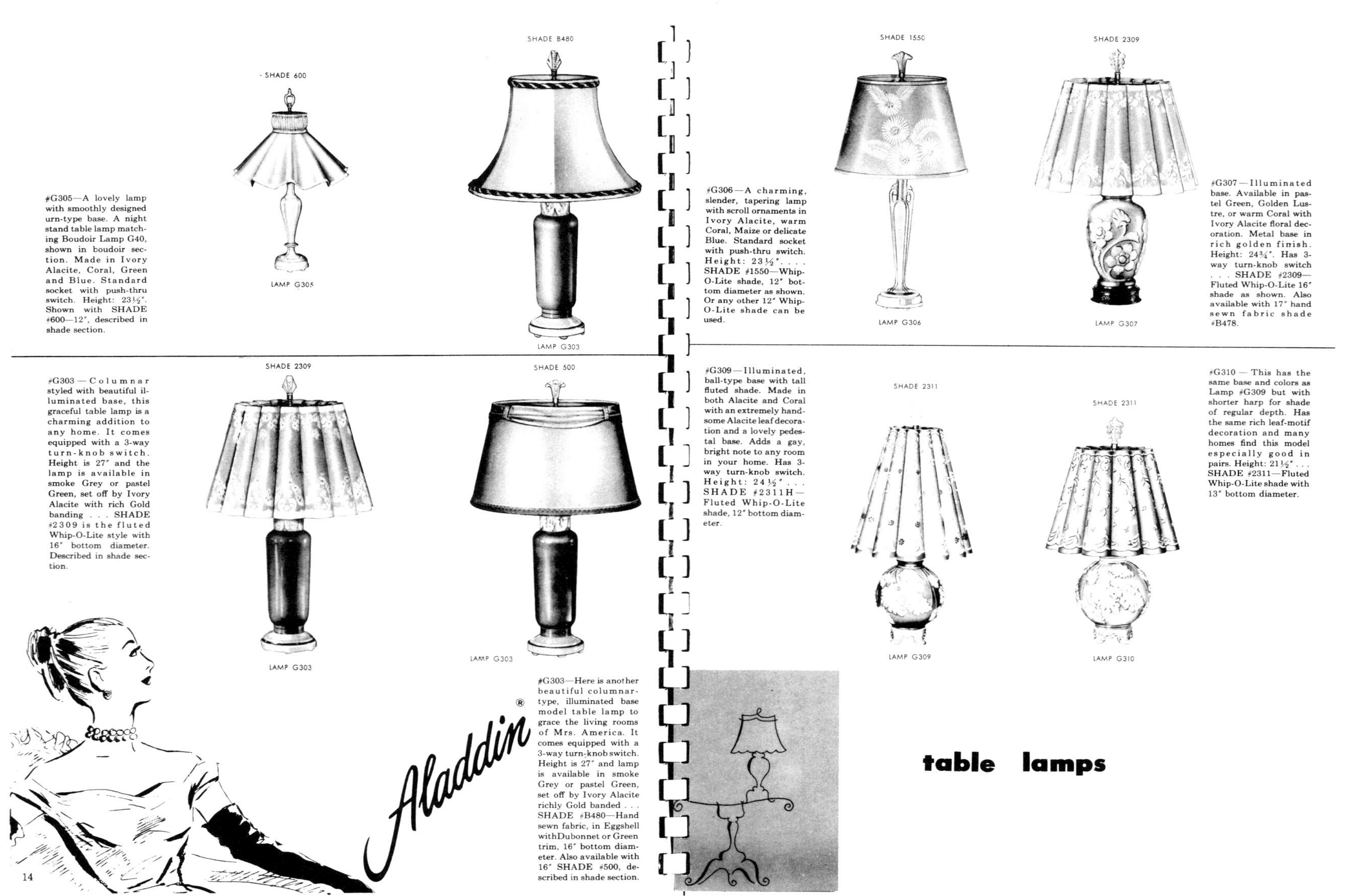

SHADE 1550

LAMP G306

#G306—A charming, slender, tapering lamp with scroll ornaments in Ivory Alacite, warm Coral, Maize or delicate Blue. Standard socket with push-thru switch. Height: 23½". . . . SHADE #1550—Whip-O-Lite shade, 12" bottom diameter as shown. Or any other 12" Whip-O-Lite shade can be used.

SHADE 2309

LAMP G307

#G307—Illuminated base. Available in pastel Green, Golden Lustre, or warm Coral with Ivory Alacite floral decoration. Metal base in rich golden finish. Height: 24¾". Has 3-way turn-knob switch . . . SHADE #2309—Fluted Whip-O-Lite 16" shade as shown. Also available with 17" hand sewn fabric shade #B478.

#G309—Illuminated, ball-type base with tall fluted shade. Made in both Alacite and Coral with an extremely handsome Alacite leaf decoration and a lovely pedestal base. Adds a gay, bright note to any room in your home. Has 3-way turn-knob switch. Height: 24½" . . . SHADE #2311H—Fluted Whip-O-Lite shade, 12" bottom diameter.

SHADE 2311

LAMP G309

#G310—This has the same base and colors as Lamp #G309 but with shorter harp for shade of regular depth. Has the same rich leaf-motif decoration and many homes find this model especially good in pairs. Height: 21½" . . . SHADE #2311—Fluted Whip-O-Lite shade with 13" bottom diameter.

SHADE 2311

LAMP G310

table   lamps

162

SHADE 909H

LAMP G186

#G186—Illuminated base. Here's a rounded base lamp which, with its matching shade, is one of our most unusual models. Richly decorated with all-over floral pattern, its effect is strikingly beautiful. Comes in Ivory Alacite only. 3-way turn-knob switch. Height: 24½″ . . . SHADE #909H— Fluted Whip-O-Lite shade, 12″ bottom diameter.

SHADE 2309

LAMP G308

SHADE B480

LAMP G308

#G308—Vase-type table lamp gracefully designed for decorative yet functional use in any room of your home. High-styled with exquisite golden finish metal base, this lovely lamp comes in exclusive Ivory Alacite, Dubonnet or Blue. The Ivory Alacite model has Rose floral decoration and striking Gold banding. Equipped with push-thru switch. Height: 26¾″ . . . SHADE #B480—Hand sewn fabric. 16″ bottom diameter. Described in shade section.

SHADE 500

LAMP G308

#G308 Gracefully designed vase-type table lamp in exclusive Ivory Alacite, Dubonnet or Blue. An exquisite high-style model with unusual golden finish metal base. Ivory Alacite model has Rose floral decoration and Gold banding. Comes with push-thru switch. Height: 26¾″ . . . SHADE #500—Is the famous Whip-O-Lite with fabric trim. In Eggshell, Dubonnet or Blue, 16″. Also in fluted Whip-O-Lite 16″ SHADE #2309 described in shade section.

SHADE 2310

LAMP G311

SHADE 500

LAMP G311

#G311—Illuminated base. Traditional, vase-on-pedestal design with gold banding on base. Comes in all-over Golden Lustre, Alacite and Dubonnet or Alacite and Blue. Has 3-way turn-knob switch. Height: 26½″...SHADE #2310— Fluted Whip-O-Lite, 14″ bottom diameter.

#G311—Illuminated base. Traditional, vase-on-pedestal design with gold banding on base. Comes in all-over Golden Lustre, Alacite and Dubonnet or Alacite and Blue. Has 3-way turn-knob switch. Height: 26½″ . . . SHADE #500 — Whip-O-Lite with fabric top trim, 14″ bottom diameter.

SHADE 500

LAMP G312

SHADE 1557

LAMP G312

#G312—A stately vase-on-pedestal design with gold banded base. Comes in Ivory Alacite, Ivory Alacite and Green or Ivory Alacite and Maize. Push-thru switch. Height: 26½″ . . . SHADE #500— Whip-O-Lite shade with draped fabric trim, 14″ bottom diameter.

#G312—A stately vase-on-pedestal design with gold banded base. Comes in Ivory Alacite, Ivory Alacite and Green or Ivory Alacite and Maize. Push-thru switch. Height: 26½″ . . . SHADE #1557— Whip-O-Lite shade, 14″ bottom diameter. Described in shade section.

table lamps

#G353—A pleasing, dainty, one-piece pin-up lamp. Made in Ivory Alacite only. Has standard socket with push-button canopy switch which minimizes tendency to jar lamp out of place when lighting . . . SHADE—Shown here with 8″ Whip-O-Lite SHADE #1550. Also available with any other 8″ Whip-O-Lite shade.

SHADE 1550

LAMP G353

SHADE 551

LAMP G268

#G268—Graceful, decorated table lamp in Ivory Alacite or Rose decorated Ivory Alacite. Its gentle flowing lines are very pleasant. Interior decorators use this lamp type with all furniture styles to create an atmosphere of charm and simplicity. Equipped with push-thru switch and standard socket. Height: 24″ . . . SHADE #B488—Fabric shade with draped top trim, 13″ bottom diameter.

SHADE B488

LAMP G268

SHADE 1550

LAMP G268

#G268—Decorated table lamp in Ivory Alacite or Rose decorated Ivory Alacite. Its gentle flowing lines are very pleasant. Push-thru switch and standard socket. Height: 24″ . . . SHADE #551—12″ Flared Bell style or SHADE #1550 12″ with fern and flower pattern may be used. Descriptions in shade section.

Aladdin®

table lamps

SHADE 2310

SHADE 500

#G313—Illuminated base. Made in Green Lustre, Gold Lustre or Coral ceramic with lovely Ivory Alacite floral decoration and gold banding. Has 3-way turn-knob switch. Height: 27″ . . . SHADE #2310—Fluted Whip-O-Lite shade, 16″ bottom diameter.

#G313—Illuminated base. Made in Green Lustre, Gold Lustre or Coral ceramic with lovely Ivory Alacite floral decoration and gold banding. Has 3-way turn-knob switch. Height: 27″ . . . SHADE #500—Whip-O-Lite shade with draped fabric trim, 16″ bottom diameter.

LAMP G313

LAMP G313

#G321—A lovely table lamp with a striking heart-shaped all-over pattern that is most intriguing. Height: 26″. Comes in Alacite, Coral, Dubonnet and Green . . . SHADE #1560—Is a 14″ Drum-type Whip-O-Lite described in shade section.

#G321—A lovely table lamp with a striking heart-shaped all-over pattern that is most intriguing. Height: 26″. Comes in Alacite, Coral, Dubonnet and Green . . . SHADE #2310—Is a 14″ Fluted Whip-O-Lite shade described in shade section.

SHADE 1560

SHADE 2310

LAMP G321

LAMP G321

SHADE 751

LAMP G202

#G202—A truly unique, modern design desk lamp of one piece construction. Here is a functional lamp with the added appeal of real beauty. Comes in gleaming Ivory Alacite with unusual antique trim. Push-button canopy switch. Height: 24″. Lamp is shown with SHADE #751, Whip-O-Lite, 12″ bottom diameter. Can be had in Dubonnet or Green.

SHADE 2310

LAMP G296-D

SHADE 600

LAMP G354

#G354 — Another charming and practical pin-up lamp. One-piece construction. Comes in Ivory Alacite only. With push-button canopy switch . . . SHADE #600 —10″ Ballerina style. Described in shade section. Also any 8″ Empire Shade.

SHADE 551

LAMP G354

#G354 — Another charming and practical pin-up lamp. One-piece construction. Comes in Ivory Alacite only. With push-button canopy switch . . . SHADE #551 —10″ Flared bell style. Described in shade section. Also any 8″ Empire Shade.

#G290-D — Illuminated base. The curving lines of this delightful lamp lend charm to any room. Beautiful floral design on Ivory Alacite. Metal base, golden finish. Has 3-way turn-knob switch . . . SHADE #2310— Fluted Whip-O-Lite, 14″ bottom diameter. Refer to shade section for complete description.

SHADE 2310

LAMP G290-D

SHADE 500

LAMP G296-D

#G294-D — Illuminated base. Comes in two finishes—Colonial scene on lighted Ivory Alacite base, gold banded; or richly finished Golden Lustre. Height: 24″. Has 3-way turn-knob switch . . . SHADE #500— Whip-O-Lite with fabric top trim, 14″ bottom diameter.

SHADE 500

LAMP G294-D

SHADE 2800

LAMP G294-D

#G294-D — Illuminated base. Comes in two finishes—Colonial scene on lighted Ivory Alacite base, gold banded; or richly finished Golden Lustre. Height: 24″. Has 3-way turn-knob switch . . . SHADE #2800— 14″. See shade section for description.

#G296-D — Illuminated base. Comes with Golden Lustre base (as shown), or with classic figure design on Ivory Alacite base, Gold banded. 3-way turn-knob switch. Height: 25″. . .Shown above with SHADE #2310—Fluted Whip-O-Lite shade with 16″ bottom diameter. Or may be had with SHADE #500—Whip-O-Lite drum type shade with fabric top trim. 16″ bottom diameter, shown below.

Aladdin®

Certified TABLE LAMPS

● EXCLUSIVE ALADDIN DESIGNS IN ALACITE CERTIFIED TABLE LAMPS

LAMP G285-C

SHADE B477-C

#G285-C—Graceful, Certified table lamp. Comes in Ivory Alacite with G-E Trigger Ring socket and switch, certified metal and glass reflector. Height: 26"... SHADE #B477-C— White fabric shade as shown with draped top trim. 16".

LAMP G295-CD

SHADE B482-C

#G295-CD—Certified. Delicate Rose floral design against Ivory Alacite. Has G-E Trigger Ring socket and switch, certified metal and glass reflector. Height: 27½"... SHADE #B482-C—Hand sewn fabric shade as shown, 16" bottom diameter, Eggshell with Green, Rose or Gold trim.

LAMP G297-C

SHADE B482-C

#G297-C—Certified. A winged-vase design mounted on golden finish metal base. Alacite vase in cool pastel Green or warm and glowing Coral effectively contrasting with Ivory decoration. Equipped with G-E Trigger Ring socket and switch, certified metal and glass reflector. Height: 28½"...SHADE #B482-C— Hand sewn fabric shade as shown, 16" bottom diameter. Eggshell with Green, Rose or Gold trim.

BUILT TO RIGID SPECIFICATIONS
OF CERTIFIED LAMP MAKERS

Aladdin has selected three outstanding table models in a variety of color combinations and built them to meet the rigid specifications established by the Certified Lamp Makers. Certified Lamps are designed to give maximum lighting performance. All Certified Lamps are equipped with a combination Certified metal and glass reflector as shown in the illustration at right. The G-E Trigger Ring switch used on Aladdin Certified Lamps is approved by Underwriters' Laboratories and tested to assure long, safe operation. Shades are rigid, withstand humidity and are also certified by the C L M.

Above illustration shows the glass and metal reflector which is exclusive on all Certified Lamps. Features the new G-E Trigger Ring socket and switch.

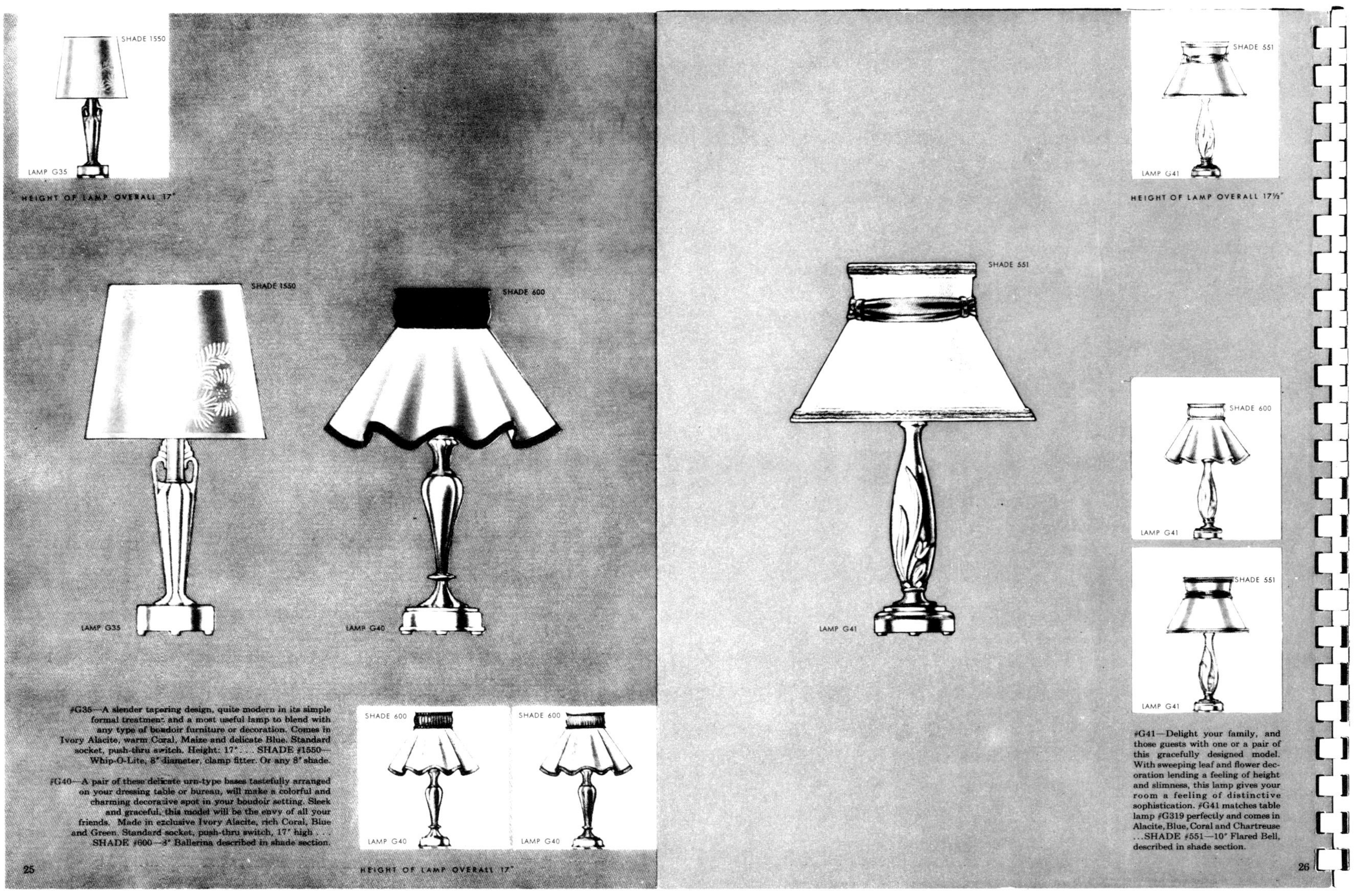

#G35—A slender tapering design, quite modern in its simple formal treatment, and a most useful lamp to blend with any type of boudoir furniture or decoration. Comes in Ivory Alacite, warm Coral, Maize and delicate Blue. Standard socket, push-thru switch. Height: 17".... SHADE #1550—Whip-O-Lite, 8" diameter, clamp fitter. Or any 8" shade.

#G40—A pair of these delicate urn-type bases tastefully arranged on your dressing table or bureau, will make a colorful and charming decorative spot in your boudoir setting. Sleek and graceful, this model will be the envy of all your friends. Made in exclusive Ivory Alacite, rich Coral, Blue and Green. Standard socket, push-thru switch, 17" high . . . SHADE #600—3" Ballerina described in shade section.

#G41—Delight your family, and those guests with one or a pair of this gracefully designed model. With sweeping leaf and flower decoration lending a feeling of height and slimness, this lamp gives your room a feeling of distinctive sophistication. #G41 matches table lamp #G319 perfectly and comes in Alacite, Blue, Coral and Chartreuse ...SHADE #551—10" Flared Bell, described in shade section.

Aladdin
floor lamps

Here are floor lamps for your every need. Distinctive appearance, a wide range of styles and surprisingly moderate prices now make it possible for you to obtain just the lamps you've been wanting for halls, living and dining rooms. Bridge lamps, luxurious Torcheres, standard floor lamps and the popular new Lounge styles so often used in pairs. Well designed and with rigid cast spindles of finest quality, Aladdin lamps are designed to give you many years of service and satisfaction.

SHADE 551

LAMP G42

SHADE 600

SHADE 1554

LAMP G42

LAMP G43

#G42—Clever combination of ball-type base blending skillfully through a flower transition into a graceful column. You'll love the looks of this charming lamp and it comes in a fascinating selection of gay colors: Alacite, soft Blue, luscious Chartreuse and Coral . . . SHADE #600—10″ Ballerina in matching colors described in shade section.

#G43—This lamp is like the preceding model in its unusual design treatment but is not as tall. Where a shorter type of boudoir lamp is required for your decorative scheme, this style is both useful and beautiful. There's a choice of fired-on ceramic finishes in Alacite, Blue, Coral and Chartreuse . . . SHADE #1554—Described in shade section.

SHADE 1554

LAMP G43

#3601—Here's a stunning new six-way floor lamp with a modern white metal stand with smooth spindle and a beautifully designed cluster arrangement. Perfect for your living room, hall, or wherever a floor lamp is needed, it comes in a lustrous Silver Plated finish or in a soft gleaming Brass Plated finish . . . SHADE #500 — 19' Dubonnet, is described in the shade section.

#3602—Another addition to the Aladdin Floor Lamp family. With its six-way control and its graceful design, you'll be proud to own this fine example of Aladdin workmanship. Made with the new "white metal" and reeded spindle section, it is smoothly patterned and is all spray painted in Ivory and Gold with Deep Bronze Candlize. Truly an outstanding lamp masterpiece . . . SHADE #3310 — 19" Dubonnet, is described in shade section.

floor lamps

*3698—The unusual treatment of the ornamental candle arms and richly designed base and spindle, makes this floor lamp the choice of decorators in many homes. 60˝ high and equipped with Mogul socket and 3 candle arms with standard sockets, it is here shown in beautiful Ivory and Gold finish . . . SHADE #R472—19˝ bottom diameter. Stretched fabric in White or Tan with smart, thin braid trim, or any other 19˝ shade can be used.

*3698—This is the same beautifully designed floor lamp, here shown in rich Oxidized Bronze with drum type shade . . . SHADE *500—Whip-O-Lite shade with draped fabric trim. 19˝ bottom diameter. Or any other 19˝ shade can be used.

*3698—Showing the versatility of this exquisitely designed lamp so popular with people everywhere, it is here shown in the all-Silver finish and with a fluted shade . . . SHADE *2310 —The rhythmic pattern of this fluted shade is excellent with this lamp, though any other 19˝ shade may be used. The 19˝ Whip-O-Lite SHADE *2310 is washable of course.

#4598—Another richly designed, luxurious Torchere in Silver or Oxidized Bronze finishes. Shown with T-171—16˝ embossed and deeply fluted glass reflector. Also available with T-168 or T-170 glass reflectors. Mogul socket with turn-knob switch. Height: 62˝. Packed one to a carton.

#4598 — Another richly designed, luxurious Torchere in Silver or Oxidized Bronze finishes. Shown with T-170—16˝ embossed with floral designed glass reflector. Also available with T-168 or T-171 glass reflectors. Mogul socket with turn-knob switch. Height: 62˝. Packed one to a carton.

SHADE 500

SHADE 1546

SHADE 1547

SHADE B483

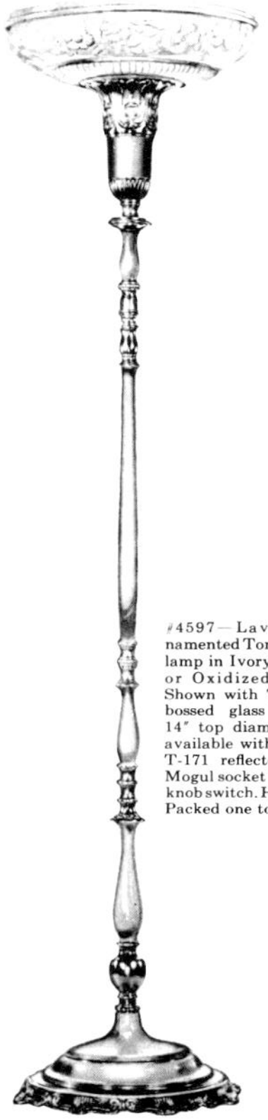

T168

SHADE 1547

LAMP 4597

LAMP 1097

LAMP 1097

LAMP 1097

LAMP 2093

#4597—Lavishly ornamented Torchere floor lamp in Ivory and Gold or Oxidized Bronze. Shown with T-168 embossed glass reflector, 14″ top diameter. Also available with T-170 or T-171 reflectors. Has Mogul socket with turn-knob switch. Height: 62″. Packed one to a carton.

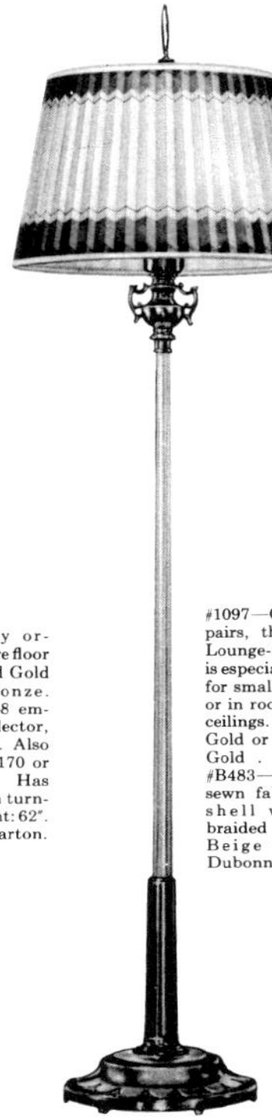

#1097—Often used in pairs, this 56″ high Lounge-type Lamp is especially desirable for small apartments or in rooms with low ceilings. In Ivory and Gold or Maroon and Gold . . . SHADE #B483—18″. Hand-sewn fabric in Egg-shell with Gold braided trim or in Beige with deep Dubonnet trim.

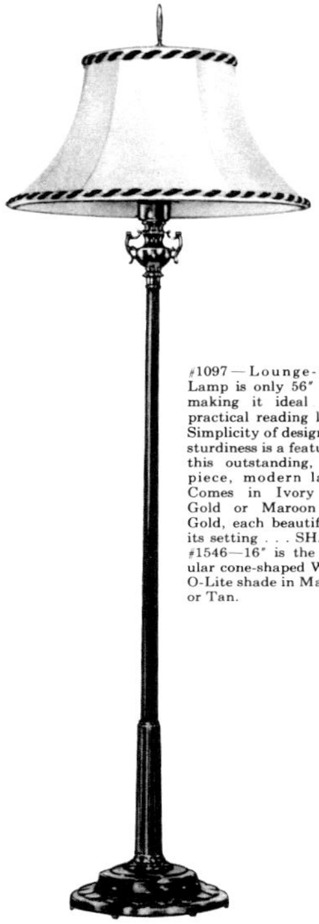

#1097—Lounge-type Lamp is only 56″ high, making it ideal as a practical reading lamp. Simplicity of design and sturdiness is a feature of this outstanding, one-piece, modern lamp. Comes in Ivory and Gold or Maroon and Gold, each beautiful in its setting . . . SHADE #1546—16″ is the popular cone-shaped Whip-O-Lite shade in Maroon or Tan.

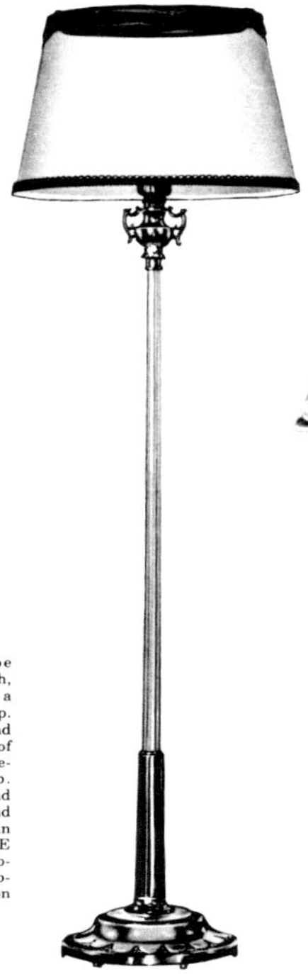

#1097—Lounge-type Lamp is rapidly gaining in popularity. Interior decorators use these lamps lavishly for many purposes as their 56″ height is so practical in small apartments or rooms with low ceilings. Available in Ivory and Gold or Maroon and Gold. . . . SHADE #500—16″ is a lovely Whip-O-Lite shade with fabric top trim. Comes in Dubonnet, Blue, Green, Rose and Tan.

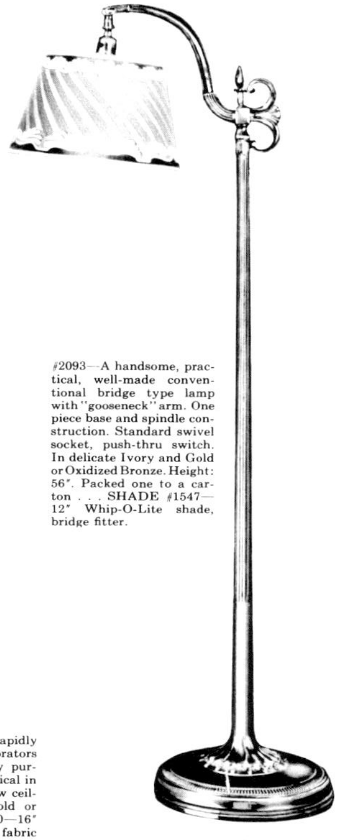

#2093—A handsome, practical, well-made conventional bridge type lamp with "gooseneck" arm. One piece base and spindle construction. Standard swivel socket, push-thru switch. In delicate Ivory and Gold or Oxidized Bronze. Height: 56″. Packed one to a carton . . . SHADE #1547—12″ Whip-O-Lite shade, bridge fitter.

G-330

G-331

G-334

G-331

G-331

G-332

G-333

G330—In classic Chinese style with an oriental symbol as an integral part of the design. Pedestal is Gold-banded. Comes with extra-wide harp to accommodate standard or reflec-tor-type bulb and has push-thru switch and socket. Height: 28½". Available in Copper Brown, Char-treuse, Chinese Red or Forest Green in fired-on Ceramic. SHADE #808 is 16" drum style in matching colors.

Lamp G330 shown with SHADE #R496, 16", fabric is also available in matching colors.

G331—A beautiful Vase design in contrasting colors. Illuminated base casts a lovely, soft glow. Comes equipped with extra-wide harp to accommodate standard or reflector-type bulb and has 3-way turn-knob switch. Height: 24½". Comes in Black and Mother of Pearl Luster with SHADE #807, 14", laminated taffeta with black lace design.

Lamp G331—In Chinese Red and Mother of Pearl Luster or Forest Green and Green Luster shown with SHADE #R495, 16", fabric in match-ing colors.

Lamp G331—In Chinese Red and Mother of Pearl Luster or Forest Green and Green Luster shown with SHADE #1604, 14", in colors to match.

G332—An inverted bud design en-circling the middle, forms two inter-esting cones in this attractive table lamp. Gold-banded. Has extra-wide harp to accommodate standard or reflector-type bulb and push-thru switch and socket. Height: 28½". Comes in fired-on Ceramic, Black, Chinese Red or Mother of Pearl. Shown with SHADE #R1602, 14" in colors to match.

G333—A graceful square-column shaped base. Has 3-way, turn-knob switch for use with 2-filament bulb. Pedestal is Gold-banded. Sculptured bas-relief figures are an attractive feature of this lamp. Height: 27½". Comes in fired-on Ceramic colors; Dubonnet, Forest Green or Gray. Shown with SHADE #809, 16", in colors to match.

G334—Shaped like lamp #G332, this attractively designed table lamp has a shorter harp to accommodate spe-cially-designed SHADE #602. Gold-banded. Equipped with push-thru switch and socket. Height: 28½". Comes in fired-on Ceramic, Gray, Forest Green or Dubonnet. SHADE #602 is 18" flared cone skirt model in colors to match.

G186—Rounded, illuminated base in Ivory Alacite with 3-way turn-knob switch. Lamp is richly decorated with all-over floral pattern. Shown with 12″ matching SHADE #909H. Overall height is 24½″.

G307—Illuminated base. Available in pastel Green, Golden Lustre or warm Coral with Ivory Alacite floral decoration. Metal pedestal in rich golden finish. Height: 24¾″. Has 3-way turn-knob switch. Shown with SHADE #2310, 16″, in colors to match.

G309—Illuminated, ball-type base available in Alacite, Coral Ceramic or Forest Green Ceramic. Extremely handsome with all-over leaf decoration and a lovely pedestal. Has 3-way turn-knob switch. Height: 24½″. Shown with SHADE #2311H, 12″, in matching colors.

Lamp G309 shown with SHADE #2312H, 12″. See Shade Section for colors.

G310—This has the same base and colors as Lamp G309 but with shorter harp. Many homes find this model especially good in pairs. Height: 21½″. Shown with SHADE #2311, 13″, of fluted Whip-O-Lite in matching colors.

G311—Traditional vase-on-pedestal design, illuminated base. Comes in all-over Golden Lustre, Alacite and Dubonnet or Alacite and Blue. Has 3-way turn-knob switch. Height: 26½″. SHADE #2310 in 14″ fluted Whip-O-Lite.

Lamp G311 shown with SHADE #500, 14″, Whip-O-Lite with fabric top trim.

G312—Stately vase-on-pedestal design with Gold-banded base. Comes in Ivory Alacite, Ivory Alacite and Green or Ivory Alacite and Maize. Push-thru switch. Height: 26½″. Shown with SHADE #500, 14″, drum style Whip-O-Lite with draped fabric trim in colors to match.

173

G319—A beautiful lamp with smooth, flowing lines. Matches perfectly, the exquisite Aladdin G41 Boudoir lamps. Fired-on Ceramic finish. Its leaf-motif base comes in Chartreuse, Blue, Coral or the exclusive Ivory Alacite. Push-thru switch and socket. Height: 25″. Shown with SHADE #551, 12″, flared bell in colors to match.

Lamp G319 shown with SHADE #600. An attractive 12″ Ballerina style in matching colors.

G322—Gracefully designed base comes in Ivory Alacite, or in fired-on Ceramic in choice of Chinese Red, Forest Green or Gray. Push-thru switch and socket. Height: 28¼″. Shown with SHADE #R494, 14″, fabric. Comes in matching colors

Lamp G322 shown with SHADE #1562 available in the 14″ popular drum style with beautiful leaf decoration in colors to match. Fluted SHADE #2312, 14″, and SHADE #805, 14″, taffeta laminated, also available in colors to match.

G323—With its repeated lines and handsome pedestal, here is a lamp that will high-spot any room. Fired-on Ceramic finish in Coral, Gold Lustre or pastel Green. Has illuminated base and 3-way turn-knob switch. Height: 28″. Extra-wide harp to accommodate standard or reflector-type bulb. Shown with SHADE #1601, 14″, in colors to match.

G324—Illuminated base imparts a warm, decorative glow and provides just enough light to relieve eye-strain when viewing television. Hammered background effect with fired-on Ceramic colors in choice of Glossy Black, Chartreuse or Chinese Red. 3-way turn-knob switch and extra-wide harp to accommodate standard or reflector-type bulbs. Height: 28″. Shown with SHADE #806, 14″, available in Chartreuse or Chinese Red.

Lamp G324 shown with SHADE #1601, 14″, Dubonnet to match the Black base.

G325—This is a popular ball-type base, always such a favorite with homemakers. Traditional in style, it blends equally well with modern furniture and drapery. Illuminated base providing a soft glow, is an important feature of this attractive lamp. Choice of Coral or Forest Green fired-on Ceramic. 3-way turn-knob switch. Height: 29″. Shown with SHADE #601H, 16″, flared bell design.

G-319

G-319

G-322

G-322

G-323

G-325

G-324

G-324

G-326

G-328

M-250

M-250

M-252

M-250

M-251

M-251

G326—Perfect with either traditional or modern furnishings. Has illuminated base that goes so well with television viewing, and 3-way turn-knob switch. Height: 22″. Comes in fired-on Ceramic, Chartreuse or Chinese Red. Shown with SHADE #1564, 18″, in matching colors and ʼrimmed at collar with interlaced etallic cord.

G328—All-over heart-shaped pattern skillfully embossed, gives this lamp a truly distinctive texture. Equipped with push-thru switch and socket. Height: 29½″. Available in Ivory Alacite, or fired-on Ceramic, Chinese Red or Forest Green. Pedestal is Gold-banded. Shown with SHADE #1600, 14″, in matching colors.

M250—Attractive metal base lamp finished in gleaming Silver. The rich elegance of this Aladdin Masterwork blends harmoniously with all furniture styles. Push-thru switch and socket. Uses standard or reflector-type bulb. Height: 28¾″. Shown with SHADE #1561. A 14″ drum with alternating color stripes.

Lamp M250 shown with SHADE #801, 14″, with Shantung fabric laminated on Whip-O-Lite.

Lamp M250 shown with SHADE #R494, 14″, fabric comes in three lovely colors. See Shade Section.

M251—Add a touch of Early American with this authentic replica. Electric of course, though it looks just like an old-fashioned kerosene lamp. All brass in a lustrous polished brass finish. Height: 23½″. Shown with SHADE #144, 14″, has Early American decorative motif.

Lamp M251 shown with glass SHADE #702, 10″, shade available in Red or Green.

M252—Another all-metal lamp with 3-way turn-knob switch, in choice of four finishes: Copper Plated with Maroon Antique, Gold Plated with Black Antique, Maroon and Gold, or Silver Plated with Black Antique. Has 3-way turn-knob switch, for use with 2-filament bulb. Height: 26½″. Shown with SHADE #1603, 14″, in matching colors.

table lamps

certified

G285-C—Created to meet the rigid specifications established by the Certified Lamp Makers, this graceful model (and all other Aladdin Certified Lamps) is designed to give maximum lighting performance. Comes in Ivory Alacite with G-E Trigger Ring socket and switch. Certified metal and glass reflector. Height: 26″. Shown with SHADE #B477-C, 16″, White fabric with draped trim.

G295-CD—Another Certified Aladdin Lamp with delicate floral design on exclusive Ivory Alacite. Certified metal and glass reflector. Has the G-E Trigger Ring socket and switch approved by Underwriters' Laboratory, tested to assure long, safe operation. Height: 27½″. Shown with hand-sewn fabric SHADE #B482-C, 16″.

Above illustration shows the glass and metal reflector which is exclusive on all Certified Lamps. Features the new G-E Trigger Ring socket and switch.

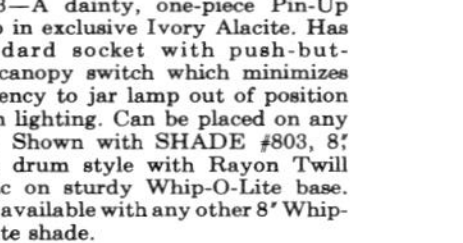

pin-up lamps

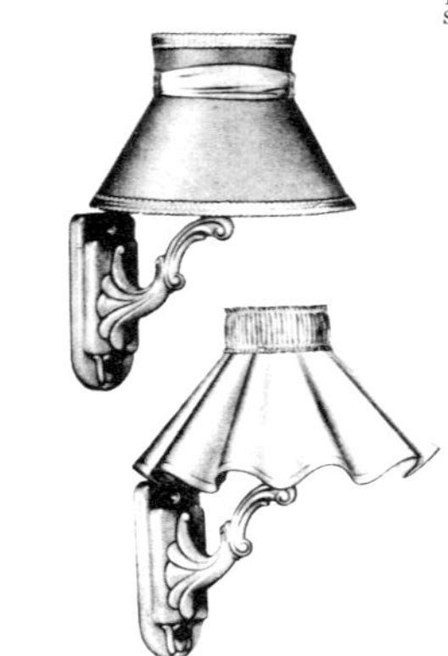

G353—A dainty, one-piece Pin-Up lamp in exclusive Ivory Alacite. Has standard socket with push-button canopy switch which minimizes tendency to jar lamp out of position when lighting. Can be placed on any wall. Shown with SHADE #803, 8″ deep drum style with Rayon Twill fabric on sturdy Whip-O-Lite base. Also available with any other 8″ Whip-O-Lite shade.

G354—Charming and practical, this go-anywhere Pin-Up lamp serves a useful function in any home. One-piece construction. Comes in Ivory Alacite only and has standard socket with push-button canopy switch. Shown with SHADE #551, 10″ flared bell style described in Shade Section. Also any 8″ Empire Shade.

Lamp G354 shown with SHADE #600, 10″ Ballerina style described in Shade Section. Also any 8″ Empire Shade.

Enchanting Aladdin Boudoir Lamps to create an atmosphere of charm and beauty. Here, where one drops day's dull care is a most important need for lamps that are friendly and soothing yet gay in design and color . . . and a pair of exquisite Aladdin Boudoir Lamps are a source of pride when party guests arrive. Sell a pair for every bedroom . . . perfect for children's rooms, too. Show them to *every* lamp customer and sales will soar!

boudoir lamps

G46—A real conversation piece, charming for children's rooms. Base is beautifully sculptured figure of Cupid in fired-on Ceramic, Mother of Pearl, Blue, Coral or Forest Green. Has push-thru switch and socket. Height: 17″. Shown with SHADE #R1602, 8″, in corresponding colors.

B45—So luxurious and so useful for reading or radio-listening, truly a delightful Bed Lamp you will always enjoy. Rubber-covered wire and hooks fully protect your furniture from scratches and there's a convenient pull-chain socket. All SHADES are laminated taffeta and trimmed with braid and tassel fringe. Available in Eggshell, Rust, Gray, Forest Green, Chartreuse or Chinese Red.

G41—A pair of these gracefully designed Boudoir Lamps will delight your family and entrance your friends. With sweeping leaf and floral decoration emphasizing its height and slimness, this style adds a distinctive note of sophistication in any setting. G41 Boudoir Lamps match the Aladdin G319 Night Table Lamp perfectly and are available in Alacite, Blue, Coral or Chartreuse. Height: 17″. Shown with SHADE #600, 10″, in the Ballerina style in colors to match.

Lamp G41 shown with SHADE #551, 10″.

G43—Unusual in design, this lamp is most attractive. Clever combination of ball-type base blending skillfully through a flower transition into a slender and graceful column. There's a choice of fired-on Ceramic finishes in Alacite, Blue, Coral or Chartreuse. Height: 17″. Shown with SHADE #1554, 8″, in colors to match. SHADE #551, 10″, may also be used.

Lamp G43 shown with SHADE #600, 10″, Ballerina model in colors to match.

G44—A charming Boudoir "ball" lamp with Illuminated Base and 3-way turn-knob switch. With either a short or tall shade, it will enhance the entire decorative effect of any bedroom. Pedestal is Gold-banded, and base is available in fired-on Ceramic Chartreuse, Chinese Red, Rust or exclusive Alacite. Overall Height: 13″ with 8″ SHADE #803 as shown.

Lamp G44 shown with SHADE #804. Shade is 7″ modern cone-type of laminated taffeta in matching colors. Height of Lamp with Shade: 17″.

#1005—A popular lounge-type Floor Lamp. Has 3-way light control with standard base socket. Night-light in Mother of Pearl bowl below shade level. Has extra-wide harp for use with reflector-type bulb. Height: 60". Comes in Gray and Gold or Oxidized Bronze. Shown with SHADE #800, 19".

Lamp #1005 shown with fabric SHADE #R497, 19". Beige with Dubonnet trim.

#3605—Slim spindle on an extremely attractive pedestal makes this a very desirable addition to decorative plans. Equipped with Mogul socket and 3 candle arms with standard sockets. 10" glass reflector. Height: 60". Available in Gray and Gold, Ivory and Gold or Oxidized Bronze. Shown with SHADE #1567, 19".

#3605—Shown with SHADE #1603, 19", with attractive design printed over laminated foil. Any other 19" shade can also be used.

#3905—A simply designed yet attractive and very practical Floor Lamp. Comes in Ivory and Gold or Oxidized Bronze finish. Equipped with Mogul socket and 3 candle arms with standard sockets. Has beam night-light in head and 10" glass reflector. Height: 60". Shown with fabric SHADE #R497, 19", in Beige background with Dubonnet trim.

Lamp #3905 shown with SHADE #805, 19". Or any other 19" shade may be used.

#7005—A very modern Swing-Arm Bridge Lamp that's equally useful for games or reading. Easily adjustable, it is equipped with Mogul socket and 8″ glass reflector for efficient light distribution. Height: 56″. Comes in Gray and Gold, Ivory and Gold or Oxidized Bronze. Matches Floor Lamps #3605 and #3905. Shown with fabric SHADE #R497, 15″.

Lamp #7005 shown with SHADE #806, 15″.

#1097—This is the Lounge-Type Floor Lamp, so popular everywhere. Interior decorators often spot them in pairs, one on each side of the entrance to a room. The 56″ height is eye-pleasing and practical in small apartments and low-ceilinged rooms. Comes in Ivory and Gold or Maroon and Gold. Equipped with extra-wide harp for use with standard or reflector-type bulb. Packed 2 of like finish to a carton. Shown with SHADE #500, 16″.

#3601—A stunning, new Floor Lamp. Modern, white-metal stand with smooth, slender spindle and a beautifully designed cluster arrangement. One-piece base and spindle construction. Perfect wherever a floor lamp is needed; living room, study, library or hall. Comes in a lovely Silver plated finish or in a soft-gleaming Oxidized Bronze. Has Mogul socket and 10″ glass reflector. Height: 60″. Shown with SHADE #500, 19″. Of sturdy, long-lasting Whip-O-Lite with fabric ribbon trim.

Lamp #3601 shown with Fabric SHADE #R489, 19″. Comes in striking Chartreuse Celanese taffeta, rayon lined.

#2093—A handsome and most practical bridge type lamp with "gooseneck" arm. One-piece base and spindle construction, well-made and durable. Has standard swivel socket and push-thru switch. Height: 56″. Comes in delicate Ivory and Gold or in Oxidized Bronze. Shown with SHADE #1555, 12″ bridge fitter only in easy-to-clean Whip-O-Lite with attractive scroll pattern in Tan or Green.

#3602—A beautiful example of fine lamp-making. Its smooth, flowing lines and raised pattern, is further enhanced with lovely color. An excellent choice for any room setting. Has 10″ glass reflector, 3 candle arms and 3-way Mogul socket. One-piece base and spindle construction. Available in Forest Green and Gold, Gray and Gold, Ivory and Gold or in Bronze. Height: 60″. Shown with SHADE #1565, 19″, Whip-O-Lite. Packed 2 of like finish to a carton.

Lamp #3602 shown with SHADE #2312, 19″, fluted Whip-O-Lite. Packed 2 of like finish to a carton.

Lamp #3602 shown with SHADE #R494, 19″, fabric. Packed 2 of like finish to a carton.

#3603—One of the Floor Lamp designs resulting from Aladdin's nationwide survey of consumer preferences. Has 3-way Mogul socket and 3 candle arms with standard sockets. Pedestal repeats the interesting pattern of the candle arm cluster. One-piece base and spindle construction, 10″ glass reflector. Height: 60″. Comes in Ivory and Gold or Oxidized Bronze. Shown with SHADE #551, 19″.

#3604—In simulated, grained Bleached Wood finish, and highlighted with sparkling Gold, this handsome Floor Lamp blends beautifully in rooms where the predominant color scheme of walls or furniture is light in shade. With darker furniture or room color, the same lamp in an Oxidized Bronze finish, is excellent. Has 3-way Mogul socket, 3 candle arms and 10″ glass reflector. Height: 60″. Matches Swing-Arm Bridge Lamp #7004. Shown with SHADE #R491, 19″.

Lamp #3604 shown with SHADE #806, 19″, laminated fabric on Whip-O-Lite.

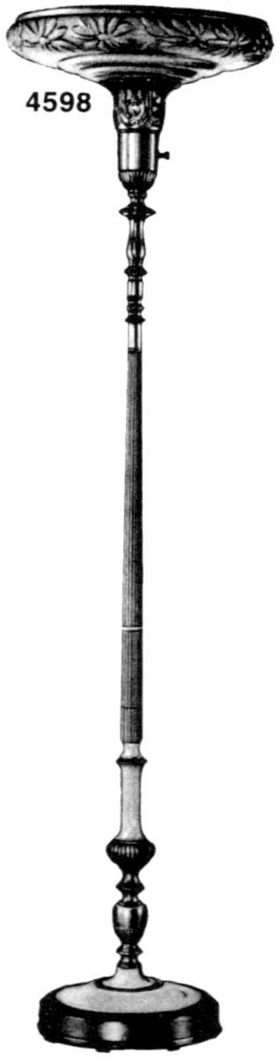

4598

T 168

4598

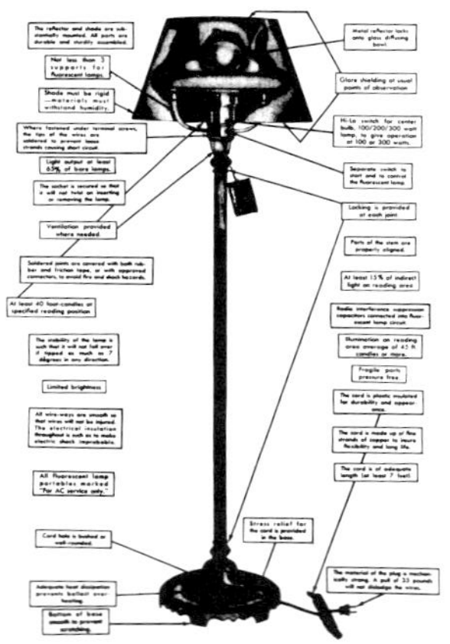

The C. L. M. Lamp

The features of Certified Lamps have been well publicized to lamp dealers within the trade and to the public at large. For your convenience, we repeat the features and specifications so that you may have them for ready reference.

7549

4898c

#4598—A richly designed, luxurious Torchere with 3-way Mogul socket. Height: 62″. May be had in soft Oxidized Bronze or gleaming Silver finish, or Ivory and Gold. Shown with REFLECTOR #T-171. Glass, 16″, embossed and beautifully fluted.

Shown alone, is REFLECTOR #T-168, another lovely, embossed, bowl-type glass, 14″ top diameter size.

Torchere #4598 shown with REFLECTOR #T-172, 16″, has beautiful embossed swirl pattern.

#7549—Cocktail Smoker. An extremely useful and beautiful Smoker, that anyone would be proud to own. At parties, or whenever guests drop in, this graceful piece with its smooth and sturdy table surface holds ash trays, cigarette boxes and drinks safely and comfortably. Height: 28¼″. Cast in White Metal, polished and plated, this stand is available in Oxidized Bronze or lovely Silver.

#7549A—Cocktail Smoker cast in durable White Metal and finished in three color combinations to match the #3602 Floor Lamp. Height: 28¼″. May be had in Forest Green and Gold, Gray and Gold or Ivory and Gold.

certified lamp

#4898C—A richly designed, luxuriously finished Certified Lamp. Has Circ-line Fluorescent tube and G-E Trigger Ring socket and switch, Certified metal and glass reflector. Height: 60″. Comes in Silver or Oxidized Bronze finishes. Shown with SHADE #R479-C, 19″, fabric with glare shielding at usual points of observation and meets all CLM specifications.

LAMP G336   SHADE 811

LAMP G337   SHADE 1571

G336 — Shown at far left with SHADE #811. The smooth flowing lines of this graceful gourd-type lamp makes it especially popular. Using a standard 9″ harp, this lamp comes in beautiful fired-on Ceramic colors; Dusty Rose, Pearl Luster, or Tan, each with Gold band trim. Equipment includes push-thru socket and switch. Height: 28½″.

G337—Shown at left with SHADE #1571. A most unusual Table Lamp with deep fluted motif set off with a wide decorative band or collar. Comes equipped with 10″ Bolite harp for use with standard or reflector-type bulb, and push-thru socket and switch. Available in Alacite, Chartreuse, Chinese Red, or Tan finishes with Gold band. Height: 28″.

lighting for television

According to latest authentic reports (November 15, 1950), there are already 8½ million television sets in use in 63 areas. Thus, millions have introduced into their homes a new element of entertainment which is also an article of home decoration. Placing of a TV set within a room is a matter of personal taste and convenience, but all users face the problem of proper room illumination. Strong contrast between the bright television screen and dark surrounding areas should be avoided in order to avoid eyestrain. Table lamps, especially those with lighted bases, are ideal for this purpose. Placed so that they do not reflect into the screen, they will provide enough illumination to prevent eye fatigue, and heighten program enjoyment. Avoid exceptionally bright spots of light on walls near set, but be sure there is sufficient general lighting.

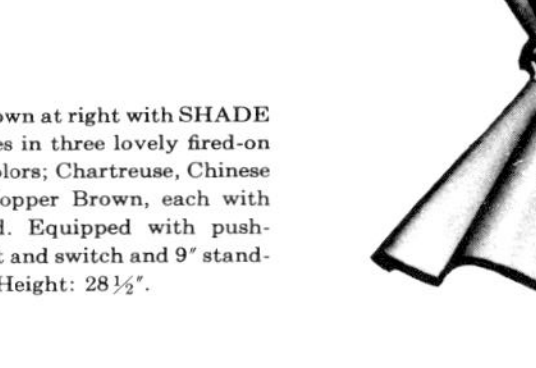

LAMP G379

G379—Shown at left is the lovely Aladdin Urn Lamp. Used everywhere by interior decorators as a design element within a room, the Urn is perfect for television viewing. Here in an exquisite show piece, is the answer to the problem of general illumination while enjoying television programs. Made in Aladdin's exclusive Alacite, the Urn casts a soft glow that is both practical and decorative. Used in pairs, Aladdin Urn Lamps are a new fashion note in useful, tasteful home lighting. Equipped with push-button canopy switch. Height: 14″, over-all.

G338—Shown at right with SHADE #R498. This handsome Table Lamp has the famous Aladdin Illuminated Base that casts a lovely glow. Has 3-way turn-knob switch and extra-wide harp for use with standard or reflector-type bulb. Comes in fired-on Chinese Red, Dusty Rose, Forest Green, or Tan, Ceramic finishes with Gold band. Height: 27″.

Lamp G338—Shown at right-center, this handsome pedestal-type lamp is here displayed with SHADE #1570.

Lamp G338—Shown at far right with SHADE #810.

LAMP G338   SHADE R498

LAMP G338   SHADE 1570

LAMP G338   SHADE 810

G339—Shown at right with SHADE #603, comes in three lovely fired-on Ceramic colors; Chartreuse, Chinese Red, or Copper Brown, each with Gold band. Equipped with push-thru socket and switch and 9′ standard harp. Height: 28½″.

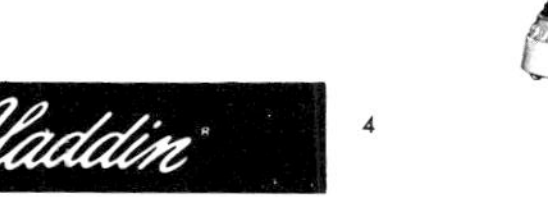

LAMP G339   SHADE 603

4

5

LAMP G186 SHADE 909H

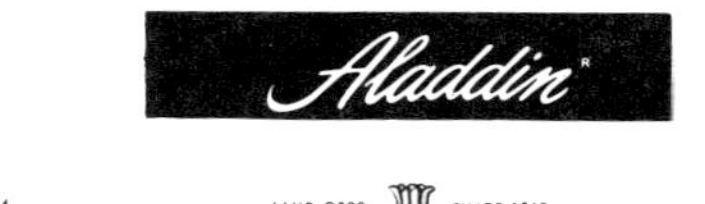

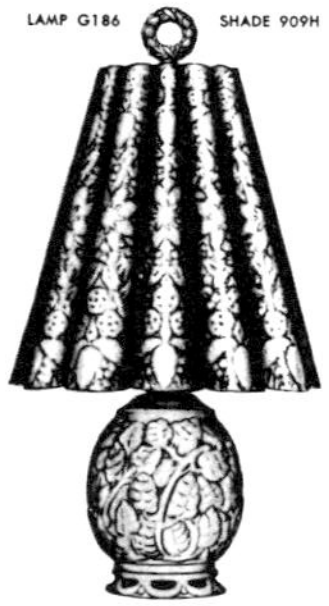

G186—Shown at left. Rounded, illuminated base in Ivory Alacite with 3-way turn-knob switch. Lamp is richly decorated with all-over leaf pattern. Shown with 12″ matching SHADE #909H. Height: 24½″, overall.

G310—Shown at right. This has the same base and colors as Lamp G309 but with shorter harp. Many homes find this model especially good in pairs. Height: 21½″. Shown with SHADE #2311, 13″, of fluted Whip-O-Lite in matching colors.

LAMP G310 SHADE 2311

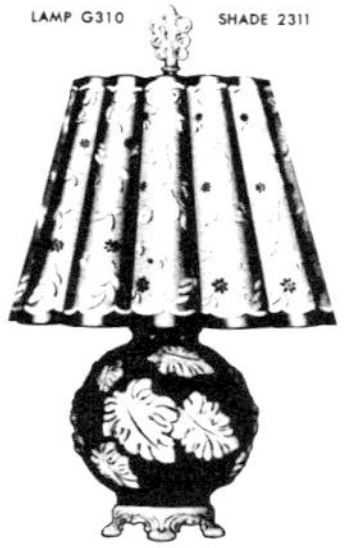

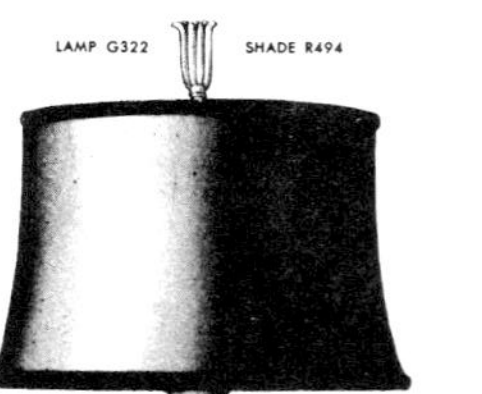

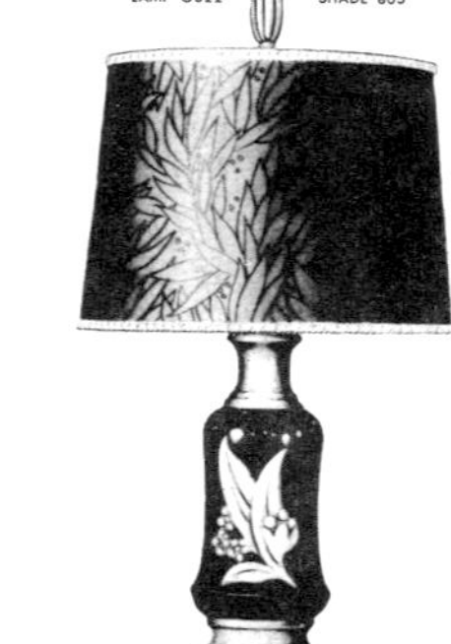

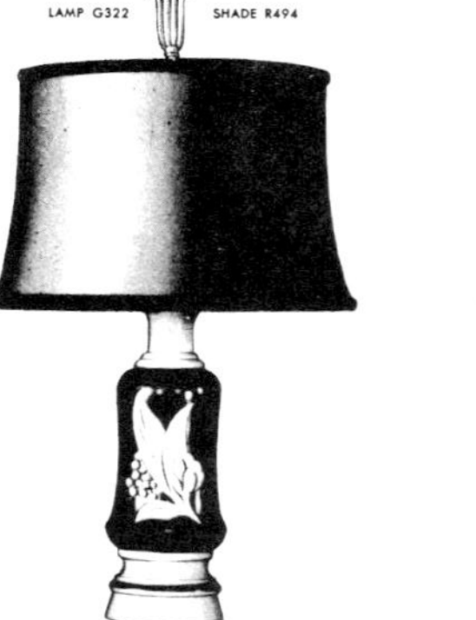

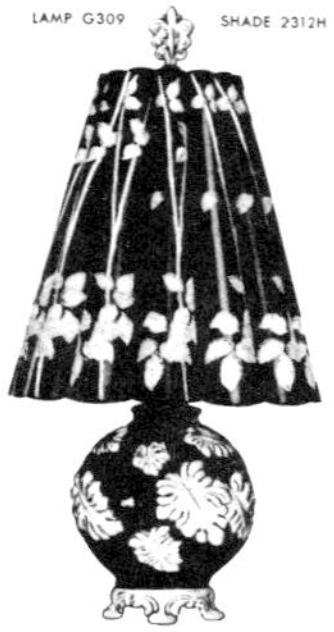

G309—Shown at right. Illuminated, ball-type base available in Alacite, or fired-on Ceramic colors; Coral, or Forest Green. Extremely handsome with all-over leaf decoration and a lovely pedestal. Has 3-way turn-knob switch. Height: 24½″. Shown with SHADE #2311H, 12″, in matching colors.

Lamp G309 shown at far right with SHADE #2312H, 12″. See Shade Section for colors.

LAMP G309 SHADE 2311H

LAMP G309 SHADE 2312H

Aladdin®

Aladdin®

G322—Shown at right. Gracefully designed base comes in Ivory Alacite, or in fired-on Ceramic in choice of Chinese Red, Forest Green or Gray. Push-thru switch and socket. Height: 28¼″. Shown with SHADE #R494, 14″, fabric. Comes in matching colors.

Lamp G322 shown at far right with SHADE #1562 which may be had in the 14″ popular drum style with beautiful leaf decoration in colors to match.

LAMP G322 SHADE R494

LAMP G322 SHADE 1562

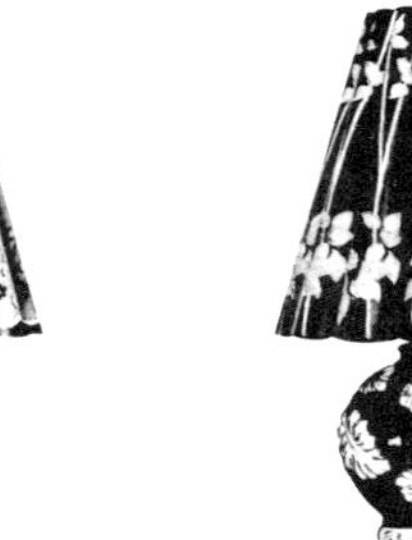

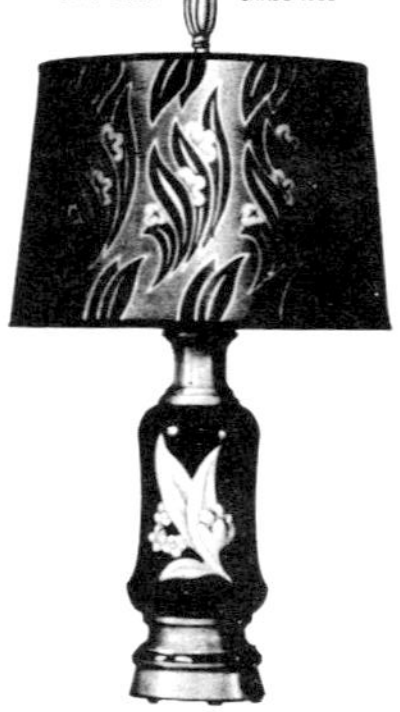

Lamp G322 is shown at right with 14″ SHADE #2312 beautifully fluted and available in matching colors.

Lamp G322 at far right is shown with SHADE #805, 14″ taffeta laminated. Also available in colors to match.

LAMP G322 SHADE 2312

LAMP G322 SHADE 805

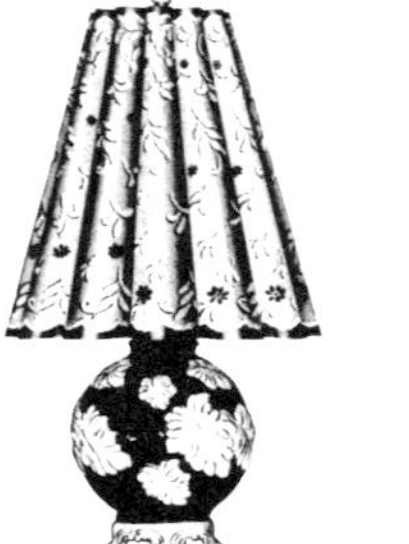

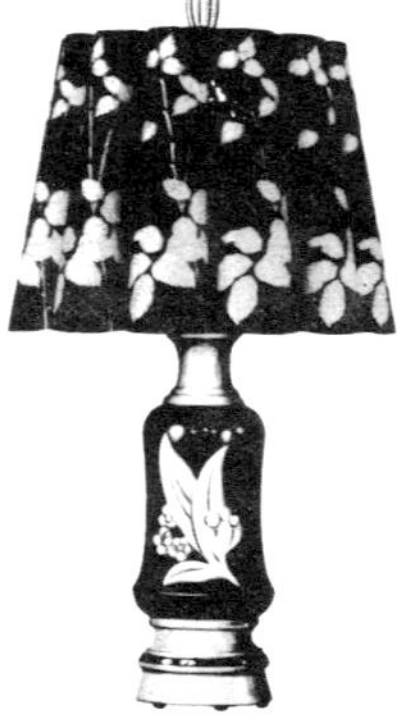

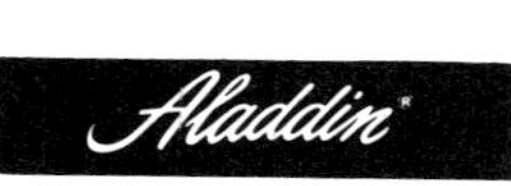

LAMP G324 — SHADE 806

LAMP G324 — SHADE 1601

G324 — Shown at far left. Illuminated base imparts a warm, decorative glow and provides enough light to relieve eye-strain when viewing television. Hammered background effect with fired-on Ceramic colors in choice of glossy Black, Chartreuse, or Chinese Red. 3-way turn-knob switch and extra-wide harp to accommodate standard or reflector-type bulb. Height: 28″. Shown with SHADE #806.

Lamp G324 shown at left with SHADE #1601, 14″, Dubonnet to match the Black base.

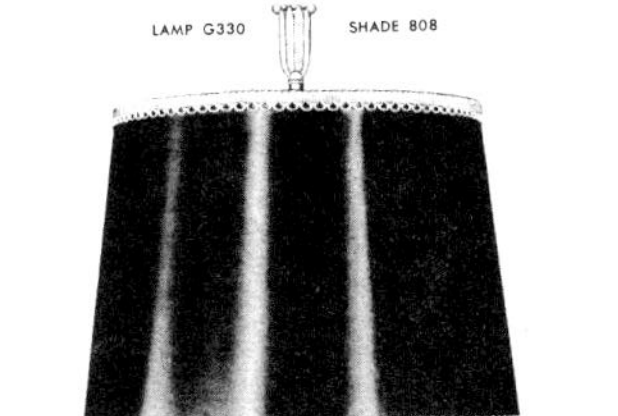

LAMP G329 — SHADE 603

G329—Shown at left. Has a lovely petal base which lends a flower-like grace to the entire lamp. Pedestal is Gold-banded. Has push-thru switch and socket. Height: 28″. Comes in beautiful fired-on Ceramic. Choice of Chartreuse, Chinese Red, or Copper Brown. SHADE #603 is of flared skirt design 18′ in matching colors.

G325—Shown at right. This is a popular ball-type base, always such a favorite with homemakers. Traditional in style, it blends equally well with modern furniture and drapery. Illuminated base, providing a soft glow, is an important feature of this attractive lamp. Choice of Coral, or Forest Green fired-on Ceramic. 3-way turn-knob switch. Height: 29″. Shown with SHADE #601H, 16″, flared bell design.

G326—Shown at far right. Perfect with either traditional or modern furnishings. Has illuminated base that goes so well with television viewing, and 3-way turn-knob switch. Height: 22″. Comes in fired-on Ceramic finishes, Chartreuse, or Chinese Red. Shown with SHADE #1564, 18″, in matching colors and trimmed at collar with interlaced metallic cord.

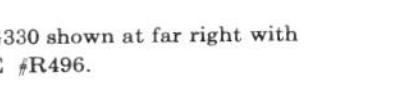

LAMP G325 — SHADE 601H

LAMP G326 — SHADE 1564

G330—Shown at right. In classic Chinese style with an oriental symbol as an integral part of the design. Pedestal is Gold-banded. Comes with extra-wide harp to accommodate standard or reflector-type bulb and has push-thru switch and socket. Height: 28½″. Available in Copper Brown, Chartreuse, Chinese Red, or Forest Green in fired-on Ceramic. SHADE #808 is 16″ drum style in matching colors.

Lamp G330 shown at far right with SHADE #R496.

LAMP G330 — SHADE 808

LAMP G330 — SHADE R496

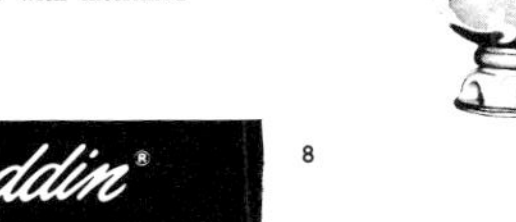

8

9

G331—Shown at far left. A beautiful Vase design in contrasting colors. Illuminated base casts a lovely soft glow. Comes equipped with extra-wide harp to accommodate standard or reflector-type bulb and has 3-way turn-knob switch. Height: 24½". Comes in Black and Mother of Pearl Luster. SHADE #807, 14", laminated taffeta with Black lace is especially designed to match this distinctive base.

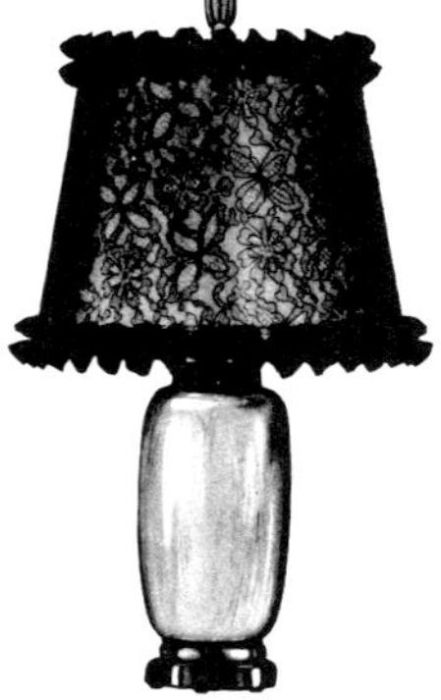

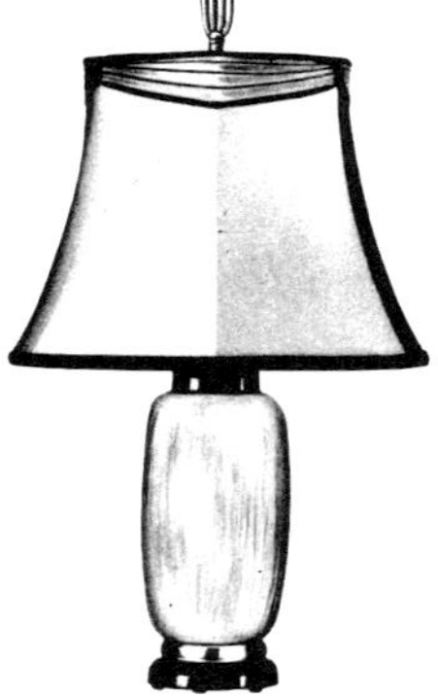

Lamp G331—Shown at left center. Comes in Chinese Red and Mother of Pearl Luster, or Forest Green and Green Luster. Shown with SHADE #R495.

Lamp G331—Shown at left with SHADE #1604. Comes in Chinese Red and Mother of Pearl Luster, or Forest Green and Green Luster.

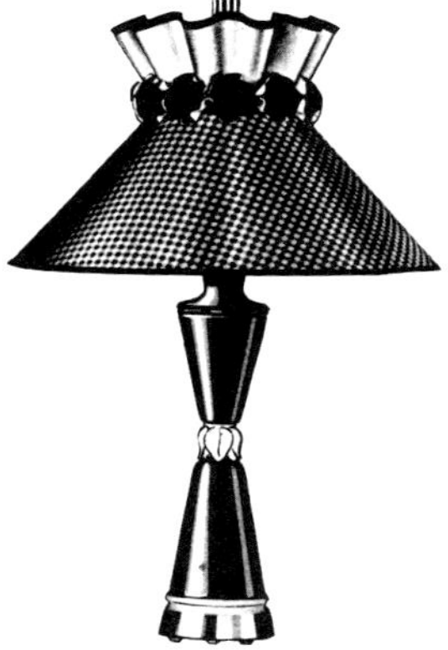

G334—Shown at left. This popular style, often referred to as the "hourglass" is very popular everywhere. Equipped with push-thru switch and socket. Height: 28½". Comes in fired-on Ceramic colors; Gray, Forest Green, or Dubonnet, each Gold-banded. Shown with SHADE #602.

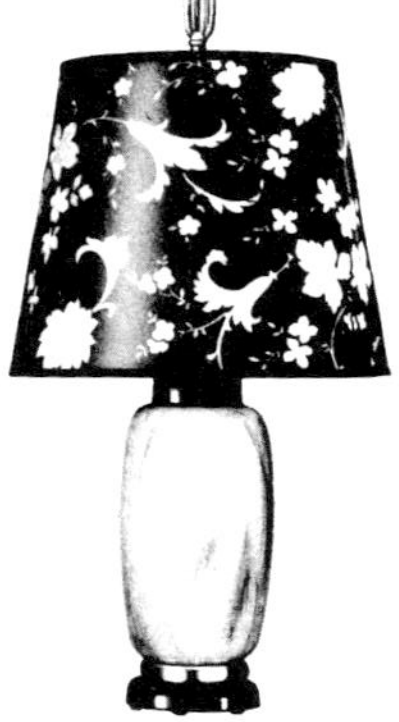

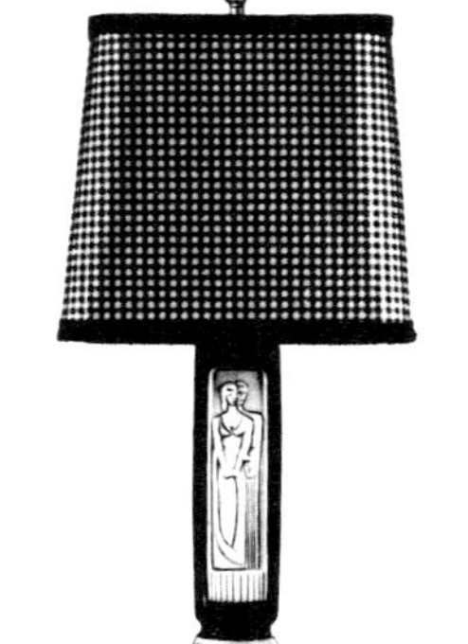

G332—Shown at right. An inverted bud design encircling the middle, forms two interesting cones in this attractive table lamp. Gold-banded. Has extra-wide harp to accommodate standard or reflector-type bulb and push-thru switch and socket. Height: 28½". Comes in fired-on Ceramic colors; Black, Chinese Red, or Mother of Pearl. Shown with SHADE #R1602, 14", in colors to match.

G333—Shown at far right. A graceful square-column shaped base. Has 3-way, turn-knob switch for use with 2-filament bulb. Pedestal is Gold-banded. Sculptured bas-relief figures are an attractive feature of this lamp. Height: 27½". Comes in fired-on Ceramic colors; Dubonnet, Forest Green, or Gray. Shown with SHADE #809.

M250—Shown at right. Attractive metal base lamp finished in gleaming Silver. The rich elegance of this Aladdin Masterwork blends harmoniously with all furniture styles. Push-thru switch and socket. Uses standard or reflector-type bulb. Height: 28¾". Shown with SHADE #1561.

Lamp M250 shown at far right with SHADE #801.

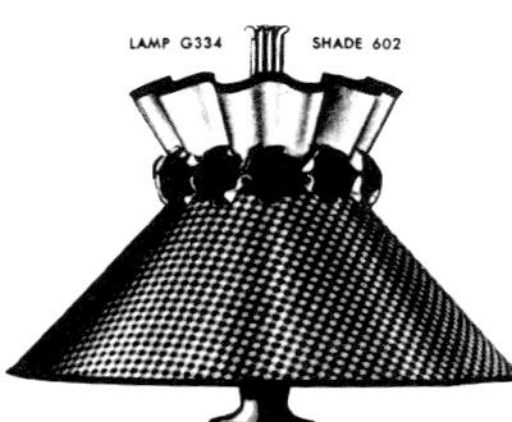

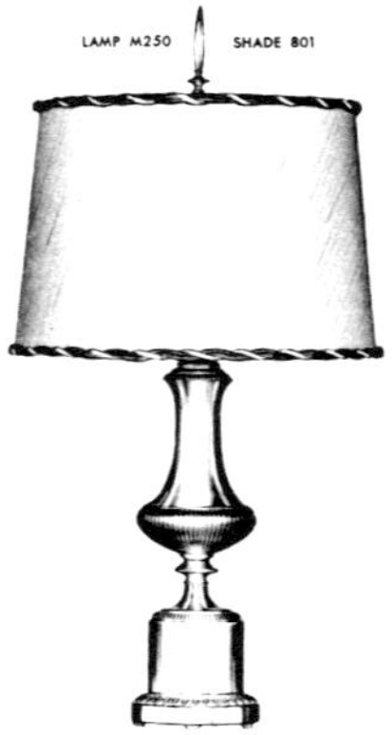

LAMP M251 — SHADE 144

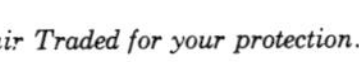

LAMP M251 — SHADE 702

M251—Shown at far left. Add a touch of Early American with this authentic replica. Electric of course, though it looks just like an old-fashioned kerosene lamp. All brass in a lustrous polished brass finish. Height: 23½". Shown with SHADE #144, 14", has Early American decorative motif.

Lamp M251 shown at left, with glass SHADE #702, 10" Shade available in Red or Green.

LAMP M252 — SHADE 1603

M252—Shown at right. Another all-metal lamp in choice of four finishes; Copper, Gold, Maroon, or Silver. Has 3-way turn-knob switch, for use with 2-filament bulb. Height: 26½". Shown with SHADE #1603, 14".

RANCH HOUSE ELECTRIC LAMPS

Here are the famous *Aladdin* HOPALONG CASSIDY Ranch House Lamps

that have the small-fry buckaroos absolutely Hoppy-eyed. The same loyal

Hoppy fans who buy Hoppy-branded items by the millions, are making

these handsome lamps literally hop off store shelves everywhere. Just the

thing to decorate a boy's or girl's room, they're sure-fire added sales

volume for your department. *Here's your opportunity to cash in*

on the greatest phenomena in the history of merchandising!

Fair Traded for your protection.

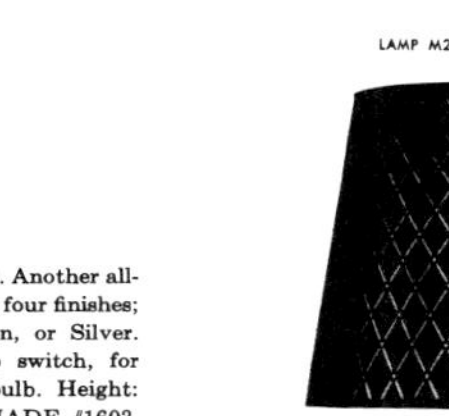

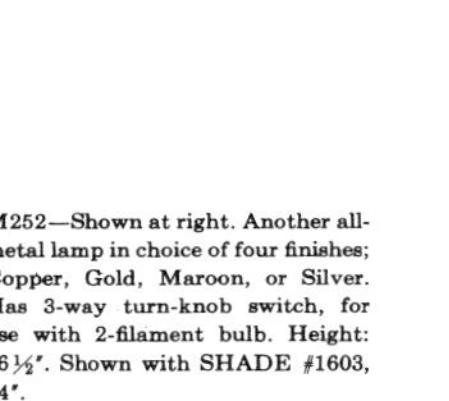

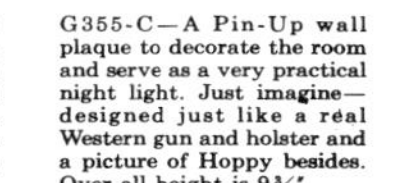

G335-C—A wonderful table lamp with sculptured head of Hoppy's horse, "Topper." The shade shows Hoppy and his pal, "California." Height: 27¼".

G47-C—Here's a beauty with Hoppy reproduced in full-color on both the base and shade. What's more, the base lights up. Every youngster will want one. Height: 17¼".

G378-C—Something really unusual, a Lighted Urn. A charming decorative touch in brother's or sister's room and there's a picture of Hopalong Cassidy that glows in full color when the urn is lighted. Height: 7½".

G355-C—A Pin-Up wall plaque to decorate the room and serve as a very practical night light. Just imagine—designed just like a real Western gun and holster and a picture of Hoppy besides. Over-all height is 9¾".

LAMP 203R SHADE 814

LAMP G340R SHADE 450R

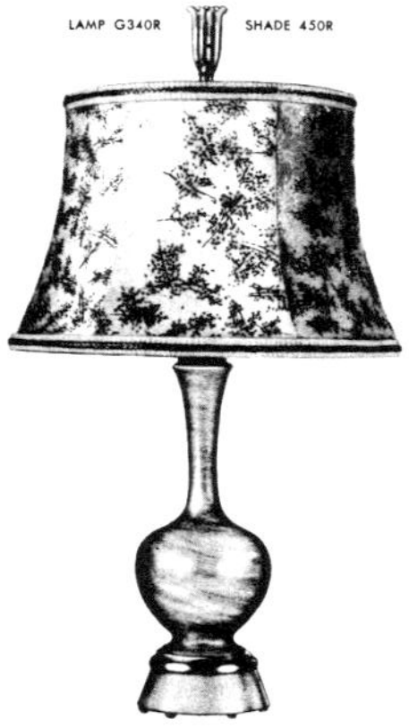

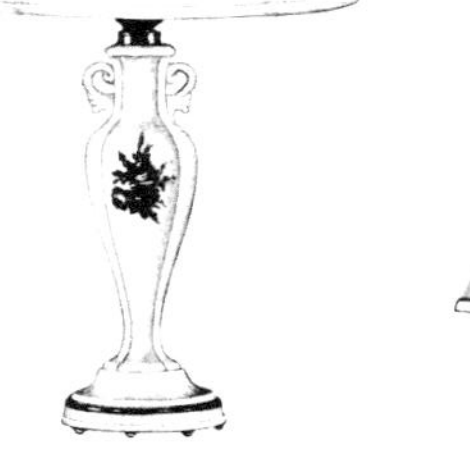

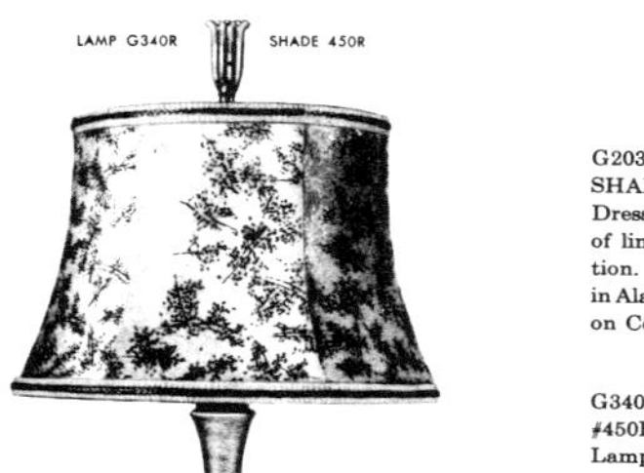

G203R—Shown at far left with SHADE #814. Here is a "Recipe" Dresser Lamp designed for beauty of line and practical light distribution. Has push-thru socket. Comes in Alacite, Coral, or Chartreuse fired-on Ceramic finishes. Height: 24½".

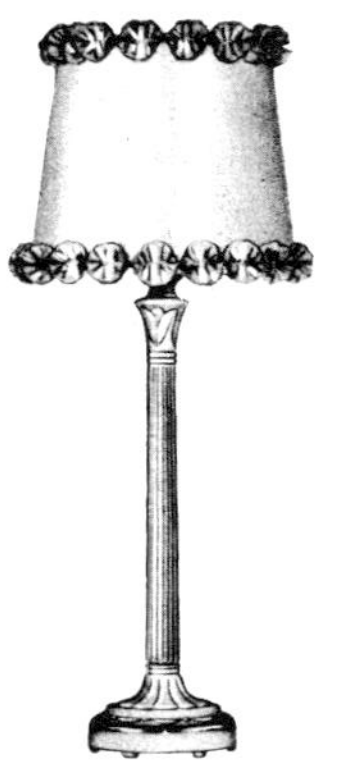

G340R—Shown at left with SHADE #450R. This is a vase-designed Table Lamp equipped with a 10" Wide harp and a turn-knob socket for use with 2-filament bulb. Available in Dusty Rose, Pearl Luster, or Tan finishes in fired-on Ceramic colors with Gold-band trim. Height: 28½".

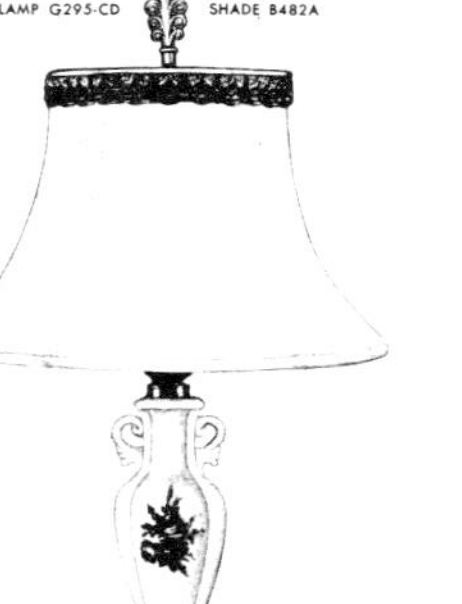

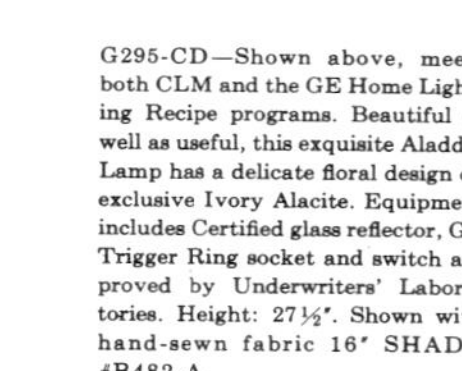

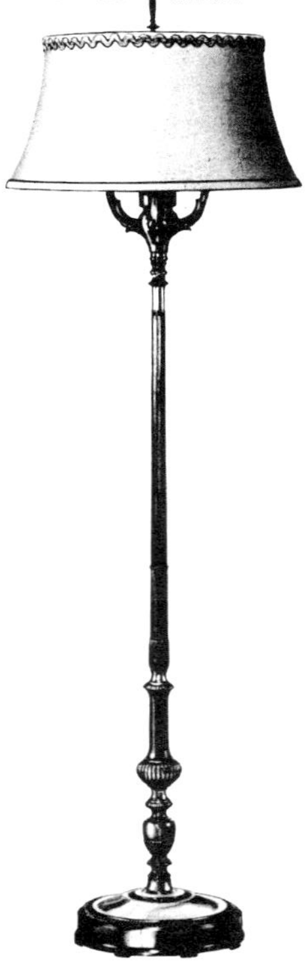

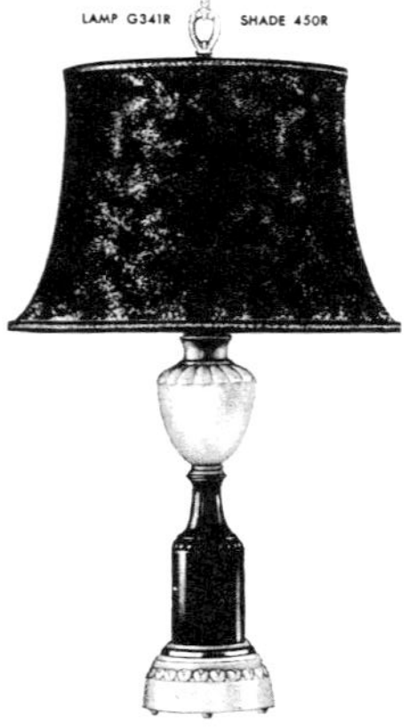

G341R—Shown at right with SHADE #450R. This Classic Table Lamp lends both dignity and charm to any decorative plan. Equipped with a 10" Wide harp and 3-way turn-knob switch for use with 2-filament bulb. Fulfills the requirements of the much publicized GE Lighting Recipe Program. Comes in attractive Chinese Red, Dusty Rose, Forest Green, or Tan in fired-on Ceramic finishes. Height: 27".

G342R—Shown at far right with SHADE #R496. Another "Recipe" Lamp designed for better lighting, better vision. More than that, this lovely lamp fits beautifully into the home as an object of true adornment. Has 10" Wide harp and 3-way socket for use with the 2-way filament bulb. Comes in Chinese Red, Copper Brown, Forest Green, or Chartreuse in fired-on Ceramic colors. Height: 28½".

LAMP G341R SHADE 450R

LAMP G342R SHADE R496

Aladdin®

Aladdin®

LAMP G295-CD SHADE B482A

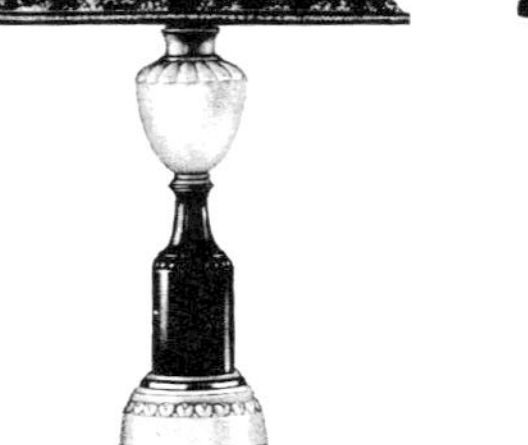

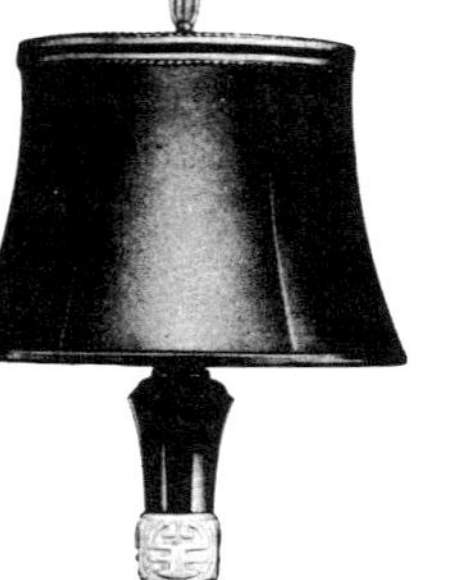

G295-CD—Shown above, meets both CLM and the GE Home Lighting Recipe programs. Beautiful as well as useful, this exquisite Aladdin Lamp has a delicate floral design on exclusive Ivory Alacite. Equipment includes Certified glass reflector, GE Trigger Ring socket and switch approved by Underwriters' Laboratories. Height: 27½". Shown with hand-sewn fabric 16" SHADE #B482-A.

#4898C—A richly designed, luxuriously finished Certified Lamp. Has Circline Fluorescent tube and GE Trigger Ring socket and switch, Certified glass reflector. Height: 60". Comes in Silver finish only. Shown with SHADE #R479-C, 19", fabric with glare shielding at usual points of observation and meets CLM and Home Lighting Recipe specifications.

LAMP 4898-C SHADE R479C

"Recipe" Lamps

With leading articles in national magazines such as Better Homes and Gardens, and supported by full-page advertisements in scores of magazines and newspapers, the General Electric Company is launching the greatest promotion of lighting for the home in the history of the industry. Public Utilities Companies in cooperation with Builders will use both new and remodeled homes to demonstrate proper lighting using both fixtures and portable lamps. Aladdin Industries, Incorporated, plays its part in this exciting promotion with its "Recipe" designed lamps, examples of which are shown in this Catalog. You can tie-in and benefit tremendously by showing Aladdin "Recipe" Lamps in your windows and/or your counter displays. Get behind this great program for bigger, more profitable Portable Lamp business from now on!

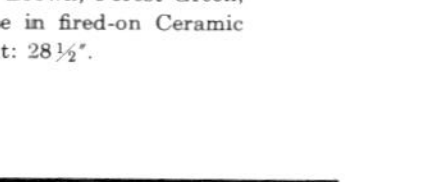

LAMP G48   SHADE R1602

LAMP G48   SHADE 1569

G48—Shown top left with SHADE #R1602. A charming Boudoir Lamp, bell-shaped and dainty, with raised leaf and floral design. Has push-thru socket and switch. Comes in Alacite and in fired-on Ceramic Blue, Chartreuse, and Coral colors. Height: 16″.

G48—Shown at bottom left with SHADE #1569.

Light and shadow . . . the fascinating

play of a bright spot of color,

texture, frilly fashion note on vanity table or dresser.

No wonder Aladdin Boudoir Lamps find such favor,

are so desirable . . . for the Aladdin Lamps shown in this section

are designed with a woman in mind . . . your customer.

LAMP G41 SHADE 600

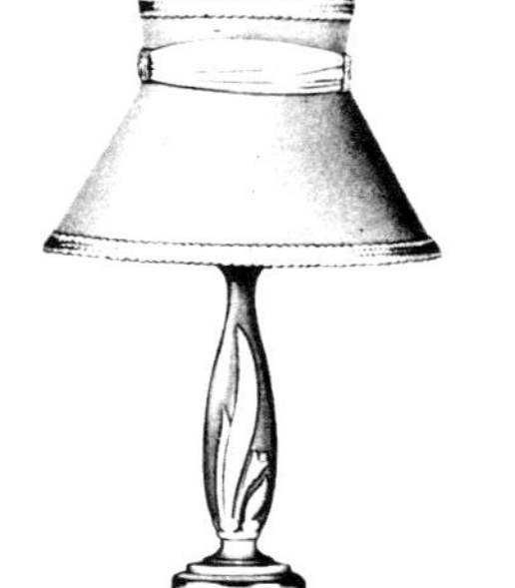

LAMP G41 SHADE 551

G41—Shown at far left. A pair of these gracefully designed Boudoir Lamps will delight your family and entrance your friends. With sweeping leaf and floral decoration emphasizing its height and slimness, this style adds a distinctive note of sophistication in any setting. G41 Boudoir Lamps are available in Alacite, Blue, Coral, or Chartreuse. Height: 17". Shown with SHADE #600, 10", in the Ballerina style in colors to match.

Lamp G41 shown at left with SHADE #551, 10".

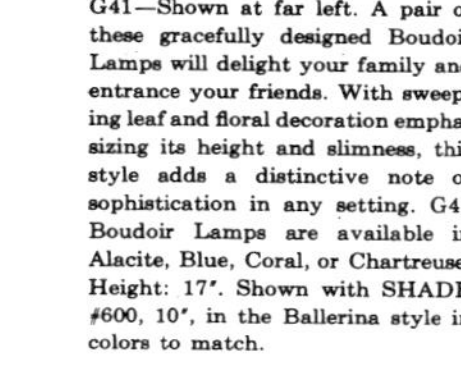

LAMP G44 SHADE 803

LAMP G44 SHADE 804

G44—Shown at far left. A charming Boudoir "ball" lamp with Illuminated Base and 3-way turn-knob switch. Pedestal is Gold-banded, and base is available in fired-on Ceramic Chartreuse, Chinese Red, Rust, or exclusive Alacite. Height: 13" with 8" SHADE #803 as shown.

Lamp G44 shown at left with SHADE #804. Shade is 7" modern cone-type of laminated taffeta in matching color. Height: 17".

G43—Shown at right. Unusual in design, this lamp is most attractive. Clever combination of ball-type base blending skillfully through a flower transition into a slender and graceful column. There's a choice of fired-on Ceramic finishes in Alacite, Blue, or Coral. Height: 17". Shown with SHADE #600, 10", Ballerina.

Lamp G43 shown at far right, this page, with SHADE #803, 8".

LAMP G43 SHADE 600

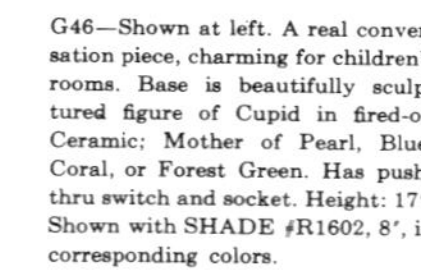

LAMP G43 SHADE 803

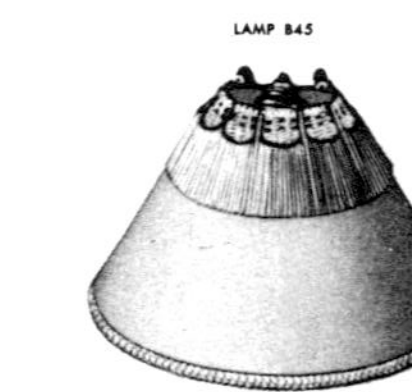

LAMP G46 SHADE R1602

G46—Shown at left. A real conversation piece, charming for children's rooms. Base is beautifully sculptured figure of Cupid in fired-on Ceramic; Mother of Pearl, Blue, Coral, or Forest Green. Has push-thru switch and socket. Height: 17". Shown with SHADE #R1602, 8", in corresponding colors.

B45—Shown at right. So luxurious and so useful for reading or radio-listening, truly a delightful Bed Lamp you will always enjoy. Rubber-covered wire and hooks fully protect your furniture from scratches and there's a convenient pull-chain socket. All shades are laminated taffeta and trimmed with braid and tassel fringe. Available in Eggshell, Rust, Gray, Forest Green, Chartreuse, or Chinese Red.

LAMP B45

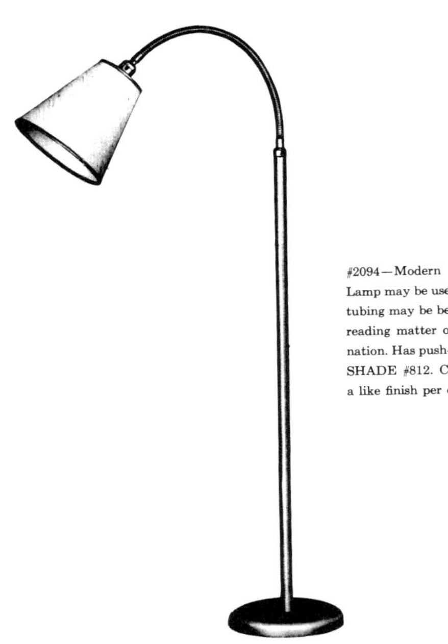

#2094—Modern as tomorrow, this flexible-tube Aladdin Floor Lamp may be used for either direct or indirect lighting effects. The tubing may be bent into graceful curves and light concentrated on reading matter or directed against the ceiling for general illumination. Has push-thru socket and switch and especially designed 9" SHADE #812. Comes in Mahogany, or Gray and packed two of a like finish per carton.

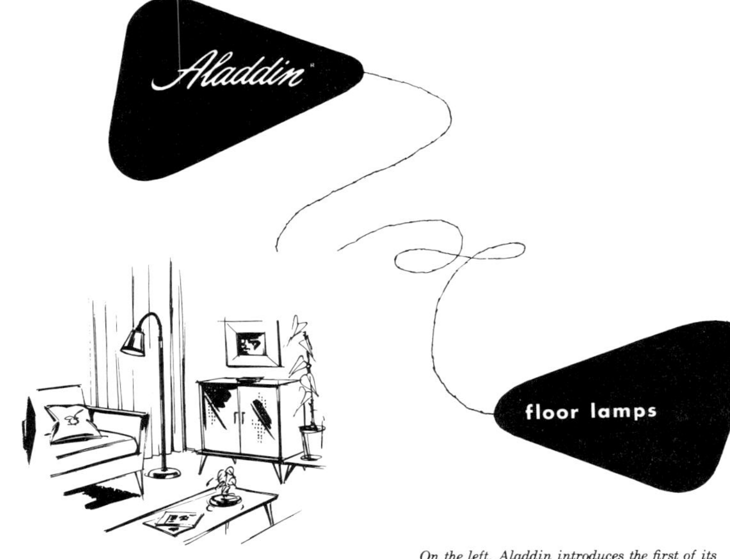

On the left, Aladdin introduces the first of its planned Contemporary Floor Lamps. On the following pages are offered new designs in the Traditional manner. Due to shortages in basic metals which naturally are being shifted to military production, Aladdin Industries this year, offers only a limited line of floor lamps. While we would like to have presented the many new models which we had designed for you, we appreciate and are completely in agreement with the nation's defense plans. No matter what the decor, your customers will find among Aladdin's famous line, floor lamps that are useful and beautiful in their homes.

#3606—A simply designed yet attractive and very practical Floor Lamp. Comes in Ivory and Gold, in Gray and Gold, and Bronze color. Is equipped with Mogul socket and three candle arms with standard sockets. The sturdy die-cast White Metal base has a beautiful filagree pattern. 10″ glass reflector. Height: 60″. Shown with SHADE #1569, 19″. Packed two of a like finish per carton.

#3606—Here shown above, with SHADE #R499, 19″. Available in Ivory and Gold, Gray and Gold, and Bronze color. Has 10″ glass reflector and is equipped with Mogul socket and three candle arms with standard sockets. White Metal base with filagree pattern. Height: 60″. Packed two of a like finish per carton.

#3606—Shown below with SHADE #2312, 19″. Mogul socket and three candle arms with standard sockets. Has 10″ glass reflector and White Metal base is decorated with beautiful filagree pattern. Height: 60″. Comes in Ivory and Gold, in Gray and Gold, and Bronze color. Packed two of a like finish per carton.

#3606—Shown here with SHADE #R497, 19″. Available in Ivory and Gold, Gray and Gold, or Bronze color. Has 10″ glass reflector and Mogul socket plus three candle arms with standard sockets. Height: 60″. Packed two of a like finish per carton.

#3606—Shown below with SHADE #805, 19″. Has 10″ glass reflector. Comes equipped with Mogul socket and three candle arms with standard sockets. Height: 60″. Available in Ivory and Gold, Gray and Gold, and Bronze color. Packed two of a like finish per carton.

#3606—Shown above with SHADE #1567, 19″. Comes in Ivory and Gold, Gray and Gold, or Bronze color. Has 10″ glass reflector. Equipped with Mogul socket and three candle arms with standard sockets. Height: 60″. Packed two of a like finish per carton.

#3606—Has a lovely motif around the base which is very decorative. The lamp is tastefully finished and can be used to good effect in any room setting. Comes in Ivory and Gold, Bronze color, or Gray and Gold. Is equipped with Mogul socket and three candle arms with standard sockets. Has 10″ glass reflector. Height: 60″. Shown below with SHADE #R489, 19″. Packed two of a like finish per carton.

LAMP 3608   SHADE R489

LAMP 3606   SHADE 1565

#3606—Shown above with SHADE #1565, 19″. Comes in Ivory and Gold, Bronze color, or Gray and Gold. Decorated base. 10″ glass reflector. Lamp is equipped with Mogul socket and three candle arms with standard sockets. Height: 60″. Packed two of a like finish per carton.

#3606—Shown below with SHADE #R490, 19″. This lamp with its decorated base is unusually attractive. Has Mogul socket and three candle arms with standard sockets. Comes equipped with 10″ glass reflector and is available in Ivory and Gold, Bronze color, or Gray and Gold. Height: 60″. Packed two of a like finish per carton.

LAMP 3606   SHADE R490

cocktail smokers

SMOKER   7549

#7549—Cocktail Smoker. Shown above. An extremely useful and beautiful Smoker, that anyone would be proud to own. At parties, or whenever guests drop in, this graceful piece with its smooth and sturdy table surface holds ash trays, cigarette boxes and drinks safely and comfortably. Height: 28¼″. Cast in White Metal, polished and plated, this stand is available in Oxidized Bronze, or lovely Silver.

#7549A—Cocktail Smoker cast in durable White Metal and finished in three color combinations. Height: 28¼″. May be had in Forest Green and Gold, Gray and Gold, or Ivory and Gold.

torchere reflectors

T-168

T-168 REFLECTOR. Shown at top, above, this 14″ diameter bowl-type, glass reflector is beautifully embossed in a gay floral and leaf pattern.

T-171

T-171 REFLECTOR. Shown at center, above. A more formal design which places accent on its bold flower motif for a rich and pleasing effect. Embossed glass, 16″ diameter.

T-172

T-172 REFLECTOR. Shown at bottom, above, this lovely 16″ glass reflector bowl is attractively embossed in a swirl pattern that makes it equally useful in both traditional and modern settings.

glass reflectors

#101—Shown above, at top. 10″ glass reflector. White mazed glass. Fits any type of floor lamp using a 10″ reflector. Packed six per carton.

#81—Shown above, at bottom. 8″ glass reflector for Swing-Arm Lamp and for Floor Lamps using reflectors of similar size. Packed six per carton.

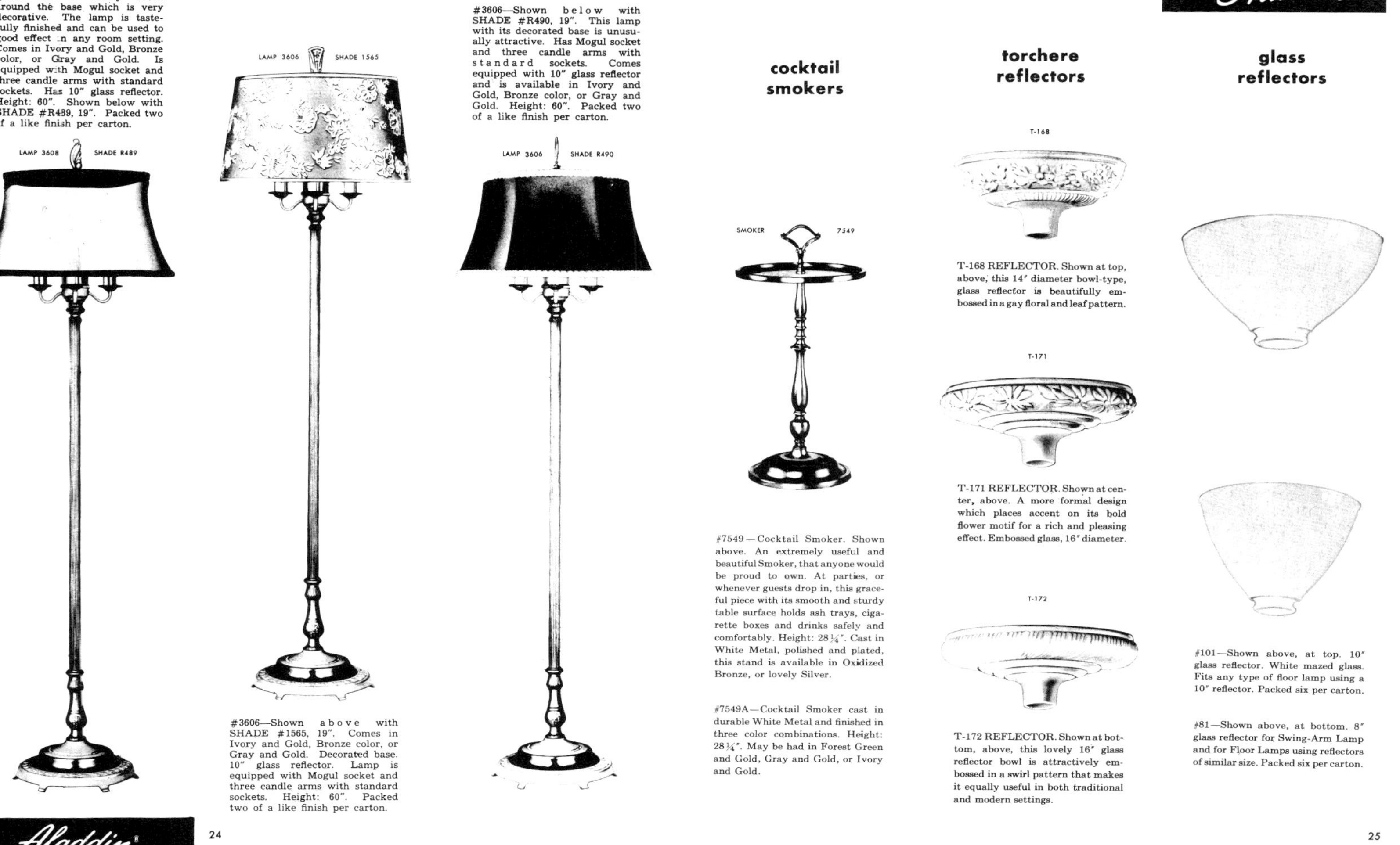

24

25

Feast your eyes upon the lovely Aladdin Table Lamps displayed on these pages. Designed especially for Aladdin by such outstanding designers as *Eugene Schwarz* and *Robert Burton*, they fill that typically American demand for both practicality and intrinsic beauty.

G348—Shown at top right. A delightful world-globe with the seas freely brushed in and the continents with their mountains raised in sculptured relief. An artist's conception —created for its decorative effect. Globe, when illuminated from within, casts a lovely glow. Wood and metal portions of lamp are finished in contrasting Black. Has 3-way socket and switch. Height: 20½". Furnished with SHADE #S348, 16"-horizontal net design.

G349—Displayed at bottom right. A most unusual and attractive Planter Lamp. Design is semi-modern and goes well with all furnishing styles. Is available in Chartreuse, Red, or Tan and each lamp comes with Flower Bowl which fits into base of lamp. Height: 32". Furnished with 20" SHADE #S349 in colors to match.

P407—Shown at far left. The design of this unusual table lamp stems from the finest designs in contemporary fine art. Sculptured forms like this may be seen in art museums all over the world. Base is highly glazed porcelain. Gray only. Comes with push-thru socket and switch. Height: 25″. Furnished with matching 16″ SHADE #S407A.

G338—Shown at left. Comes in fired-on Chinese Red, Dusty Rose or Forest Green, Ceramic finishes. Lighted base. Has 3-way turn-knob switch. Height: 27″. Furnished with washable Whip-O-Lite SHADE #1570—15″.

G359—At far left. Semi-Modern. The gracefully flowing lines of this excellent table lamp attracts attention wherever shown. Available in Chartreuse or Red. Has push-thru socket and switch. Height: 27½″. Furnished with 16″ rectangular shaped fabric SHADE #S359.

G363—Shown at left. Design is raised, formalized leaf pattern. Pedestal is Gold band trimmed. Has push-thru switch. Comes in Avocado Green only. Packed 4 to a carton. Height: 29½″. Furnished with 15″ matching SHADE #S363.

G361—Shown at right. A simple yet unusual design that is both bright and gay. Has lighted base, so useful for TV viewing or as a night light. Matches G50 Boudoir Lamp. Comes in Chartreuse, Ivory, or Rose finishes. Height: 25½″. 15″ matching SHADE #S361 has fabric laminated over Whip-O-Lite.

P401—Shown at far right. An excellent example of semi-modern styling. The open spaces accented by rhythmically swirling lines make this an unusually outstanding lamp. Has highly glazed porcelain luster finish. Has push-thru socket and switch. Available in Gray, Green or Tan. Height: 27″. Furnished with matching 15″ SHADE #S401 —vertical net design.

G360—Shown at right. Harp-like in design, this graceful table lamp adds a decorative note to any home. Colors are strikingly beautiful. Comes in Chocolate or Forest Green. Height: 27½″. Furnished with genuine Polyplastex SHADE #S360—15″ drum shape in matching colors.

G364—Shown at far right. The striking raised leaf pattern blends subtly into the deeper tones of the base and the bright band at the bottom. Packed 4 to a carton. Comes in Autumn Gold finish only. Has push-thru socket and switch. Height: 29½″. Furnished with 15″ matching SHADE #S364.

G326—Shown at far left. Perfect with either traditional or modern furnishings. Has illuminated base—so useful with television viewing, and 3-way turn-knob switch. Height: 22″. Comes in Chartreuse, Amber or Jade Green. Furnished with SHADE #S326, 18″.

G338—At left. Illuminated Gold banded base in Tan only. A Traditional "vase-on-pedestal" design. Its conservative dignity adds quiet charm to any room. Height: 27″. SHADE #810—15″, is of Shantung fabric laminated to translucent Whip-O-Lite.

P406—Shown at right. A modern, free-form abstract design in highly glazed porcelain. The deep Sandlewood color of the pedestal changes subtly to more tawny hues in the fascinating contours of the base. Has push-thru socket and switch. Height: 25″. Furnished with matching 16″ SHADE #S406.

P404—Shown at far right. An unusual example of free-form design—modern as tomorrow. Highly glazed porcelain finish in a rich Chocolate Brown. Push-thru socket and switch. Height: 28½″. 15″ SHADE #S404 is Plaid taffeta laminated on durable Whip-O-Lite.

P403—Shown at far left. A graceful, plume design. Semi-modern. Base has highly glazed porcelain luster finish and push-thru socket and switch. Comes in Cerise, Tan or a lovely Green. Height: 24″. Complete with horizontal net SHADE #S403—16″.

W347—At left. Exquisite solid oak table lamp with grain accented in choice of two lovely finishes, Limed Oak or Silver Fox. Has push-thru socket and switch. Height: 28″. 15″ SHADE #S347 in Black tapestry design on Swedish Red or Chartreuse.

G336—Displayed at right. A graceful and popular gourd-type lamp. Comes in beautiful fired-on Ceramic colors; Dusty Rose, Pearl Luster, or Tan, each with Gold band trim. Equipment includes push-thru socket and switch. Height: 28½″. Furnished with SHADE #811 —18″ in matching colors.

G350—Shown at far right. Modern, yet conservatively styled, this attractive Planter Lamp can be used in either traditional or contemporary surroundings. Comes equipped with Flower Bowl. Lamps available in Red, Tan, or Chartreuse. Height: 28½″. Complete with specially designed oval fabric SHADE #S350—16″.

G186—Shown at far left. Illuminated ball-type base in Ivory Alacite. Striking, all-over leaf design. Height: 24½″. Exclusive fluted Whip-O-Lite SHADE #S186H—12″, is flock decorated.

W346—At left. Solid oak table lamp with square pedestal and rounded vase design. Hand polished, grained finish. Forms flow pleasingly into one another, and the entire effect is one of graceful dignity. Push-thru socket and switch. Comes in Limed Oak or Silver Fox. Height: 28″. Furnished with SHADE #S346—15″, in Cherry Red, Chartreuse or Tawny Beige—Butcher Linen laminated on Whip-O-Lite.

G362—Shown at far left, An outstanding ball-type lamp combining both traditional and modern. Has lighted base. Stripe design offers unusual contrast. Available in Jade Green, Autumn Gold, or Chartreuse. Height: 26″. Furnished with genuine Polyplastex SHADE #S362—14″.

P408—Illustrated at left. An unusual free-form porcelain glaze base Planter Lamp. For those who love growing plants in decorative settings, this table lamp is ideal. Equipped with push-thru socket and switch. Comes in Volcanic Green, Volcanic Red and Volcanic Gray finish. Height: 27½″. Furnished with 13″ SHADE #S408 in colors to match.

G337—Shown at right. A most unusual table lamp with deep fluted motif set off with a wide decorative band or collar. Push-thru socket and switch. Available in Alacite, Chartreuse, Chinese Red, or Tan finishes with Gold band. Height: 28″. Furnished with SHADE #1571—15″.

G344—At far right. Another unique table lamp making use of oval design forms on a rectangular shape. Has push-thru socket and switch. Available in Chartreuse, Flame Red, or exclusive Alacite finishes, each Gold banded. Height: 27½″. Matching SHADE #S344—15″, in cross-hatch design with piping top and bottom.

G343—Displayed at right. Lovely figurine with superbly flowing lines. Definitely a table lamp that will add charm in any surrounding. Comes decorated in choice of Flame Red or Pearl Green, both finishes accented with Gold bands. Has push-thru socket and switch. Height: 27″. Furnished with gracefully pleated 18″ SHADE #S343.

P402—Shown at far right. One of Aladdin's finest creations. A lovely lamp in highly glazed porcelain. Has push-thru socket and switch. Comes in Cocoa, Turquoise, or Willow Green. Rounded pedestal is Gold finished. Height: 27½″. Furnished with SHADE #S402—15″. Shade is Shantung laminated on Whip-O-Lite with double piping. Matching trim top and bottom.

G365—Shown at far left. The sculptured flower and leaf design, makes this lighted base table lamp an outstanding item. Has Gold band trim. Comes in Chartreuse only. Height: 29½″. Furnished with 15″ matching SHADE #S365. Packed 4 to a carton.

M367—Shown at left. A modern approach to a Hurricane Type Lamp. Has many uses. Base in Black Iron. Spun glass washable shade—7″ in diameter. Has pull-chain socket. Height: 18″.

P409—Shown at far left. A truly aristocratic lamp in highly glazed porcelain pottery. Available in Blended Green or Blended Tan. Furnished with 18″ SHADE #S409. Shade material is of "Polly-Wisp," a laminated fiber glass of unusual texture. Height over all 32½″.

P410—At left. Flask shape is accented allowing color to run freely. Comes in Volcanic Brown or Volcanic Green. SHADE #S410, 16″, is burlap, sometimes called Calcutta, laminated on both sides with Vinylite. Height over all 35″.

M251—Shown at right. Add a touch of Early American with this authentic replica. Electric of course, though it has all the charm of an old-fashioned kerosene lamp. Solid brass in a lustrous polished finish. Height: 23½″. Furnished with glass SHADE #703—10″, in Red, Green or White. Specify shade color when ordering.

P405—Shown at far right. Contemporary porcelain base table lamp. Design is in the latest abstract fashion now so popular. Has push-thru socket and switch. This lamp comes in an exquisite Chartreuse finish. Height: 28½″. Furnished with matching 15″ SHADE #S405—vertical net design.

G340R—Shown at right. A Recipe lamp meeting all General Electric lighting specifications. Beautiful vase-on-pedestal design. Has 3-way socket for use with 2-filament bulb. Comes in Dusty Rose, Pearl Luster, or Tan, with Gold band trim. Height: 28½″. Matching fabric SHADE with Gold fleck # 450R —16″.

G345R—Displayed at far right, is another Aladdin "Recipe" lamp designed to fit in with the GE national promotion. The unusual Pineapple motif is extremely attractive and the lamp may be had in Brown, Flame Red, or Forest Green, each with Gold band trim. Has wide harp for use with standard or reflector type bulb. Push-thru socket and switch. Height: 28″. Furnished with 16″ SHADE #S345 in gleaming plastic with colored ruching trim at top.

Aladdin boudoir lamps add a touch of magic . . . a note of gayety . . . delightful charm . . . to every bedroom. Your customers will want them in matching pairs for vanity and night tables and for dressers in every room. Show the Aladdin Planter Lamps, too . . . so attractive in either traditional or contemporary settings.

G49—Shown at right. A boudoir lamp with an unusually fresh and charming design. Ideal for children's bedrooms, too, this gay little lamp appeals to everyone. Comes in Chartreuse, Rose, or Jade Green. Height: 18″. Packed 2 of a color to a carton. Furnished with 8″ washable Whip-O-Lite SHADE #S49, Boucle trimmed.

G355C—Shown at far right. A Pin-up wall plaque to decorate any youngster's room and serve also as a practical night light. Designed like a real Western gun and holster with a picture of *Hopalong Cassidy*. Height: 9¾″.

G44—Shown at right. Available in Chartreuse, Ivory, or Rose. Ever-popular, illuminated ball-type base for decorative lighting. Height: 17″. Packed 2 of a color to a carton. Modern cone-type SHADE of laminated taffeta #S44—7″.

G48—Displayed at far right. A charming boudoir lamp, bell-shaped and dainty, with raised leaf and floral design. Has push-thru socket and switch. Comes in Ivory, Blue, Chartreuse, or Rose. Height: 16″. Packed 2 of a color to a carton. Furnished with SHADE #S48—8″, net trim top and bottom.

LAMP G203R   SHADE 814

LAMP G50   SHADE S50

LAMP B45

G203R—Displayed at far left. Here is a "Recipe" Dresser Lamp, ideal for the boudoir, designed for beauty of line and correct light distribution. Has push-thru socket. Comes in Alacite, Coral, or Chartreuse. Height: 24½". Furnished with laminated SHADE #814—9".

G50—Shown at left. Comes in Chartreuse, Ivory or Rose. Matches night stand lamp #G361. Has lighted base. SHADE #S50—8" is fabric laminated over Whip-O-Lite with Boucle trim top and bottom. Height: 18". Packed 2 of a color per carton.

B45—Shown at left. Luxurious and useful for reading or radio-listening, truly a delightful Bed Lamp. Rubber-covered wire and hooks fully protect furniture from scratches and there's a convenient pull-chain socket. All shades are laminated taffeta. Available in Eggshell, Rust, Chartreuse, Rose, Beige, or Copper Brown.

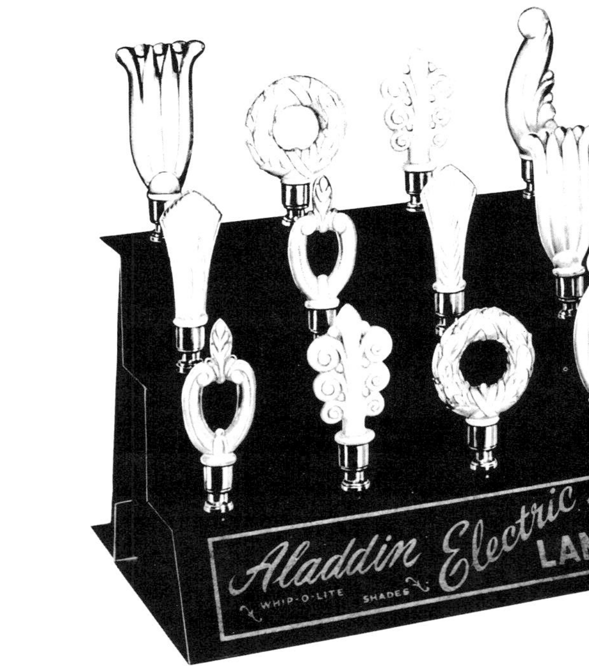

FINIAL ASSORTMENT

A complete assortment for the convenience of your customers. Here is a well-designed display stand that makes it easy to sell finials. All are equipped with studs and can be used on floor as well as table lamps. Dealers may have this display stand without charge with their first order of a dozen or more finials.

16   17

To please your customers, to satisfy the requirements of both traditional and contemporary decoration, Aladdin presents this series of exquisite floor lamps. In tune with the trend of bringing the "outdoors" into the home, Aladdin designers have made greater use of natural woods than ever before. Note especially, that many of Aladdin's modern lamps go equally well in traditional settings.

#3510—Displayed at right. Slender, beautifully grained, Solid Oak floor lamp. Has 3-way Mogul socket and 10″ Glass Reflector. Height: 60″. Comes in Limed Oak or the somewhat darker Palamino finish. Furnished with 23″ SHADE #S552. Packed one to a carton.

#3613—Shown at center, right. Traditional 6-Way all-metal floor lamp, available in Gray and Gold or Ivory and Gold finishes. Has 10″ Glass Reflector and 3-way Mogul socket plus three candle arms with standard sockets. Height: 60″. Furnished with 19″ SHADE #1572. Packed two of a like finish per carton.

#7011—At far right. Modern in design, yet so classic in its simplicity that it can be used in any atmosphere, this Swing Arm Solid Oak floor lamp is finished in Limed Oak or Silver Fox. A companion to Floor Lamp #3511. Equipped with socket for use with 2-filament bulb. Requires no Glass Reflector. Height: 58″. Furnished with SHADE #S346, drum type 16″. Packed one to a carton.

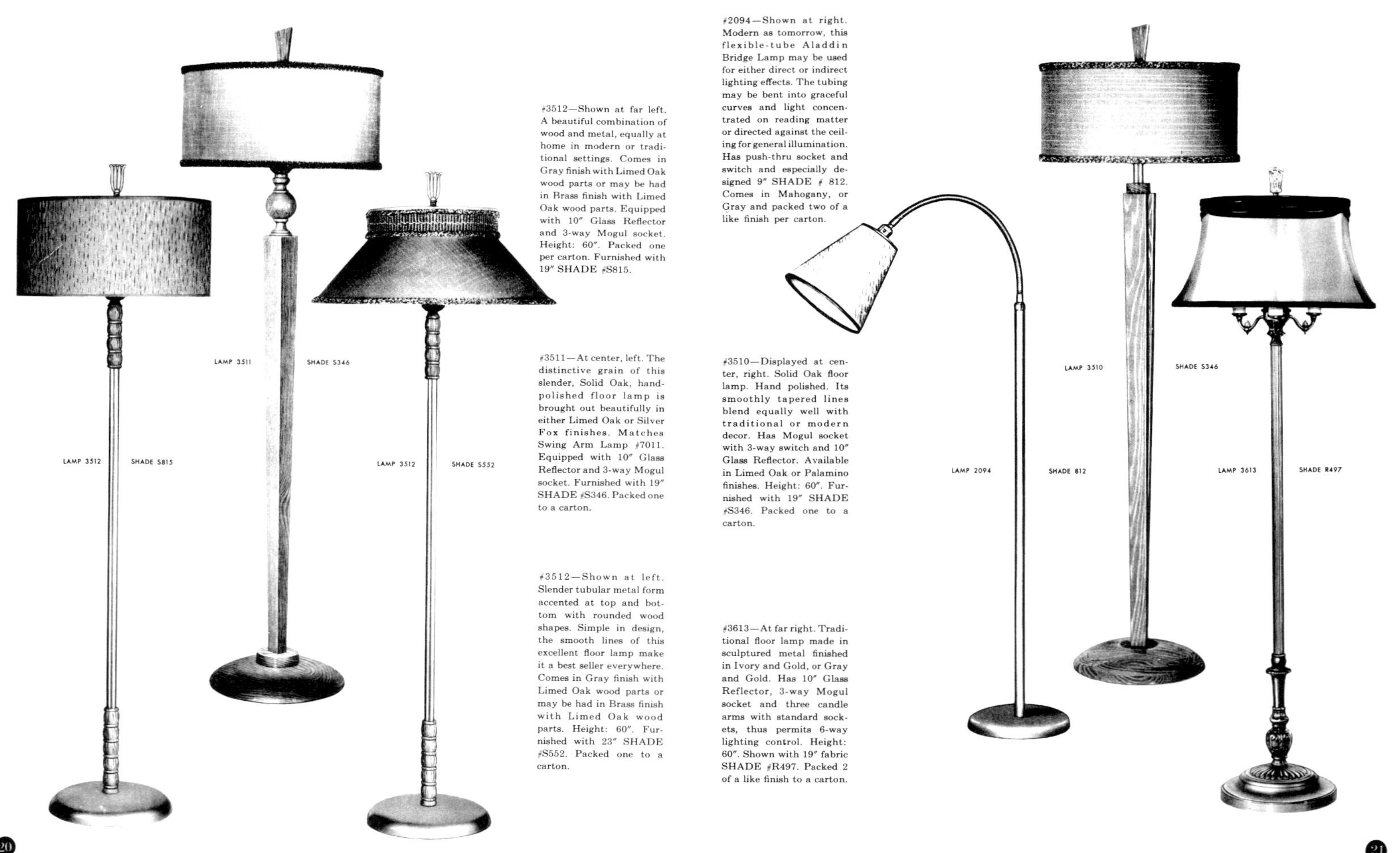

#3512—Shown at far left. A beautiful combination of wood and metal, equally at home in modern or traditional settings. Comes in Gray finish with Limed Oak wood parts or may be had in Brass finish with Limed Oak wood parts. Equipped with 10″ Glass Reflector and 3-way Mogul socket. Height: 60″. Packed one per carton. Furnished with 19″ SHADE #S815.

#3511—At center, left. The distinctive grain of this slender, Solid Oak, hand-polished floor lamp is brought out beautifully in either Limed Oak or Silver Fox finishes. Matches Swing Arm Lamp #7011. Equipped with 10″ Glass Reflector and 3-way Mogul socket. Furnished with 19″ SHADE #S346. Packed one to a carton.

#3512—Shown at left. Slender tubular metal form accented at top and bottom with rounded wood shapes. Simple in design, the smooth lines of this excellent floor lamp make it a best seller everywhere. Comes in Gray finish with Limed Oak wood parts or may be had in Brass finish with Limed Oak wood parts. Height: 60″. Furnished with 23″ SHADE #S552. Packed one to a carton.

#2094—Shown at right. Modern as tomorrow, this flexible-tube Aladdin Bridge Lamp may be used for either direct or indirect lighting effects. The tubing may be bent into graceful curves and light concentrated on reading matter or directed against the ceiling for general illumination. Has push-thru socket and switch and especially designed 9″ SHADE # 812. Comes in Mahogany, or Gray and packed two of a like finish per carton.

#3510—Displayed at center, right. Solid Oak floor lamp. Hand polished. Its smoothly tapered lines blend equally well with traditional or modern decor. Has Mogul socket with 3-way switch and 10″ Glass Reflector. Available in Limed Oak or Palamino finishes. Height: 60″. Furnished with 19″ SHADE #S346. Packed one to a carton.

#3613—At far right. Traditional floor lamp made in sculptured metal finished in Ivory and Gold, or Gray and Gold. Has 10″ Glass Reflector, 3-way Mogul socket and three candle arms with standard sockets, thus permits 6-way lighting control. Height: 60″. Shown with 19″ fabric SHADE #R497. Packed 2 of a like finish to a carton.

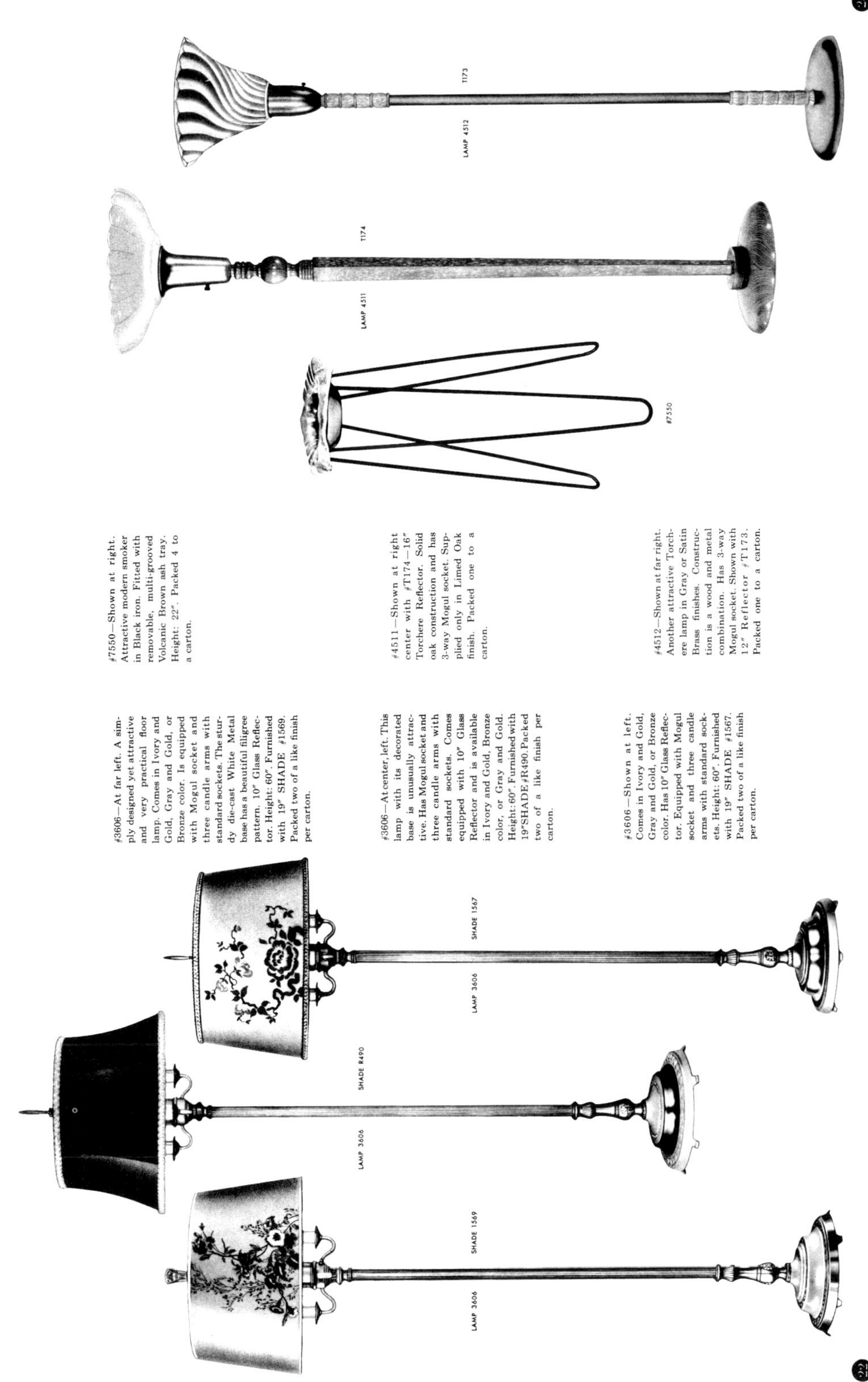

#7550—Shown at right. Attractive modern smoker in Black iron. Fitted with removable, multi-grooved Volcanic Brown ash tray. Height: 22". Packed 4 to a carton.

#4511—Shown at right center with #T174—16" Torchere Reflector. Solid oak construction and has 3-way Mogul socket. Supplied only in Limed Oak finish. Packed one to a carton.

#4512—Shown at far right. Another attractive Torchere lamp in Gray or Satin Brass finishes. Construction is a wood and metal combination. Has 3-way Mogul socket. Shown with 12" Reflector #T173. Packed one to a carton.

#3606—At far left. A simply designed yet attractive and very practical floor lamp. Comes in Ivory and Gold, Gray and Gold, or Bronze color. Is equipped with Mogul socket and three candle arms with standard sockets. The sturdy die-cast White Metal base has a beautiful filigree pattern. 10" Glass Reflector. Height: 60". Furnished with 19" SHADE #1569. Packed two of a like finish per carton.

#3606—At center, left. This lamp with its decorated base is unusually attractive. Has Mogul socket and three candle arms with standard sockets. Comes equipped with 10" Glass Reflector and is available in Ivory and Gold, Bronze color, or Gray and Gold. Height: 60". Furnished with 19"SHADE #R490. Packed two of a like finish per carton.

#3606—Shown at left. Comes in Ivory and Gold, Gray and Gold, or Bronze color. Has 10" Glass Reflector. Equipped with Mogul socket and three candle arms with standard sockets. Height: 60". Furnished with 19" SHADE #1567. Packed two of a like finish per carton.

On this and the following pages are displayed a variety of Aladdin Shades styled in Whip-O-Lite, fabric, and fabric laminated on Whip-O-Lite. Exclusive, patented Whip-O-Lite is greaseless and glare-free. Easy to maintain, Whip-O-Lite may be cleaned in a jiffy with a damp cloth. Aladdin fabric shades are exquisitely tailored and made in a wide range of Shantungs, Twills and Rayons.

SHADE S44

SHADE S813

SHADE S48

SHADE S49

SHADE S50

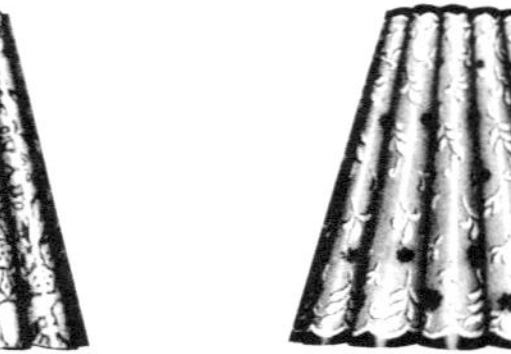

SHADE S186H

SHADE 2311H

#61—6″ Glass Reflector. White mazed glass. Fits any type of table lamp using a 6″ reflector. Packed six per carton.

#81—8″ Glass Reflector for Swing Arm Lamps and for floor lamps using reflectors of similar size. Packed six per carton.

#101—10″ Glass Reflector. White mazed glass. Fits any type floor lamp using a 10″ reflector. Packed six per carton.

T-172 — Reflector. This lovely 16″ Glass Reflector bowl is attractively embossed in a swirl pattern that makes it equally useful in both traditional and modern settings.

T-173—12″ Glass Reflector beautifully styled in a wide vase design for maximum direction of light toward the ceiling. Spreads a soft radiance throughout the room.

T-174—Smooth and graceful in its design, this 16″ Glass Reflector adds a touch of loveliness to any torchere. Goes well with either modern or traditional bases.

#S44—Shown at right, top row. 7″, Clamp fitter. Boucle trimmed Whip-O-Lite Boudoir shade laminated with Butcher Linen available in Beige or Chartreuse. Also laminated with Taffeta available in Rose.

#S813—At far right, top row. 7″, Clamp fitter. Taffeta fabric laminated on Whip-O-Lite. Has Eggshell ruching at bottom and wide braid trim at top. Comes in Brown, Chartreuse, or Eggshell. Packed two of each color, six per carton.

#S48—At right, center row. 8″, Clamp fitter. Boudoir shade available in Blue, Chartreuse, Ivory, or Rose. Made of sturdy, lasting Whip-O-Lite with lovely net trim at top and bottom.

#S49—Shown at center, center row. 8″, Clamp fitter. Whip-O-Lite Boudoir shade with Boucle trim top and bottom. Comes in Chartreuse, Jade Green, or Rose.

#S50—At far right, center row. Clamp fitter. Taffeta fabric laminated to patented Whip-O-Lite with dainty Ivory Boucle top and bottom. This 8″ Boudoir shade is available in Chartreuse, Rose or Ivory.

#S186H—Shown at right, bottom row. Washer fitter. An attractively fluted 12″ shade of easy to clean Whip-O-Lite. Available in White, only. Made for use on Lamp G186.

#S2311H—At far right, bottom row. 12″, Washer fitter. Fluted Whip-O-Lite shade. Made in Forest Green, Rose or White.

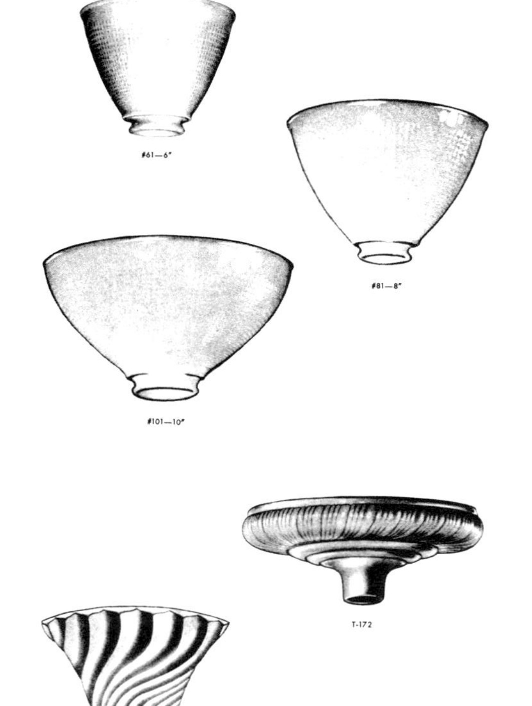

#61—6″

#81—8″

#101—10″

T-172

T-173

T-174

G-203R. *Glass Base, 24½"* High. Colors, Ivory, Coral, Chartreuse. 9" Laminated Shade. **$3.25**

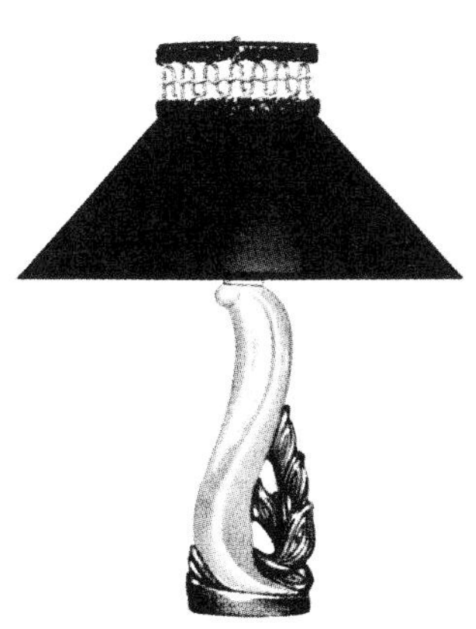

P-411. *Ceramic Base, 25"* High. Colors, Gray, Brown, Tan, Green. 20" Laminated Shantung Shade. **$6.95**

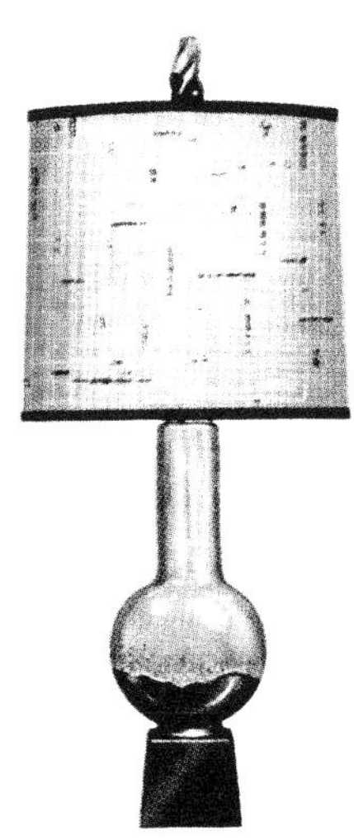

P-410. *Ceramic Base, 35"* High. Colors, Volcanic Brown, Volcanic Green. 16" Burlap Shade, Laminated with Vinylite. **$12.95**

G-345R. *Glass Base, 28"* High. Colors, Brown, Flame Red, Forest Green. 16" Plastic Ribbon Shade. **$3.95**

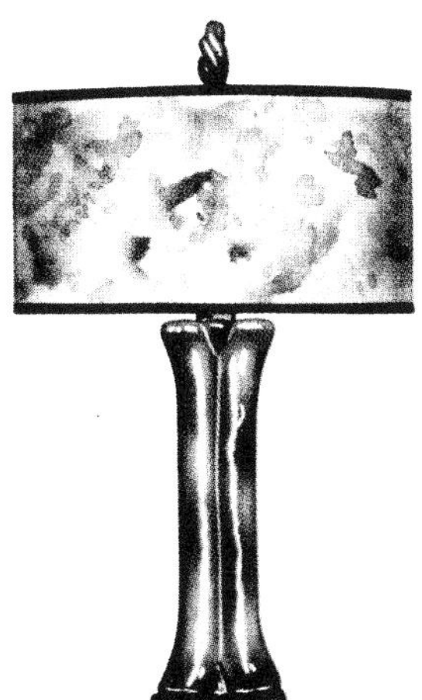

P-409. *Ceramic Base, 32½"* High. Colors, Blended Green, Blended Brown. 18" "Poly-Wisp" Fiberglass Shade. **$11.95**

G-336. *Glass Base, 28½"* High. Colors, Dusty Rose, Pearl Lustre, Tan. 18" Matching Whip-O-Lite Shade. **$5.45**

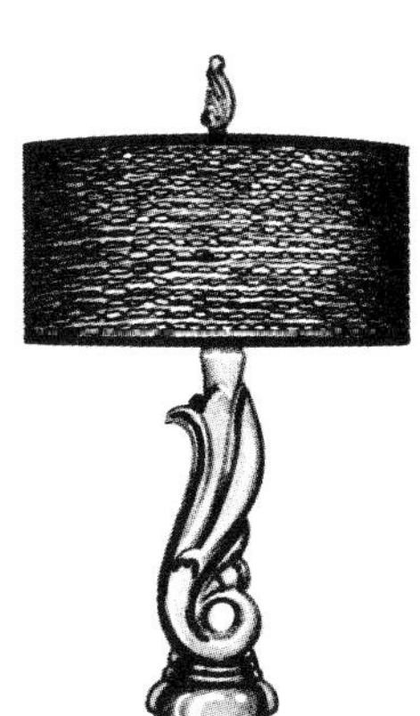

P-403. *Ceramic Base, 24"* High. Colors, Cerise, Tan, Green. 16" Shade of patented Whip-O-Lite. **$5.95**

The Aladdin

1952 LINE

All prices shown are quoted at wholesale. F.O.B. Portland, Ore. or Alexandria, Ind. Terms 1% 10—Net 30 days.
(Prices slightly higher West of the Rockies.)

Turn the page for more promotional sales items.

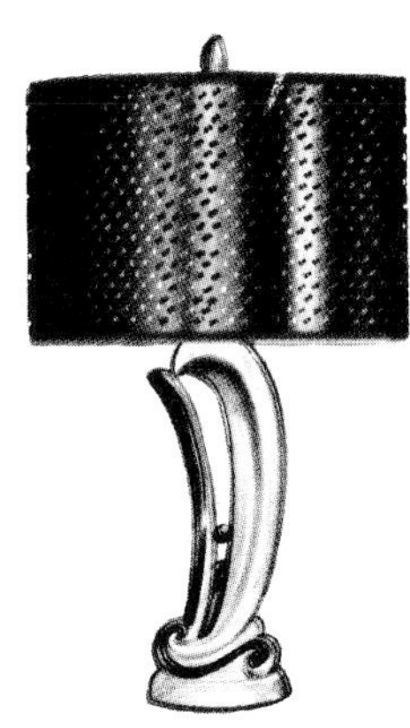

P-413. *Ceramic Base*, 24½″ High. Colors, Cerise, Green, Pearl. 15″ Pierced-glazed parchment shade. **$5.95**

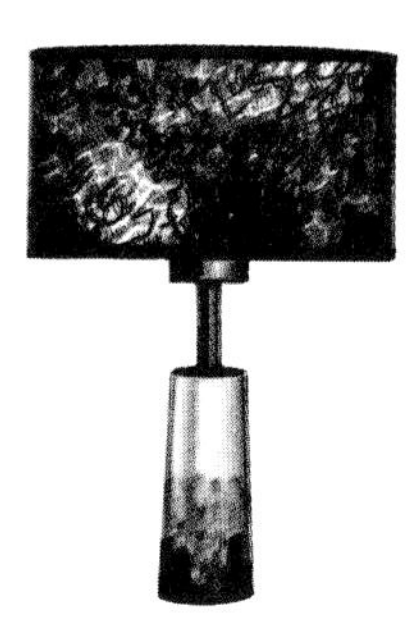

P-51. *Ceramic Base*, 18″ High. Colors, Black and White, Yellow and Chartreuse, Agate Brown. 12″ Vinylite Laminated Shade. **$4.95**

P-421. *Ceramic Base*, 25″ High. Colors, Terra Cotta, Leaf Green. 16″ Tree-bark Fabric Shade. **$9.95**

M-251. 23½″ High. Brass Base with Red, Green or White 10″ Glass Shade. **$8.95**

P-53. *Ceramic Base*, 17″ High. Colors, Tan, Green, Pearl. 13″ Laminated Shantung Shade. **$3.95**

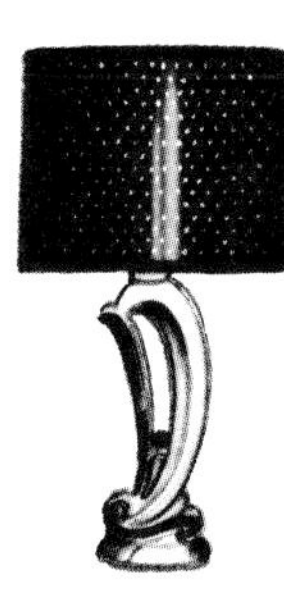

P-52. *Ceramic Base*, 16″ High. Colors, Pearl Lustre, Green, Cerise. 9″ Pierced-glazed parchment shade. **$3.75**

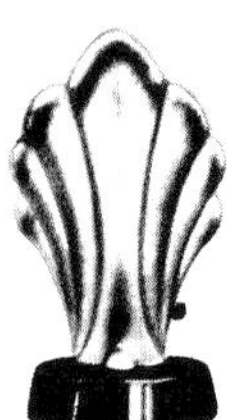

TV-380. *Ceramic Base*, 12½″ High. Colors, Green, Brown. Packed 2 of each color to carton. **$3.95**

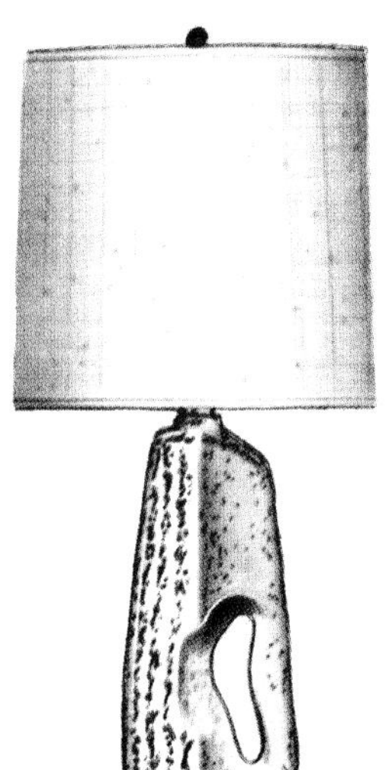

P-420. *Ceramic Base*, 32″ High. Colors, Sandalwood, Gray, Green. 3 Way Socket. 16″ Laminated Homespun Shade. **$10.95**

P-408. *Ceramic Base*, 27½″ High. Colors, Volcanic Red, Green, or Gray. 13″ Modern Whip-O-Lite Cone Shade. **$7.95**

M-367. 18″ High. Black Iron Base with Spun Glass Shade. **$3.50**

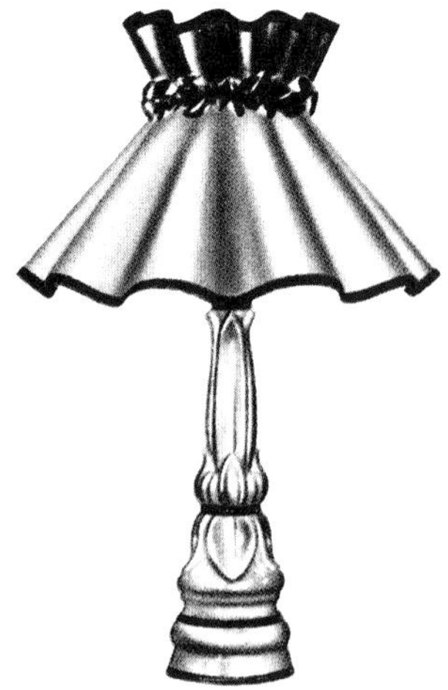

P-414. *Ceramic Base*, 29″ High. Colors, Maroon, Gray, Chartreuse. 18″ Fluted Flare Shade of Laminated Taffeta. **$7.95**

P-415. *Ceramic Base, 25"* High. Colors, Green, Dubonnet, White. 20" Printed Whip-O-Lite Shade. **$7.95**

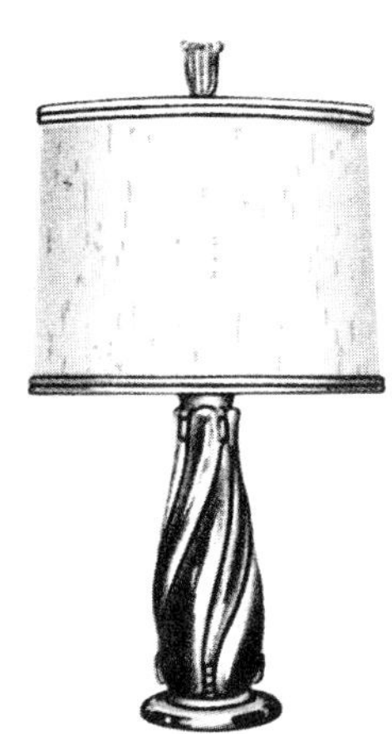

P-402. *Ceramic Base, 27½"* High. Colors, Cocoa, Turquoise, Willow Green. 15" Shantung Laminated Shade. **$7.95**

G-340R. *Glass Base, 28½"* High. Colors, Dusty Rose, Pearl Lustre, Tan. 16" Gold Flecked Matching Fabric Shade. **$6.95**

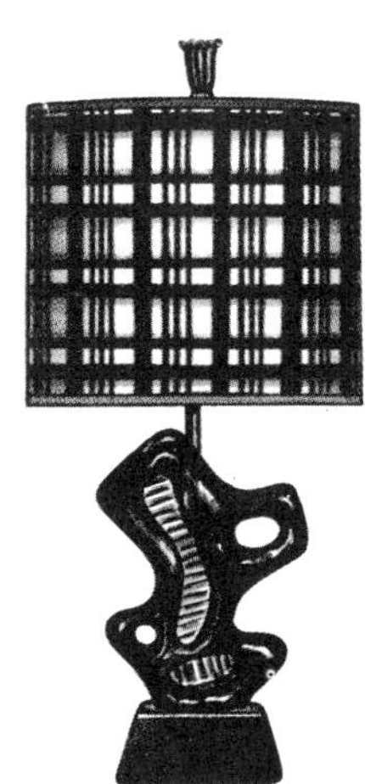

P-404. *Ceramic Base, 28½"* High. Color, Chocolate. 15" Plaid Taffeta Laminated Shade. **$8.95**

Style... Quality ...Price

And variety that assures your store a wide selection for your customers. Quality material, quality workmanship, throughout. The 1952 *Aladdin* Line is the direct result of research and design development to satisfy current market demands that will mean quicker turnover, sure profits, for you!

Prices are slightly higher West of the Rockies.

Showrooms

CHICAGO
1224 MERCHANDISE MART
BOSTON
101 TREMONT STREET
SAN FRANCISCO
WESTERN MERCHANDISE MART
HIGH POINT, N. C.
SOUTHERN EXPOSITION BLDG.

P-407. *Ceramic Base, 25"* High. Color, Gray. 16" Shade of Translucent Whip-O-Lite Material. **$7.95**

P-419. *Ceramic Base, 29½"* High. Brown & Mustard, Chartreuse and White, White and Yellow. 3 Way Socket. 15" Laminated Treebark Shade. **$10.95**

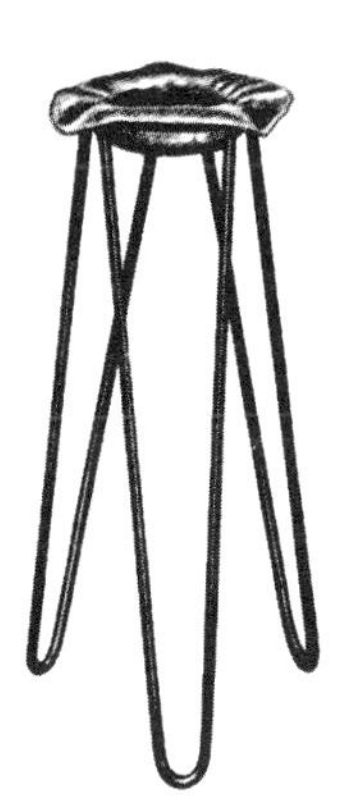

7550. 22" High. Smoker with Black Iron Base and Volcanic Brown Ash Tray. Packed 4 to a carton. **$2.95**

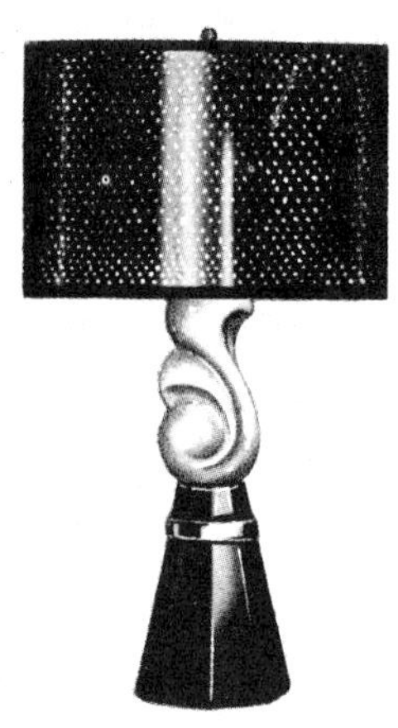

P-417. *Ceramic Base*, 26″ High. Colors, Maroon, Cream, Green. 15″ Pierced-glazed parchment shade. **$6.95**

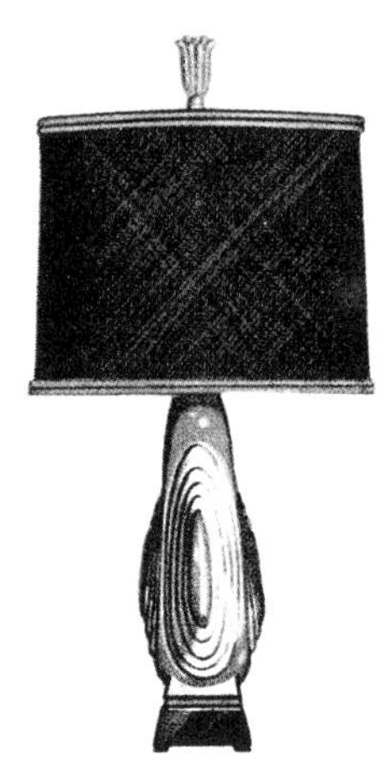

G-344. *Glass Base*, 27½″ High. Colors, Chartreuse, Flame Red, Ivory. 15″ Washable Whip-O-Lite Shade. **$5.95**

P-422. *Ceramic Base*, 22″ High. Colors, Cream, Cream and Terra Cotta, Black and Gold. 17″ Oval Shantung Fabric Shade. **$9.95**

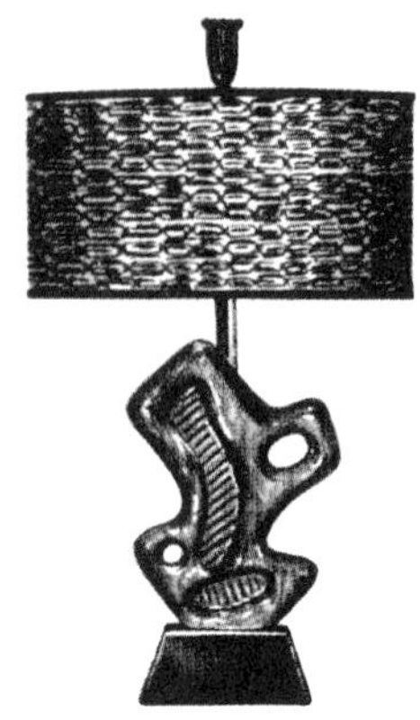

P-406. *Ceramic Base*, 25″ High. Color, Sandalwood. 16″ Drum Style with Horizontal Net design. **$7.95**

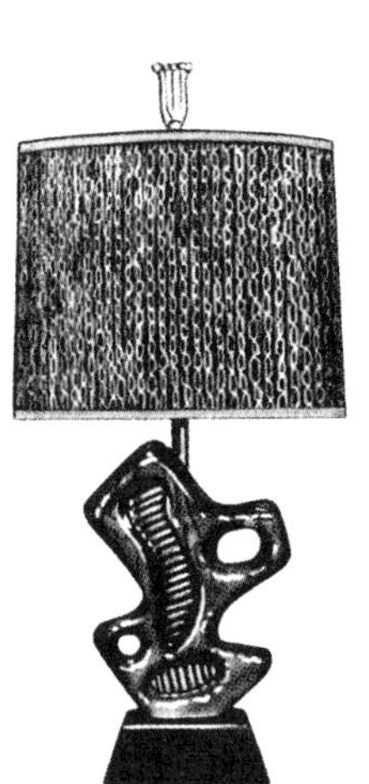

P-405. *Ceramic Base*, 28½″ High. Color, Chartreuse. 15″ Drum Type Whip-O-Lite Shade. **$7.95**

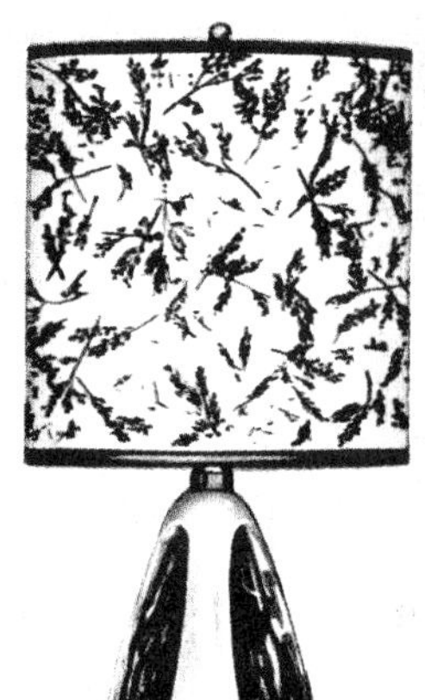

P-423. *Ceramic Base*, 29½″ High. Color, White and Brown. 3 Way Socket. 15″ Vinylite Laminated Shade, Heather design. **$11.95**

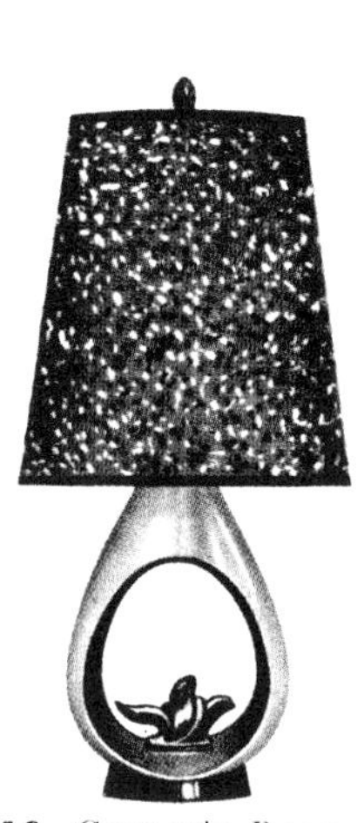

P-412. *Ceramic Base*, 25″ High. Colors, Chartreuse, Mulberry, Taffy Tan, Lemon Yellow. Lighted base. 13″ Polyplastex Splatter-dash Shade. **$8.95**

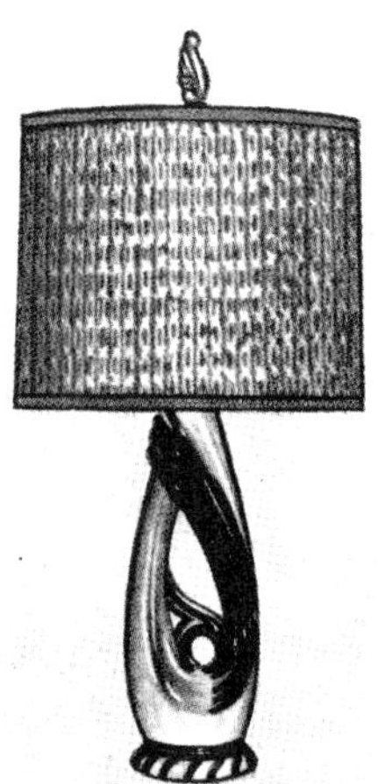

P-401. *Ceramic Base*, 27″ High. Colors, Gray, Green, Tan. 15″ Washable Whip-O-Lite Shade. **$5.95**

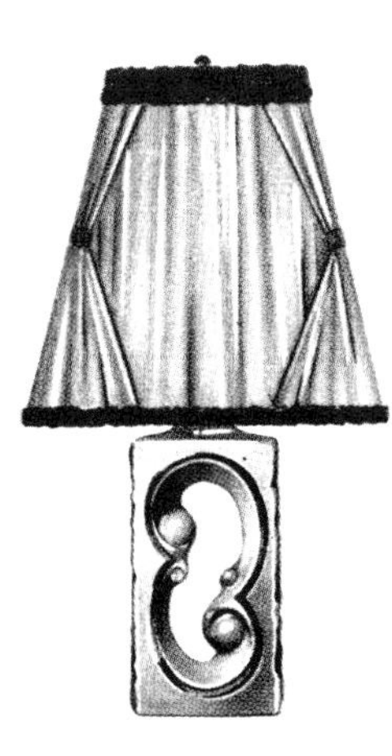

P-418. *Ceramic Base*, 28″ High. Colors, Chartreuse, Black. 15″ x 11″ Rectangular Plastic Ribbon Shade. **$5.95**

P-416. *Ceramic Base*, 20″ High. Colors, Agate Brown, Gray. 20″ Shade. Laminated Homespun. **$9.95**

G-343. *Glass Base*, 27″ High. Colors, Flame Red, Pearl Green. 18″ Pleated Shade. **$6.95**

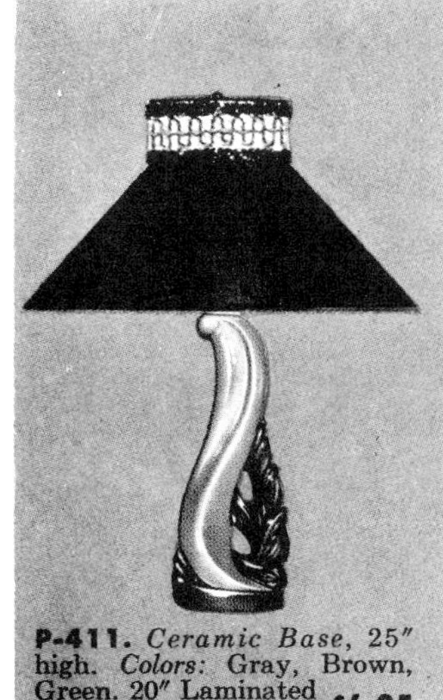

P-411. *Ceramic Base,* 25″ high. *Colors:* Gray, Brown, Green. 20″ Laminated Shantung Shade. **$6.95**

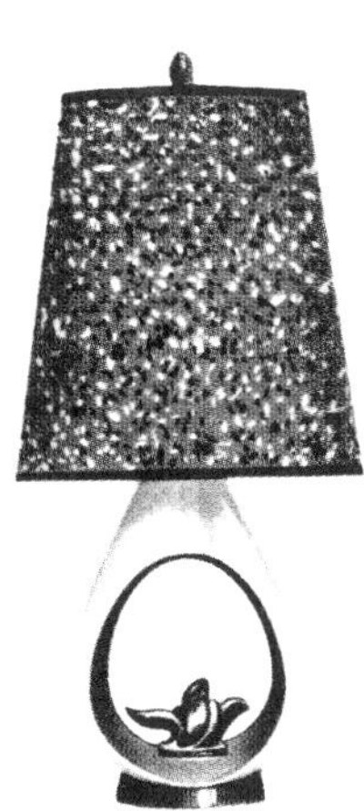

P-412. *Ceramic Base,* 25″ high. *Colors:* Chartreuse, Mulberry, Taffy Tan, Lemon Yellow. Lighted base. 13″ Polyplastex Splatterdash Shade. **$8.95**

P-51. *Ceramic Base,* 18″ high. *Colors:* Black and White, Yellow and Chartreuse, Agate Brown. 12″ Vinylite Laminated Shade. Packed 2 of a color per carton. **$4.95**

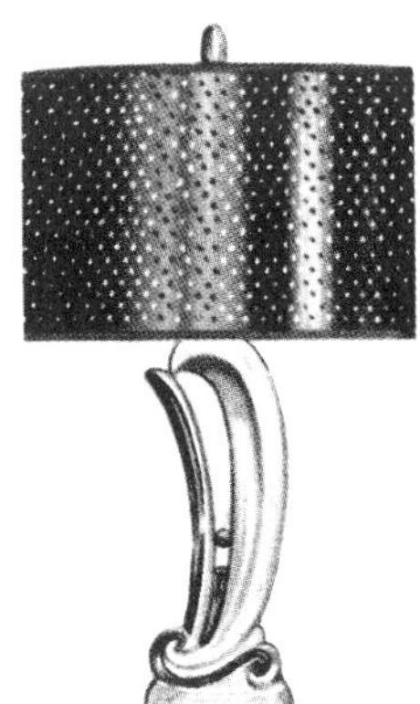

P-413. *Ceramic Base,* 24½″ high. *Colors:* Cerise, Green, Pearl. 15″ Pierced-glazed Parchment Shade. **$5.95**

P-439. *Ceramic Base,* 27″ high. *Colors:* Ivory, Gray. 3-Way Socket. 16″ Shantung Fabric Shade. **$7.95**

P-434. *Ceramic Base,* 26″ high. *Colors:* Gray with Red Shade, Green with Chartreuse Shade. 15″ Laminated Butcher Linen Shade. **$7.95**

P-433. *Ceramic Base,* 25″ high. *Color:* Ivory and Gold. 16″ washable Whip - O - Lite Shade. Packed 4 per carton. **$4.95**

P-438. *Ceramic Base,* 25″ high. *Colors:* Chestnut Brown, Green. 15″ washable Whip-O-Lite Shade. **$5.95**

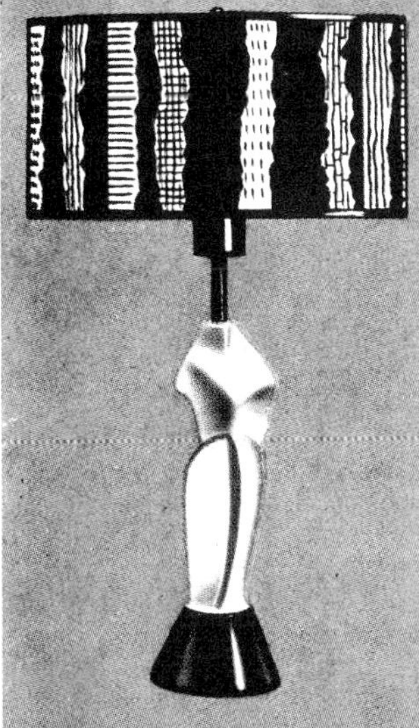

P-437. *Ceramic Base,* 28″ high. *Color:* Black and White. 17″ Drum-Style washable Whip-O-Lite Shade. **$9.95**

Your Feature Line for '53

Aladdin® Lamps

Every lamp a standout in styling and sales appeal

TURN THE PAGE FOR THE FULL PICTURE OF THIS MAGNIFICENT NEW LINE

P-55. *Ceramic Base,* 21″ high. *Colors:* Black, Yellow. 9″ Polyplastex Synskyn Shade. Packed 2 of a color per carton. **$3.95**

P-415. *Colors:* Dubonnet, White. 20″ Printed Whip-O-Lite Shade in Green, Brown and Dubonnet. **$7.95**

P-54. *Ceramic Base,* 19″ high. *Colors:* Carnation Pink, Dresden Blue, White. 11″ Tinted Whip-O-Lite Shade. Packed 2 of a color per carton. **$3.95**

P-53. *Ceramic Base,* 17″ high. *Colors:* Tan, Green, Pearl. 13″ Laminated Shantung Shade. Packed 2 of a color per carton. **$3.95**

P-421. *Ceramic Base,* 25″ high. *Colors:* Terra Cotta, Leaf Green. 16″ Treebark Fabric Shade. **$9.95**

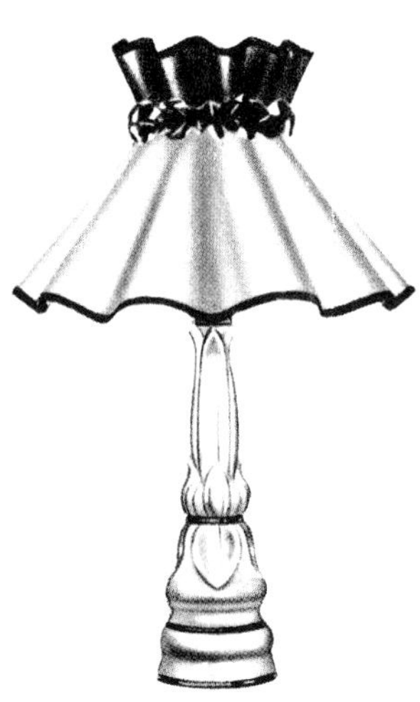

P-414. *Ceramic Base,* 29″ high. *Colors:* Maroon, Gray, Chartreuse. 18″ Fluted Flare Shade of Laminated Taffeta. **$7.95**

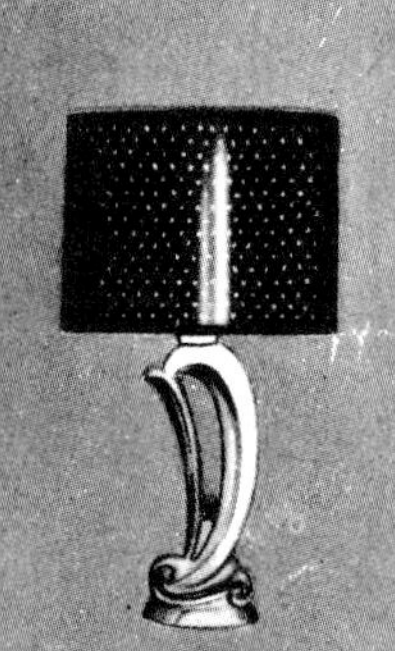

P-52. *Ceramic Base,* 16″ high. *Colors:* Pearl Lustre, Green, Cerise. 9″ Pierced-glazed Parchment Shade. Packed 2 of a color per carton. **$3.75**

P-436. *Ceramic Base,* 22″ high. *Color:* Aztec Brown. 16″ Laminated Madagascar Cloth Shade. **$8.95**

P-428. *Ceramic Base,* 22″ high. *Color:* Aztec Green. 16″ Laminated Shade, Aztec Print. **$8.95**

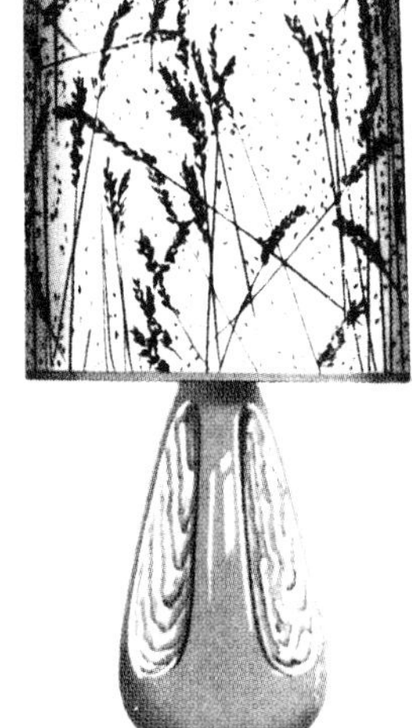

P-443. *Ceramic Base,* 29½″ high. *Colors:* White and Yellow, Chartreuse and White. 3-Way Socket. 15″ Vinylite Laminated Scattergrass Shade. **$11.95**

TV-380. *Ceramic Base,* 12½″ high. *Colors:* Green, Brown. Packed 2 of each color per carton. **$3.95**

P-427. *Ceramic Base,* 19″ high. *Colors:* Frosted Black, Embassy Green, Chestnut Brown. Pierced Satin-finish Parchment Shade. **$7.95**

M-451. Contemporary Free Form Black Metal Base, 24″ high. 17″ Matching Shade.
$7.95

M-448. Black Metal Tripod Base, 24″ high. 16″ Polyplastex Synskyn Shade.
$8.95

M-445. White Sphere on Black Metal Base, 21″ high. 13″ Polyplastex Synskyn Shade. Packed 2 per carton.
$7.95

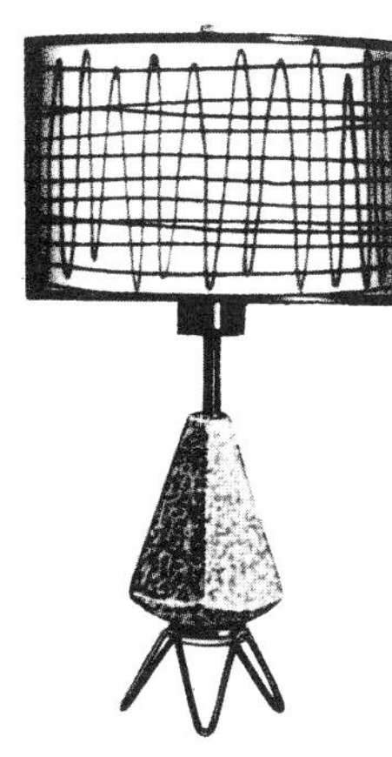

M-446. White and Green Ceramic Pyramid on Metal Base, 22″ high. 13″ Polyplastex Synskyn Shade. Packed 2 per carton.
$7.95

M-449. Contemporary Black Metal Base, 26″ high. 17″ Matching Whip-O-Lite Shade.
$9.95

M-447. Black and Yellow or Mat Green Ceramic on Metal Base, 21″ high. 15″ Shade of Laminated Vinylite Polyplastex.
$9.95

M-367. Black Iron Base, 18″ high. White Synskyn Shade.
$3.50

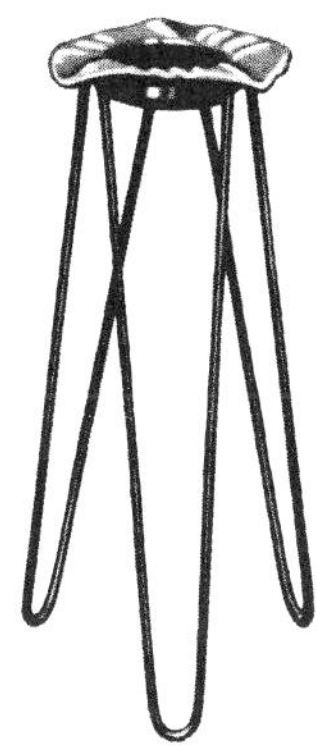

7550. Smoker with Black Iron Base, 22″ high. Volcanic Black and White Ash Tray. Packed 4 per carton.
$2.95

P-442. *Ceramic Base, 21″ high. Colors: Chartreuse, Forest Green, Gray. 14″ Butcher Linen Laminated Shade. Packed 2 of a color per carton.*
$5.95

M-251. Brass Base, 23½″ high. Red, Green or White 10″ Glass Shade.
$8.95

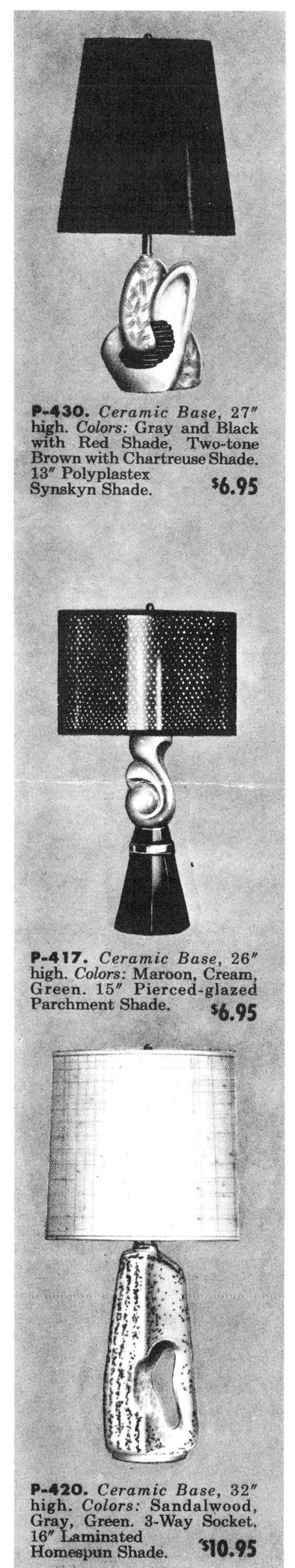

P-430. *Ceramic Base,* 27″ high. *Colors:* Gray and Black with Red Shade, Two-tone Brown with Chartreuse Shade. 13″ Polyplastex Synskyn Shade. **$6.95**

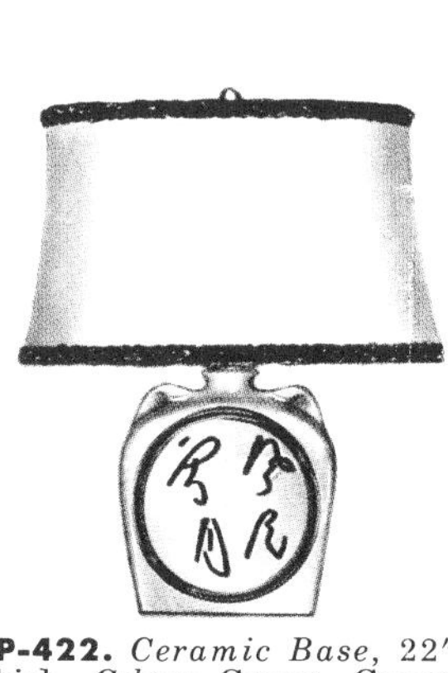

P-422. *Ceramic Base,* 22″ high. *Colors:* Cream, Cream and Terra Cotta, Black and Gold. 17″ Oval Shantung Fabric Shade. **$9.95**

P-431. *Ceramic Base,* 27″ high. *Colors:* Black, Mulberry, Chartreuse. 13″ Polyplastex Splatterdash Shade. **$6.95**

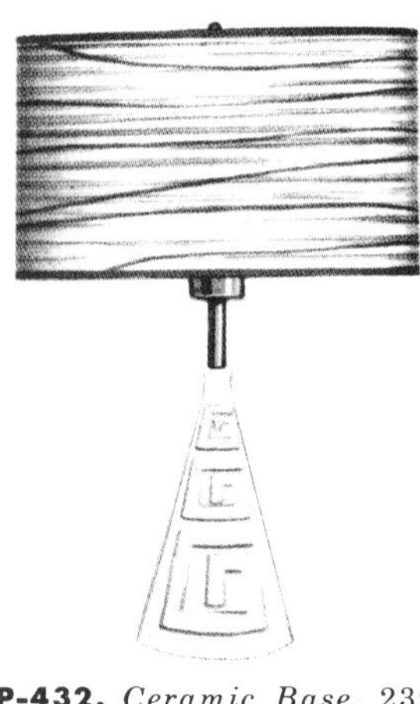

P-432. *Ceramic Base,* 23″ high. *Colors:* Frosted Black, Frosted Citron Yellow. 16″ Polyplastex Synskyn Shade. **$7.95**

P-417. *Ceramic Base,* 26″ high. *Colors:* Maroon, Cream, Green. 15″ Pierced-glazed Parchment Shade. **$6.95**

P-435. *Ceramic Base,* 29″ high. *Colors:* Nile Green and White, Jonquil Yellow and White. 3-Way Socket. 15″ Treebark Laminated Shade. **$7.95**

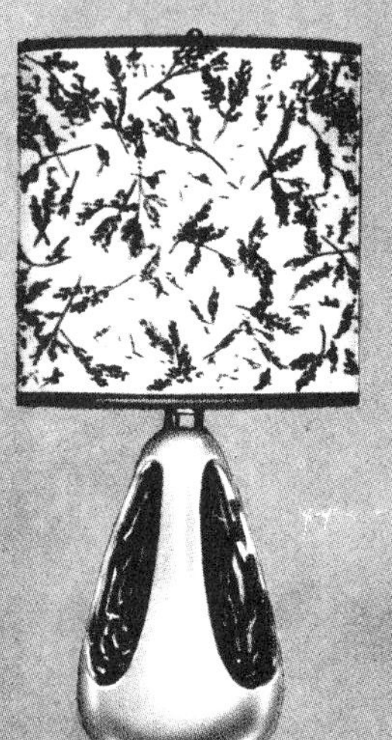
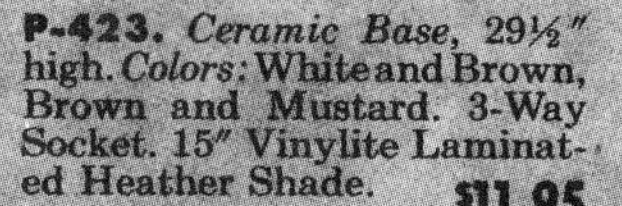

P-423. *Ceramic Base,* 29½″ high. *Colors:* White and Brown, Brown and Mustard. 3-Way Socket. 15″ Vinylite Laminated Heather Shade. **$11.95**

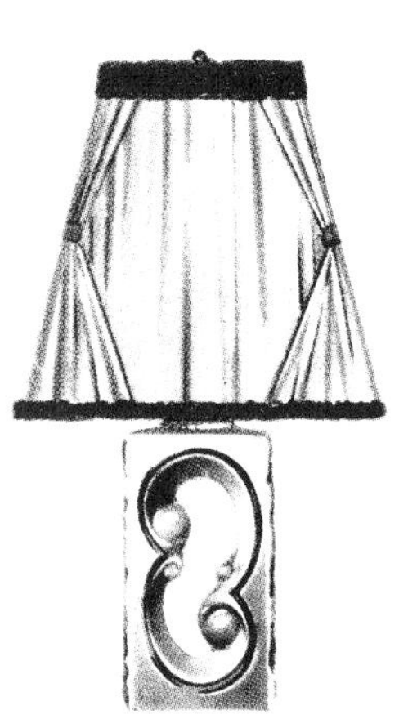

P-418. *Ceramic Base,* 28″ high. *Colors:* Chartreuse, Black. 15″ x 11″ Rectangular Plastic Ribbon Shade. **$5.95**

P-420. *Ceramic Base,* 32″ high. *Colors:* Sandalwood, Gray, Green. 3-Way Socket. 16″ Laminated Homespun Shade. **$10.95**

P-444. *Ceramic Base* with Elm Leaf Pattern, 25″ high. *Colors:* Maize, Tan. 15″ washable Whip-O-Lite Shade with Harmonizing Pattern. **$6.95**

The *Aladdin* ® 1953 Line

All prices shown are quoted at wholesale. F.O.B. Nashville, Tenn. or Portland, Ore. Terms 1% 10—Net 30 days.

Prices slightly higher West of the Rockies

P-439 *Ceramic Base,* 27" high. *Colors:* Ivory, Gray. 3-Way Socket. 16" Shantung Fabric Shade. **$8.25**

P-441 *Ceramic Sculptured Base,* 29" high. *Color:* Ivory. 3-Way Socket. 16" Shantung Fabric Shade. **$12.95**

P-410 *Ceramic Base,* 35" high. *Colors:* Green or Brown with Burlap Vinylite Shade. Swedish Gray with Tarlatane Vinylite Shade. 3-Way Lighting. **$11.95**

P-419 *Ceramic Base,* 29½" high. *Colors:* Brown & Mustard, Chartreuse and White, White and Yellow. 3-Way Socket. 15" Laminated Tree-bark Shade. **$9.50**

P-433 *Ceramic Base,* 25" high. *Color:* Ivory and Gold. 16" washable Shade. Packed 4 per carton **$5.25**

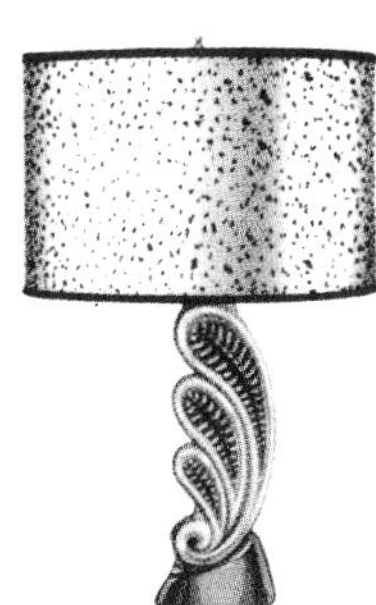

P-459 *Ceramic Base,* 22" high. *Colors:* Cerise, Green. 15" Confetti Shade. **$6.35**

P-460 *Ceramic Base,* 25" high. *Colors:* Cream and Brown, Chartreuse and Forest Green. 13" Shantung Laminated Shade. **$6.35**

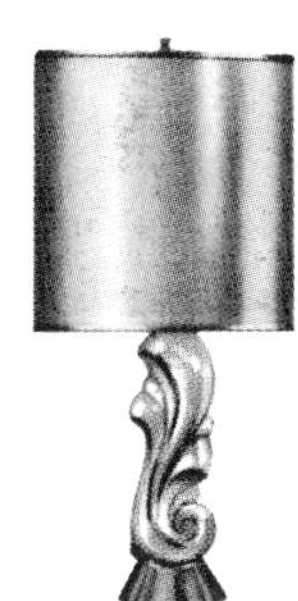

P-461 *Ceramic Base,* 26" high. *Color:* Cerise. 13" Taffeta Laminated Shade. **$6.15**

Slightly higher West of the Rockies

P-471 *Ceramic Base,* 27" high. *Colors:* Mat Brown, Mat Green. 3-Way Lighting. 13" Shantung Laminated Shade. **$8.50**

P-465 *Ceramic Base,* 26" high. *Color:* White and Black. 3-Way Lighting. 13" Free-form design shade. **$8.50**

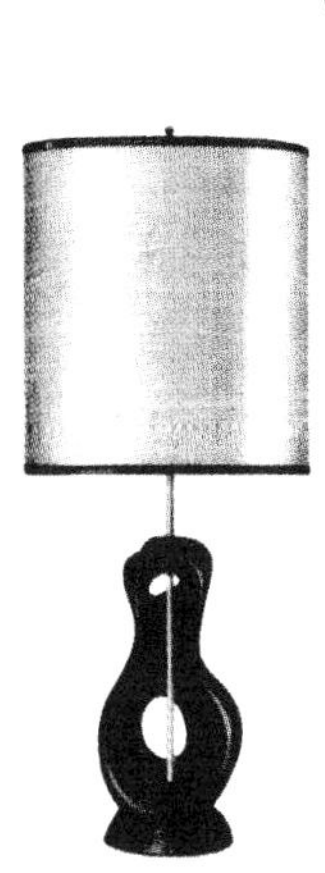

P-467 *Ceramic Base,* 30" high. *Color:* Fruitwood finish. 3-Way Lighting. 13" Shade of Laminated Madagascar cloth. **$9.95**

P-416 *Ceramic Base,* 20" high. *Colors:* Agate Brown, Gray. 20" Shade of Laminated Homespun. **$9.95**

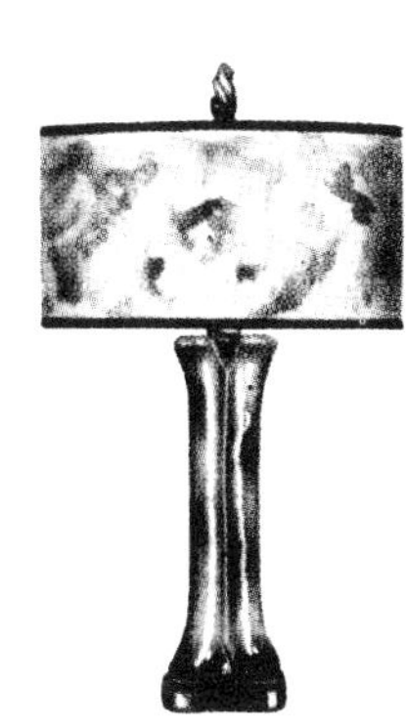

P-409 *Ceramic Base,* 32½" high. *Colors:* Blended Green, Blended Brown. 3-Way Lighting. 18" "Poly-Wisp" Fiberglass Shade. **$10.50**

213

P-51 *Ceramic Base.* 18″ high. *Colors:* Black and White, Yellow and Chartreuse, Agate Brown. 12″ Vinylite Laminated Shade. Packed 2 of a color per carton. **$5.50**

P-58 *Ceramic Base,* 17″ high. *Colors:* Black and White, Citron Yellow and White. 9″ Decorated Shade. Packed 2 of a color per carton. **$4.75**

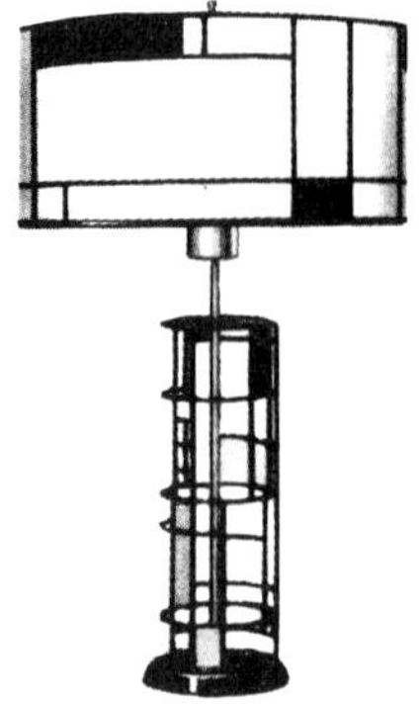

M-449 *Contemporary Black Metal Base,* 26″ high. 17″ Matching Shade. **$9.95**

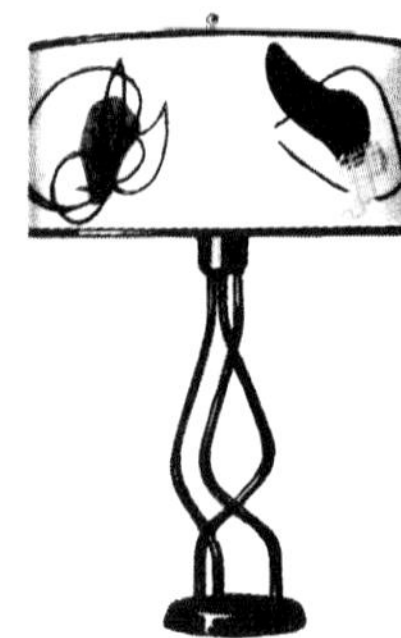

M-451 *Contemporary Free Form Black Metal Base,* 24″ high. 17″ Matching Shade. **$7.95**

P-56 *Ceramic Base,* 17″ high. *Colors:* Cerise, Chartreuse, Green. 8″ shade with matching trim. Packed 2 of a color per carton. **$3.75**

P-60 *Ceramic Base,* 19″ high. *Colors:* Black and White, Brown and Mustard. 9″ Laminated Madagascar Cloth Shade. Packed 2 of a color per carton. **$5.95**

M-447 *Black and Yellow or Mat Green Ceramic on Metal Base,* 21″ high. 15″ Shade of Laminated Vinylite Polyplastex. **$9.95**

M-251 *Brass Base,* 23½″ high. Red, Green or White 10″ Glass Shade. **$9.50**

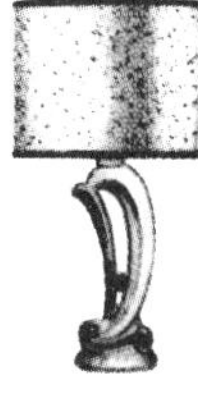

P-61 *Ceramic Base,* 16″ high. *Colors:* Pearl Lustre, Green, Cerise. 8″ Shade. Packed 2 of a color per carton. **$3.75**

M-381 11″ high. Black Base, Glasschop Vinylite Laminated Shade. Packed 4 units per carton. **$2.95**

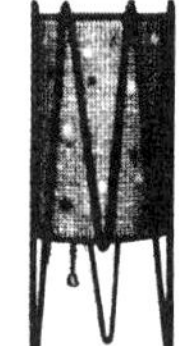

M-469 *Black Iron,* 15″ high. Shade of Laminated Tarlatane. Packed 4 units per carton. **$3.85**

M-367 *Black Iron Base,* 18″ high. White Synskyn Shade. **$3.50**

TV-380 *Ceramic Base,* 12½″ high. *Colors:* Green, Brown. Packed 2 of each color per carton. **$4.25**

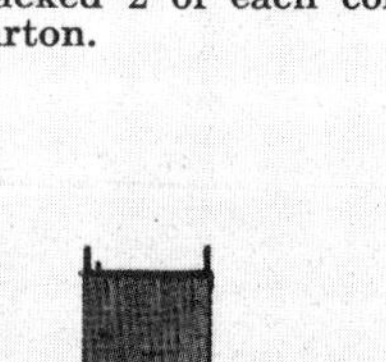

TV-382 *Ceramic Base,* 10″ high. *Colors:* Mat Black, Fruitwood. For TV use. Packed 2 of each color per carton. **$4.50**

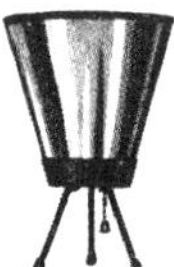

TV-426 11″ high. Black Base, Opaque gold foil paper shade for TV use. Packed 4 units per carton. **$2.95**

M-452 *Cabana lamp,* 14″ high. Black Iron. Has Ceramic ash tray. Laminated Denim Shade. Packed 2 per carton. **$7.95**

M-458 *Ceramic Base with Black Iron,* 24″ high. *Colors:* Swedish Gray, Swedish Brown. 14″ Laminated Terrycloth Shade. **$7.95**

M-446 *White and Green Ceramic Pyramid on Metal Base,* 22″ high. 13″ Polyplastex Synskyn Shade. Packed 2 per carton. **$7.95**

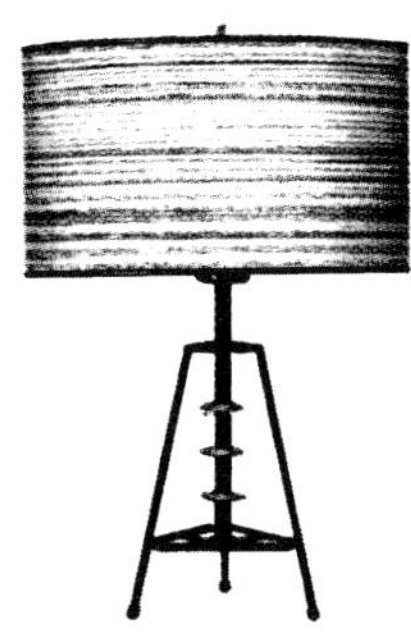

M-448 *Black Metal Tripod Base*, 24″ high. 16″ Polyplastex Synskyn Shade. **$8.95**

M-453 *Deluxe Cabana lamp*, 19½″ high. Black Iron. Has 2 Ceramic ash trays. Laminated Denim Shade. **$9.95**

M-454 32″ high. *Ceramic Base with matching Metal Base.* In Ivory and Gold, Black and White. 3-Way Lighting. 11″ Drum Shade. **$7.95**

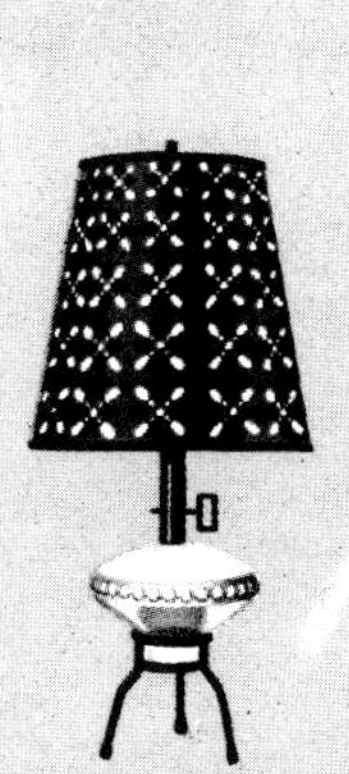

M-455 *Black Iron and Cream Ceramic Colonial Modern Base*, 26″ high. 12″ Green or Nasturtium shade. **$9.35**

M-445 *White Sphere on Black Metal Base*, 21″ high. 13″ Polyplastex Synskyn Shade. Packed 2 per carton. **$7.95**

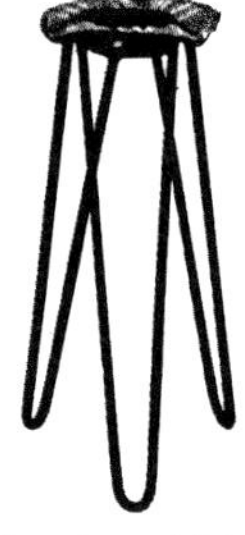

7550 *Smoker with Black Iron Base*, 22″ high. Volcanic Black and White Ash Tray. Packed 4 per carton. **$3.60**

Now

Aladdin® Lamps

ARE...

PRE-PAID A history-making move. Freight prepaid by *Aladdin* on shipments of 100 lbs. and over! Prices shown are at wholesale.*

PRE-PACKED Every *Aladdin* lamp packed with shade in individual cartons. Simplifies inventory, reduces damage, eliminates your packing problems.

PRE-SOLD *Aladdin* is the best known name in lamps. Backed by over 40 years of consistent national advertising.

Slightly higher
West of the Rockies

P-425 *Ceramic Base*, 21″ high. *Colors:* White and Black. 14″ Terry-cloth Laminated Shade. Packed 2 per carton. **$6.75**

P-424 *Ceramic Base*, 27″ high. *Colors:* Black and White, Mulberry and White. 13″ Confetti Shade. **$7.25**

P-423 *Ceramic Base*, 29½″ high. *Colors:* White and Brown, Brown and Mustard. 3-Way Socket. 15″ Vinylite Laminated Heather Shade. **$11.95**

P-420 *Ceramic Base*, 32″ high. *Colors:* Sandalwood, Gray, Green. 3-Way Socket. 16″ Laminated Homespun Shade. **$10.50**

P-415 *Ceramic Base,* 25″ high. *Colors:* Dubonnet, White. 20″ Printed Shade in Green, Brown, Dubonnet. **$8.50**

P-421 *Ceramic Base,* 27″ high. *Colors:* Terra Cotta, Leaf Green. 16″ Treebark Fabric Shade. **$8.75**

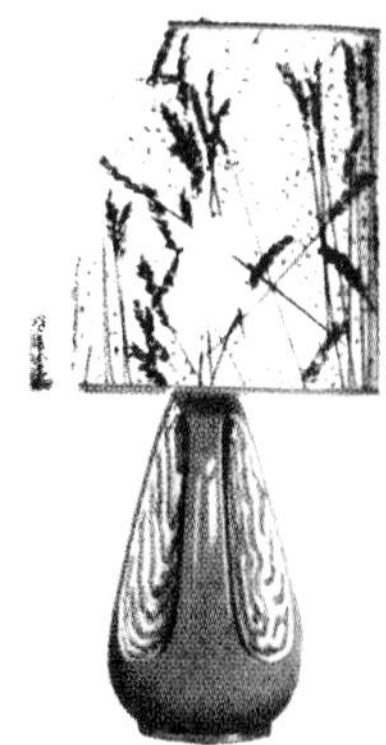

P-443 *Ceramic Base,* 29½″ high. *Colors:* White and Yellow, Chartreuse and White. 3-Way Socket. 15″ Vinylite Laminated Scattergrass Shade. **$11.95**

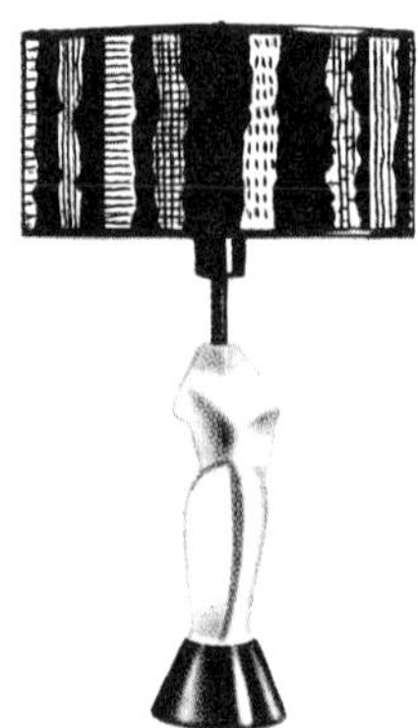

P-437 *Ceramic Base,* 28″ high. *Color:* Black and White. 17″ Drum-Style Shade. **$9.95**

P-436 *Ceramic Base,* 22″ high. *Color:* Aztec Brown. 15″ Laminated Madagascar Cloth Shade. **$9.50**

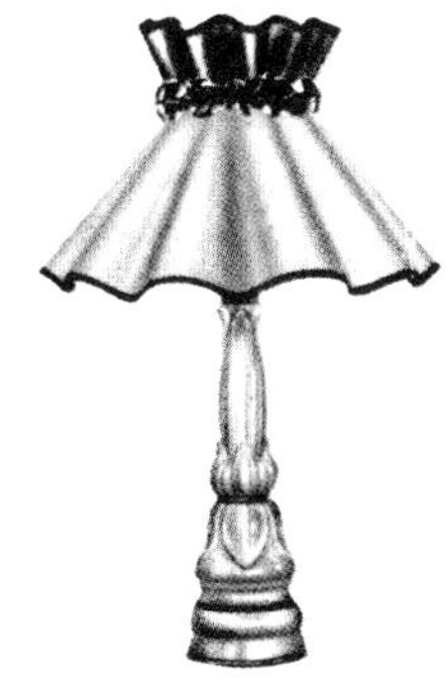

P-414 *Ceramic Base,* 29″ high. *Colors:* Maroon, Gray, Chartreuse. 18″ Fluted Flare Shade of Laminated Taffeta. **$7.75**

P-427 *Ceramic Base,* 19″ high. *Colors:* Frosted Black, Embassy Green, Chestnut Brown. Pierced Satin-finish Parchment Shade. **$8.25**

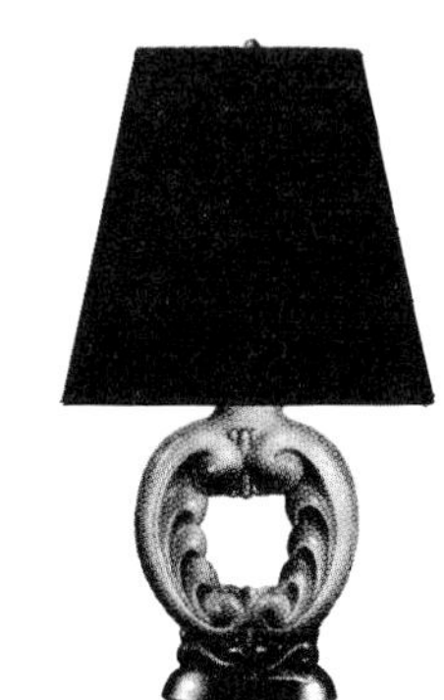

P-434 *Ceramic Base,* 26″ high. *Colors:* Gray with Red Shade, Green with Chartreuse Shade. 15″ Laminated Butcher Linen Shade. **$8.35**

P-422 *Ceramic Base,* 22″ high. *Colors:* Cream, Cream and Terra Cotta, Black and Gold. 17″ Oval Shantung Fabric Shade. **$8.95**

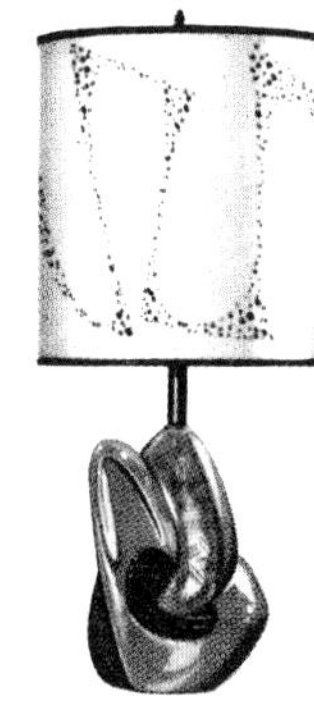

P-429 *Ceramic Base,* 27″ high. *Colors:* Gray and Black, Two-tone Brown. 12 matching Shades. **$7.35**

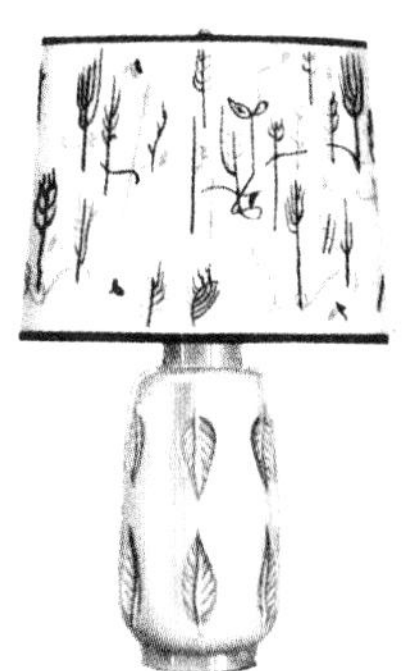

P-444 *Ceramic Base with Elm Leaf Pattern,* 25″ high. *Colors:* Maize, Tan. 15″ Shade with Harmonizing Pattern. **$7.35**

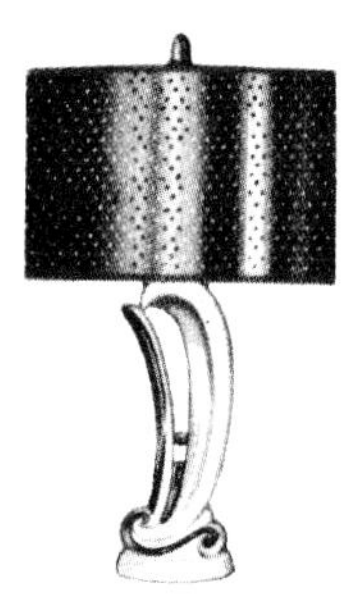

P-413 *Ceramic Base,* 24½″ high. *Colors:* Cerise, Green, Pearl. 15″ Pierced-glazed Parchment Shade. **$6.20**

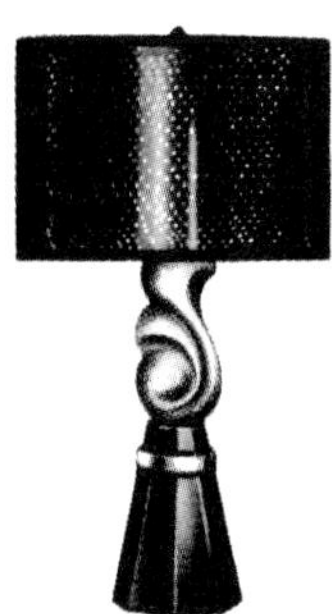

P-417 *Ceramic Base,* 26″ high. *Colors:* Maroon, Cream, Green. 15″ Pierced-glazed Parchment Shade. **$6.95**

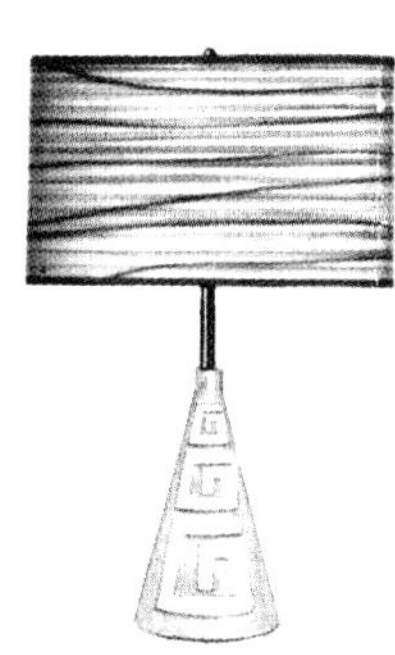

P-432 *Ceramic Base,* 23″ high. *Colors:* Frosted Black, Frosted Citron Yellow. 16″ Polyplastex Synskyn Shade. **$8.25**

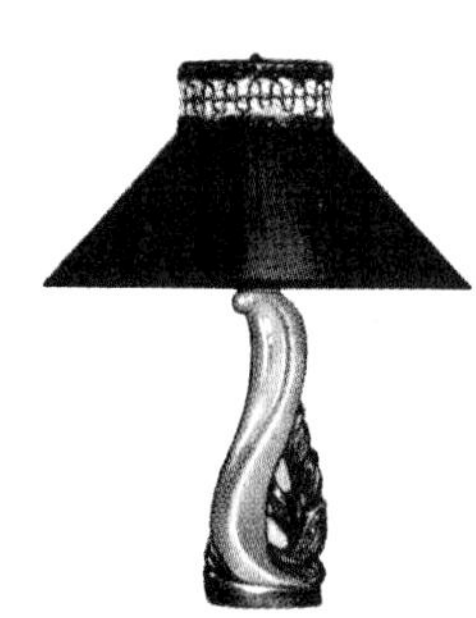

P-411 *Ceramic Base,* 25″ high. *Colors:* Gray, Brown. 20″ Laminated Shantung Shade. **$7.95**

P-438 *Ceramic Base,* 25″ high. *Colors:* Chestnut Brown, Green. 15″ washable Shade. **$6.25**

M.T.509 Magic Touch Lamp. Ceramic Base, 28″ high. *Colors:* Black and Gold, Green and Silver, White and Gold. 16″ Shade of Laminated Omar Fabric. 3-way lighting.

The most outstanding development in the lamp industry. *Aladdin's* new "MAGIC TOUCH" lamps will sell like magic. These "MAGIC TOUCH" lamps go on or off at the slightest touch. No need to turn a knob or pull a chain. They work like magic, they pull like magic. They create interest, build traffic in your lamp department. And . . . they SELL. What's more, they help sell every other *Aladdin* lamp in your store.

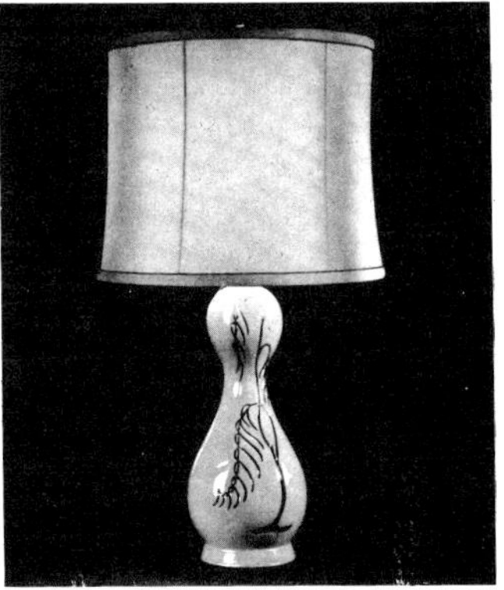

M.T.507 Magic Touch Lamp. Ceramic Base, 27″ high. *Colors:* Sandstone and Gold, White and Gold. 15″ Shantung Fabric Shade. 3-way lighting.

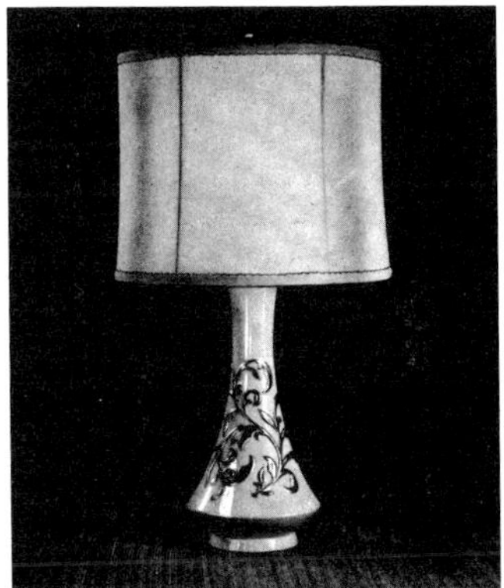

M.T.508 Magic Touch Lamp. Ceramic Base, 27″ high. *Colors:* White and Gold, Green and Gold. 15″ Shantung Fabric Shade. 3-way lighting.

ALADDIN INDUSTRIES, INCORPORATED • Nashville, Tennessee

Space 1224, Merchandise Mart, Chicago; 1726 Flint Ave., Portland, Oregon; Southern Exposition Bldg., High Point, N. C.; Western Merchandise Mart, San Francisco. **Factory Shipping Points:** Nashville, Tennessee; Portland, Oregon. *Available in Canada from Aladdin Industries, Incorporated, 1401 The Queensway, Toronto, Ontario*

P-459 Ceramic Base, 22″ high. *Colors:* Cerise, Gray, Green. 15″ Printed Shade. Packed 2 of a color per carton.

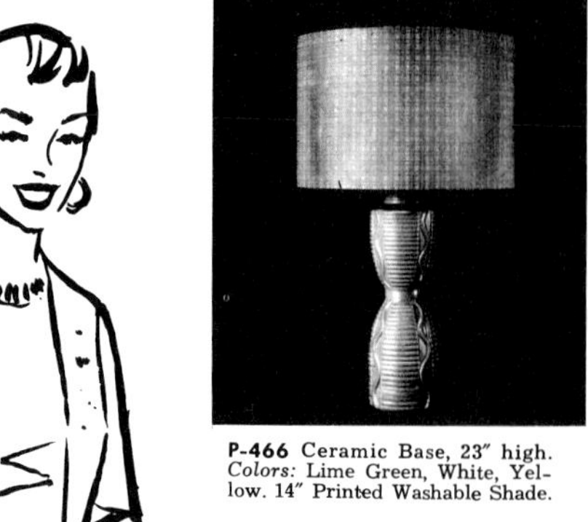

P-466 Ceramic Base, 23″ high. *Colors:* Lime Green, White, Yellow. 14″ Printed Washable Shade.

P-487 Ceramic Base, 26″ high. *Colors:* White and Gray, White and Green. 3-way lighting. 16″ Shade of Laminated Seanet. Packed 2 of a color per carton.

P-478 Ceramic Base, 27″ high. *Colors:* Pearl and Gold, Ivory and Gold. 17″ Laminated Tondoe Casement Shade. 3-way lighting.

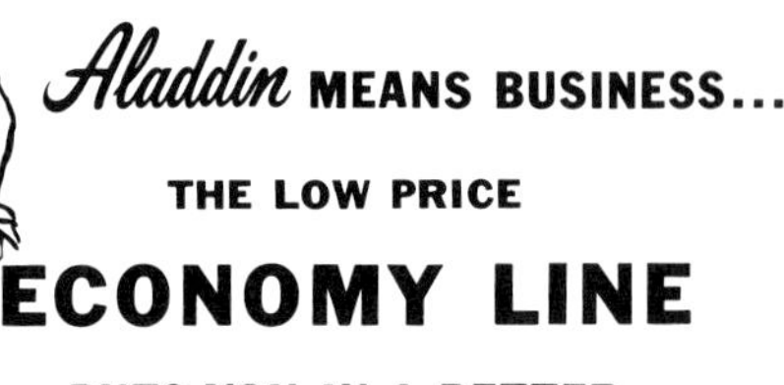

M-367 Black Iron Base, 13″ high. White Synskyn Shade.

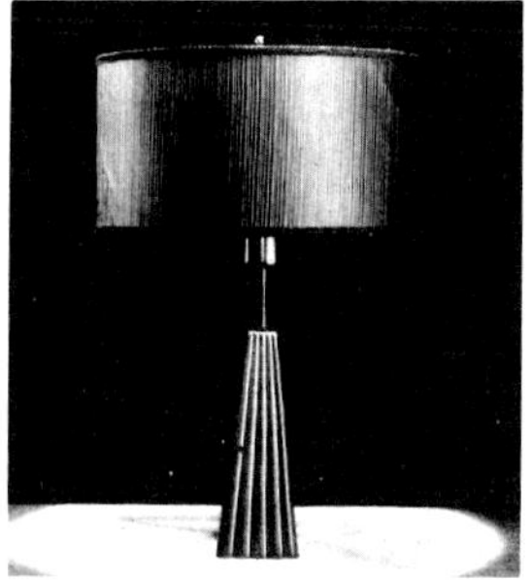

P-470 Reeded Ceramic Base, 24″ high. *Colors:* Ivory, Chartreuse, Beige. 15″ Laminated Satin Repp Shade. 2 of a color per carton.

P-483 Ceramic Base, 24″ high. *Colors:* Green, Mustard. 20″ Coolie Shade of Laminated Champagne Cloth. 2 of a color per carton.

P-471 Ceramic Base, 27″ high. *Colors:* Mat Brown, Mat Green. 13″ Shantung Laminated Shade. 3-way lighting.

M-469 Black Iron, 15″ high. Shade of Laminated Tarlatane. Packed 4 units per carton.

P-484 Ceramic Base, 29″ high. *Colors:* Black and White, Green and White. 16″ Shade of Laminated Delhi Cloth. 3-way lighting.

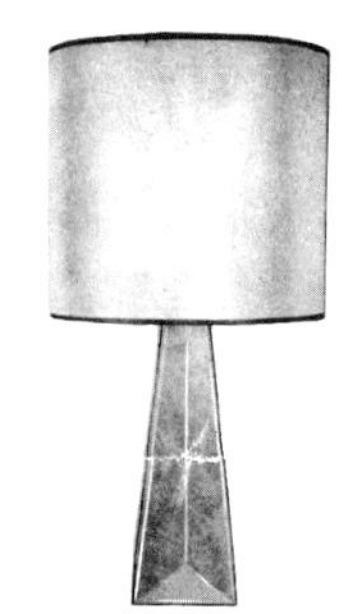

P-489 Ceramic Base, 28″ high. *Colors:* Black, Mother of Pearl, Olive Green. 3-way lighting. 14″ Veiled Pattern Washable Shade.

P-497 Brass and Ceramic Base, 25″ high. *Colors:* Green, Pearl, Tan. 15″ Laminated Shade. 3-way lighting. Packed 2 of a color per carton.

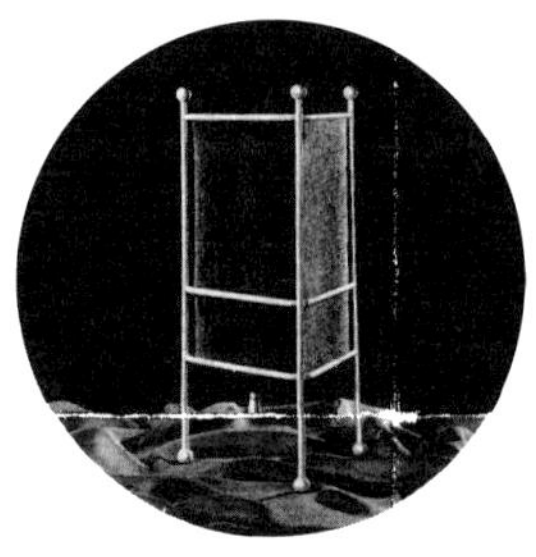

M-480 Triangle Casual Modern in Black Iron. 15″ high. *Colors:* White Frame with Laminated Charcoal Denim, Black Frame with Laminated Gold Seanet. Packed 4 of a color per carton.

P-482 Ceramic Base, 29″ high. *Colors:* White and Black, White and Brown, White and Yellow. 3-way lighting. 14″ Shade of Laminated Delhi.

P-430 Ceramic Base, 25″ high. *Colors:* Gray and Black, Brown and Black. 13″ Matching Shade.

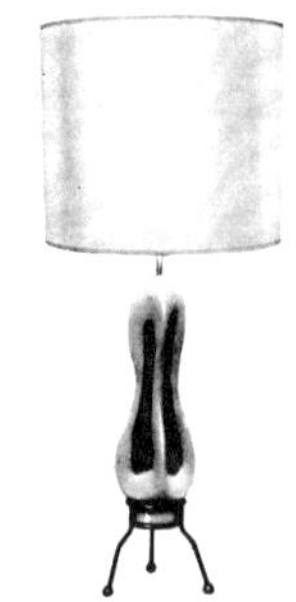

P-491 Sculptured Ceramic with Black Iron Base, 32″ high. *Colors:* White and Brown, White and Mauve. 3-way lighting. 14″ Shade of Laminated French Straw Cloth.

M-452 Cabana Lamp, 11″ high. Black Iron. Has Ceramic Ash Tray. Laminated Denim Shade. Packed 2 per carton.

P-433 Ceramic Base, 25″ high. *Color:* Ivory and Gold. 16″ Washable Shade. Packed 4 per carton.

P-432 Ceramic Base, 23″ high. *Colors:* Frosted Black, Frosted Citron Yellow. 16″ Polyplastex Synskyn Shade.

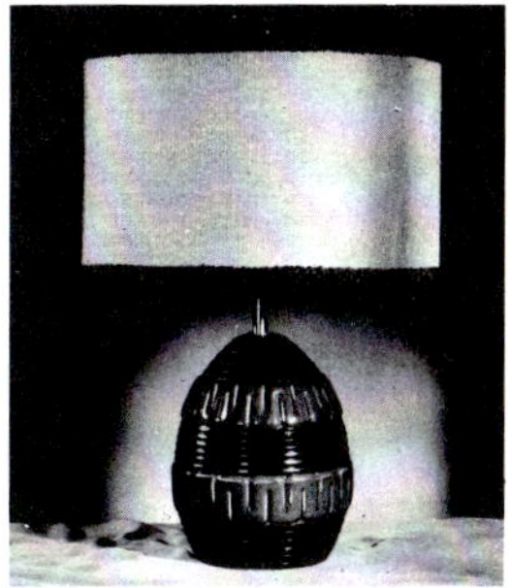

P-436 Ceramic Base, 22″ high. *Colors:* Brown, Gray. 15″ Laminated Madagascar Cloth Shade.

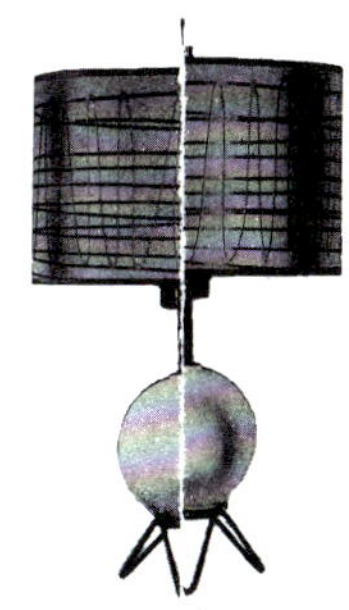

M-445 White Sphere on Black Metal Base, 21″ high. 13″ Polyplastex Synskyn Shade. 2 per carton.

M-468 Contemporary. Ceramic with Metal, 28″ high. *Colors:* Black and White, Black and Lime. 14″ Printed Whip-O-Lite Shade. 3-way lighting.

P-486 Ceramic Base, 28″ high. *Colors:* Black with Gold, Brown and White, Forest Green with Gold. 3-way lighting. 14″ shade of Laminated Yucatan.

P-493 Ceramic Base, 26″ high. *Colors:* Green, Tan. 3-way lighting. 15″ Shantung Fabric Shade.

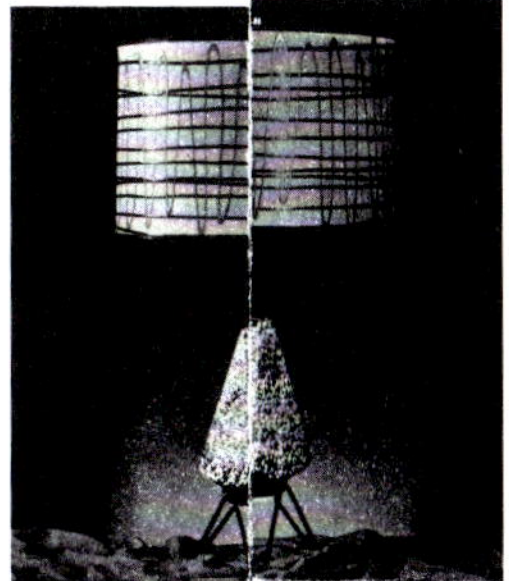

M-446 White and Green Ceramic Pyramid on Metal Base, 22″ high. 13″ Polyplastex Synskyn Shade. Packed 2 per carton.

M-463 Ivory Ceramic with Black Iron Base, 26″ high. 12″ Flocked Shade. 3-way lighting.

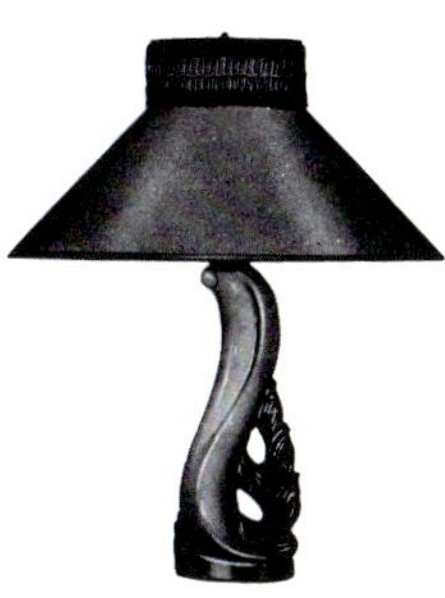

P-411 Ceramic Base, 27″ high. *Colors:* Gray, Brown, Green. 20″ Laminated Shantung Shade.

M-454 32″ high. Ceramic with Metal Base. *Colors:* Ivory and Gold, Black and White. 11″ Drum Shade. 3-way lighting.

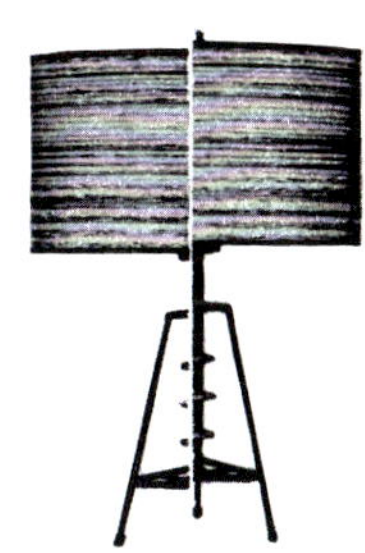

M-448 Black Metal Tripod Base, 24″ high. 16″ Polyplastex Synskyn Shade.

P-464 Ceramic Base, 21″ high. *Color:* White and Black. 14″ Washable Whip-O-Lite Shade. Packed 2 per carton.

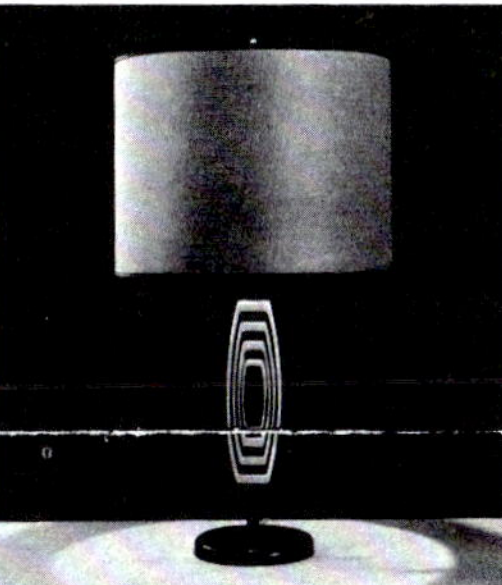

M-456 Contemporary. Ceramic with Metal, 27″ high. *Colors:* Brown and White, Black and White. 14″ Laminated Madagascar Cloth Shade. 3-way lighting.

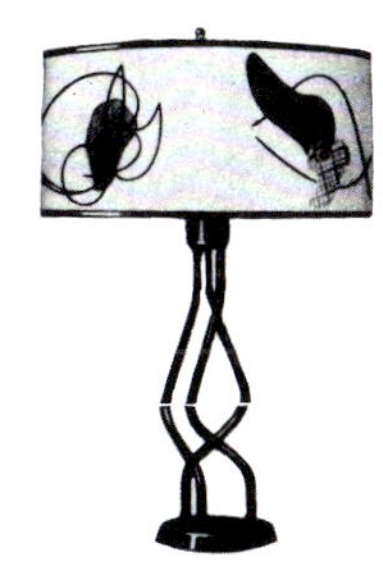

M-451 Contemporary Free-Form Black Metal Base, 24″ high. 17″ Matching Shade.

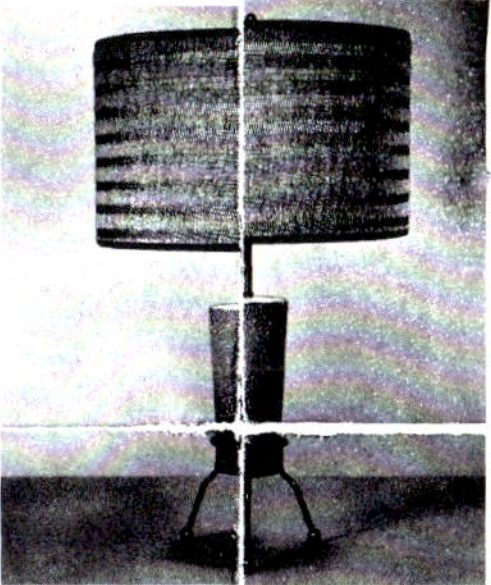

M-458 Ceramic Base with Black Iron, 24″ high. *Colors:* Swedish Gray, Swedish Brown. 14″ Laminated Terry-Cloth Shade.

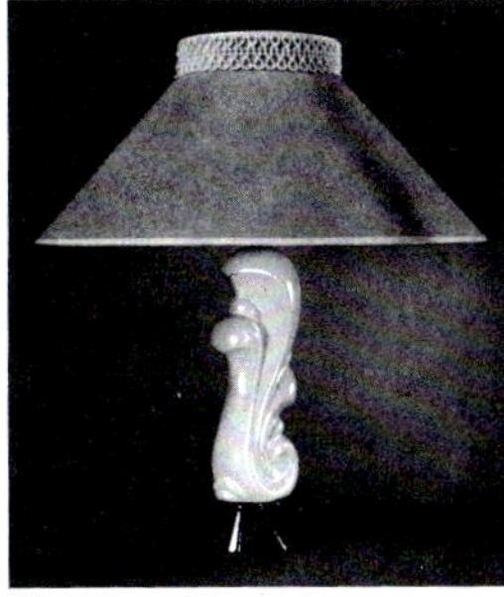

P-481 Ceramic Base, 24″ high. *Colors:* Black and White, Cerise. 20″ Laminated Fabric Shade.

Aladdin **MEANS BUSINESS...**

WITH A NEW, MORE DIVERSIFIED LAMP LINE, A LAMP FOR EVERY ROOM, EVERY TASTE, EVERY BUDGET

P-419 Ceramic Base, 29½″ high. *Colors:* Chartreuse and White, White and Yellow. 3-way lighting. 15″ Laminated Tree-bark Shade.

P-465 Ceramic Base, 26″ high. *Color:* White and Black. 13″ Shade. Free-form Design. 3-way lighting.

P-423 Ceramic Base, 29½″ high. *Colors* White and Brown, Brown and Mustard. 15″ Laminated Heather Shade. 3-way lighting.

P-473 Contemporary. Ceramic Base, 26″ high. *Colors:* Mat Black with White Veiling, White with Brown Veiling. 18″ Laminated Fabric Shade. 3-way lighting.

M-505 Brass Lamp 24″ high. *Colors* Brown and Brass, White and Brass. 16″ Shade of Laminated Champagne Cloth. 3-way lighting.

P-420 Ceramic Base, 32″ high. *Colors:* Sandalwood, Gray, Green. 3-way Lighting. 16″ Laminated Homespun Shade.

P-506 Brass and Ceramic, 29″ high. *Colors:* Brown and White, Gray and Black. 14″ Shade of Laminated Fireglow Fabric. 3-way lighting.

M-447 Black and Yellow or Frosted Green Ceramic on Metal Base, 21″ high. 15″ Laminated Vinylite Polyplastex Shade.

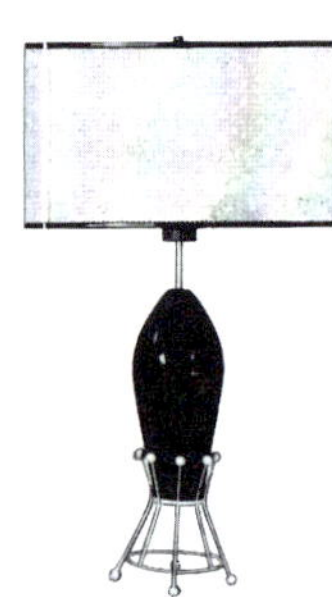

M-475 Ceramic with Black Iron Base, 30″ high. *Colors:* Black with White Base, Yellow with Black Base, White Crackle with Black Base. 17″ Laminated Seanet Shade. 3-way lighting.

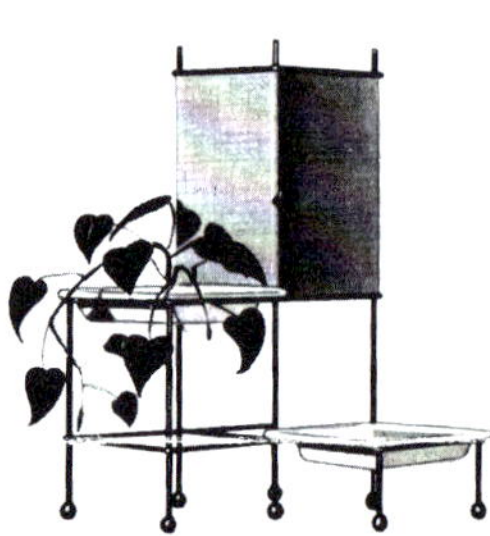

M-453 De Luxe Cabana Lamp, 19½″ high. Black Iron. Has 2 Ceramic Ash Trays. Shade of Laminated Tangerine Denim.

P-504 Ceramic Base, 26″ high. *Colors:* Charcoal, White. 18″ Shade of Laminated Down-Beat Cloth. 3-way lighting.

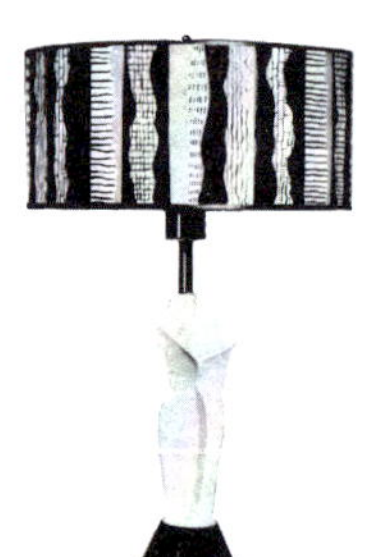

P-437 Contemporary Figurine. Ceramic. *Color:* Black and White. 28″ high. Drum-Style Shade.

P-488 Ceramic Base, 26″ high. *Colors:* Black and White, Two-tone Green, Sandalwood. 3-way lighting. 15″ Shantung Shade.

P-485 Ceramic Base, 30″ high. *Colors:* Black and Gold, Green and White, White and Gold. 16″ Shade of Laminated Omar Cloth. Flexible 3-way lighting.

P-499 Ceramic Base with Brass, 29″ high. *Colors:* Black and White, Brown and White, Striped White. 14″ Shade of Laminated Delhi cloth. 3-way lighting.

P-467 Ceramic Base, 30″ high. *Colors:* Fruitwood finish. 3-way lighting. 13″ Shade Laminated Madagascar Cloth.

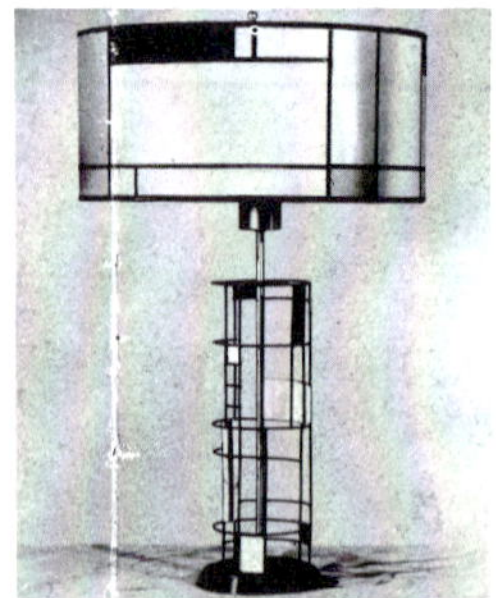

M-449 Contemporary Black Metal. 26″ high. 17″ Matching Shade.

W-501 Solid Wood with Brass Trim in Cherry, Pine, Walnut. Height: 27″. 16″ Shade of Laminated Chintz. 3-way lighting.

P-500 Ceramic Base, 31″ high. *Color:* Black and White. 16″ Shantung Fabric Shade. 3-way lighting.

W-502 Solid Wood, 29″ high. *Finishes:* Cherry with Brass, Walnut with Silver. 16″ Shantung Fabric Shade. 3-way lighting.

M-494 Black Metal with Brass, 26″ high. 3 Circuit Switch in Base. 16″ Shade of Laminated Pongee.

W-503 Solid Wood with Ceramic, 29″ high. *Finishes:* Cherry, Walnut. 18″ Shade of Laminated Chintz. 3-way lighting.

M-495 Brass Metal Lamp, 29″ high. *Colors:* Brass with Brown, Brass with White. 3-way lighting. 16″ Shade of Laminated Delhi.

P-410 Ceramic Base, 35″ high. In Swedish Gray with 15″ Tarlatane Vinylite Shade. 3-way lighting.

M-476 Contemporary Abacus Lamp. 27″ high. 18″ Laminated Charcoal Tweed Shade. 3-way lighting.

M-450 Contemporary Lamp with Night-Light, 24″ high. 16″ Laminated Lyme Casement Shade. 3-way lighting.

7550   7552   7553

7550 Smoker with Black Iron Base, 22″ high. Volcanic Black and White Ceramic Ash Tray. Packed 4 per carton.

7552 Contemporary Smoker, 24″ high. Wrought Iron Stand Tipped with Wood Ball. *Colors:* Black, White. Packed 4 of a color per carton.

7553 Smoker. White Ceramic Ash Tray and Black Iron. 28″ high. Packed 4 per carton.

TV-384

TV-386

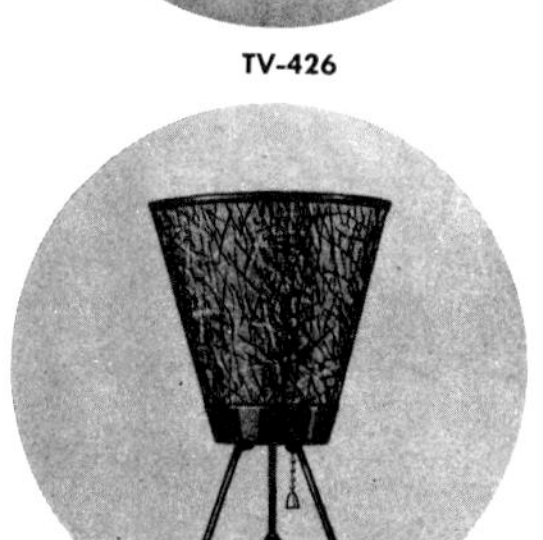

TV-426

TV-385

M-381

TV-386 Ceramic Base, 5″ high. Combination planter and TV lamp. *Colors:* Oyster, Sandalwood. Packed 2 of each color per carton.

TV-384 Ceramic Base, 9½″ high. For TV use. *Colors:* Pearl, Green. Packed 2 of each color per carton.

TV-426 11″ high. Black Base. Variegated Shade. Packed 4 units per carton.

TV-385 Ceramic Base, 10½″ high. *Colors:* Mustard, Gray. Packed 2 of each color per carton.

M-381 Black Iron Base, 11″ high. Glasschop Vinylite Laminated Shade. Packed 4 units per carton.

Aladdin MEANS BUSINESS

...AND WE MEAN RIGHT NOW! PLACE YOUR ORDER TODAY— GET YOUR SHARE OF PROFITS NOW! USE THE SIMPLIFIED, ENCLOSED ORDER FORM

M-62 Contemporary, 20″ high. *Colors:* Black with Brass, White with Brass. 7″ Gold Veiled Shade with Matching Trim. Packed 2 of a color per carton.

P-71 Ceramic Base, 17″ h'gh. *Colors:* Beige, Pink, Green. 9″ Laminated Shade of Jubilee Cloth with Net Trim. 2 of a color per carton.

M-59 Colonial Modern Candlestick, 18″ high. *Colors:* Black and Brass, Pink and Black, Black and Yellow. 7″ Laminated Plaid Taffeta Shade. 4 of a color per carton

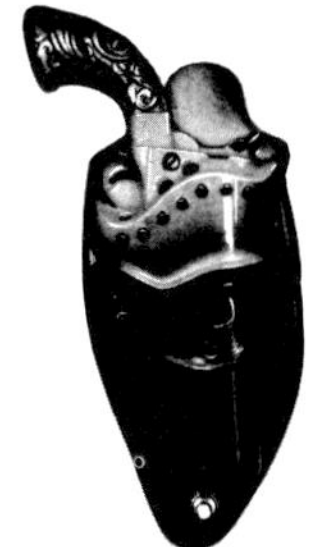

P-51 Ceramic Base, 18″ high. *Colors:* Black and White, Yellow and Chartreuse, Agate Brown, 12″ Vinylite Laminated Shade. Packed 2 of a color per carton.

P-60 Ceramic Base, 19″ high. *Colors:* Black and White, Brown and Mustard. 9″ Laminated Madagascar Cloth Shade. Packed 2 of a color per carton.

P-57 Gun-n-Holster Pin-Up, 10″ high. Push button switch for 6-watt bulb. Packed 12 per carton.

P-56 Ceramic Base, 17″ high. *Colors:* Cerise, Chartreuse, Green. 8″ Whip-O-Lite Shade with Matching Trim. 2 of a color per carton.

P-68 Ceramic Base, 18″ high. *Colors:* Ivory, Pink, Yellow. 8″ Net Trim Printed Shade. Packed 2 of a color per carton.

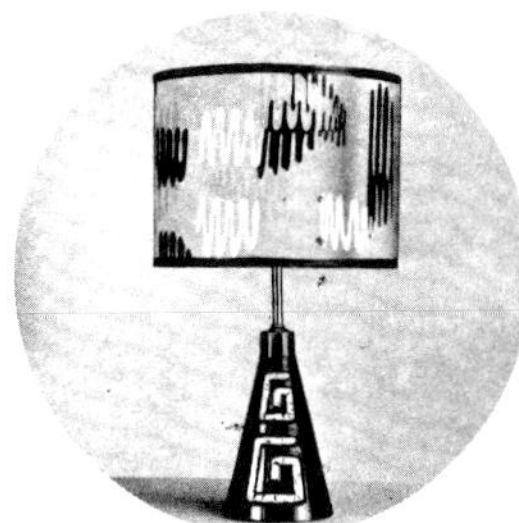

P-58 Ceramic Base, 17″ high. *Colors:* Black and White, Citron Yellow and White. 9″ Decorated Shade. Packed 2 of a color per carton.

P-64 Ceramic Base, 18″ high. *Colors:* Black, Pearl, Pink, 8″ Veiled pattern washable shade. Packed 2 of a color per carton.

M-70 Ceramic & Metal, 22″ high. *Colors:* Black & Brass, White & Brass. 9″ Laminated Shade of Pongee. Packed 2 of a color per carton.

F-200 Black metal accented with white discs and gold stars. 18″ white taffeta shade. Large size harp for 3-way bulb. Height 56″. Packed 2 per carton.

F-201 Black metal with brass trimmings. Fiberglas reflector. 18″ Laminated Lubbock Casement Cloth Shade. 3-way lighting. Height 53″. Packed 2 per carton.

F-202 Black metal with brass trimmings. Fiberglas reflector. 18″ laminated Lubbock Casement cloth shade. 3-way lighting. Adjustable height from 53″ to 64″. Simply slide up or down. No gadgets or gimmicks to adjust. Packed 2 per carton.

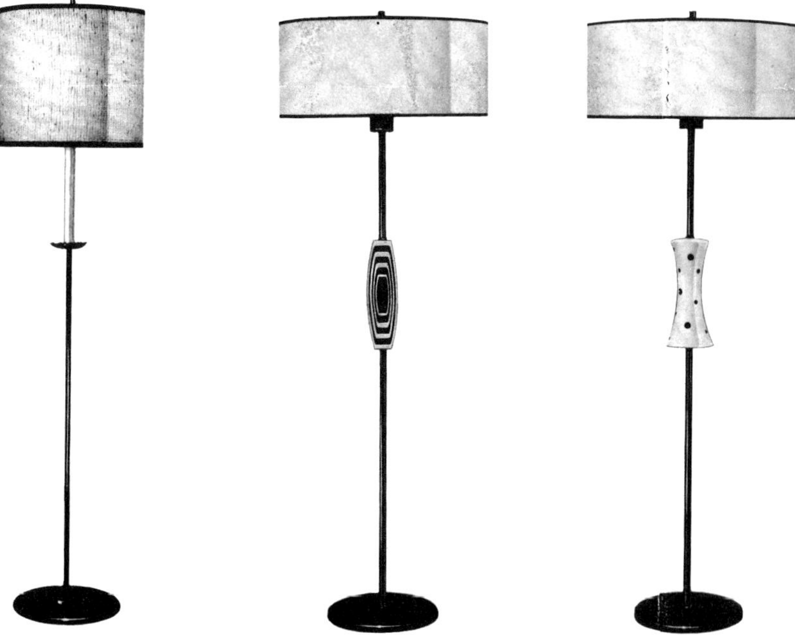

F-203 Colonial Modern, black metal base with brass ornaments. Metal candle of white. 14″ laminated Lyme Casement cloth shade. Large size harp for 3-way bulb. Height 54″. Packed 2 per carton.

F-204 Black metal with ceramic break. Matches Aladdin Table Lamp M-456. 18″ Laminated Madagascar cloth shade. Large size harp for 3-way bulb. Height 53″. Packed 2 per carton.

F-205 Black metal with ceramic break. Matches Aladdin Table Lamp M-468. 18″ Laminated Madagascar cloth shade. Large size harp for 3-way bulb. Height 53″. Packed 2 per carton.

Index